Up to Speed with Swing

Up to Speed with Swing

User Interfaces with Java Foundation Classes

STEVEN GUTZ

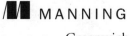 MANNING

Greenwich
(74° w. long.)

For electronic browsing and ordering of this, and other Manning books, visit:
http://www.manning.com.

The publisher offers discounts on this book when ordered in quantity.
For more information, please contact:

Special Sales Department
Manning Publications Co.
3 Lewis Street
Greenwich, CT 06830

Fax: (203) 661-9018
email: orders@manning.com

∞ Recognizing the importance of preserving what has been written, it is Manning's policy to have the books we publish printed on acid-free paper, and we exert our best efforts to that end.

Library of Congress Cataloging-in-Publication Data
Gutz, Steven J.
    Up to speed with Swing : user interfaces with Java Foundation Classes /
Steven Gutz.
      p.   cm.
    Includes bibliographical references and index.
    ISBN 1-884777-64-3 (alk. paper)
    1. User interfaces (Computer systems) 2. Swing (Computer file) 3. Java
(Computer program language) 4. Java foundation classes. I. Title.
  QA76.9.U83G88 1998
  005.13'3--dc21   98-6652
               CIP

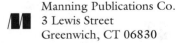
Manning Publications Co.
3 Lewis Street
Greenwich, CT 06830

Copyeditor: Leslie Aickin
Typesetter: Dorothy Marsico
Designer: Leslie Haimes

Second, corrected printing
Printed in the United States of America
  2 3 4 5 6 7 8 9 10 – CR – 00 99 98

For Sharon, who found me when I was lost

Contents

2   *Swing basics* 29

PART II   *Swing components* *53*

3 *Panels and panes* 55

9 List boxes 283

PART III   *Advanced topics*   391

12   *Creating custom look-and-feel*   393

Preface

An "early technology adopter" (also known as a techno-geek) like myself is usually ready to evaluate an exciting new API the day it is released (if not sooner). In late 1994, while attending a software developers' conference in California, I encountered a past acquaintance who, at the time, was employed by Sun Microsystems. As I am apt to do, I began complaining to him about the generally inadequate state of the business, and, in particular, the coding effort and portability weaknesses in languages such as C and C++. After listening to my droning for a while, my friend told me about a particularly interesting programming language coming from Sun Microsystems in just a couple of months. A new language from Sun? Aren't they a UNIX workstation company? What does a hardware company know about building computer languages? I was skeptical about trying to use any language produced by Sun Microsystems.

The language my friend was referring to was Java 1.0, which, as he predicted, was shipped at the beginning of 1995. In late January of 1995, I connected to Sun's World Wide Web site, pulled down the first version of the Java Development Kit (JDK), and immediately began tinkering. Although I didn't yet understand the overall vision of Java, I was impressed with the platform independence, and with the speed at which I could build relatively complex prototypes. In these early stages, I viewed Java as a replacement for Microsoft's Visual Basic as a prototyping tool; however, I was soon to appreciate the capabilities of this new language. Java 1.0 was still far from that utopian software world that I was searching for, but it demonstrated some real promise as an object-oriented language, and Sun's commitment to future enhancements convinced me that Java was the language for me. In spite of the many skeptics around me, I was hooked.

I continued to use Java 1.0, noting its weaknesses and doing my best to work around them. I eventually discovered some serious limitations in Java, but, when I was almost ready to give up on the language, Sun released Java 1.1 featuring a totally new event model and offering significant new features like internationalization and keyboard support. As an early technology adopter, I downloaded the 1.1 release, and my confidence in Java was renewed. Applications that crawled in the Java 1.0 Virtual Machine (VM) raced, once they were adapted to the new event model. However, like many other early adopters, I became exceedingly annoyed with the lack of power of Java's Abstract Windowing Toolkit (AWT). Still, I persisted because, in my mind, Java's potential was so great.

My interest in Java continued, and, in April 1997, I attended my first JavaOne conference, quickly getting lost among the thousands of other attendees. The conference spanned all levels of developer expertise, and much of what I saw was familiar to me. However, I heard many people (mostly Sun and JavaSoft employees) talking about something code-named Swing. The (as yet) unreleased Swing was Sun's attempt to improve Java's AWT and standardize the user interface components for future versions of Java. Discarding my original plans for the conference, I attended every session concerning Swing so that I could learn more about Sun's new Swing class library. Most of these sessions were primarily promotional, but a few of the Swing demos caught my eye.

By June 1997, Sun finally made a public alpha release of Swing, which coincided with the start of a software project for which I wanted to employ Java. After considering several user interface (UI) class libraries from third-party vendors and completely disregarding Sun's warnings that the API would change, I decided to take a big risk and use Swing for my project. Through several subsequent alpha and beta releases of Swing, my project paralleled its progress. Each time Sun offered a new release, I had to spend a day fixing my code broken by the changes they made. It was often frustrating, but I was steady in my resolve to integrate Swing into my application.

My persistence paid off. My application shipped about the same time that Sun published the final release of Swing, and my work received a very positive response from my peers. While still basking in my success, I began to realize that I had invested a significant number of hours learning to make effective use of the Swing classes. So, as an early technology adopter who had successfully conquered the learning curve, I decided to share my knowledge with others, now that the Swing technology was in the mainstream. The results of my efforts are presented in this book, and it is my sincerest hope that it will help smooth out some of the bumps that developers may hit when starting to use Swing.

In late February 1998, Sun shipped the finished Swing code; however, Swing is a significant part of a larger group of technologies named Java Foundation Classes (JFC). For developers using Java 1.1, JFC is available for downloading as a separate package from JavaSoft's web site. Java 1.2 users will discover that JFC is integrated into the Java run time, so no additional installations will be required.

Intended audience

This book is intended to help Java developers who want to build user interfaces with Java, regardless of their level of expertise. However, this book is not a Java tutorial, so, if you are a novice, you will certainly require some additional references to assist with the basic language syntax. In the appendices of this book, you will find several good Java language resources. If you are an expert user, this book will serve as a resource which you can keep close at hand, referring to it when you hit a real snag.

Regardless of your level of expertise, I will assume that you have some experience building simple applications and/or applets with version 1.1 (or later) of Java. One of the early chapters of this book is a Java AWT refresher course, but it is by no means a complete tutorial for the language. This chapter will serve only to help contrast Java, as it was with AWT, to Java as it now exists with Swing.

Since the last chapter of this book will discuss optimization of Java code using multithreading, I will also assume that you have a solid understanding of how to write Java code with threads and of the inner workings of multithreading in general. Multithreading is a complex mechanism which can be either your most indispensable optimization tool or your worst debugging nightmare. You must use extreme caution when writing multithreaded applications, and, though we will examine multithreading from the Swing perspective, this book will not help you understand the pitfalls that multithreading can introduce into a Java application.

Finally, I will assume that you possess a thirst to learn. Though this book will cover some advanced topics related to Swing, there will still be much to learn on your own. Swing is brimming with interesting classes that can save you hours of work, but to adequately describe each individual class would require a much larger book. Don't be afraid to throw together some small test programs to test aspects of the Swing classes which you do not immediately understand.

How this book is organized

This book consists of three parts. We begin with a bit of background on Java and Swing, then look at the basic user interface functionality. Finally, we examine some of the more advanced capabilities of Swing. I've also included a chapter to help you with optimization. The book is organized as follows:

Part I contains all of the information you require to get started with Swing, including a description of the software packages you need and how to set them up. We will also have a quick Java refresher course for those who need it. Then, we will examine the architecture of Swing and start to talk about some of the advanced capabilities it offers.

Part II contains details about the typical classes you will utilize in the process of creating your own Swing applications. We will look at each of the common components and how to best use them, as well as techniques that can extend and enhance them to better suit your needs.

In Part III, we look at more advanced topics. We will describe how to create components with a custom look-and-feel, and take a look at several ways to make your Java code run faster.

NOTE: Throughout this book, you will see sections containing partial information regarding the Swing component APIs, including brief descriptions of the contents of significant groups of methods. Although you can find complete information in the online documentation provided with the JFC and JDK toolkits, the partial reference allows you to quickly review the API for a given class without requiring access to a computer.

Conventions

In order to present the information contained in this book in a consistent manner, the following conventions are used throughout:

The text contains many guidelines, recommendations, and warnings to indicate where you might want to pay some special attention. For example:

FYI Though significant in scope, Swing represents only one of many parts of a larger technology group called Java Foundation Classes (JFC).

The following table summarizes the types of information you will find within these messages:

UI Guideline	**User Interface Guideline.** These tips are only guidelines—not rules. Feel free to accept or ignore any of these suggestions.
FYI	**For Your Information**. These messages provide information that may be of interest to you as you read the book or work with the examples. Messages of this type include tips, warnings, and general observations.
IMHO	**In My Humble Opinion.** These messages contain editorial comments and recommendations from the author which may not reflect the opinions of Sun or other Java developers.

Except where noted, user-entered commands are capitalized (for example, DIR).

Except where noted, filenames may use both upper and lower case. Java can be sensitive about the case of file names (for example, SampleClassFile.java)

All Universal Resource Locators (URLs) will be shown with Courier font, such as the following web site address for IBM VisualAge for Java:

```
http://www.software.ibm.com/ad/vajava/.
```

The source code in this book will follow a particular coding convention based on the *Java Coding Standards* written by AmbySoft, Inc. Much of this standard is based loosely on Hungarian Notation, and was originally devised for the C programming language by Charles Simonyi of Microsoft, Inc. If you are unfamiliar with this coding convention, you can find out more about it at the web site:

```
http://www.ambysoft.com.
```

Variables will be prefixed with a type designator as follows:

Prefix	Data Type
off	Offset
len	Length
b	Byte
c	Character
d	Double
f	Float
l	Long
o	Object
s	String
v	Arbitrary value

Methods will be named with full English names according to the AmbySoft coding convention (for example, `isBordered()`, `setValue()`, or `testForOccurrence()`). Constants will be names in hyphenated, uppercase text (for example, `MAXIMUM_OFFSET`).

All source code will appear in Courier font. For example:

```
//
// Sample program, main entry point
//
public void main( String args[] )
{
      TestFrame myFrame = new TestFrame();
      myFrame.setVisible( true );
}
```

Obtaining the source code

This book includes many sample applications, including all of the source code for each sample. If you feel the need, you can type in the samples yourself, but fortunately, there is a much better alternative. Manning Publications, Inc. has provided a site on the World Wide Web:

```
http://www.manning.com/Gutz2
```

from which any owner of this book can download the example source code, including any updates to correct bugs. This will save you the time and effort required to type in the samples you want to run.

All of the code in this book is 100 percent pure Java code, and should compile in any Java environment on any platform. Additionally, the compiled code should run on any Java virtual machine meeting the Sun Java 1.1 (or later) specification. Some of the samples from the book may not run in conjunction with the Microsoft virtual machine.

The Manning web site also includes the entire text of this book in searchable format, allowing you to keep the book on hand while you work and giving you the capability to perform full-text searches for information.

Author Online

Purchase of *Up to Speed with Swing* includes free access to a private Internet forum where you can make comments about the book, ask technical questions, and receive help from the author and from other Swing users. To access the Swing forum, point your web browser to:

`http://www.manning.com/Gutz2`

where you will be able to subscribe to the forum. This site also provides information on how to access the forum once you are registered, what kind of help is available, and the rules of conduct on the forum.

I have tried to be complete and accurate within the limits of this book; however, errors and omissions are inevitable. If you find mistakes in this book, or if you think I have left something out, please let me know. There may be another edition of this book, and, if so, I would like to make as many corrections and implement as many suggestions as possible. Please direct them to me using the Author Online forum.

Special thanks

A book is never created by a single person. In my case, I had help from many people who deserve special recognition. These people have gone above and beyond the call of duty to offer assistance and encouragement, or they have played a significant role in the development of Java or Swing.

To James Gosling, the father of Java. Many thanks for the ingenuity and persistence you invested to take a seemingly obscure idea and use it to create an industry.

To Adam Abramski, a JFC Evangelist (they have such interesting job titles in California) with Sun Microsystems. Without Adam, I could never have bent Sun's ear the way I did. Thanks for listening.

To Steve Wilson and Michael Albers of JavaSoft, who provided lots of welcome assistance developing the chapter dealing with custom look-and-feel. I am not able to say enough about the contributions they provided.

To Roger Chang, for taking time out of his busy schedule to add the user interface tips and guidelines. I hope that you will find Roger's insights as valuable as I do.

To Randy Westman, who took the time to proofread my manuscript and provide technical input. Thank you for the effort you made, even though I know your spare time was scarce.

To Manning Publications for producing such a fine book. Special thanks to the efforts of Marjan Bace, Ted Kennedy, Mary Piergies, Leslie Aickin, Dottie Marsico, Elizabeth Martin, and everyone else at Manning who contributed to the task of producing this book.

To the "Fulcrum Thursday Night Club" (you know who you are). Thanks for the weekly reality check.

To all of the brilliant people at Sun Microsystems who helped to design, implement, and support Java and Swing—their efforts are quite amazing when you realize what they have accomplished in such a short time. Keep up the great work.

Finally, to the thousands of Java developers out there—without you there would be no reason for this book. I hope I am able to teach you things which will help you prove that Java is a real contender for application development.

Review process for this book

Manning recognizes the importance to you of accurate, relevant and useful content in the books you buy. We therefore put considerable emphasis on submitting each manuscript we develop to an exhaustive technical and editorial review. This book was reviewed in two phases: early, while in partial manuscript form, and again, after the completed manuscript reached us.

Partial manuscript review led to some important realignments in the book's focus. Making those changes at mid-point, rather than after the final manuscript had been completed, saved the author time-consuming revision—and got the book into your hands more quickly.

Complete manuscript review—in an orgy of opinion and occasional counter-opinion—corrected, improved, and caused us to drop from and add to the manuscript at tremendous rates that only an experienced author and confident expert like Steve Gutz could sustain. An intense review such as this can help a draft manuscript to mature in mere weeks into a balanced, reasoned, and correct work ready for publication. Thanks to Steve's commitment to first rate results, that's exactly what happened in this case.

Reviewer comments were analyzed by Manning staff and the author and in many cases multiple exchanges with the reviewers led to clarifications and improved understanding of individual problems. Along the way we gained a firsthand feeling for the intensity of interest that Swing generates among people who know it.

Speed is critical in getting a book like this to market during the window when readers want it most. Even the most adroit author must have substantial experience with a technology in order to present the reader with a useful treatment, and that requires time—to which the long process of writing, reviewing, revising, and production must be sequentially added before a manuscript can become a book.

Our manuscript review was done entirely online, resulting in valuable time savings that would otherwise have gone into transporting paper copies between us and our reviewers. Online review also lets us avoid the additional delays and paperwork associated with shipping documents to overseas reviewers, so that this book reflects, quite literally, world-class feedback.

The following six people participated in the technical review of the partial manuscript:

James Begole, USA

Tom Bergman, USA

David Karr, USA

Martin Naedele, Austria

Michael Shimer, USA

William Wake, USA

For the complete manuscript review, we had the benefit of advice from the following seven people:

David Anderson, Singapore

Jaideep Bafna of Dataware Technologies, USA

David Karr, USA

Alexis Moussine-Pouchkine, France

Michael Neylon of the University of Michigan, USA

Travis Shirk of Dimensional, USA

Vaino Vaher of IBM Sweden

David Karr graciously offered to help with both review phases.

Additionally, the following five members of the AWT/Swing Team at JavaSoft, USA, offered detailed suggestions, complaints, corrections, and advice:

Michael Albers

Jeff Dinkins

Georges Saab

Will Walker

Steve Wilson

Altogether eighteen individuals donated their valuable time to this effort, resulting in improvements that would have been impossible to achieve without them. Our sincere thanks go to all the reviewers whose contributions helped keep us and the author focused on what readers want and need. In addition, the following seven individuals assisted with corrections to the first printing:

Jim George

Matt Robinson

Dion Gillard

Kevin Snow

Mark Stewart

Khalid S. AL-Khater

George Aguiar

On the western shores of northern Scotland, Laurence Vanhelsuwe devoted several focused days to proofing the entire book and contributed numerous corrections to the text and source code.

About the cover illustration

"Homme de Javan" (Java Man), the cover illustration, is from the 1805 edition of Sylvain Maréchal's four-volume collection of men's and women's regional dress customs. This book was first published in Paris in 1788, one year before the French Revolution. Its title alone required no less than 30 words:

> "Costumes Civils actuels de tous les peuples connus dessinés d'après nature gravés et coloriés, accompagnés d'une notice historique sur leurs coutumes, moeurs, religions, etc., etc., redigés par M. Sylvain Maréchal"

The four volumes include an annotation on the illustrations: "gravé à la manière noire par Mixelle d'après Desrais et colorié."

Clearly, the engraver and illustrator deserved no more than mention of their last names—after all they were mere technicians. The workers who colored each illustration by hand remain nameless.

The remarkable diversity of this collection reminds us vividly of how distant and isolated the world's towns and regions were from each other just 200 years ago. Dress codes have changed everywhere and the diversity by region, so rich at the time, has practically disappeared. It is now hard to tell the inhabitant of one continent from another. Perhaps we have traded off some cultural diversity for a richer and more varied personal life—including an incredibly interesting technology environment.

Dubbed the "Java Man Book," this is the first Manning title to be illustrated with Sylvain Maréchal's people of the past. At a time when it is hard to tell one computer book from another, Manning celebrates the inventiveness and initiative of the world of software with a new series of covers based on the rich diversity of regional life brought back to life by these pictures. Just think, Maréchal's was a world so different from ours people would take the time to read a book title 30 words long.

Related Manning books

Manning publishes several related books and has others in development. Because of its cover illustration, *Up to Speed with Swing* is often referred to as the "Java Man Book." *Up to Speed with Swing* is a tutorial on how to develop applications using the Swing piece of Java Foundation Classes. Manning also has a companion book, the "Java Woman Book," by Stephen Drye and William Wake which is primarily a Swing reference.

The Java Man Book brings the beginner and intermediate Swing programmer up to speed on this important part of the JFC. As such, it will probably be most useful to you while you are learning this environment.

The Java Woman Book is a programmer's companion for the long run. It is a reference work with a short tutorial section in part one of the book for those who can get going without too much hand holding. We expect it to be used by intermediate and advanced Java programmers who want concise, cross-referenced sources of factual information interlaced with examples.

For many, the Swing online documentation simply isn't enough. Programming effectively in Swing may require significant experimentation and reading of the raw source code, for which they may not have adequate time. The authors of the Java Man Book and the Java Woman Book have done this work for the reader. They relate their experience and gleaned know-how in these two books.

The Java Woman Book API descriptions contain everything in the Swing JavaDoc, amplified with the authors' pointers and examples derived from their cumulative experience in developing fully featured applications with Swing. The Reference section of the book includes discussions of how a given class relates to the rest of the API, as well as full descriptions of the use of each field and method call. It also features a cross-reference index at the end of each class description, which provides links to other classes in the Swing API used by the class in question. These features should prove valuable to the programmer in his daily work environment.

Manning also publishes the second edition of its *Java Network Programming*. The success of the first edition has led us to update this book to make it even more useful to network programmers. The encryption framework of the first edition has been extended and moved to a new book, *Applied Java Cryptography*. The space saved has allowed the second edition of JNP to offer a more complete treatment of network programming in Java. The second edition details the Java platform support for networked and distributed computing, with many supporting examples. It develops advanced network clients and servers and a sophisticated messaging library; it includes significantly extended examples including DNS and finger clients, and an advanced Web server. This new edition covers comprehensively the features of JDK 1.1 and introduces the new features that will be in JDK 1.2. It is a resource for the advanced networking questions that developers will encounter when they start writing complex networked applications, including details of advanced stream programming, implementation of complex Internet protocols, RMI and CORBA.

Manning publishes a growing list of advanced titles in the Java field. Manning's *Server-Based Java Programming* is a guide to the increasing use of Java for server applications. *Java Servlets by Example* covers the use of Java for client/server applications that can be too difficult or too time consuming to even consider without the servlet technology. As an example, it covers how CGI scripts, the inefficient, memory-hungry, slow processes, can be replaced with leaner, faster, portable and easy to maintain Java servlets. Both of these titles are planned for Summer 1998.

Manning's *The Awesome Power of Java Beans*, to be released May 98, is a second generation Java Beans book. It transmits to the reader the maturity in understanding derived from the now available experience with Java's component technology, teaching not only bean use and reuse but also bean development. It includes a selection of completed and tested beans for use by the reader. Manning's *Distributed Java Applications Programming* discusses how to develop sophisticated applications that run on two or more computers. It includes discussions of low-level sockets, RMI, CORBA using Visigenic's Java VisiBroker, and Mobile Agents using ObjectSpace's Voyager. Its release is planned for Fall 1998.

Manning's companion to the book you are holding, *Java Foundation Classes: Swing Reference*, alias the Java Woman Book, will be available July 1998.

Part I

Getting started

*P*art I of this book contains the introductory information required to start you down the road to building your own applications with Java and Swing. I begin by describing the tools you will need or may choose to use. Then, I will review some of Java's key features. Finally, we will start to examine the concepts upon which the Swing class library is built.

NOTE: This part contains a review of the more basic areas of Java, AWT, and Swing. If you are an experienced Java developer, much of part 1 will be review, so you will probably use this material for reference only.

A Java refresher

1

1.1   What is Java?

To many people, Java is simply a tool used to create insignificant applets to embellish web pages. By now, everyone using the Web has probably visited at least one web site implementing a Java applet to scroll text, play a video file, or display real-time stock quotations. Java is certainly well suited as an applet builder.

To application developers, Java is a relatively new language which permits complex implementations of large programs. Many companies are now delivering Java-based products into the mainstream of corporate and home use (such as office suites and games). Companies like IBM, Sun Microsystems, and Hummingbird Communications are building Java programs which do not depend on the presence of a web browser at all. Most current Java applications are still related to the Web in some way (network administration, for example), but Java is quickly evolving into an applications language that permits high speed animation, audio capabilities, and much more. Java, then, is an application language as well.

But is Java more than this? Sun Microsystems and JavaSoft certainly think it is. Over the past two years, Sun has been investing in the concept of Java as an operating system platform. Figure 1.1 illustrates the architecture used to develop JavaOS. Notice that large portions of the operating system are written in Java, suggesting that the operating system could easily be ported to many different platforms. JavaOS is a compact and powerful operating system which has the ability to scale down to the smallest personal digital assistant (PDA) or SmartCard and up to the largest mainframe. JavaOS will run programs written in Java, and has been tuned to ensure that performance is at its best.

Sun is also developing central processing units (CPUs) that execute the Java bytecode natively. This represents a potentially massive performance boost for Java applications running on computers with this chip. The Java processors are available in several versions, with some suitable for SmartCard and PDAs, others for PC coprocessor cards, and still others for stand-alone workstation systems. Java is also now becoming part of the hardware platform.

Java can be many things to many people. Sun and JavaSoft are committed to Java in every conceivable way, and they are certainly not alone. IBM, Netscape, Oracle, and several other large companies interested in Java's market potential are investing heavily in the effort started by Sun. For the purposes of this book, though, we will assume that the Java world is limited to building applications and applets, though one should be aware that all code described by this book will execute in any Java environment which supports a graphical user interface (GUI).

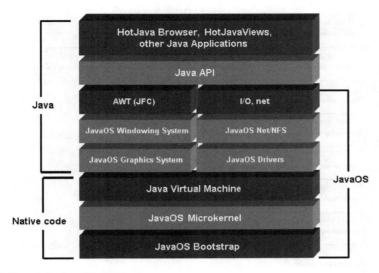

Figure 1.1   JavaOS architecture

1.2   What is AWT?

The AWT is the part of JDK responsible for the user interface, and since all Swing components are based on AWT, we need to quickly review what functionality AWT offers us as future Swing developers. AWT is a set of classes providing everything a developer requires in order to create a front end for an applet or application. Currently, AWT includes over sixty classes, but with each new release, the class library evolves to include new features. All of the user interface components are derived from the Component class (see figure 1.2) which is responsible for all aspects of configuration and display common to all components.

AWT is a collection of high level classes intermingled with classes that provide a much lower level of functionality. Too often, a class that you would expect to find is absent from AWT, resulting in an unexpected effort to write volumes of new code. In the version 1.0 release of Java, the AWT event model was horrendous. Every event for every control passed through the `handleEvent()` method—even those events that eventually got processed by some default handler internal to the virtual machine. Sun recognized and acknowledged the shortcomings of Java 1.0 and promised a solution in future releases of the language.

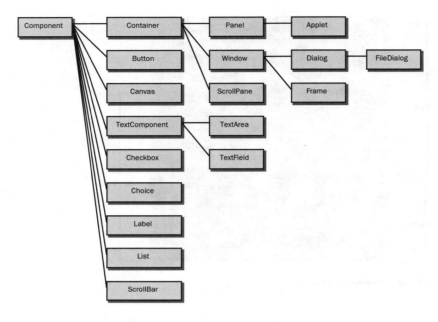

Figure 1.2   A partial AWT class hierarchy

Sun did correct many of the known version 1.0 limitations with Java 1.1, but it was becoming clear that if they wanted developers to build applications on a par with those available on the Microsoft Windows and UNIX X Windows platforms, Sun had to provide a new class library. This new class library would eventually become known as *Swing*, and would include all of the advanced classes that developers expect. Swing is still not a perfect API, but it is certainly a technological leap forward.

1.3   The Java event models

Throughout its brief history, Java has had two event models, and this represents the most significant difference between versions 1.0 and 1.1 of the language. Version 1.2 of Java uses the same event model as 1.1. Understanding the 1.1 event model is crucial to successfully building JFC applications, since most Swing components either generate events or recognize that events have occurred.

In this section, we will review the differences between the two event models, and explain the advantages and disadvantages of each. Unless you are building an applet that must be compatible with an older version of Netscape Navigator or Microsoft Internet Explorer, you should be writing code supporting the Java 1.1 event model, and if you are writing JFC code, as we are, you *must* use the 1.1 event model. The 1.1 and 1.2 Java Virtual Machines still support the 1.0 event model, but Sun could remove this backward compatibility from future versions of the language specification, so you should avoid building code supported only by Java 1.0.

1.3.1   Java 1.0

Java 1.0 offered developers a simple event model. As shown in figure 1.3, all event handling is performed by a single mechanism implemented as a cascading series of test conditions. This is the same technique used by Windows to handle window actions.

Although easy to understand, the Java 1.0 event model is inefficient, since every event passes through the event handler for testing and possible action processing. The event model requires the developer to implement a method called `action` with the following format:

```
public boolean action( Event actionEvent, Object oObj )
{
```

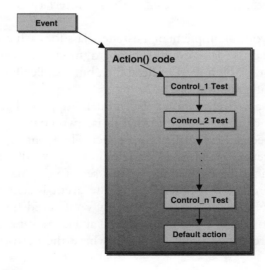

Figure 1.3
Java 1.0 event handling

```
// Handle actions for MyControl
if(actionEvent.target instanceof myControl )
{
    // Process event for MyControl

    return true;
}

// Handle other actions

// Action code didn't handle this event, so let Java do it.
return false;
}
```

Since some frames within a typical application may have dozens of user action-able controls, the length of the `action()` method can become quite unmanageable. This can easily result in tedious debugging, and poor application performance.

1.3.2   Java 1.1 and beyond

Fortunately, Sun's developers resolved to correct the crippling weaknesses in the 1.0 event model. The result, in the Java 1.1 virtual machine, was a completely revamped model, called the delegation event model, which delivered greatly improved performance. The basic change to the event model in 1.1 was the addi-tion of listener classes to detect activity on a per control basis. Listeners are devel-oper written classes which implement one or more of the Java 1.1 abstract listener classes which listen for events (usually) initiated by some user action. For example, to intercept actions for a button, the `ActionListener` interface must be implemented.

It is important to note that you can implement a listener class for each control, or one class for all actions, or one class for all events (keyboard, mouse, actions, and so on). The 1.1 event model allows a high level of flexibility, but this flexibility can cause some confusion when creating applications.

Figure 1.4 illustrates the Java 1.1 delegation event model. Suppose that Main Class is a user interface object, such as a frame, and that it has two components (a list box and a button) that have been added to the frame panel. The Control_1 class has been configured to handle events for the list box and Control_2 handles events for the button. When the user clicks the button, an event is sent to the main class, which internally determines where the event should go. The event is sent to the Control_2 class for processing. Notice that, unlike similarly configured frames in Java 1.0, the code to detect list box activity was not executed at all, resulting in bet-ter performance. Figure 1.4 represents a simple example where the performance increase would be almost imperceptible. However, as the frame becomes more complex, with many more components, the increase in speed becomes proportionately more significant. The following listing shows the Java code to implement the display in figure 1.4.

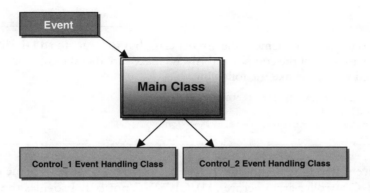

Figure 1.4
Java 1.1 event handling

```
class MainClass extends Frame
{
   // Set up the frame
   .
   .
   .

   // Create the list box
   listbox = new List();
   add( listbox );
   listbox.addItemListener( new Control_1() );

   // Create the button
   button = new Button( "OK" );
   add( button );
   button.addActionListener( new Control_2() );

   }

class Control_1 implements ItemListener
{
   public void itemStateChanged( ItemEvent event )
   {
       // Handle list box selection events
   }
}
```

```
class Control_2 implements ActionListener
{
    public void actionPerformed ( ActionEvent event )
    {
        // Handle button events
    }
}
```

FYI It is common to implement the listener class, but to forget to add the listener to the instance of the component. Always make sure that the components are created with code like the following:

```
button = new Button( "OK" );
add( button );
button.addActionListener( new Control_2() );
```

This new event handling technique in Java 1.1 is part of a larger scheme called the Model-View-Controller architecture (MVC). MVC not only provides the delegation event model, but also introduces an observer/observable model which allows the uncoupling of the application, interface, and control elements. The intent of MVC is to separate the user display from the control of the user input. This really suggests that the user interface's look-and-feel can be modified without altering its operation. Figure 1.5 illustrates the MVC architecture implemented in Java 1.1. The following table summarizes the components of the MVC architecture and their basic purposes:

Component	Purpose
Model	Represents the underlying data of the object Notifies the view that its state has changed, forcing the view to be redrawn
View	Accesses the data from the model and specifies how it is displayed
Controller	Determines how user interactions with the view cause data in the model to change

Note that the Swing class library makes extensive use of the MVC architecture to permit the creation of user interface components featuring a custom look-and-feel and/or custom data model. We will be delving into these aspects of Swing in

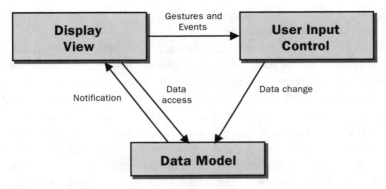

Figure 1.5   Model-View-Controller architecture

later chapters, but I should point out that tinkering with MVC is an advanced skill, and it should be approached with due caution.

Custom data models are more commonly implemented than custom look-and-feel. You will undoubtedly use this aspect of MVC (and Swing) quite often. The default data models for Swing components, though complete, are limited in scope, so you will certainly want to implement your own.

Unless you are concerned with building corporatewide applications running across multiple platforms, and have a desire to maintain the same look-and-feel everywhere, you may not want to get mired down in the custom look-and-feel aspects of MVC. However, there may be times when you just want to create a checkbox with a slightly different appearance, and since the functionality for a checkbox already exists, you can alter the user interface rather than building an entirely new component. Though it is possible that you may never build an application with components that implement custom user interfaces or data models, it is important to understand the concepts of MVC because it is fundamental to Java today and into the future. We will examine these in more detail in the next chapter.

1.4   JavaBeans

Most of us love to find shortcuts to make our jobs easier, simpler, and faster, and that coincides with the demands placed on us to build software in less time, for less money. So, it was no accident that the software industry developed ways to "componentize" code, usually in the form of software objects. This allows us to take existing software components, and, with relatively little coding effort, plug them together to create a useful application.

The component model for software development was made popular by applications like Microsoft Visual Basic, and it has quickly become the way most application environments generate code. Microsoft grew so enamored with the component model concept that they developed the Component Object Model (COM) for their Windows product, and now COM is embedded into almost everything Microsoft does (and many other companies, as well). Unfortunately, COM is plagued by a horrendous learning curve. Any developer who claims to be a COM guru is probably lying, unless they have been completely immersed in it for at least a year. COM is, without question, the single most difficult part of Windows programming to understand.

As part of the Java 1.1 effort, Sun decided that the language needed a standard component model; however, they realized that a technology similar to COM would probably fail miserably. Sun needed to re-examine the way programmers build code, and then create a new component technology, while at the same time minimizing the learning curve. The result was a totally new component model which Sun dubbed JavaBeans. Since we are concerned with creating Swing applications in this book, we need to appreciate that all Swing components are based on the JavaBeans technology. Though you will not need to understand the inner workings of Java-Beans, we do need understand what beans are and how we can use them.

JavaBeans is simple to implement (at least when compared to COM), and it integrates into most visual environments quite well. The most important distinction between COM and JavaBeans is that applying JavaBeans' technology does not alter the existing language syntax. All aspects of the language work as they do without beans, and the developer is not required to think differently when working with beans. The same cannot be said for COM.

Creating a bean does not require any advanced knowledge or training. So, as a simple introduction to Java beans, here is an example of a simple JavaBean:

```java
public class BeanExample implements java.io.Serializable
{
   private int beanValue;

   public BeanExample()
   {
      beanValue = 0;
   }

   public void setBeanValue( int newValue )
```

```
{
    beanValue = newValue;
}
public int getBeanValue()
{
    return beanValue;
}
}
```

BeanExample is a real bean that is complete. It has no visual representation (not a requirement for a bean), but it does have a state (represented by the bean-Value attribute) which is automatically saved by the JavaBeans' persistence mechanism. It also implements a property called "Value" that will appear in any JavaBeans compliant visual programming environment which loads this bean.

This is really all that JavaBeans is about. It offers the same capabilities as COM, but does not require developers to absorb volumes of knowledge before they realize any return on their time investments. I have presented a simple view of JavaBeans to demonstrate that the technology is much easier to comprehend than COM, though, in practice, JavaBeans development is more complicated than what I have shown here. However, if you compare the JavaBeans example here to a similar COM example written in C, you will immediately appreciate JavaBeans.

1.5   A review of components, listeners, and events

You have already seen some examples of component use in the sample code shown earlier in this chapter, but we should take some time to quickly review the typical procedures for using components and listeners. Component use in Java 1.0 was much easier than it is with the delegation event model introduced in Java 1.1. All you had to do was create a new instance of a component, add it to a panel, and it will intercept any events it generated using the `handleEvent()` method. With Java 1.1, things become a bit more convoluted.

In version 1.1 or later, a component is created in essentially the same way as it was with Java 1.0, and it is also added to the panel the same way; however, event handling is vastly different, and it is also unlike most other windowing environments. We have already touched on the Model-View-Controller architecture of Java 1.1, and briefly discussed event listeners, but we should examine these in a bit more detail. As shown previously, the basic code to create any component and listen for action events is:

```
button = new Button( "OK" );
add( button );
button.addActionListener( new Control_2() );
```

Action listeners are only one of several types of listeners provided by the Java API (for example, selecting an item in a list box generates an `ItemEvent`, which is intercepted by any `ItemListener` attached to the list box control). Note, however, that list boxes can generate `ActionEvent` instances as well, so you may need to attach multiple listeners to a component, depending on your needs. Below is a list of AWT components and possible events and listeners for each:

Component	Events	Listeners
Button	ActionEvent	ActionListener
Checkbox	ItemEvent	ItemListener
Choice	ItemEvent	ItemListener
Container	ContainerEvent	ContainerListener
Window, Dialog, Frame	WindowEvent	WindowListener
List	ActionEvent ItemEvent	ActionListener ItemListener
ScrollBar	AdjustmentEvent	AdjustmentListener
TextComponent TextArea	TextEvent	TextListener
TextField	TextEvent, ActionEvent	TextListener, ActionListener

Handling an `ActionEvent` requires that you implement an `actionPerformed()` method in your listener class, for example:

```
public void actionPerformed( ActionEvent event )
{
   if( event.getSource() == buttonOK )
     Action_OK();
   if( event.getSource() == buttonCancel )
     Action_Cancel();

}
```

But if, for example, you want to handle a more advanced event, such as intercepting the string within a text field and using it to control the enabled state of a button, you need to implement a `TextListener` rather than an `ActionListener`. The following example code determines whether or not a text field contains information. If it does, an OK button is enabled; otherwise, the button is disabled. This is the type of code you would typically use within a dialog box to prevent the user from omitting a required field value.

```
class DialogOfMine
    extends Dialog
    implements TextListener
{
    private TextField textField = null;>

    public DialogOfMine()
    {
        super( "MyDialog", true );
        .
        .
        .

        // Create the text field
        textField = new TextField();
        add(textField);
        textField.addTextListener( this );
        .
        .
        .

    }
    public void textValueChanged( TextEvent event )
    {
        if( event.getSource() == textField)
        {
            if(textField.getText().length() == 0 )
                button.setEnabled( false );
            else
                button.setEnabled( true );
        }
    }
}
```

The example adds a `TextListener` to the `textField` attribute. Since the listener is implemented within the DialogOfMine class, the "implements `TextListener`" clause has been added to the class definition. To implement a TextListener, the dialog code must supply a `textValueChanged()` method, which is called any time the user adds text or removes characters from the text field. With this method, we can examine the contents of the field, and disable the OK button if the field is empty.

1.6 Layout manager refresher

If you have been using AWT for a while, then you know that UI components are inserted into a panel. There are many ways to accomplish this simple task. In most windowing environments, components are added to their owner windows by using hard-coded X-,Y-coordinates. Java supports this mechanism, but suppose we wanted to add components to a resizable window? We don't really want to concern ourselves with having to handle a resize event to manually recalculate the sizes and positions of the window's components.

Fortunately, unlike most windowing environments, Java offers several classes, called layout managers, which are responsible for managing how UI components get displayed within a panel. Layout managers alleviate many of the pains developers experience when attempting to build their user interfaces, and are one of the features that separate Java from other languages.

AWT supports five different layout managers, and Swing implements an additional four. We will examine the Swing layout managers in chapter 3. For now, let's review the layouts supported by AWT in Java 1.1.

1.6.1 BorderLayout

Panels configured with a border layout add components by accepting a geographical position: north, south, east, west or center (see figure 1.6). When the Java Virtual Machine (JVM) shows the panel, the components around the edges are given as much size as they require, and the component in the center gets whatever space remains.

The listing below creates five AWT buttons and applies them to each of the valid positions in a frame which has been configured with the border layout. The result is the output shown in figure 1.6.

```java
import java.awt.*;

class TestFrame extends Frame
{
   public TestFrame()
   {
      super();
      setSize( 200, 200 );
      setLayout( new BorderLayout() );

      add( new Button( "North" ), BorderLayout.NORTH );
      add( new Button( "South" ), BorderLayout.SOUTH );
      add( new Button( "East" ), BorderLayout.EAST );
```

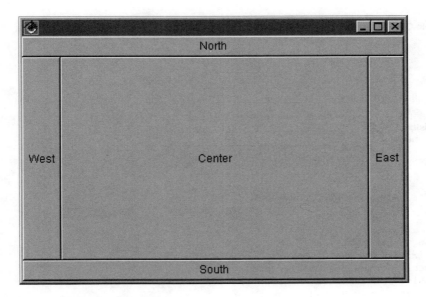

Figure 1.6   BorderLayout sample

```
        add( new Button( "West" ), BorderLayout.WEST );
        add( new Button( "Center" ), BorderLayout.CENTER );
    }
}
```

If you ran this program, you would notice that, as the frame window is resized, the internal components are automatically resized to accommodate the change in their parent's size.

1.6.2   CardLayout

The CardLayout manager is not like the others provided by Java. When you add components to a frame configured for card layout, they are not displayed at the same time. Instead, the components are stacked like cards, so only the topmost component is visible. Think of a panel with a CardLayout manager as a slide show viewer, except that, in addition to sequential viewing, cards in the card layout can be accessed randomly, as well.

Figure 1.7 illustrates how card layout works. In a stack of several cards, only the topmost card is visible. The code to generate a stack like the one shown in figure 1.7 is as follows:

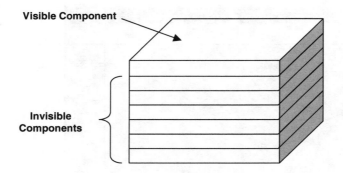

Figure 1.7   A diagram showing CardLayout

```
setLayout( new CardLayout() );
add( "first", new Button( "First" );
add( "second", new Button( "Second" );
add( "third", new Button( "Third" );
add( "fourth", new Button( "Fourth" );
show( this, "first" );

// Step to the next pane
next( this );
```

CardLayout manager is a bit obscure, but can be an incredibly useful mechanism for displaying one of several panels. Though you probably will not use Card-Layout often, we cannot ignore its significance, so it is important that you understand how it works. This layout manager is particularly useful for building composite components, like tabbed panels.

1.6.3   FlowLayout

Figure 1.8   FlowLayout sample

The most basic of all Java layout classes is FlowLayout, and it is the default layout for all panels. With FlowLayout, components are added to the owner panel in a left to right fashion, wrapping to the next row when necessary. The alignment of rows can be specified, but, by default, each row is centered within the panel. The following code generates a simple frame of buttons that has the Flow-Layout manager applied. The results are shown in figure 1.8.

```java
import java.awt.*;

class TestFrame extends Frame
{
   public TestFrame()
   {
      super();
      setSize( 200, 200 );
      setLayout( new FlowLayout() );
      setBackground( Color.lightGray );

      add( new Button( "One" ) );
      add( new Button( "Two" ) );
      add( new Button( "Three" ) );
      add( new Button( "Four" ) );
      add( new Button( "Five" ) );
   }
}
```

1.6.4 GridLayout

The GridLayout manager allows developers to better control how and where components are placed within a panel. The panel is divided into a configurable number of equally sized rectangles organized into a row and column matrix. The X,Y cell location of each component can be determined according to the order in which it was added to the panel.

The following code sample creates a simple framed window containing five AWT buttons applied to a panel supporting a GridLayout manager. The display in figure 1.9 shows the resultant output. Notice that, like FlowLayout, the grid is filled by row, and wraps to the new row when required.

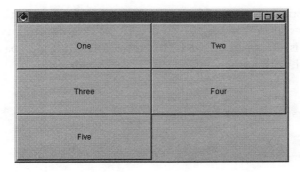

Figure 1.9
GridLayout sample

```
import java.util.*;

class TestFrame extends Frame
{
    public TestFrame()
    {
        super();
        setSize( 200, 200 );
        setLayout( new GridLayout( 3, 2 ) );
        setBackground( Color.lightGray );

        add( new Button( "One" ) );
        add( new Button( "Two" ) );
        add( new Button( "Three" ) );
        add( new Button( "Four" ) );
        add( new Button( "Five" ) );
    }
}
```

1.6.5 GridBagLayout

The GridLayout manager requires that all components have the same dimensions. Realizing that, for some applications, this limitation can be too restrictive, Sun Microsystems decided to add a more advanced layout manager to AWT. Like Grid-Layout, the GridBagLayout manager contains a dynamic rectangular grid of cells, but each component added to the panel can occupy one or more cells.

To accomplish this task, GridBagLayout uses a helper class called GridBag-Constraints which specifies how the components are laid out within the panel's display area. The placement of each component depends on the GridBagConstraints object associated with it, and upon the minimum size and the preferred size of the component's container.

The following code listing creates a frame window using the GridBagLayout manager. To this frame, several buttons are applied with varying constraints. The output of this code sample is shown in figure 1.10. Notice that Button5 spans the entire width of the panel, while the other buttons use only a single cell.

```
import java.awt.*;

class TestFrame extends Frame
{
    public TestFrame()
    {
        super();
```

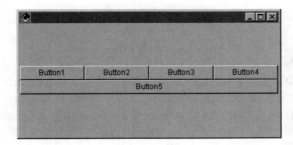

Figure 1.10
GridBagLayout sample

```
// Create the grid bag layout manager instance and
// an associated constraints object
GridBagLayout gridBag = new GridBagLayout();
GridBagConstraints gridConstraints =
                new GridBagConstraints ();

setSize( 200, 200 );
setLayout( gridBag );
setBackground( Color.lightGray );

// Create some buttons, adding them to the grid bag
// using three equal portions
gridConstraints.fill = GridBagConstraints.BOTH;
gridConstraints.weightx = 1.0;
createButton( "Button1", gridBag, gridConstraints );
createButton( "Button2", gridBag, gridConstraints );
createButton( "Button3", gridBag, gridConstraints );

// The fourth button on this line gets the space that's left
gridConstraints.gridwidth =
        GridBagConstraints.REMAINDER;
createButton( "Button4", gridBag, gridConstraints );

// Create another button on the next line that uses
// the entire width.
gridConstraints.weightx = 0.0;
createButton( "Button5", gridBag, gridConstraints );
gridConstraints.gridwidth = GridBagConstraints.RELATIVE;
}

protected void createButton( String sName,
                GridBagLayout gridBag,
                GridBagConstraints gridConstraint )
{
    Button button = new Button( sName );
    gridBag.setConstraints( button, gridConstraint );
```

```
        add( button );
    }
}
```

1.6.6 Combining multiple layouts

Most Java developers know that AWT fundamentally depends on the Component class, and almost everything AWT displays is, at some level, based on this powerful class. In this section, the recurring theme (when talking about layout managers) is the AWT Panel, which is also derived from the Component class. We have seen how a specific layout can be applied to a panel, but in all of the layout examples shown so far, our frame had only one panel and hence, one layout manager.

Fortunately, the people at Sun decided that Java should allow windows to contain more than one panel. Since each panel has its own layout, we can easily create some complex frames without the need to intercept window resize events and manipulate the size or position of our components.

The following sample code creates a frame using multiple panels to create a much more complex user interface. Notice that, although the user interface appears to be much more complicated, the code to create it is straightforward. This example applies the BorderLayout manager to the frames' main panel in the same way as the border layout example shown previously. To the north pane of this panel, a rudimentary tool bar has been added by creating a secondary panel with a FlowLayout manager.

```
import java.awt.*;

class TestFrame extends Frame
{
    public TestFrame()
    {
        super();

        setSize( 200, 200 );
        setLayout( new BorderLayout() );
        setBackground( Color.lightGray );

        // Create a subpanel for the toolbar
        Panel toolbar = new Panel();
        toolbar.setLayout( new FlowLayout() );
        toolbar.add( new Button( "Button 1" ) );
        toolbar.add( new Button( "Button 2" ) );
        toolbar.add( new Button( "Button 3" ) );
        toolbar.add( new Button( "Button 4" ) );
        toolbar.add( new Button( "Button 5" ) );
```

```
        // Add the toolbar to the main panel
        add( toolbar, BorderLayout.NORTH );

        // Add a multi-line editor to the reset of the panel
        add( new TextArea(), BorderLayout.CENTER );
    }
}
```

The resulting display, after compiling and executing this source code, is shown in figure 1.11.

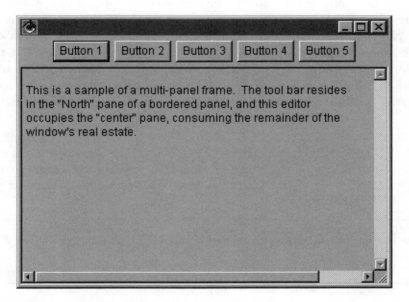

Figure 1.11   A multiple layout sample

1.7   Minimum software requirements

Building software is the focus of this book, and most readers will need to know what minimum set of software tools is required to start designing, building, and testing JFC-based Java applications. From this point forward, we will be designing complete JFC and Java applications, so now is a great time to review the software requirements.

The list of the minimum software packages required for Java development is quite small. Most operating systems ship with a simple text editor, (for example Microsoft Windows or UNIX). In the case of Windows, the NOTEPAD or WORDPAD applications are adequate to get started, though a better editor capable of showing line and column numbers, and managing some of the typical programming features (like auto indenting) is a definite asset.

Since much of the information regarding Java is on the World Wide Web, the development system requires the installation of a browser. There is a continuing argument among computer users about which browser is best, but any of the popular web browsers will be adequate for our purposes. Note that, if building Java applets is planned, the web browser must support the Java 1.1 specification. Microsoft's Internet Explorer does not support some key features of Java 1.1, and it has extensions not supported in the Java language specification, so caution should be observed when using this browser for Java development. Production applets should be tested on all available browsers, so testing can detect any language conflicts.

IMHO Microsoft Internet Explorer 4.0 has some relatively serious bugs in its virtual machine. If you build or find an applet that does not appear to operate correctly in IE 4.0, try it with Netscape Communicator or Sun's HotJava browser.

Below is a list of common web browsers and URLs where they can be downloaded.

Netscape Communicator	`http://www.netscape.com/download/client_download.html`
Microsoft Internet Explorer	`http://www.microsoft.com/ie/download/`
Sun HotJava	`http://java.sun.com/products/hotjava/index.1_0.html`

Finally, a copy of the latest Java Development Kit is required. The JDK includes all of the basic tools needed to compile Java code. Swing applications require JDK 1.1.2 or later; however, this book will assume that JDK 1.2 is being used, which is the most recent release. The JDK can be downloaded free from the Sun Microsystems web site at `http://www.javasoft.com/jdk`.

With this limited set of tools, any imaginable Java application can be created. For creating applications that depend heavily on the user interface, consideration should be given to some form of visual authoring tool. Appendix A includes a partial list of visual tools currently available.

1.8 Delivering a final product

Until Java 1.1 was released, deployment of applications built with Java was tedious and usually involved a great deal of effort sorting out which files from the JDK were necessary and which ones could be omitted. In addition, until Java 1.1, the only mechanism for grouping class files was to store them (without compression) in a ZIP archive file. This meant that it was necessary to add the 9MB CLASSES.ZIP file to the application build, as well as any other ZIP files required to run your program.

To resolve some of the issues associated with delivering a Java-based product, JavaSoft released the Java Runtime Environment (JRE). JRE includes a collection of run-time classes, a virtual machine, and other miscellaneous files necessary to deliver a Java application. This package significantly reduces the amount of work effort, allowing you to quickly package your application. Since Java 1.1 supports compressed .JAR files, the large CLASSES.ZIP file is no longer necessary, and the resultant application footprint is much smaller. In addition, Sun broke the run-time classes into two pieces to help further reduce the size of the final application. The RT.JAR file contains the required run-time classes, and the I18N.JAR file contains classes that are required only for internationalized applications. By utilizing the JRE, a typical English-only application written in Java can now have a delivered footprint of about 1.5MB.

To use JRE, you do not have to do anything special to create your application. Build your code as you normally would, using the JDK, running with the JavaVM application. When your application is complete, create a product directory structure like the one shown in figure 1.12.

Where:

App-Dir	The root directory for your application
App-Dir/bin	An optional directory containing any binary executables you may have.
App-Dir/lib	Contains any .JAR files, classes, properties, or other support files used by your application
App-Dir/jre/bin	Contains the binary files for JRE. This is usually a complete copy from the JRE installation

App-Dir/jre/lib	Contains the JRE .JAR files and other support files. This is usually a complete copy from the JRE installation.

There are two ways to start your application using JRE. Sun recommends creating a small starter application in C, which can be as simple as:

```
void main( void )
{
    system( "jre/bin/jre -classpath .;./lib;./jre/lib "
                         "MyApplication" );
}
```

This simple boot program does not set any environment variables or accept any command line parameters, so you may need to add a few more lines, but regardless, the start-up program will remain quite simple.

A second way is to create a shell script under UNIX or a .BAT file for Windows (or a .CMD file for Windows NT) to accomplish the same task. You might find this technique more useful during the alpha and beta cycles of a project, since it allows you to quickly edit the file to change class paths and other start-up parameters without having to recompile the boot program.

FYI   **Microsoft Windows Native Libraries.** If your application uses a native Windows library (.DLL), this file must be located in the executable search PATH so the JRE's virtual machine can find it.

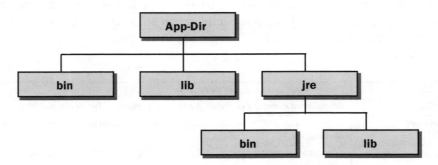

Figure 1.12 A typical JRE-based product directory structure

FYI **Solaris Native Libraries.** Sun issues the following warning. Your .so should be placed in the App-Dir/lib/$(ARCH)/$(THREADS_TYPE) subdirectory, where $(ARCH) denotes the target architecture (for this example, the architecture is "sparc"), and $(THREADS_TYPE) is the type of threads the Solaris VM is using (for now, this must be "green_threads").

The Java Runtime Environment has no royalty fees associated with it, and is available for free download from the Sun Microsystems Java World Wide Web site at `http://java.sun.com/products/jdk/1.1/jre`. At this site, you will also find details about JRE installation and some examples of its use.

1.9 Just-In-Time compilers

The most common complaint among users of Java-based applications relates to performance. Java is well known for its platform independence, but this capability comes with a significant associated cost. Java compilers do not build native executables; rather, they compile source code to produce class files of Java bytecode. Like p-code produced by many Pascal compilers several years ago, Java bytecode is interpreted at run time, which can result in slower performance than expected.

Once again, JavaSoft (and many other Java tool vendors) offers a solution to this problem in the form of a Just-In-Time compiler (JIT). A JIT is embedded into the Java virtual machine, and its purpose is to quickly compile Java classes into native machine code as they are loaded into memory. There is a minor time penalty paid for the JIT compilation, but the resultant code runs significantly faster than Java code interpreted by other compilers. Sun claims that the performance increase with the JIT can be as much as 10 times faster than running the same application without it. Your mileage may vary depending on the type of application you are writing.

The beauty of the Just-In-Time compilers associated with Java is that they require no special design or coding effort on the part of a developer. Like most other aspects of Java, JITs just work! The JIT compiler for Windows 95/NT, created by JavaSoft with assistance from Symantec, can be freely downloaded from their Java web site at the URL `http://java.sun.com/products/jdk/1.1/`. Sun refers to the package as the Win32 Performance Pack. If you are a UNIX user you may have to hunt a bit for a Just-In-Time compiler, but it should be available for most platforms.

FYI On a system running Microsoft Windows, the JDK should be installed first, followed by the Java Runtime Environment, and finally, the Performance Pack. If the Performance Pack is not installed last, the installation program will not be able to update JRE

After installing the Performance Pack, the Java Runtime Environment will automatically be updated to include the JIT. You can also use the JIT with the developer's version of the virtual machine shipped with the JDK.

FYI On a system running Microsoft Windows, if you are planning to run the Just-In-Time compiler in conjunction with the JDK, remember to set the following environment variable:

```
set JAVA_COMPILER=symcjit
```

1.10 Chapter summary

In this chapter, we have reviewed the Java language, AWT, and the details surrounding the Java 1.1 delegation event model. We have also briefly examined JavaSoft's component object technology called JavaBeans, and, presented a simple example of a bean. The layout manager section of this chapter presented an overview of the layout managers included with AWT, though you will see additional layouts in chapter 3. Finally, we reviewed the Java Runtime Environment and how you can use it to create stand-alone applications.

You have briefly heard about Sun's new user interface library, Swing, but in the next chapter we will begin to learn more about it, and you will start to see more examples using Swing code. From this point on, you should consider AWT passé. As you will see, Swing provides all the components required for building portable, lightweight applications and applets.

Swing basics

In this chapter

- What is Swing?
- Model-View-Controller architecture
- The JComponent class

2.1 What is JFC?

As you know, Sun shook the computing world in 1995 with the introduction of an object-oriented language for building client-side browser applets. That language now spans the entire client/server space and the application space previously dominated by programs written in C and C++. Unfortunately, in Java 1.0 and 1.1, some debilitating weaknesses prevented Java from becoming the mainstream industrial-strength language it needed to be in order to survive. Realizing these weaknesses, Sun began an initiative in late 1996 and early 1997 to fill in some of the gaps in the Java language, and they eventually settled on what is known as JFC.

Sun (with the assistance of IBM, Netscape, and Lighthouse Designs) created JFC to help address many of the issues about Java's platform independence and about its user interface consistency. The result is an AWT super-set framework of prebuilt user interface components (written in 100 percent pure Java) which greatly simplify the task of building application front ends. The JFC components, shown in figure 2.1, provide developers with a completely portable set of user interface tools delivered as part of the core Java 1.2 platform.

2.2 What is Swing?

Though this book will periodically discuss the pluggable look-and-feel support in JFC, the primary concern is the top-most Swing layer. Swing is a subset of the Java Foundation Classes, and consists of lightweight components to enhance existing

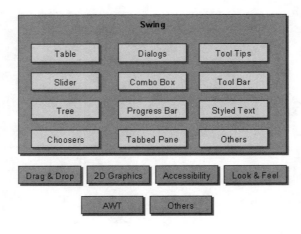

Figure 2.1
Java Foundation Classes

AWT components and to provide advanced controls such as tables and hierarchical trees. The class structure of Swing mimics that of AWT in that all user interface components are derived from a single parent called JComponent (which is derived from the existing AWT Container class).

Figure 2.2 shows a partial hierarchy for the Swing class library. At first, it appears fairly complex; but, if this diagram is compared to the AWT class structure shown in the last chapter, you will see many similarities. Swing (a superset of AWT) provides similar components; however, most components in Swing have been extended and enhanced. Fortunately, the method structure for Swing is similar to AWT, so you should already know how to use Swing for the common components, such as text fields and labels.

 Since JComponent, and hence all Swing components, are derived from the AWT container class, they can contain other UI components. For example, a table object can contain an instance of a button, a label, or even a graphic image. This is an important distinction between Swing and AWT.

2.2.1 Swing package overview

In part 2 of this book, we will begin to use Swing components in earnest; however, before this can be attempted, a quick overview of the Swing package organization is needed. The following table identifies each Swing package and briefly describes its purpose.

`com.sun.java.swing`	This highest level package contains the basic Swing components, default component models, and interfaces delegate and model classes.
`com.sun.java.swing.border`	This package specifies the interfaces and classes that define and render specific border styles.
`com.sun.java.swing.event`	The event package contains all Swing-specific event types and listeners. Swing components can also support events specified in `java.awt.event`.
`com.sun.java.swing.plaf`	The plaf package contains the pluggable look-and-feel API used to define custom user interfaces. It includes libraries to emulate the look-and-feel of Windows, Macintosh, Motif, and some custom interfaces created by Sun.
`com.sun.java.swing.table`	The table package contains interfaces and classes which support the Swing JTable control.

`com.sun.java.swing.text`	The text package consists of support classes for the Swing document framework.
`com.sun.java.swing.text.html`	This extension of the text package contains classes specific to HTML text components.
`com.sun.java.swing.tree`	The tree package contains interfaces and classes to support the Swing JTree hierarchical tree class.
`com.sun.java.swing.undo`	The undo package contains support classes to implement undo/redo functionality in Swing.

2.3 Why use Swing?

For many developers, the resistance to change to a new user interface class library may be too great; however, all Java programmers should seriously consider implementing future applications with Swing rather than AWT. Swing makes the development of Java-based programs both possible and attractive by offering capabilities that simply do not exist with AWT. JFC has advantages over AWT that will be examined in detail in this section.

2.3.1 JavaBeans compliance

All Swing components are JavaBeans compliant. The JavaBeans specification is a crucial segment of the Java 1.1 architecture used to create standard visual and non-visual software components. JavaBeans components have a consistent property API and a common event handling mechanism which permit interoperability and code reuse. What this means is that most visual environments will be able to load and use Swing components without the need for software updates or complicated library creation procedures.

2.3.2 Lightweight framework

The most difficult task that Sun faced, when building a portable user interface library for Java, was how to handle the differences from one platform to another. For example, a button on the Microsoft Windows platform differs in both operation and appearance from a similar control on an X-Motif screen, and the Apple Macintosh interface is unlike either of these. In the past, any attempts to allow portability usually involved creating an interface with functionality reduced to the lowest common denominator of all platforms, leaving the developer at the mercy of the target platform for nonstandard components. Sun devised a different solution that implemented a platform specific look-and-feel, while still providing a common Java

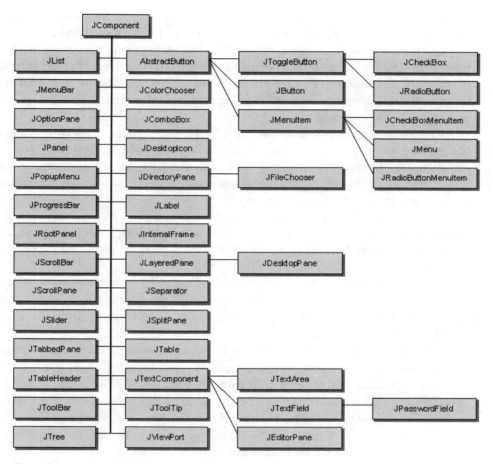

Figure 2.2　Partial Swing class structure

API. This technique required a thin veneer layer to implement the Java API, and a somewhat larger native code layer (called a peer class) to map the Java API to the platform specific component. Controls of this nature have become known as heavy-weight components.

When creating Swing, the architects at Sun decided that restricting an application to the look-and-feel provided by the target platform was no longer desirable. Despite all the efforts of the AWT developers, several problems with cross-platform applications persisted. For example, the use of scroll bars is not consistent on different platforms. Though platform specific look-and-feel is still desirable for some applications, a common look-and-feel across all platforms is becoming increasingly important. Sun addressed these demands by introducing a lightweight component framework that does not require platform-specific peer classes and is written entirely in Java. Lightweight components provide a consistent interface across all platforms, while remaining completely portable.

In addition to platform consistency, lightweight components offer some other distinct advantages. First, because lightweight components are "light," they make much more efficient use of resources in the virtual machine, resulting in smaller program footprints and somewhat faster code. Second, unlike AWT components (which are always opaque), lightweight components can have transparent pixels. This means that several components can be overlain to give the perception of a much more complex component. In addition, pixel transparency means that components no longer have to be rectangular—we can create round or oval buttons if desired.

All Swing components implement a lightweight framework to eliminate the restrictions of the peered interface in AWT. Since Swing components are not necessarily restricted to the platform's native user interface, you can configure the look-and-feel in any way desired.

Sun does not recommend mixing Swing components with older heavyweight components because of some known conflicts. With the advantages that lightweight Swing components offer, one would wonder why anyone would need to use heavyweight components, but there will be times when this is necessary. For example, if you are integrating a third-party heavyweight component, such as a three-dimensional chart, you hit an unavoidable boundary between the lightweight and heavyweight worlds, which will inevitably cause you grief.

The problem between these two clashing technologies is one of Z-orders. All graphical components are drawn according to a specified Z-order (the layers on which certain components are drawn). Lightweight components reuse the screen real estate of their nearest heavyweight ancestor, and, as a result, are restricted to the same Z-order position. Since heavyweight components each receive their own unique Z-order position, they can conflict with any lightweight components drawn within the same panel.

For example, assume you create an AWT Label and a Swing JLabel instance within a panel. The JLabel receives the same Z-order position as its parent panel, while the AWT Label is drawn at a higher Z-order position. Since layers are drawn lowest to highest, the Label can cover its Swing sibling, obscuring the output of the application.

Since we will probably never be able to completely eliminate heavyweight components from our designs, we have to learn to live with the limitations they pose on a lightweight architecture. To help you address these issues, try to adhere to the following four guidelines:

1 When possible, avoid mixing heavyweight and lightweight components in containers where the lightweight component may overlap the heavyweight. Swing offers replacement components for those defined in AWT. Use Swing whenever possible.

2 Never place heavyweight AWT components inside a lightweight container such as a JScrollPane. To scroll heavyweight components, use AWT's ScrollPane class.

3 Never add a heavyweight component to a Swing internal frame (JInternalFrame) instance.

4 Be careful with pop-up components such as menus. If you use a pop-up menu in a container holding heavyweight components, you need to force them to display at the top of the Z-order. To control this for a JPopupMenu object, use the `setDefaultLightWeightPopupEnabled()` method before the instance has been realized.

2.3.3 Interaction with external resources

A major drawback of early versions of Java and AWT was an inability to properly interact with external resources, such as a mouse or keyboard. Java 1.1 partially addresses these problems, but Swing further enhances these features by fully implementing interactions with the mouse and keyboard. In particular, Swing now offers full support for keyboard accelerators and mnemonics for menu items and most other components. Additionally, Swing offers support for users with special needs who are either unable to use a keyboard or unable to read the display.

2.4 Model-View-Controller architecture

Chapter 1 briefly noted the existence of the MVC architecture introduced in Java 1.1, but included little insight about the inner workings of MVC. Lightweight component technology is also part of the MVC mechanism, though this may not be obvious. This section collects the many pieces of MVC into a single model to help you better understand this technology. Understanding MVC is not critical to using Swing; however, it is necessary for some of the advanced aspects of Swing, such as pluggable look-and-feel.

2.4.1 How MVC works

MVC is a well known object-oriented design structure originally adopted and modified from SmallTalk to create and manage Java GUI components. The basic concept of MVC is that every component consists of three parts: a Model, a View, and a Controller. (see figure 2.3)

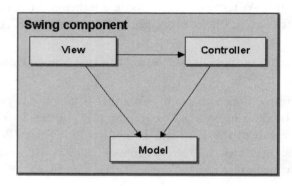

**Figure 2.3
Simplified anatomy of
a Swing component**

The Model is responsible for maintaining all aspects of the component state. This includes, for example, such values as the pressed/unpressed state of a push button, or the currently selected item for a list box.

The View determines the visual representation of the component's model. This is the "look" of the object. For example, the View displays the correct color of a component, whether the component appears raised or lower (in the case of a button), or the rendering of the desired font.

The Controller performs event handling for the entire component. This is the "feel" of the component, and it determines what actions are performed when the component is used. In the case of a push button component, the Controller detects the button press from the user, and informs the Model that the state has changed. The Model then tells the View to repaint to reflect the new Model data.

2.4.2 What can MVC accomplish?

You may ask, "Why do I care about MVC?" The short answer is, "You don't have to," as long as you are willing to accept the default MVC provided by Swing for each component. In this simple scenario, you can blindly implement user interfaces with Swing components without any knowledge of MVC; however, you will soon realize that the default Swing MVC for most components is unacceptable for many applications. For example, let's assume that you want one column of a table to contain a simulated tree control. The existing MVC for a Swing JTable offers nothing resembling this capability, so you need to implement this yourself by enhancing, or completely replacing, the default MVC.

Understanding and using MVC offers two distinct capabilities: the ability to change the look-and-feel of a component, and the ability to change the data Model that a component uses. The next two sections describe these concepts in more detail.

2.4.3 Custom rendering

Figure 2.4
Two views of a radio button component

The primary point of interest for MVC, is the custom look-and-feel of a component. The more advanced part of the Swing API permits developers to completely replace the look-and-feel (View and Controller) with a new functionality. There are two main advantages to doing this. First, the user interface can be made consistent across several platforms, rather than relying on the target platform to render the application's user interface using the GUI controls provided by the operating system. Second, since the Model and Controller parts of the component can remain unchanged, completely different components can be devised by reusing much of a component that already exists. Figure 2.4 shows the same radio button group using two different user interfaces. The important point to make about figure 2.4 is that the code underneath the UI did not change at all to create the different views.

A more subtle and simple use of MVC is custom rendering. This allows the developer to intercept the drawing mechanism of a component and attach new code. This is useful for rendering one column, or one cell of a table, differently from the rest. In the example shown in figure 2.5, the columns of a table containing stock market data are rendered. Note that the Stock column contains a larger font than the others do, and that the color of each column is rendered independently.

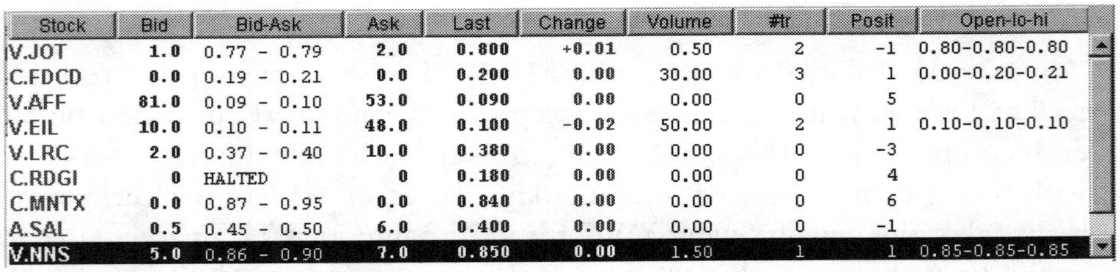

Stock	Bid	Bid-Ask	Ask	Last	Change	Volume	#tr	Posit	Open-lo-hi
V.JOT	1.0	0.77 - 0.79	2.0	0.800	+0.01	0.50	2	-1	0.80-0.80-0.80
C.FDCD	0.0	0.19 - 0.21	0.0	0.200	0.00	30.00	3	1	0.00-0.20-0.21
V.AFF	81.0	0.09 - 0.10	53.0	0.090	0.00	0.00	0	5	
V.EIL	10.0	0.10 - 0.11	48.0	0.100	-0.02	50.00	2	1	0.10-0.10-0.10
V.LRC	2.0	0.37 - 0.40	10.0	0.380	0.00	0.00	0	-3	
C.RDGI	0	HALTED	0	0.180	0.00	0.00	0	4	
C.MNTX	0.0	0.87 - 0.95	0.0	0.840	0.00	0.00	0	6	
A.SAL	0.5	0.45 - 0.50	6.0	0.400	0.00	0.00	0	-1	
V.NNS	5.0	0.86 - 0.90	7.0	0.850	0.00	1.50	1	1	0.85-0.85-0.85

Figure 2.5 Example of custom rendering

Additionally, one column or cell could contain a bitmap with, or without, additional text. When we examine the use of tables in a later chapter, you will see how simple custom rendering can be.

2.4.4   Custom data models

The second key aspect of MVC is the provision to modify or replace the data model. In a previous example, we wanted to create an instance of a table with one column containing a simulated hierarchical tree. To accomplish this task, we need to understand that the data model requires some enhancement. For example, a tree introduces the concept of nodes, and these nodes can usually be in either an expanded or collapsed state. Additionally, a given node typically has at least one child and, possibly, a parent as well. All of these rudimentary tree features must be integrated into an expanded data model for the table. Fortunately, almost every Swing UI component provides a method to apply a different data model. As you will see throughout part 2 of this book, applying new or enhanced data models to a Swing component is usually a simple task.

For each component that supports a custom data model, Swing implements an associated default data model which it uses if you do not elect to create your own. The default model helps to simplify the creation of these fairly complex components.

For example, if you write code to create a simple table (we will examine this in chapter 11), Swing uses the default data model for a table. As a result, you can create and load the table with data using just a few lines of code by specifying your table's headers and column data in vectored arrays. The table's default data model accepts these data vectors and knows how to use them to display the title of each column, how to display the correct data for each cell, and so on. As a developer, you have minimal involvement after the instance is created.

Custom data models allow you to change the default behavior to suit your own needs. In our table example, you may want to associate additional attributes, such as the color of the font, with each cell, or, if you are displaying numbers, perhaps you need to add an attribute to the model to control the format of the display. There is really no limit to what can be accomplished with a custom data model.

Since custom data models are such an important part of Swing, we will examine them in much greater detail as we progress through this book. Specifically, we will design and implement custom data models for Swing's list, hierarchical tree, and table components.

2.5 Delegates

By now, you have probably realized that the diagram in figure 2.3 was an overly simplified view of a Swing component. In practice, the path between the View and Controller is not limited to a single data path. Many tasks demanded by the user of the Controller can affect the visual representation of a component, resulting in a complex and, possibly, intertwined series of connections between the Controller and the View. As a result, the diagram from figure 2.3 must be modified to create a truer representation of the component (see figure 2.6).

2.5.1 What are delegates?

Sun's solution to this complexity was to simplify the components' internal communications paths by wrapping the View and Controller parts with a new mechanism which outwardly exhibits the original simple model shown in figure 2.3. The class

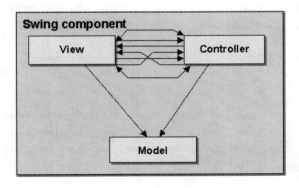

Figure 2.6
More realistic anatomy of a
Swing component

that combines the View/Controller part of the Model is called a delegate. The result is a component representation like that shown in figure 2.7.

From the outside, the Viewer and Controller appear to be a single delegate entity, and this offers some distinct advantages. The combined View/Controller allows both the appearance and behavior (the look-and-feel) of a component to be handled as a single unit.

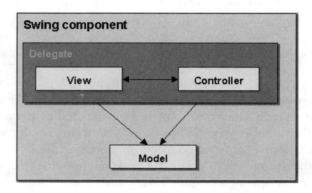

Figure 2.7
Real anatomy of a
Swing component

2.5.2 The ComponentUI class

You now know that every Swing UI object wraps its View/Controller code with a delegate to better package its look-and-feel; however, you may be unclear about how this happens. In Swing, the delegate part of a component is derived from a class named ComponentUI. With a few simple method calls to a ComponentUI instance, you can change the look-and-feel of any associated Swing component object. For example, to assign a new delegate to a component (again, this refers to a component's look-and-feel), you can call the ComponentUI `setUI()` method. The following table identifies some ComponentUI methods and their purposes.

Method	Purpose
`installUI(JComponent c)`	Installs this ComponentUI for the specified component
`uninstallUI(JComponent c)`	Removes this ComponentUI from the specified component
`paint(Graphics g, JComponent c)`	Allows access to the Graphics instance associated with the specified component

Method	Purpose
`getPreferredSize(JComponent c)`	Return the preferred size for the specified component based on this ComponentUI
`getMinimumSize(JComponent c)`	Return the minimum size for the specified component based on this ComponentUI
`getMaximumSize(JComponent c)`	Return the maximum size for the specified component based on this ComponentUI

2.6 Pluggable LookAndFeel

In a Swing-based application, a class called LookAndFeel characterizes the pluggable look-and-feel of all GUI components. It accomplishes this task by creating delegates for each component through the instantiation of ComponentUI objects.

Even though LookAndFeel manages all the mundane work required to create new View-Controllers for Swing components, it is complicated to change the complete set of ComponentUI classes for the look-and-feel of an application. This can be a tedious operation using ComponentUI, and is not for the faint of heart.

Fortunately, the developers of Swing created a much simpler mechanism for changing the entire look-and-feel for an application. A class called UIManager is used to manage the complete pluggable look-and-feel, and, with it, you can easily change the appearance of your application. To do this, you simply call the UIManager's `setLookAndFeel()` method. Here is an example:

```
try {
    UIManager.setLookAndFeel(
        "com.sun.java.swing.motif.MotifLookAndFeel" );
    SwingUtilities.updateComponentTreeUI( myFrame );
}
catch (Exception  e)
{
    System.err.println( "Could not load LookAndFeel" );
}
```

The call to `SwingUtilities.updateComponentTreeUI()` informs all components in the UI hierarchy of the application that the look-and-feel has changed. In response to this, each component discards its current ComponentUI instance and creates one associated with the new interface.

Swing currently supports five different pluggable user interfaces:

Windows	This interface provides a look-and-feel conforming to the Microsoft Windows 95 user interface.
Motif	The Motif look-and-feel conforms to the X Windows Motif interface found on many UNIX workstations.
Organic	This pluggable look-and-feel interface is cross platform compatible. It presents a user interface that some might find objectionable, but it may suit your tastes. The Organic look-and-feel is available in several themes, including Santa Fe, Vancouver, Dallas, and Darkroom, all of which simply modify the color palette.
Metal	This look-and-feel resembles the Macintosh user interface, but has a distinctly chiseled appearance.
Macintosh	This interface allows developers to create applications with an Apple Macintosh look-and-feel.

 The Windows and Macintosh pluggable look-and-feel libraries are supported only on their native platforms. Attempts to use them on other platforms will result in an UnsupportedLookAndFeel exception when the application calls the `UIManager.setLookAndFeel()` method.

According to Sun, this limitation is artificial, and is in place only because Microsoft will neither confirm nor deny the right to present the Windows interface on non-Windows platforms.

 The Organic look-and-feel library is not currently part of the Swing release, but will be available separately from the JavaSoft web site.

2.7   Creating UI objects

In the previous section, you heard a lot about a class named ComponentUI. What you didn't hear about were all of the child classes derived from ComponentUI. For the pluggable look-and-feel interface to work, each component must have a UI class derived from ComponentUI (which contains the user interface code).

The diagram in figure 2.8 shows the hierarchy in place for the ButtonUI family. Note that, for each pluggable look-and-feel library (Windows, Motif, Metal, and so on), there is a ButtonUI class to generate the user interface. If you do the math, taking each GUI component into account, you will realize that Swing supplies a large number of classes derived from ComponentUI. So, if you decide to create an entire pluggable look-and-feel, be prepared to invest some time and effort. Fortunately, this is usually a simple task.

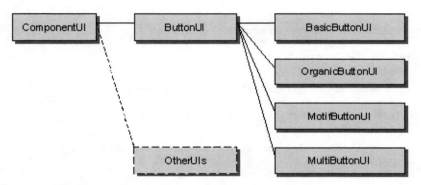

Figure 2.8   ComponentUI hierarchy for a JButton

2.7.1   Creating a simple component

We will deal with the task of creating a custom look-and-feel in greater detail in a later chapter, so, for now, we will just create a simple custom component interface for a button. Listing 2.1 derives a new class from ButtonUI that creates a button with a flat face.

```
// Imports
import java.awt.*;
import com.sun.java.swing.*;
import com.sun.java.swing.plaf.*;

class MyButtonUI extends ButtonUI
{
    public void installUI( JComponent component )
    {
        System.out.println( "MYButtonUI:installUI" );
    }
```

Listing 2.1   A custom UI example

```
public void uninstallUI( JComponent component )
{
    System.out.println( "MYButtonUI:uninstallUI" );
}

public Insets getDefaultMargin( AbstractButton button )
{
    return button.getInsets();
}

public Insets getInsets( JComponent component )
{
    return new Insets( 5, 5, 5, 5 );
}

public Dimension getMaximumSize( JComponent component )
{
    return getPreferredSize( component );
}

public Dimension getMinimumSize( JComponent component )
{
    return getPreferredSize( component );
}

public Dimension getPreferredSize( JComponent component )
{
    Graphics     g      = component.getGraphics();
    Dimension    rect   = new Dimension();
    FontMetrics  fm     = g.getFontMetrics();
    Insets       insets = component.getInsets();

    rect.width = fm.stringWidth(
                    ((JButton)component).getText() )
                            + insets.left + insets.right;
    rect.height = fm.getHeight() + insets.top + insets.bottom;

    return rect;
}

public void paint( Graphics g, JComponent component )
{
    Dimension    rect = new Dimension();
    FontMetrics  fm = g.getFontMetrics();
    Insets       insets = component.getInsets();

    g.setColor( Color.white );
    g.fillRect( 0, 0, size.width - 1, size.height - 1 );
```

Listing 2.1   A custom UI example (continued)

```
        g.setColor( Color.black );
        g.drawString( ((JButton)component).getText(),
                insets.left, insets.top + fm.getAscent() );
    }
}
```

Listing 2.1   A custom UI example (continued)

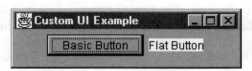

Figure 2.9
Example of a custom button

The results of using component look-and-feel in a Java program are shown in figure 2.9. Note that the example code in listing 2.1 does not handle mouse events, such as "mouse over" or "mouse click" operations, so the custom button acts more like a label than a button; however, the example does show how a custom look-and-feel can be implemented with relative ease.

The example in figure 2.9 shows a simple application containing two buttons. The button on the left, labeled "Basic Button", is a standard JButton component from the Swing class library, while the button on the right is an instance of the class MyButtonUI (from the previous code fragment) to implement the custom appearance.

2.8   JComponent, the mother of Swing

We already know that all AWT components stem from a single parent (called Component) which is responsible for all generic component manipulation. Swing derives a new class, named JComponent, to further enhance the capabilities of a component. As shown in figure 2.2, all Swing components are derived from JComponent. Since understanding JComponent contributes greatly to the knowledge needed to utilize Swing effectively, this section describes the details of the key facets of this class. JComponent provides much of the functionality of all Swing components, supplying many features common to all graphical controls.

2.8.1   Pluggable look-and-feel

We have already discussed the ability to create custom user interfaces, so we won't dwell on this feature. It is enough to say that JComponent is responsible for all of the pluggable look-and-feel logic of a Swing component, and that these user interface characteristics can be specified by the developer, or optionally by the user, at run time.

2.8.2 Keystroke handling

The architecture of JComponent was designed to handle keyboard events for each component. Additionally, keyboard events can be nested such that the component's owner processes all events. For example, the top level panel (the owner of a component) can manage the keyboard event generated by pressing the <F1> key. This way the <F1> will be recognized regardless of which child component of the panel currently has the focus.

2.8.3 Action objects

Action-interface objects provide a single control point for actions generated by the user. For example, if an application provides a toolbar button and a menu option that perform the same task, they can be configured to point to the same action object. If the action is disabled, all GUI items that reference that object are automatically disabled. This capability can greatly reduce the amount of code required to manage toolbars and menus.

2.8.4 Borders

JComponent fully supports borders. The border can be a single border, such as a raised bevel, or can be a compound border which consists of two different border styles applied to the control at the same time. For example, a raised bevel combined with a lowered bevel creates a border with a thin raised edge, much like that of a typical status bar.

2.8.5 Accessibility

Though noncommercial developers may downplay the need to support users with special needs, others, particularly those involved with government projects, understand these needs and are required to design applications accessible to everyone. All Swing components are compatible with Assistive Technologies (a standard that provides alternative interfaces, such as Braille). This is accomplished using the Swing `Accessible` interface and, where necessary, the `AccessibleText` interface. We will not delve into the details of accessibility in this book, though these features will be mentioned, when appropriate.

Sun provides an excellent article on the subject of accessibility. This details not only the relevance that accessibility has, but also the design concepts and guidelines you can apply to your own applications. You can find this article on Sun's web site at `http://www.sun.com/access/updt.HCI.advance.html`.

2.8.6 Other features of JComponent

There are a number of other features provided by JComponent. These features include: internationalization/localization, ToolTips, automatic scrolling (for trees, tables, and so on), double buffering of components (for faster repaints), and slow-motion graphics rendering (for debugging component rendering bugs).

2.8.7 Controlling component size

AWT offers a single mechanism for controlling the size of a component—set-Size(), which sets the absolute size in pixels. This technique works fine for heavyweight components, where the look-and-feel of the user interface is constant, but can cause problems when applied to the flexible user interfaces of Swing.

For backward compatibility, JComponent does provide all of the original sizing APIs from the AWT Component class, but Sun discourages the use of these methods for absolute sizing and positioning of Swing components. In Swing-based applications, the look-and-feel can be changed dynamically, and, as a result, applying absolute sizes is inappropriate. To address this issue, Swing provides three sizing methods that will be used extensively in the examples in this book. These methods are outlined below.

`setPreferredSize()` `getPreferredSize()`	This method sets the desired size of the component when drawn. In response to this method, Swing will make its best attempt to lay out the component such that this size is accommodated. If the current look-and-feel is incapable of drawing the component at the preferred size, it will adjust the dimensions to offer a best fit.
`setMinimumSize()` `getMinimumSize()`	This method determines the minimum dimensions with which the component can be drawn. During lay out, the component will still make its best effort to draw at the preferred size, but in circumstances where the preferred dimensions are smaller than the minimum size, the minimum dimensions will be used.
`setMaximumSize()` `getMaximumSize()`	This method controls the maximum dimensions at which a component can be drawn. If, during component lay out, the current size exceeds the maximum, the component size will default to the specified maximum value.

Controlling the minimum, maximum, and preferred sizes of a component object allows layout managers to resize dimensions without being concerned about the current look-and-feel in place, or the potential that this user interface may be changed at run time.

The JComponent sizing methods are particularly useful for embedding components inside a container object, such as, a split pane. Setting the minimum and maximum sizes of embedded components controls the range of the divider within the splitter pane, for example, preventing divider positioning to invalid or inappropriate positions.

2.8.8 JComponent constants

JComponent includes a number of constants used to control how the `register-KeyboardAction()` method behaves. This method intercepts keyboard accelerator activity for a component. The component can be configured to intercept keys when the window is focused, or if the key is pressed while one of the component's children have the focus. The constants are as follows:

```
public static final int WHEN_FOCUSED
public static final int WHEN_ANCESTOR_OF_FOCUSED_COMPONENT
public static final int WHEN_IN_FOCUSED_WINDOW

public static final int UNDEFINED_CONDITION
```

This constant is used by some of the API methods to indicate that no condition is defined.

```
public static final String TOOL_TIP_TEXT_KEY
```

This constant contains the comment to display when the cursor is over the component, also known as a *value tip*, *flyover help*, or *flyover label*.

2.8.9 JComponent variables

```
protected transient ComponentUI ui
```

This variable contains the associated instance of the UI component. This value is dependent on the selected look-and-feel in use.

```
protected EventListenerList listenerList
```

This variable holds the list of event listeners associated with this JComponent instance.

```
protected AccessibleContext accessibleContext
```

This variable is used by the accessibility support mechanism. JComponent contains all of the methods in interface `Accessible`, though it won't actually implement the interface for them. Implementation is the responsibility of the individual objects that extend JComponent.

2.8.10 JComponent constructors

```
JComponent()
```

The default constructor creates an instance of a JComponent. JComponent is an abstract class, and, as such, only derived child classes may call this constructor.

2.8.11 JComponent significant method groupings

```
public void updateUI()
protected void setUI(ComponentUI x)
public String getUIClassID()
```

These pluggable look-and-feel methods are used to configure and control the user interface being used.

```
protected Graphics getComponentGraphics(Graphics g)
protected void paintComponent(Graphics g)
protected void paintChildren(Graphics g)
protected void paintBorder(Graphics g)
public void update(Graphics g)
public boolean isPaintingTile()
public Graphics getGraphics()
public void setDebugGraphicsOptions(int debugOptions)
public int getDebugGraphicsOptions()
public void repaint(long tm, int x, int y, int width,
                                    int height)
public void repaint(Rectangle r)
public boolean isOptimizedDrawingEnabled()
public void paintImmediately(int x, int y, int w, int h)
public void paintImmediately(Rectangle r)
```

This group of methods offers support for handling the graphics instances and repainting the component.

```
public boolean isFocusCycleRoot()
public void setNextFocusableComponent(Component aComponent)
public Component getNextFocusableComponent()
public void setRequestFocusEnabled(boolean aFlag)
public boolean isRequestFocusEnabled()
public void requestFocus()
public void grabFocus()
```

```
public boolean requestDefaultFocus()
public boolean isFocusTraversable()
protected void processFocusEvent(FocusEvent e)
public boolean hasFocus()
```

This group of methods controls how the component reacts to the focus. Like the AWT Component class, Swing components support a series of methods to handle the keyboard focusing mechanism. Components can request focus, or simply grab it. Additionally, JComponent can enable or disable the focus to prevent instances from receiving focus. For example, labels should never receive the keyboard focus because they do not support any form of editing.

```
public void setBorder(Border border)
public Border getBorder()
```

These methods manage the border applied to a component. The next chapter will illustrate that each JComponent derivative supports the capability to own a border. Border management of all Swing components is controlled at the JComponent level.

```
public void setPreferredSize(Dimension preferredSize)
public Dimension getPreferredSize()
public void setMaximumSize(Dimension maximumSize)
public Dimension getMaximumSize()
public void setMinimumSize(Dimension minimumSize)
public Dimension getMinimumSize()
public Insets getInsets()
public float getAlignmentY()
public void setAlignmentY(float alignmentY)
public float getAlignmentX()
public void setAlignmentX(float alignmentX)
public void setBounds(int x, int y, int w, int h)
public void setBounds(Rectangle r)
public Rectangle getBounds(Rectangle rv)
public Dimension getSize(Dimension rv)
public Point getLocation(Point rv)
public int getX()
public int getY()
public int getWidth()
public int getHeight()
```

JComponent controls all sizing, positioning, and alignment for all Swing-based components. This group of methods controls such aspects of a component as its minimum, maximum, and preferred size, and the alignment of the object.

```
public void registerKeyboardAction(ActionListener anAction,
```

```
                       KeyStroke aKeyStroke, int aCondition )
public void unregisterKeyboardAction(KeyStroke aKeyStroke)
public KeyStroke[] getRegisteredKeyStrokes()
public int getConditionForKeyStroke(KeyStroke aKeyStroke)
public ActionListener getActionForKeyStroke(
                              KeyStroke aKeyStroke)
public void resetKeyboardActions()
```

This method group manages keyboard actions for the component. Each JComponent derivative inherently supports keyboard accelerator handling. Keyboard actions for any user-enterable character can be intercepted and assigned a particular action. Actions for each component can be registered or unregistered.

```
public void setToolTipText(String text)
public String getToolTipText()
public String getToolTipText(MouseEvent event)
public Point getToolTipLocation(MouseEvent event)
public JToolTip createToolTip()
```

ToolTips, also known as fly-over help or fly-over labels, are a trait of every Swing-based UI component. As this list shows, JComponent supports a number of methods to create and manage ToolTip text for the component instance.

```
public void setDoubleBuffered(boolean aFlag)
public boolean isDoubleBuffered()
```

Unlike AWT, Swing components support double buffering. This simplifies dynamic user interface aspects, such as animation. AWT demanded custom code to manage display buffering, but for components derived from JComponent, double buffering is simply controlled by these two methods.

```
public Accessible getNextAccessibleSibling()
public Accessible getPreviousAccessibleSibling()
public Accessible getAccessibleAt(Point p)
public String getAccessibleName()
public void setAccessibleName(String s)
public String getAccessibleDescription()
public void setAccessibleDescription(String s)
public AccessibleStateSet getAccessibleStateSet()
public AccessibleRole getAccessibleRole()
public Number getAccessibleValue()
public boolean setAccessibleValue(Number n)
public Number getMinimumAccessibleValue()
public Number getMaximumAccessibleValue()
public Accessible getAccessibleParent()
public void setAccessibleParent(Accessible a)
public int getAccessibleChildrenCount()
```

```
public Accessible getAccessibleChild(int i)
public int getAccessibleActionCount()
public String getAccessibleActionDescription(int i)
public boolean doAccessibleAction(int i)
public AccessibleText getAccessibleText()
public int getAccessibleSelectionCount()
public Accessible getAccessibleSelection(int i)
public void addAccessibleSelection(int i)
public void removeAccessibleSelection(int i)
public void clearAccessibleSelection()
public void selectAllAccessibleSelection()
```

Accessibility is significant if your applications will be used by people requiring additional assistance, such those who are blind. Though we will not examine these capabilities in this book, all Swing components derived from JComponent support Assistive Technology as a result of this group of methods.

For a description of other method groupings provided by the JComponent class, see the online API description included with the JFC product.

2.9   Chapter summary

In this chapter, we have covered all of the basic concepts of the Swing class library, starting with a definition of Swing and its component classes. Then, we reviewed the Model-View-Controller architecture and applied it to the Swing class library. This led to a quick study of pluggable look-and-feel, accompanied by a simple example of a component with a custom user interface.

Then, we looked at the internals and features of JComponent, and we examined the capabilities built into every Swing component. The use of these capabilities will become more apparent in part 2 of this book, as we begin to create applications using Swing components.

Finally, we briefly described each of the packages that make up the Swing class library. The contents and use of these packages will become clear as you progress through the remainder of this book.

Part II

Using Swing
components

*P*art 2 of this book contains the details required to use each of the key Swing components. You will start by looking at Swing panels and panes (the most basic components) and then build on this knowledge to include buttons, menus, and more. Finally, we will examine more complex components, such as tables and hierarchical trees. When appropriate, we will also look at some of the more subtle aspects of Swing. The concepts you will learn in this part of the book can be applied to your own applications for either visual effect or performance enhancement.

3

Panels
and panes

In this chapter, you will begin to learn about some of the common components built into Swing. If you are familiar with AWT, then you know that you require either an instance of Frame or Applet as a starting point, and from there you can add additional panels and components to complete the code.

With Swing, all user interface component class names begin with the letter J, and, where possible, the name is the same as the AWT class it replaces. So, the basic starting point for a Swing-based program is either JFrame or JApplet. We will examine both of these classes, followed by a discussion of JPanel (a replacement for the AWT Panel class), the various flavors of panes provided by Swing, and the new layout managers supplied in the Swing class library.

3.1   JFrame

Simply put, if you know how to use the AWT Frame class, then you can use JFrame. JFrame is an extended version of Frame that adds support for special painting behavior, and for child components that are managed by a JLayeredPane (you will learn a little more about this class later in the chapter). Additionally, JFrame has support for Swing MenuBars, allowing them to be placed not only at the top of the window, but also anyplace within the frame (though, if the menu is attached to the frame using the `setMenuBar()` method, it will always be located at the top of the window).

All objects associated with a JFrame are managed by its only child, an instance of JRootPane. JRootPane is a simple container for all other panes for the JFrame instance. The following hierarchy shows the nesting of objects within a JFrame instance:

        JFrame
                JRootPane
                        glassPane
                        layeredPane
                                [menuBar]
                                contentPane

3.1.1   A JFrame application

As with the AWT Frame class, you use an instance of JFrame to build the primary window of applications rather than applets. Of course, a JFrame can also be used to create secondary windows to an application or an applet. The code below creates a very simple application class using JFrame.

```
import java.awt.*;
import com.sun.java.swing.*;

class TestFrame
        extends JFrame
{
    public TestFrame()
    {
        setTitle( "Test Application" );
        setSize( 100, 100 );
        setBackground( Color.gray );

        Panel topPanel = new Panel();
        topPanel.setLayout( new BorderLayout() );
        getContentPane().add( topPanel );

        // Create a label to look at
        Label labelHello = new Label( "Hello World!" );
        topPanel.add( labelHello, BorderLayout.NORTH );
    }

    // Main program started
    public static void main( String args[] )
    {
        // Create an instance of the Test application
        TestFrame mainFrame = new TestFrame();
        mainFrame.setVisible( true );
    }
}
```

Listing 3.1   "Hello World!" using JFrame

Listing 3.1 creates a very simple Java application using JFrame. Although Swing provides its own panel and label classes, they have been intentionally left out of this example. Instead, the AWT equivalents have been used. The result of this application is shown in figure 3.1.

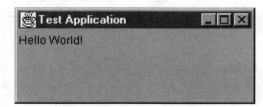

Figure 3.1
The "Hello World!" application

It is possible to mix AWT components and Swing components within a Swing-based application; however, due to Z-order limitations, you may experience some annoyances during screen repaints. AWT components appear to get quickly painted in the upper-left corner of the frame before being correctly positioned, resulting in unexpected flicker.

When possible avoid using AWT components in Swing applications. Use the Swing equivalents instead.

The example in listing 3.1 appears pretty much as expected, containing code as it would exist using AWT. There is one significant difference, however. The line:

```
getContentPane().add( topPanel );
```

appears a bit odd, and, in particular, the call to `getContentPane()`. JFrame exhibits a slight incompatibility when compared to the AWT Frame class because it contains only a single child (which is an instance of JRootPane). In order to add any other components to the JFrame instance, they must be added to the root pane. This is unlike the AWT Frame class which creates an instance of a Panel automatically, allowing components to be added directly to the frame instance. To access the root pane, JFrame provides a method called `getContentPane()`.

FYI It is impossible to add components directly to a JFrame using the following syntax:

```
frame.add( component );
```

Instead you must always use this notation:

```
frame.getContentPane().add( component );
```

Failure to add components using the `getContentPane()` mechanism will result in the generation of an exception. The best solution to this problem is to create a panel, add it to the content pane, then add all components to the new panel.

The JFrame class offers some other interesting features. In addition to the content pane, JFrame also provides two other panes: a layered pane and a glass pane. We will examine JLayeredPane in more detail later in this chapter.

The glass pane allows you to display components in front of the existing JFrame instance, which can be useful in some applications. For example, suppose you want to create a network application that allows users on different computers to draw on a common "white board." You can display the local user's drawing on the content pane of the application, while on the glass pane, you could display the remote user's mouse pointer and any drawing he or she performs.

Another practical use for the glass pane is in game development. The background of your game can be shown in the content pane, and any animated items can be drawn on the glass pane. Building your game in this way greatly simplifies the redrawing you must do when an image moves on the screen.

3.1.2   JFrame variables

```
protected JRootPane rootPane
```

This variable contains an instance of the root pane associated with the frame. Note that all components owned by the frame must be added to the root pane, which is unlike the technique familiar to AWT users.

```
protected boolean canAdd
```

This variable controls whether or not components can be added directly to the frame. Under most circumstances, this variable will contains a false value.

```
protected AccessibleContext accessibleContext
```

The `accessibleContext` variable contains an instance of the context used by the Assistive Technology mechanism of the component. In most situations, this variable will be unused.

3.1.3   JFrame constructors

```
JFrame()
```

This constructor creates a new JFrame instance that is initially invisible.

```
JFrame( String title )
```

This constructor creates a new JFrame instance that is initially invisible. The title of the frame (shown in the title bar of the frame) is assigned the text specified by the title parameter.

3.1.4   JFrame significant method groupings

```
public void setJMenuBar( JMenuBar menu );
```

Like its AWT cousin, JFrame will support a single application menu bar. We will see how menus are created in chapter 7; however, once created, they can be added with the `setMenuBar()` method.

```
public void setDefaultCloseOperation(int operation);
public int getDefaultCloseOperation();
```

A unique feature of JFrame is the ability to assign how the window's close operation works. JFrame implements a method to set and get the value of the default close operation.

```
protected JRootPane createRootPane();
protected void setRootPane(JRootPane root);
public JRootPane getRootPane();
public Container getContentPane();
public void setLayeredPane(JLayeredPane layered);
public JLayeredPane getLayeredPane();
public void setGlassPane(Component glass);
public Component getGlassPane();
```

A JFrame instance can contain three different panes: a layered pane, a glass pane, and a root pane. We've already talked about the root pane. The layered pane is the invisible pane on top of the frame's root pane. It can be accessed to display dynamic items (such as cursors) above the frame contents.

3.2   JApplet

JApplet is the Swing equivalent of the AWT Applet class. Much like JFrame, JApplet has extensions to allow for interposing input and special painting behavior, and also supports child components that are managed by a root pane (recall the root pane description in the previous section) . Unlike the AWT applet class, JApplet permits the addition of menu bars and toolbars. This is a feature sorely lacking from AWT in previous versions of Java.

3.2.1   A JApplet sample applet

The code shown in listing 3.2 performs the same task as the example for JFrame shown previously; however, this code executes within the AppletViewer or a browser. Note that the restrictions of JFrame with regard to `getContentPane()`

apply equally to JApplet. The output produced by executing the code in listing 3.2 is shown in figure 3.2.

```java
import java.awt.*;
import com.sun.java.swing.*;
public class TestApplet
        extends      JApplet
{
    public TestApplet()
    {
    }
    public void init()
    {
        setSize( 100, 100 );
        setBackground( Color.gray );

        Panel topPanel = new Panel();
        topPanel.setLayout( new BorderLayout() );
        getContentPane().add( topPanel );
        Label labelHello = new Label( "Hello World!" );
        topPanel.add( labelHello, BorderLayout.NORTH );
    }
}
```

Listing 3.2   "Hello World!" using JApplet

3.2.2   JApplet variables

```java
protected boolean canAdd
```

This variable controls whether or not components can be added directly to the applet. Under most circumstances, this variable will contain a false value.

```java
protected AccessibleContext accessibleContext
```

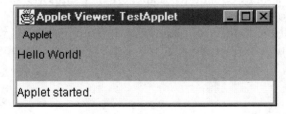

Figure 3.2
The "Hello World!" applet

The `accessibleContext` variable contains an instance of the context used by the Assistive Technology mechanism of the component. In most situations, this variable will be unused.

3.2.3 JApplet constructors

```
JApplet()
```

This constructor creates a new JApplet instance.

3.2.4 JApplet significant method groupings

```
public void setJMenuBar( JMenuBar menu );
public JMenuBar getJMenuBar();
```

If you have written AWT applets in the past, then you realize that it was impossible to assign a menu bar to an applet. With Swing, this limitation is a thing of the past.

```
public void setContentPane(Container contentPane);
public Container getContentPane();
public void setLayeredPane(JLayeredPane layered);
public JLayeredPane getLayeredPane();
public void setGlassPane(Component glass);
public Component getGlassPane();
protected void setRootPane(JRootPane root);
public JRootPane getRootPane();
protected JRootPane createRootPane();
```

A JApplet instance, like a JFrame, can contain three different panes: a layered pane, a glass pane, and a root pane. The methods in this group manage these panes for the JApplet, allowing you to control where various panels, components, and pop-ups are placed within the hierarchy of the window.

3.3 Creating simple panels

The Swing equivalent of AWT's Panel class is JPanel. With few exceptions, everything you know about Panel applies equally to JPanel. JPanel supports all of the AWT layout managers and also the new layouts provided by Swing.

For example, if you recall the GridLayout source code from chapter 1, we can rewrite this as a Swing application in the following way:

```
import java.awt.*;
import com.sun.java.swing.*;

class TestFrame
```

```
        extends JFrame
{
    public TestFrame()
    {
        setSize( 200, 200 );
        setBackground( Color.gray );

        JPanel topPanel = new JPanel();
        topPanel.setLayout( new GridLayout( 3, 2 ) );
        getContentPane().add( topPanel );
        topPanel.setBackground( Color.lightGray );

        topPanel.add( new Button( "One" ) );
        topPanel.add( new Button( "Two" ) );
        topPanel.add( new Button( "Three" ) );
        topPanel.add( new Button( "Four" ) );
        topPanel.add( new Button( "Five" ) );
    }
}
```

Notice that the TestFrame class is now derived from JFrame rather than from Frame, and it creates a JPanel to which the GridLayout manager is applied. The buttons are now added to the JPanel instance, rather than to the main frame.

 An instance of JPanel is double buffered by default. Developers of AWT code will appreciate this, since it simplifies dynamic aspects of a panel, such as animation, and reduces flicker while repainting. Double buffering can be turned off with a call to the following method from the JComponent class:

```
        topPanel.setDoubleBuffered( false );
```

3.3.1 JPanel constructors

```
JPanel( LayoutManager layout, boolean isDoubleBuffered )
```

This constructor creates a new JPanel instance with the specified layout. The double buffering capabilities of the panel are controlled by the specified boolean value.

```
JPanel( LayoutManager layout )
```

This constructor creates a new JPanel instance with the specified layout.

```
JPanel( boolean isDoubleBuffered )
```

This constructor creates a new JPanel instance with a default FlowLayout and the specified double buffering configuration.

```
JPanel()
```

This constructor creates a new JPanel instance with a default FlowLayout and the double buffering enabled.

3.4   Simple border types

Borders can be applied to any Swing component, but in most instances it is a panel instance that gets a specific border style, so we will discuss these styles in this section. All of the information in this section applies to all other Swing components; for example, you can apply a border to a label or text field using the techniques described in this section.

Swing implements several distinct border styles, shown in the following table:

Border	Description
BevelBorder	A 3-D border that supports a raised or lowered appearance
CompoundBorder	A border consisting of nested borders. The next section of this chapter discusses this special case.
EmptyBorder	A border permitting you to specify reserved space for an invisible border
EtchedBorder	A border that has the appearance of an etched line
LineBorder	A single color line of an arbitrary thickness
MatteBorder	A border allowing tiling of a specified icon or color
SoftBevelBorder	A border like BevelBorder, but having softer edges
TitledBorder	A border allowing a title string to be displayed on one of several orientations and alignments

Figure 3.3 shows all of the simple border styles provided by the Swing class library. These borders range from the ordinary to the obscure. To set the border of a JPanel, use code similar to the following fragment:

```
import com.sun.java.swing.*;
import com.sun.java.swing.border.*;
{
   .
   .
   .
   JPanel myPanel = new JPanel();
```

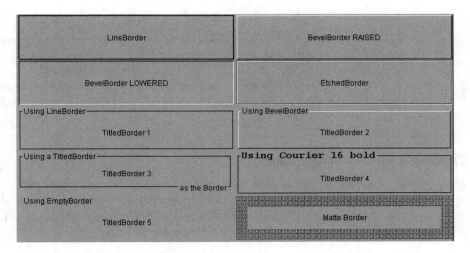

Figure 3.3 Simple border styles supported by Swing

```
    myPanel.setBorder( new BevelBorder ( BevelBorder.RAISED ) );
    .
    .
    .
}
```

Swing provides a shortcut class specifically for creating borders. This class, named BorderFactory, can be accessed by importing the `com.sun.java.swing.border` package. The following code fragment sets a raised, beveled border using Border-Factory:

```
import com.sun.java.swing.*;
import com.sun.java.swing.border.*;

{
    .
    .
    .
    JPanel myPanel = new JPanel();
    myPanel.setBorder( BorderFactory.createRaisedBevelBorder() );
    .
    .
    .
}
```

Use borders to create group boxes. Bordered panels may then be used to group functionality and visually segregate UI components. They could be used to enclose a set of related UI objects, such as radio buttons or check boxes. The contents of a group box are usually at a lower level of detail than is the label in the group box title. Use 3-D bevel border types to give the application a less dated look.

3.4.1 Creating a custom border class

The borders supplied by Swing are adequate (and standard) enough for most applications, but there may be times when a custom border is desirable. You can derive new borders by designing a class that implements the Border interface. This task is relatively simple if you use the following code sample as a base:

```
class MyBorder implements Border
{
    private Color color;

    public MyBorder( Color color )
    {
        this.color = color;
    }

    public void paintBorder( Component component,
                             Graphics g, int iX, int iY,
                             int iWidth, int iHeight )
    {
        Insets insets = getBorderInsets( component );

        g.setColor( color );
        g.fillRect( iX, iY, 3, iHeight );
        g.fillRect( iX, iY, iWidth, 3 );
        g.setColor( xcColor.darker() );
        g.fillRect( iX + iWidth - insets.right, iY,
                        3, iHeight );
        g.fillRect( iX, iY + iHeight - insets.bottom
                        iWidth, 3 );
    }

    public Insets getBorderInsets( Component component )
    {
        return new Insets( 3, 3, 3, 3 );
    }
    public boolean isBorderOpaque()
    {
```

```
        return false;
    }
}
```

3.5 Compound border creation

Swing also supports compound borders (multiple borders applied to the same component). The need for this feature may not be immediately obvious, but there will certainly be times when you will want to create a component with a lowered border inside a raised border. Think of a status line, for example. You can create a status line by adding a text field to a raised panel, but this requires several lines of code and the creation of at least one superfluous panel. You will also find a compound border useful for applying an EmptyBorder around some other border type in order to create a larger-than-normal white space around a component.

A better solution is to use a compound border. The code fragment below implements a compound border by combining a raised bevel with one that is lowered.

```
import com.sun.java.swing.*;

{
    .
    .
    .
    JPanel myPanel = new JPanel();
    myPanel.setBorder( BorderFactory.createCompoundBorder(
            new BevelBorder ( BevelBorder.RAISED ),
            new BevelBorder ( BevelBorder.LOWERED ) ) );
    .
    .
    .
}
```

FYI The first parameter to `createCompoundBorder()` represents the outside border, and the second parameter is the inside border.

Another example of a compound border is a border that possesses a visual style (an etched edge, for example) and also requires a title. Swing provides a slightly different interface to achieve this type of border. As shown in the following code fragment, the constructor of the TitledBorder class accepts a Border type as a parameter. This border can be any of the current borders supplied by Swing, or can be one of your own design if you create a class that extends Border.

```
import com.sun.java.swing.*;
import com.sun.java.swing.border.*;

{
  .
  .
  .
    myPanel.setBorder( new TitledBorder(
                 new EtchedBorder(), "Border Title" ) );
  .
  .
  .
}
```

Finally, let's take a look at some code that generates a very complex border. Study the following code fragment to see if you can determine its results. Note that the code could have been written as one continuous line, but that the use of the temporary variable helps clarify its purpose.

```
import com.sun.java.swing.*;

import com.sun.java.swing.border.*;

{
  .
  .
  .
    Border border1 = new TitledBorder( new EtchedBorder(),
                            "A very complex title" );
    myPanel.setBorder( new TitledBorder( border1, "Another Title",
                  TitledBorder.RIGHT, TitledBorder.BOTTOM ) );
  .
  .
  .
}
```

Did you get it right? Figure 3.4 shows the actual output from these two lines of code. As you can see, the TitledBorder class, and Swing border classes in general, provides the flexibility to create a border in almost any way you choose.

3.6   Swing layout managers

In chapter 1, we reviewed layout managers provided by AWT in Java 1.1. Though the AWT managers are completely compatible with Swing, and will be sufficient for most

Figure 3.4
A very complex border

applications, Swing supports four additional layout managers to meets its own needs. The following table summarizes the Swing layout managers and their purposes:

Layout Manager	Description
BoxLayout	A layout manager that aligns components along the X- or Y- axis of a panel. It attempts to use the preferred width and height of components during the layout process.
OverlayLayout	Arranges components one on top of another, aligning the base point of each component in a single location
ScrollPaneLayout	A layout manager specific to scrolling panes
ViewportLayout	A layout manager specific to view ports within scrolling panes

Of the layout managers listed here, only BoxLayout will be useful in typical application development. The other layout managers discussed in the previous table may be useful to advanced Swing users, though these managers are quite specific and are usually applicable only to the components for which they are intended. Unless you are writing a new scrolling pane, you are unlikely to be able to apply the ViewportLayout manager to any other panel.

Since BoxLayout will be useful, we should look at it in a bit more detail. The BoxLayout organizes the components it manages along either the X- or Y-axis of the owner panel. The alignment of these components can be left or right justified, or centered (the default). The code in listing 3.3 creates two panels that support the BoxLayout. The upper panel aligns its components along the Y-axis, and the lower panel aligns along the X-axis. To each of these panels, we add three components of varying sizes so we can note the effects they have on the BoxLayout manager.

```
import java.awt.*;
import com.sun.java.swing.*;

class TestFrame
```

Listing 3.3   Sample using BoxLayout

```
        extends JFrame
{
    public TestFrame()
    {
        setTitle( "BoxLayout Application" );

        JPanel topPanel = new JPanel();
        topPanel.setLayout( new BorderLayout() );
        getContentPane().add( topPanel );

        // Create panels to display X- and Y-
        // axis box layouts
        JPanel yAxisPanel = createYAxisPanel();
        topPanel.add( yAxisPanel, BorderLayout.CENTER );
        JPanel xAxisPanel = createXAxisPanel();
        topPanel.add( xAxisPanel, BorderLayout.SOUTH );
    }

    public JPanel createYAxisPanel()
    {
        JPanel panel = new JPanel();
        panel.setLayout( new BoxLayout( panel, BoxLayout.Y_AXIS ) );
        panel.setBackground( Color.lightGray );
        // Add some components to this panel
        panel.add( new JButton( "Button 1" ) );
        panel.add( new TextArea( "This is a text area" ) );
        panel.add( new JCheckBox( "Checkbox 1" ) );

        return panel;
    }

    public JPanel createXAxisPanel()
    {
        JPanel panel = new JPanel();
        panel.setLayout( new BoxLayout( panel, BoxLayout.X_AXIS ) );
        panel.setBackground( Color.gray );

        // Add some components to this panel
        panel.add( new JButton( "Button 1" ) );
        panel.add( new TextArea( "This is a text area" ) );
        panel.add( new JCheckBox( "Checkbox 1" ) );

        return panel;
    }

    // Main program started
    public static void main( String args[] )
    {
```

Listing 3.3 Sample using BoxLayout (continued)

```
        // Create an instance of the test application
        TestFrame mainFrame = new TestFrame();
        mainFrame.pack();
        mainFrame.setVisible( true );
    }
}
```

Listing 3.3   Sample using BoxLayout (continued)

The output produced by this example is shown in figure 3.5. Notice how the components are laid out in each of the panels. In the upper panel, components are displayed vertically, and are centered horizontally. In the lower window (dark gray) the components are centered vertically, but are laid out in a horizontal direction,

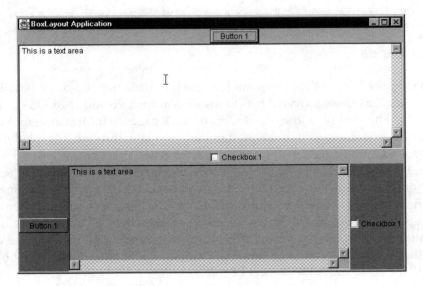

Figure 3.5   BoxLayout program output

much like the FlowLayout manager would do it. Unlike FlowLayout, however, the BoxLayout manager will not wrap components to the next line. Instead, components will be reduced to the limits permitted by their specified minimum sizes, and if there is still insufficient panel real estate, the layout manager will simply clip components. This applies equally to panels with a vertical box layout.

Since some Swing components are ideally suited to the BoxLayout manager, we will examine a more practical implementation later. When adding Swing check boxes or radio buttons to a panel, it is highly recommended that you use the Box-Layout, particularly if you have several components to lay out in tabular form. If you want to peek ahead to see an example using BoxLayout, you will find the source code in chapter 4, listing 4.5.

To make using the BoxLayout manager easier, Swing also provides a class named Box that creates a container with the BoxLayout manger applied. To quickly construct a panel of this type, use code similar to the following:

```
// Create a new panel
Box boxPanel = new Box(BoxLayout.Y_AXIS );

// Add components
boxPanel.add( new JButton( "Button 1" ) );
boxPanel.add( new TextArea( "This is a text area" ) );
boxPanel.add( new JCheckBox( "Checkbox 1" ) );
```

3.7 Tabbed Panes

The tabbed pane is one of the most unique controls made popular by graphical user interfaces (such as those provided by Microsoft Windows 95 and IBM OS/2 Workplace Shell). This control allows developers to stack pages of information into a single point of reference, and it helps the user navigate through the plethora of features found in most modern software applications.

Until the introduction of Swing, Java developers were forced to either live without the conveniences of the tabbed control, or they had buy, or write, one that met their needs. Of course, since most of us are unwilling to write a tabbed pane control and likely too miserly to pay to use someone else's code, we tend to find other solutions. Fortunately, Swing offers Java developers a free tabbed pane component that is both complete and powerful. This component is implemented by the JTabbedPane class, and is the subject of this section.

As far as we are concerned, a tabbed pane is just like any other Swing component. We can add it to a panel, and we can add components to it, usually in the form of pages. To each of the pages in a tabbed pane, we can associate any other Java UI components, panes, or even other tabbed panes, and since the JTabbed-Pane control extends JComponent, it derives a lot of functionality for special features (such as tool tips, keyboard handling, and so on).

Avoid stacking tabs. If you are in need of more than six tabs in a single row, consider that you may need another dialog. Users find it disconcerting to hunt for items in many tabs, especially when they are stacked and a row of tabs shifts forwards when selected. A common mistake is to overload a dialog with tabs for new features.

The best place to see an example of Swing's tabbed pane component and the capabilities it provides is the SWINGSET demonstration program that ships with the Swing product. Figure 3.6 shows one of the many pages included in the SWINGSET application tabbed pane. Notice that the tabs for each page have a title, and can optionally also include graphics. The pages themselves can own an array of graphical components. In the case of the page shown in figure 3.6, this includes a very fancy list box, radio buttons, check boxes, and buttons.

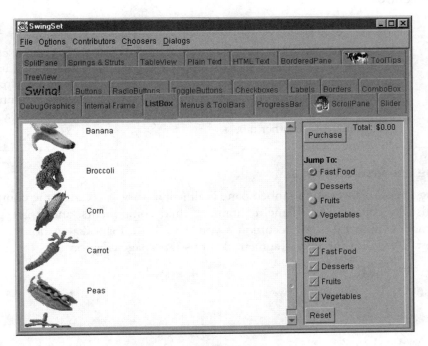

Figure 3.6   Use of a tabbed pane in SWINGSET

3.7.1   Creating a tabbed pane

In spite of its apparent complexity, creating a tabbed pane is a simple exercise. The following code fragment creates an instance of JTabbedPane:

```
import com.sun.java.swing.*;

{
    .

    .

    .

    tabbedPanel = new JTabbedPane();
    topPanel.add( tabbedPanel, BorderLayout.CENTER );
    .

    .

    .

}
```

Note that this sample does not yet create any pages for the tabbed pane. The code would run properly, but would produce a gray box where you would expect to see the control.

Use tabs to group functionality within modal dialogs. In general, tabs are found in modal dialogs, such as property sheets, rather than being used to drive an entire application. Try to order the tabs from left to right by frequency or by importance of use. Don't overload a tab with too many controls; if you are running out of space, consider that you may need to invoke another dialog or create another tab.

3.7.2   Adding and inserting pages

Adding pages to an existing tabbed pane is almost as easy as creating the control. A page usually consists of a JPanel containing child components, and it is typically constructed using the same techniques you would use for a dialog box or frame window. The following code fragment demonstrates page creation.

```
import com.sun.java.swing.*;

{
    .

    .

    .

    // Create the page panel
    pagePanel = new JPanel();
```

```
pagePanel.setLayout( new BorderLayout() );
pagePanel.add( new JLabel( "Sample Label" ),
               BorderLayout.NORTH );
pagePanel.add( new JTextArea( "" ),
               BorderLayout.CENTER );
pagePanel.add( new JButton( "Button 1" ),
               BorderLayout.SOUTH );

// Add the panel to the tabbed pane
tabbedPanel.addTab( "Page 1", pagePanel );
   .
   .
   .

}
```

You would, of course, use similar code for every page you want to add to the tabbed pane. Note, however, that this code adds pages sequentially, a process that may not always be appropriate. There may be occasions, while in the process of executing an application, when you need to insert a page. In addition to adding pages, the Swing JTabbedPane class also provides a mechanism to insert pages anywhere within the page hierarchy. To accomplish this, the actual page creation is performed using JPanel just as it was for the add operation, but the insertion is invoked with a line of code similar to the following:

```
// Insert the panel into the tabbed pane
tabbedPanel.insertTab( "Inserted Page",
                       new ImageIcon( "image.gif" ),
                       pagePanel,
                       "My tooltip text",
                       iLocation );
```

In this example, the variable iLocation represents the page index (position) where the page will be inserted. This example also slides in a couple of new features you have not previously seen. The new ImageIcon("image.gif") parameter loads a GIF file into an instance of the ImageIcon class and attaches it to the tab. This is exactly how the graphics were added to the tabs in the figure 3.6 SWING-SET sample.

FYI   All pages contained by a JTabbedPane are indexed starting at 0. For example, in a tabbed pane with five pages, the first page is 0 and the last page is four. Many of the JTabbedPane methods refer to page indices.

3.7.3 Removing pages

Pages contained by a JTabbedPane component can also be removed at run time. This is accomplished using a line of code similar to the following:

```
tabbedPanel.removeTabAt( iLocation );
```

where `iLocation` is the index of the page to be removed. If, for some reason, you want to remove all pages from the tabbed pane, you need to keep track of the number of pages remaining, otherwise the Java VM will generate an unexpected exception. To do this, use code similar to this:

```
while( tabbedPanel.getTabCount() > 0 )
    tabbedPanel.removeTabAt( 0 );
```

The `getTabCount()` method returns an integer containing the total number of pages in the panel.

3.7.4 Selecting pages

There are two mechanisms to select a page. The first and easier (since it involves no additional code) is for the user to click the desired tab. When this operation is performed, the JTabbedPane instance automatically moves the selected page to the front of the pane and updates the tabs.

However, as a developer, you can also write code to force any page in the tabbed pane to move to the front of the page stack. To do this, call the `setSelectedIndex()` method with the index of the page you want up front. Use code similar to this:

```
tabbedPanel.setSelectedIndex( iLocation );
```

A second method to accomplish this uses the component reference of the page. The component reference is typically the instance of the panel that was referenced when the page was added. Assuming you know the value of this instance, you can utilize the following code:

```
tabbedPanel.setSelectedComponent( pagePanel );
```

3.7.5 A complete JTabbedPane example

So far, all you have seen are snippets of code to handle a few of the functions of a tabbed control using the Swing JTabbedPane class. So before we move on, let's put some of these features together to create a simple application.

```
import java.awt.*;
import com.sun.java.swing.*;

class TestFrame
      extends JFrame
{
    private    JTabbedPane tabbedPane;
    private    JPanel panel1;
    private    JPanel panel2;
    private    JPanel panel3;
    public TestFrame()
    {
        // NOTE: to reduce the amount of code in this example, it uses
        // panels with a NULL layout. This is NOT suitable for
        // production code since it may not display correctly for
        // a look-and-feel.

        setTitle( "Tabbed Pane Application" );
        setSize( 300, 200 );
        setBackground( Color.gray );

        JPanel topPanel = new JPanel();
        topPanel.setLayout( new BorderLayout() );
        getContentPane().add( topPanel );

        // Create the tab pages
        createPage1();
        createPage2();
        createPage3();

        // Create a tabbed pane
        tabbedPane = new JTabbedPane();
        tabbedPane.addTab( "Page 1", panel1 );
        tabbedPane.addTab( "Page 2", panel2 );
        tabbedPane.addTab( "Page 3", panel3 );
        topPanel.add( tabbedPane, BorderLayout.CENTER );
    }

    public void createPage1()
    {
        panel1 = new JPanel();
        panel1.setLayout( null );

        JLabel label1 = new JLabel( "Username:" );
        label1.setBounds( 10, 15, 150, 20 );
        panel1.add( label1 );

        JTextField field = new JTextField();
```

Listing 3.4   Sample application with JTabbedPane

```
        field.setBounds( 10, 35, 150, 20 );
        panel1.add( field );

        JLabel label2 = new JLabel( "Password:" );
        label2.setBounds( 10, 60, 150, 20 );
        panel1.add( label2 );

        JPasswordField fieldPass = new JPasswordField();
        fieldPass.setBounds( 10, 80, 150, 20 );
        panel1.add( fieldPass );
    }

    public void createPage2()
    {
        panel2 = new JPanel();
        panel2.setLayout( new BorderLayout() );

        panel2.add( new JButton( "North" ), BorderLayout.NORTH );
        panel2.add( new JButton( "South" ), BorderLayout.SOUTH );
        panel2.add( new JButton( "East" ), BorderLayout.EAST );
        panel2.add( new JButton( "West" ), BorderLayout.WEST );
        panel2.add( new JButton( "Center" ), BorderLayout.CENTER );
    }

    public void createPage3()
    {
        panel3 = new JPanel();
        panel3.setLayout( new GridLayout( 3, 2 ) );

        panel3.add( new JLabel( "Field 1:" ) );
        panel3.add( new TextArea() );
        panel3.add( new JLabel( "Field 2:" ) );
        panel3.add( new TextArea() );
        panel3.add( new JLabel( "Field 3:" ) );
        panel3.add( new TextArea() );
    }

    // Main method to get things started
    public static void main( String args[] )
    {
        // Create an instance of the test application
        TestFrame mainFrame = new TestFrame();
        mainFrame.setVisible( true );
    }
}
```

Listing 3.4   Sample application with JTabbedPane (continued)

The application code in listing 3.4 creates an instance of JTabbedPane with three pages, all based on the JPanel class mentioned earlier in this chapter. Each of these pages uses a different AWT layout manager in order to demonstrate that each page's appearance is independent of others within the tabbed pane.

The third page includes instances of the AWT TextArea class to show that AWT components can be intermixed with Swing without any serious drawbacks. Note that in the source code in listing 3.4, you will also see instances of classes that you may not recognize, such as JTextField and JPasswordField. These are user interface component classes supplied by Swing which will be examined in more detail in the coming chapters. The result of executing the code contained in listing 3.4 is shown in the screen captures in figure 3.7.

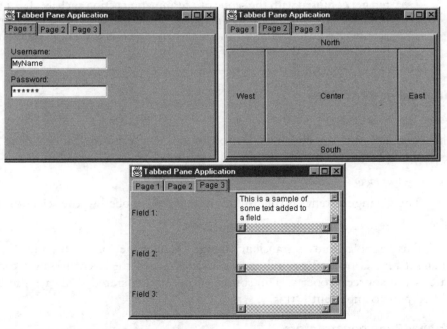

Figure 3.7   Sample JTabbedPane application output

IMHO Though the current release of Swing supports mixing AWT components with Swing, you may notice some flicker when selecting tab pages containing them. Swing appears to paint AWT components into the upper-left corner of a JPanel before repainting them in the correct position. This seems to be a bug, but it is actually related to some limitations on the Z-order positioning of heavyweight components. If possible, you should use AWT components only when you absolutely must.

UI GUIDELINE **Place buttons that terminate a tabbed dialog in a nontabbed area, typically, below the tabs.** The biggest problem with tabs is that the user can often get confused with the scope of a terminating action such as OK or Cancel. For example, when you make changes to multiple tabs, pressing OK or Cancel now has an ambiguous meaning when placed inside a tab. Actions applied in the nontabbed area map to changes made to all tabs.

3.7.6 JTabbedPane variables

```
protected SingleSelectionModel model
```

This variable holds the current selection model in use by the tabbed pane. If the developer specifies no model, Swing will assign a default selection model.

```
protected ChangeListener changeListener
```

The ChangeListener is the listener that will be applied to the selection model.

```
protected transient ChangeEvent changeEvent
```

This variable holds a transient change event value for a tab pane. Only one ChangeEvent is needed per tab pane instance, since the event's only (read-only) state is the source property. The source of events generated is always the current tabbed pane component ("this").

3.7.7 JTabbedPane constructors

```
JTabbedPane()
```

This constructor creates a new JTabbedPane instance with no pages.

3.7.8 JTabbedPane significant method groupings

```
protected ChangeListener createChangeListener();
public void addChangeListener(ChangeListener l);
public void removeChangeListener(ChangeListener l);
```

These methods control the presence of a ChangeListener for the tabbed pane. The listener is used to detect page selection changes and other events generated by the control.

```
public void insertTab( String title, Icon icon,
           Component component, String tip, int index );
public void addTab( String title, Icon icon,
           Component component, String tip );
public void addTab(String title, Icon icon, Component component );
public void addTab( String title, Component component );
public void removeTabAt( int index );
```

This group of methods is used to add and remove pages to the tabbed pane component instance. Each tab can contain a title string and/or an icon image. Additionally, a ToolTip string can be assigned to each pane.

```
public int getSelectedIndex();
public void setSelectedIndex(int index);
public Component getSelectedComponent();
public Component getComponentAt(int index);
public void setComponentAt(int index, Component component );
public void setSelectedComponent( Component c );
public int indexOfTab( String title );
public int indexOfComponent( Component component );
```

Each tab in the tabbed page is assigned a unique index number starting with zero and increasing in value. With this group of methods, the index of a specific page can be determined or selected. Note that the last two methods in this list will return the index of a page with the specified title or with the specified component instance value.

```
public int getTabCount();
```

This method returns the number of pages within the tabbed pane instance.

```
public SingleSelectionModel getModel();
public void setModel(SingleSelectionModel model);
```

The selection model, though initially defaulted by Swing, can be set to a custom model, if desired. Additionally, the current selection model can be retrieved.

```
public String getTitleAt(int index);
```

```
public Icon getIconAt(int index);
public void setTitleAt(int index, String title);
public void setIconAt(int index, Icon icon);
```

As previously mentioned, each tab can have an optional string or icon image. This method group provides the capability to set and retrieve the tab's title and icon.

3.8　Scrolling panes

Using some window environments, creating scrolling windows can be a painful experience because, after the window is created, the environment tells the application that something needs repainting. It is entirely the developer's responsibility to recognize these messages from the windowing environment, determine exactly what needs to be repainted, and then manage the repaint by collecting a set of drawing rectangles. This is a relatively primitive way in which to keep the screen updated, and it can result in countless hours of debugging time.

As usual, Java has the answer. Swing introduces a new class called JScrollPane that manages almost all aspects of a scrollable view. There is no need to determine drawing rectangles, and it is not necessary to intercept window movement events. Simply put, JScrollPane makes a developer's life much easier.

Figure 3.8 shows an example of a scrolling pane from the SWINGSET demo provided with the Swing product. Notice that this example contains both horizontal and vertical scroll bars with which the user can manipulate the view. The presence of the scroll bars can be controlled either programmatically or automatically (depending on the size of the window).

The most important point to make with an application utilizing a scrolling view is that the developer is responsible only for populating the pane. After this is accomplished, Swing manages all of the movement, repainting, and resize activities associated with the pane. You can simply create the view and be done with it!

GUIDELINE　　**Favor vertical scrolling over horizontal scrolling in panes.** Users tend not to enjoy scrolling, but when users are forced into a scrolling situation, they almost always scroll downward first rather than toward the right. Initially, place the object being scrolled at the top-left most position, and then, place more viewable information in a vertical path downward.

Figure 3.8   Example of a scrolling pane

Another key feature of a scrolling pane is that it is not limited to a static image like the one shown in figure 3.8. An instance of JScrollPane can contain a series of buttons, images, JPanels, or any other UI components. A special layout manager called ScrollPaneLayout manages component layout in the JScrollPane, and another class named JViewPort manages the actual viewing area of the scrolling pane.

These concepts are illustrated in figure 3.9. The JViewPort class maintains size information for the view and tracking information for the view port. With this data, JScrollPane determines if there is a requirement for scroll bars, and, if so, it draws them in the pane. Typically you will never want to handle the scrolling yourself, but JViewPort does offer the flexibility to allow developers to access its internals.

3.8.1   An example using JScrollPane

Listing 3.5 constructs an example using the JScrollPane class. In this example, we create a scrolling pane, and to it we add a JLabel instance showing a rather larger image. Since this image is too large for the panel to display entirely, scroll bars will

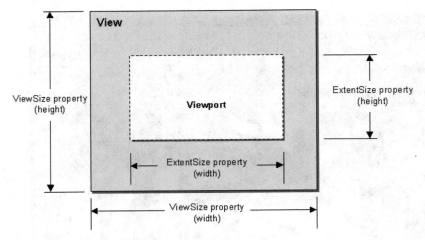

Figure 3.9 Scrolling a viewport through a view

automatically appear. Without any coding effort on our part, these scroll bars are active, and any attempts to move them will result in the graphic scrolling smoothly though the viewing region. The output produced by this application is shown in figure 3.10.

```
import java.awt.*;
import com.sun.java.swing.*;

class TestFrame
      extends    JFrame
{
    private       JScrollPane scrollPane;

    public TestFrame()

    {
        setTitle( "Tabbed Pane Application" );
        setSize( 300, 200 );
        setBackground( Color.gray );

        JPanel topPanel = new JPanel();
        topPanel.setLayout( new BorderLayout() );
        getContentPane().add( topPanel );

        Icon image = new ImageIcon( "main.gif" );
```

Listing 3.5   Sample application with JScrollPane

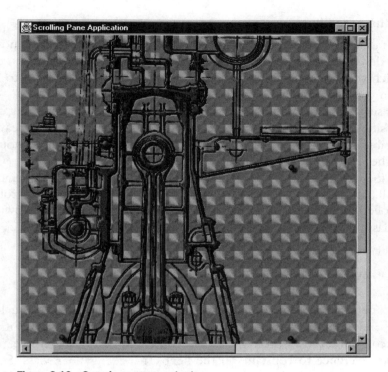

Figure 3.10 Sample program output

```
    JLabel label = new JLabel( image );

    // Create a scroll pane
    scrollPane = new JScrollPane();
    scrollPane.getViewport().add( label );
    topPanel.add( scrollPane, BorderLayout.CENTER );
}

public static void main( String args[] )
{
    // Create an instance of the Test application
    TestFrame mainFrame = new TestFrame();
    mainFrame.setVisible( true );
}
}
```

Listing 3.5 Sample application with JScrollPane (continued)

3.8.2 Controlling the scroll bars

As convenient as it is to have scroll bars appear in a scrolling pane, you may not find this behavior desirable in some situations. For example, if you are writing an application in which you want to supply separate controls (like VCR buttons) to scroll the pane, then you need to be able to hide the scroll bars.

In other situations, you may elect to show the scroll bars at all times, regardless of their necessity. Many Windows applications (NOTEPAD, for example), leave the scroll bars visible at all times in order to avoid screen repainting as the amount of information they contain increases or decreases.

Swing's JScrollPane class offers a mechanism to control the visibility characteristics of its scroll bars, and the presence or absence of horizontal and vertical scroll bars can be controlled individually. To manage the scroll bar policy, as it is known, the JScrollPane class provides two methods. These can be used as follows:

```
scrollPane.setVerticalScrollBarPolicy(
            ScrollPaneConstants.VERTICAL_SCROLLBAR_NEVER );
scrollPane.setHorizontalScrollBarPolicy(
            ScrollPaneConstants.HORIZONTAL_SCROLLBAR_ALWAYS );
```

In this code fragment, the first line sets the vertical scroll bar policy such that the scrolling pane never displays a vertical scroll bar, regardless of the size of its contents. The second line causes the horizontal scroll bar to always be visible. These methods make reference to constants in the `ScrollPaneConstants` class. See the Swing online documentation for more details regarding this class.

3.8.3 Controlling the scrolling programmatically

Since you can now eliminate the scroll bars from a JScrollPane instance, you now need to know how to scroll the view by using code resembling the following:

```
Point pos = scrollPane.getViewport().getViewPosition();
pos.y -= 50;
scrollPane.getViewport().setViewPosition( pos );
```

In this code fragment, the value of "pos" is loaded with the current viewport position. To this, we add 50 (pixels) to the vertical value and then set the new viewport position.

Some components you can add to a scrolling pane will implement the Scrollable interface. This allows the scroll pane to query the component for the preferred pixel size of a unit or block scroll increment. This is how the JScrollPane class scrolls a list box or table instance by one line at a time.

3.8.4 Creating scrollable components

If you notice the scrolling characteristics in the previous example, you will observe that clicking the unit increment arrows in the scroll bars moves the item just a single pixel at a time. While the smooth scrolling is appealing in some situations, there will be times when you expect a unit increment to move more than this. For example, in a list box it is desirable to move the view by the equivalent of one line of text.

The problem with the previous example arises as a result of displaying the image within a JLabel instance. To apply correct scrolling, the component added to the scrolling pane should implement an interface called Scrollable. This is what Swing components like JTable, JList, and JTree do to apply appropriate scrolling sizes. Scrollable is an interface class which requires the implementation of five methods, shown in the table below.

Method	Purpose
getPreferredScrollableViewportSize	This method returns the preferred size of the viewport for a view component. For example, in JList, this method returns the dimensions of the viewport required to display all of the rows.
getScrollableBlockIncrement	This method is called by the scrolling pane code when the user selects one of the block increments in the scroll bar (a page up or page down). The caller supplies the direction of movement and a parameter indicating the horizontal or vertical orientation of the movement.
getScrollableUnitIncrement	This method is called by the scrolling pane code when the user selects one of the unit increments in the scroll bar. The caller supplies the direction of movement and a parameter indicating the horizontal or vertical orientation of the movement.
getScrollableTracksViewportWidth	This boolean method should return true if you want the viewport to force the width of the scrollable component to match the width of the viewport.

Method	Purpose
getScrollableTracksViewportHeight	This boolean method should return true if you want the viewport to force the height of the scrollable component to match the height of the viewport.

To improve the scrolling characteristics of the previous example, we need to implement a new class (which we will arbitrarily name ScrollLabel) which implements the Scrollable interface. We can then use this class, instead of the Jlabel, to implement a better image scroller. The ScrollLabel class is shown in the following code fragment.

```
class ScrollLabel extends JLabel implements Scrollable
{
    public ScrollLabel( Icon s )
    {
        // We will implement only the image constructor.
        super( s );
    }

    public Dimension getPreferredScrollableViewportSize()
    {
        // Return a predefined preferred viewport size
        return new Dimension( 120, 120 );
    }

    public int getScrollableBlockIncrement(
                Rectangle visibleRect, int orientation,
                int direction)
    {
        // When doing block increments, scroll by 30 pixels
        return 30;
    }

    public int getScrollableUnitIncrement(
                Rectangle visibleRect, int orientation,
                int direction)
    {
        // When doing a unit increment, scroll by 10 pixels
        return 10;
    }

    public boolean getScrollableTracksViewportWidth()
    {
        return false;
    }

    public boolean getScrollableTracksViewportHeight()
```

```
        {
            return false;
        }
    }
```

3.8.5 JScrollPane constructors

```
JScrollPane ( Component view, int vsbPolicy, int hsbPolicy )
```

This constructor creates an instance of a scrolling pane containing the specified component within its view. The scroll bar policies are also specified.

```
JScrollPane( Component view )
```

This constructor creates an instance of a scrolling pane containing the specified component within its view.

```
JScrollPane ( int vsbPolicy, int hsbPolicy )
```

This constructor creates an empty instance of a scrolling pane with the specified scroll bar policies.

```
JScrollPane()
```

This constructor creates an empty instance of a scrolling pane.

3.8.6 JScrollPane significant method groupings

```
public int getVerticalScrollBarPolicy()
public void setVerticalScrollBarPolicy(int x)
public int getHorizontalScrollBarPolicy()
public void setHorizontalScrollBarPolicy(int x)
public JScrollBar createHorizontalScrollBar()
public JScrollBar createVerticalScrollBar()
public JScrollBar getHorizontalScrollBar()
public JScrollBar getVerticalScrollBar()
```

This method group manages the scroll bars associated with the scrolling pane. The policies of the scroll bars can be retrieved or set, and the scroll bars can be constructed with the creation methods.

```
public Border getViewportBorder()
public void setViewportBorder(Border viewportBorder)
protected JViewport createViewport()
public JViewport getViewport()
public void setViewport(JViewport x)
public void setViewportView(Component view)
```

With these methods, all aspects of the viewport, which is the visible portion of the view, can be managed.

```
public JViewport getRowHeader()
public void setRowHeader(JViewport x)
public void setRowHeaderView(Component view)
public JViewport getColumnHeader()
public void setColumnHeader(JViewport x)
public void setColumnHeaderView(Component view)
```

The viewport of the scrolling pane can have a column header view added to it. This is typically used by the JTable component (a child of JComponent used to display tabular information), but it can be added to the scrolling pane any time you need to identify the contents. The methods in this group control the presence and content of the column view.

3.9 Split panes

Occasionally, in the quest for that perfectly designed user interface, you need to perform some really fancy layout operations. Many programs feature split frames that let the user view two or more pieces of information simultaneously and, with the drag of a mouse, resize any of the frames to view more or less data.

A late addition to the beta versions of Swing was a class named JSplitPane which provides this capability, while at the same time doing most of the work for you. As you will see, with just a few lines of code, you can add this functionality to your applications.

JSplitPane is used to divide two components which, by user intervention, can be resized interactively. The split pane can be divided left-to-right using an orientation setting of `JSplitPane.HORIZONTAL_SPLIT`, or top-to-bottom with the orientation set to `JSplitPane.VERTICAL_SPLIT`.

 JSplitPane will divide two, and only two, components. However, if you require a more complex interface, you can nest one JSplitPane inside another. This provides the capability to intermix horizontally and vertically split panes.

The divider can be adjusted by the user using the mouse, or it can be set in the software with a call to the `setDividerLocation()` method. When the divider is moved by the user, the minimum and maximum size setting of the contained components is used to determine the movement limits. Hence, if the minimum size of the two components is greater than the size of the split pane, the JSplitPane code will prevent resizing of the frames separated by the divider.

 Refer to the `JComponent.setMinimumSize()` method in the Swing online documentation for a description of a component's minimum size and the techniques used to alter it.

```
import java.awt.*;
import com.sun.java.swing.*;
class TestFrame
        extends JFrame
{
    private     JSplitPane splitPaneV;
    private     JSplitPane splitPaneH;
    private     JPanel       panel1;
    private     JPanel       panel2;
    private     JPanel       panel3;

    public TestFrame()
    {
        setTitle( "Split Pane Application" );
        setBackground( Color.gray );

        JPanel topPanel = new JPanel();
        topPanel.setLayout( new BorderLayout() );
        getContentPane().add( topPanel );

        // Create the panels

        createPanel1();
        createPanel2();
        createPanel3();

        // Create a splitter pane
        splitPaneV = new JSplitPane( JSplitPane.VERTICAL_SPLIT );
        topPanel.add( splitPaneV, BorderLayout.CENTER );

        splitPaneH = new JSplitPane( JSplitPane.HORIZONTAL_SPLIT );
        splitPaneH.setLeftComponent( panel1 );
        splitPaneH.setRightComponent( panel2 );
```

Listing 3.6   Sample application with JSplitPane

```java
        splitPaneV.setLeftComponent( splitPaneH );
        splitPaneV.setRightComponent( panel3 );
    }
    public void createPanel1()
    {
        panel1 = new JPanel();
        panel1.setLayout( new BorderLayout() );

        // Add some buttons
        panel1.add( new JButton( "North" ), BorderLayout.NORTH );
        panel1.add( new JButton( "South" ), BorderLayout.SOUTH );
        panel1.add( new JButton( "East" ), BorderLayout.EAST );
        panel1.add( new JButton( "West" ), BorderLayout.WEST );
        panel1.add( new JButton( "Center" ), BorderLayout.CENTER );

    }

    public void createPanel2()
    {
        panel2 = new JPanel();
        panel2.setLayout( new FlowLayout() );

        panel2.add( new JButton( "Button 1" ) );
        panel2.add( new JButton( "Button 2" ) );
        panel2.add( new JButton( "Button 3" ) );
    }

    public void createPanel3()
    {
        panel3 = new JPanel();
        panel3.setLayout( new BorderLayout() );
        panel3.setPreferredSize( new Dimension( 400, 100 ) );
        panel3.setMinimumSize( new Dimension( 100, 50 ) );

        panel3.add( new JLabel( "Notes:" ), BorderLayout.NORTH );
        panel3.add( new JTextArea(), BorderLayout.CENTER );
    }

    public static void main( String args[] )
    {
        // Create an instance of the test application
        TestFrame mainFrame = new TestFrame();
        mainFrame.pack();
        mainFrame.setVisible( true );
    }
}
```

Listing 3.6 Sample application with JSplitPane (continued)

Listing 3.6 contains a complete application to demonstrate the use of JSplit-Pane. The example has a bit of added complexity to show how to manage split panes contained within other split panes.

GUIDELINE

Allow user configuration of split panes. The user may wish to completely hide a portion of the split window or never invoke one in the first place. Consider making this a user configurable option in the UI, either by invoking view modes or by allowing the user to move the splitter until the view is fully hidden and then easily reopen the closed pane. Should the user resize the dialog, scroll bars should appear in the splitter pane dynamically when the viewable region of any pane is compromised.

Notice that, as the dividers are moved, the panels they contain are automatically resized, including the buttons in the case of a panel with BorderLayout. Also notice that the horizontal divider can be moved only a finite amount up or down. This limit is imposed on the split pane by the minimum sizes of the component panels (the minimum size of the buttons in the upper direction and the minimum size of the panel holding the text area object in the lower window). The output of this example is shown in figure 3.11.

3.9.1 Intercepting JSplitPane events

There may be situations when you need to know that the divider in a split pane has moved; however, if you examine Sun's online documentation for JSplitPane, you will notice that this class does not offer any method like addChangeListener(). So how, then, do you detect divider movement?

The answer to this question is not obvious; though, if you shift your focus a bit, you will see that you can detect changes to the splitter pane. A JSplitPane is really just a container for other components, and that is where the solution to this problem can be found. If you examine the JComponent class, you will notice a method called addAncestorListener(), which is used to notify a component when its owner has changed.

In any application supporting a JSplitPane instance, you can implement an AncestorListener for one of the components it owns. The interface requires the implementation of three methods, and one of these methods is called to notify the component that its owner (the split pane in this case) has changed. We can implement this code as follows:

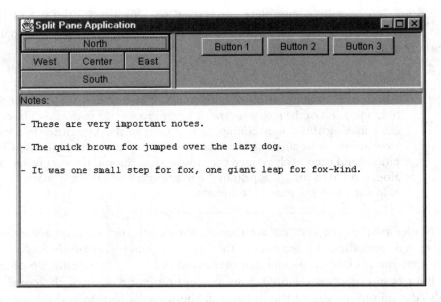

Figure 3.11   Sample program output

```
class MyPanel
   extends    JPanel
   implements AncestorListener
{
   // Add any special code for this component

   // Ancestor Listener support
   public void ancestorMoved( AncestorEvent event )
   {
       // Add code here to handle a split pane divider movement
   }

   // Not used
   public void ancestorAdded( AncestorEvent event )
   {
   }
   public void ancestorRemoved( AncestorEvent event )
   {
   }
}
```

The MyPanel class can then be added to one side of the split pane and will faithfully detect any changes to the divider.

3.9.2 JSplitPane constants

```
public static int VERTICAL_SPLIT
public static int HORIZONTAL_SPLIT
```

These constants are used to control the type of split used. The splitter bar dividing the two contained components can be oriented either vertically or horizontally.

```
public static String LEFT
public static String RIGHT
public static String TOP
public static String BOTTOM
public static String DIVIDER
```

These constants are used to specify where a component will be added to the split pane. The pane accepts two components that will be either TOP/BOTTOM or LEFT/RIGHT oriented. The third option is to add a component (DIVIDER type) that will represent the divider.

```
public static final String ORIENTATION_PROPERTY
public static final String CONTINUOUS_LAYOUT_PROPERTY
public static final String DIVIDER_SIZE_PROPERTY
public static final String ONE_TOUCH_EXPANDABLE_PROPERTY
public static final String LAST_DIVIDER_LOCATION_PROPERTY
```

These constants specify the names of properties that are used by the split pane component.

3.9.3 JSplitPane variables

```
protected int orientation
```

This method contains the orientation of the splitter component's divider. It contains either HORIZONTAL_SPLIT or VERTICAL_SPLIT.

```
protected boolean continuousLayout
```

This value is set if the split pane is configured to show continuous layout. In this mode, the splitter pane is repainted continuously during resize operations.

```
protected Component leftComponent
protected Component rightComponent
```

These variables hold the instances of the two components on either side of the divider.

`protected int dividerSize`

This variable holds the size of the divider in pixels. It is controlled with the `setDividerSize()` method.

`protected boolean oneTouchExpandable`

This variable is a flag that controls the expanded and collapsed state of the split pane.

`protected int lastDividerLocation`

This variable contains the previous location of the split pane's divider relative to the origin of the pane.

3.9.4 JSplitPane constructors

`JSplitPane()`

This constructor creates a new JSplitPane instance configured to vertically divide the child components.

`JSplitPane( int newOrientation )`

This constructor creates a new JSplitPane instance with a divider configured as specified by the orientation parameter.

```
JSplitPane( int newOrientation, Component newLeftComponent,
                       Component newRightComponent)
```

This constructor creates a new JSplitPane instance with a divider configured as specified by the orientation parameter. The components for each side of the divider are specified as method parameters.

```
JSplitPane( int newOrientation, boolean newContinuousLayout,
                        Component newLeftComponent,
                        Component newRightComponent )
```

This constructor creates a new JSplitPane instance with a divider configured as specified by the orientation parameter. The components for each side of the divider are specified as method parameters. Additionally, the caller can specify the use of continuous layout for the components.

3.9.5 JSplitPane significant method groupings

```
public void setDividerSize(int newSize)
public int getDividerSize()
public void setLastDividerLocation(int newLastLocation)
public int getLastDividerLocation()
public void setDividerLocation(int location)
public int getDividerLocation()
public int getMinimumDividerLocation()
public int getMaximumDividerLocation()
public void resetToPreferredSizes()
```

This group of methods controls the divider present within the split pane. The divider size can be retrieved or set to a specific location. Additionally, the minimum and maximum positions of the divider can be determined.

```
public void setLeftComponent(Component comp)
public Component getLeftComponent()
public void setTopComponent(Component comp)
public Component getTopComponent()
public void setRightComponent(Component comp)
public Component getRightComponent()
public void setBottomComponent(Component comp)
public Component getBottomComponent()
```

This group of methods controls the components displayed within the split pane.

```
public void setOrientation(int orientation)
public int getOrientation()
```

The orientation of the split window can be changed from horizontal to vertical, or vice versa. Also, the current orientation can be determined with the getOrientation() method.

```
public void setContinuousLayout(boolean newContinuousLayout)
public boolean isContinuousLayout()
```

These methods control the continuous layout mechanism within the split pane.

```
public void remove(Component component)
public void remove (int index)
public void removeAll()
```

This group of methods is used to remove components from the split pane. Components can be specified by component instance or index, or, if desired, both components can be removed.

```
protected void addImpl( Component comp,
                        Object constraints, int index )
```

If orientation of the split pane is LEFT/TOP or RIGHT/BOTTOM, and a component with that identifier was previously added, the old component will be removed, and then the specified component will be added in its place. If constraint is not one of the known identifiers, the layout manager will throw an `IllegalArgumentException`.

3.10 Advanced scrolling

We have described some of the workings of a simple application utilizing the JScrollPane and JSplitPane components, but neither of these examples was especially inspiring or advanced. Since these components (particularly JScrollPane) are heavily used throughout most Swing-based applications, it would be useful to see how they interact in a more advanced program.

The application shown in listing 3.7 implements a JFrame containing a splitter pane. Within this splitter, there are two subpanels, each containing an instance of a Swing component. I purposely selected a text field and a graphic for this example to illustrate that the contents of the scrolling panes can be almost anything you choose.

For now, ignore the code inside the `CreateTopPane()` method. It creates a Swing-based text area and loads it with a file. You will see this code reviewed in chapter 5 when we examine the JTextArea component.

The remainder of the code in listing 3.7 should be straightforward; however, there is a bit of code in the `stateChanged()` method to calculate the scale differences between the two scrolling panes. Actually, the scale calculation in this example is inaccurate, since it does not completely account for the size of the panes. Move the horizontal scroll bar in the top pane for a demonstration of this inaccuracy. With a bit more math, you can compensate for this error. Experiment with the JViewport `getViewPosition()` and `getExtentSize()` methods to correct the calculation.

```
import java.io.*;
import java.awt.*;
import com.sun.java.swing.*;
import com.sun.java.swing.event.*;

class TestFrame
        extends         JFrame
        implements      ChangeListener
```

Listing 3.7   Advanced scroller source code

```
{
    private    JSplitPane    splitPaneV;
    private    JSplitPane    splitPaneH;
    private    JScrollPane   scrollPane1;
    private    JScrollPane   scrollPane2;

    public TestFrame()
    {
        setTitle( "Advanced Scoller Application" );
        setSize( 300, 200 );

        setBackground( Color.gray );
        JPanel topPanel = new JPanel();
        topPanel.setLayout( new BorderLayout() );
        getContentPane().add( topPanel );

        // Create a text area for the top pane
        createTopPane();

        // Load a graphics for the bottom pane
        createBottomPane();

        // Create a split pane
        splitPaneV = new JSplitPane( JSplitPane.VERTICAL_SPLIT );
        topPanel.add( splitPaneV, BorderLayout.CENTER );

        // Add the components to the splitter pane
        splitPaneV.setLeftComponent( scrollPane1 );
        splitPaneV.setRightComponent( scrollPane2 );
    }

    public void stateChanged( ChangeEvent event )
    {
        // Event in the top pane??
        if( event.getSource() == scrollPane1.getViewport() )
        {
            // Get the current viewport position for the top pane
            Point point = scrollPane1.getViewport().getViewPosition();

            // Determine the correct scaling for the views
            Dimension dim1 = scrollPane1.getViewport().getViewSize();
            Dimension dim2 = scrollPane2.getViewport().getViewSize();
            float fXScale = 1;
            float fYScale = 1;
            if( dim1.width > dim2.width )
            {
                fXScale = (float)dim1.width / (float)dim2.width;
                fYScale = (float)dim1.height / (float)dim2.height;
```

Listing 3.7 Advanced scroller source code (continued)

```
                // Scale the movement
                point.x /= fXScale;
                point.y /= fYScale;
            }
            else
            {
                fXScale = (float)dim2.width / (float)dim1.width;
                fYScale = (float)dim2.height / (float)dim1.height;

                // Scale the movement
                point.x *= fXScale;
                point.y *= fYScale;
            }
            // Move the other viewport accordingly
            scrollPane2.getViewport().setViewPosition( point );
        }
    }

    private void createBottomPane()
    {
        // Load a graphic into the display
        Icon image2 = new ImageIcon( "main.gif" );
        JLabel label2 = new JLabel( image2 );

        // Create a tabbed pane
        scrollPane2 = new JScrollPane();
        scrollPane2.setVerticalScrollBarPolicy(
                ScrollPaneConstants.VERTICAL_SCROLLBAR_NEVER );
        scrollPane2.setHorizontalScrollBarPolicy(
                ScrollPaneConstants.HORIZONTAL_SCROLLBAR_NEVER );
        scrollPane2.getViewport().add( label2 );
        scrollPane2.getViewport().addChangeListener( this );
    }

    private void createTopPane()
    {
        // Create a text area
        JTextArea area = new JTextArea();

        // Load a file into the text area, catching any exceptions
        try {
            FileReader fileStream = new FileReader( "TestFrame.java" );
            area.read( fileStream, "TestFrame.java" );
        }
        catch( FileNotFoundException e )
        {
            System.out.println( "File not found" );
```

Listing 3.7   Advanced scroller source code (continued)

```
        }
        catch( IOException e )
        {
            System.out.println( "IOException occurred" );
        }

        // Create the scrolling pane for the text area
        scrollPane1 = new JScrollPane();
        scrollPane1.getViewport().add( area );
        scrollPane1.getViewport().addChangeListener( this );
    }

    public static void main( String args[] )
    {
        // Create an instance of the test application
        TestFrame mainFrame = new TestFrame();
        mainFrame.setVisible( true );
    }
}
```

Listing 3.7   Advanced scroller source code (continued)

You can run the program and stretch out the frame so you can see both panes (similar to the sample shown in figure 3.12). Now, move the vertical scroll bar in the top pane and study the effect. Notice that the view in the bottom pane tracks with the scroll bar activity in the top.

Though the example shown here is impractical, it illustrates how to track one scrolling pane with respect to another. The need for this type of functionality is quite common in applications, and now you know how easy it is to create.

Another, more subtle aspect of this program is the absence of the scroll bars from the lower window, even though the image is larger than the viewport. This is accomplished by setting the horizontal and vertical scroll bar policies which we examined earlier in this chapter.

3.11 Layered panes

We are delving into relatively obscure territory for the remainder of this chapter. The panes described from here on are classes that you may never need, and they are discussed here only to be thorough. These classes are used predominately for internal functions in Swing, but Sun has made them available in the event that you require additional capability. These pane classes are for advanced users only.

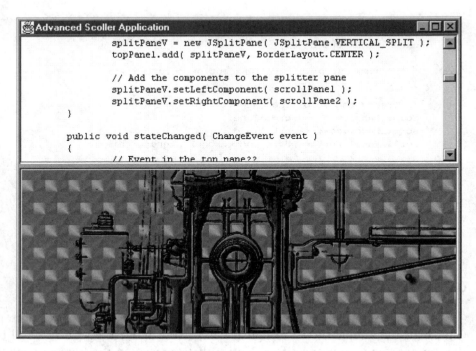

Figure 3.12   Advanced scroller output

The first of these panes is the JLayeredPane class, which was briefly noted in the section describing JFrame at the beginning of this chapter. JLayeredPane manages a list of children in the same manner as the Container does; however, it allows for the definition of several layers within itself. Child components belonging to the same layer are managed exactly the same way as a normal Container object, but components in higher layers display above lower ones. A distinct integer number identifies each of the layers of a JLayeredPane.

The layer attribute can be predefined for a Component by passing an Integer object during the add operation. For example:

```
xcLayeredPane.add( xcComponent, JLayeredPane.DEFAULT_LAYER );
```

Or

```
xcLayeredPane.add( xcComponent, new Integer( 5 ) );
```

Additionally, the layer attribute can be set on a Component object by calling:

```
xcLayeredPane.setLayer( xcComponent, 4 );
```

 The layer of a component should be set before the component is added to the JLayeredPane instance.

The layer of a component can be determined anytime with the call:

```
int iLayer = xcLayeredPane.getLayer( xcComponent );
```

JLayeredPane supports other methods for determining layers, component references, and so on, but we won't be going into any more detail here. The Swing online documentation describes the methods supported by this class.

3.11.1 JLayeredPane constants

```
public static final Integer DEFAULT_LAYER
public static final Integer PALETTE_LAYER
public static final Integer MODAL_LAYER
public static final Integer POPUP_LAYER
public static final Integer DRAG_LAYER
public static final Integer FRAME_CONTENT_LAYER
```

These constants are used to identify the layers within the layered pane. Each of these predefined layers has a specific purpose that is dependent on the type of pane over which it is applied.

3.11.2 JLayeredPane variables

```
protected boolean paintBackground
```

This boolean value controls the requirement to paint the background of the layered pane during a repaint. If the layered pane is transparent, this value will be false.

3.11.3 JLayeredPane constructors

```
JLayeredPane()
```

This default constructor creates a new instance of a layered pane.

3.11.4 JLayeredPane significant method groupings

```
public void setLayer(Component c, int layer)
public void setLayer(Component c, int layer, int position)
```

```
public int getLayer(Component c)
public int highestLayer()
public int lowestLayer()
public static void putLayer(JComponent c, int layer)
public static int getLayer(JComponent c)
public Component[] getComponentsInLayer(int layer)
protected int insertIndexForLayer( int layer, int position )
public int getComponentCountInLayer(int layer)
```

The methods within this group are used to manage the particular layers within the pane. With these methods, the current, highest, or lowest layers can be determined. Also, new components can be assigned to specific layers.

```
public int getIndexOf( Component c )
public void moveToFront( Component c )
public void moveToBack( Component c )
public void setPosition( Component c, int position )
public int getPosition( Component c )
```

This group of methods controls the position of components within the layers of the pane.

3.12 Directory panes

Swing provides another pane that may have more use in your applications than JLayeredPane. If you have ever needed to implement a file dialog in an application, you could use the standard FileDialog class provided by AWT; however, you may want to create an application that embeds this functionality into a larger dialog. Perhaps you just want to create your own file management interface instead using FileDialog.

Swing provides a class called JDirectoryPane that does most of the work for you. An instance of this class creates a scrollable window containing a list of files and directories. You can control the starting path of the list using the correct constructor, and the class also implements a method interface to allow you to intercept events that occur as a result of some user interaction.

IMHO   As of the JFC 1.0 release, the JDirectoryPane class is not officially included in the Swing library. Sun will not support the use of any classes in the `com.sun.java.swing.preview` package, and this information may be subject to change. You should not use this class to build production code.

We won't go into the complete details of JDirectoryPane here; however we can quickly look at an example of some code that creates a directory pane. Listing 3.8 creates a panel to which it adds an instance of JDirectoryPane. Additionally, this code provides an action listener to intercept events from the directory listing. If the user double clicks on a file, the `actionPerformed()` code displays the details of the file selected. Note that double clicking on a directory generates a different event (`doubleClickContainer`) which you can intercept independently of file actions. For other events supported by JDirectoryPane, see the Swing online documentation.

```java
import java.awt.*;
import java.awt.event.*;
import com.sun.java.swing.*;
import com.sun.java.swing.preview.*;

class TestFrame
        extends     JFrame
        implements ActionListener
{
    private      JDirectoryPane      directoryPane;

    public TestFrame()
    {
        setTitle( "Directory Pane Application" );
        setSize( 300, 200 );
        setBackground( Color.gray );

        JPanel topPanel = new JPanel();
        topPanel.setLayout( new BorderLayout() );
        getContentPane().add( topPanel );

        directoryPane = new JDirectoryPane();
        topPanel.add( directoryPane, BorderLayout.CENTER );

        directoryPane.addActionListener( this );
    }

    public void actionPerformed( ActionEvent event )
    {
        // Get the event action string
        String sAction = event.getActionCommand();
        if( sAction != null )
        {
            // Did the user double click on a file
            if( sAction.equals( "doubleClick" ) )
            {
```

Listing 3.8 Sample application with JDirectoryPane

```
                    // Display the selected file
                    TypedFile file = directoryPane.getSelectedFile();
                    System.out.println( "Selected=" + file.toString() );
            }
        }
    }

    public static void main( String args[] )
    {
        // Create an instance of the test application
        TestFrame mainFrame = new TestFrame();
        mainFrame.setVisible( true );
    }
}
```

Listing 3.8   Sample application with JDirectoryPane (continued)

The resulting application output of this listing is shown in figure 3.13. Notice the presence of the vertical scroll bar which is automatically applied to the window when the listing becomes too large for the window's viewport.

3.12.1 JDirectoryPane variables

`protected DirectoryModel directoryModel`

This variable hold the directory model used for the pane instance.

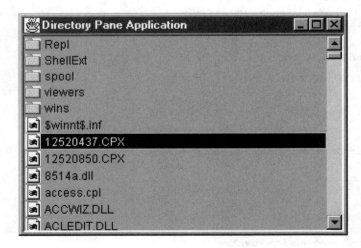

Figure 3.13
Sample program output

```
protected ListSelectionModel listSelectionModel
```

This variable holds the list selection model. Swing defaults this model if no user written model is specified.

```
protected transient JDirectoryPane.Redirector redirector
```

This transient variable contains an instance of the redirector for this instance. The redirector listens to property changes from the directory model and rebroadcasts them with this instance as their source.

```
protected transient JDirectoryPane.SelListener selListener
```

This transient variable contains an instance of the selection listener for this instance. The selection listener reacts to value changes from list selection models and fires an action, if appropriate.

```
protected String command
protected String doubleClickCommand
protected String doubleClickContainerCommand
```

These variables hold the command strings associated with specific events within the directory pane.

3.12.2 JDirectoryPane constructors

```
JDirectoryPane()
```

This constructor creates a JDirectoryPane instance beginning at the user's home directory.

```
JDirectoryPane( String path )
```

This constructor creates a JDirectoryPane instance beginning at the directory specified by the string parameter.

```
JDirectoryPane( File directory )
```

This constructor creates a JDirectoryPane instance beginning at the directory given by the File parameter.

3.12.3 JDirectoryPane significant method groupings

```
public TypedFile getSelectedFile()
public Vector getSelectedFiles()
public File getCurrentDirectory()
public void setCurrentDirectory(File dir)
```

These methods are used to manage the file and directory selections within the directory pane instance.

```
public void setActionCommand(String command)
public String getActionCommand()
public void setDoubleClickCommand(String command)
public String getDoubleClickCommand()
public void setDoubleClickContainerCommand(String command)
public String getDoubleClickContainerCommand()
public Action getGoUpAction()
public ActionListener getDefaultActionListener()
public void performDoubleClick()
public void goUp()
```

The methods within this group manage the action events associated with the directory pane. For example, when the user clicks on a directory in the listing, a doubleClick event is generated.

3.13 Chapter summary

This chapter has covered a lot of the preliminary ground required to understand Swing. You now know how Swing wraps the AWT application framework classes to create JFrame and JApplet, and have seen examples using these new classes.

This chapter also presented the JPanel class which, like AWT's Panel class, is used in almost every conceivable application. You saw how to take simple components (including AWT components) and add them to a JPanel instance to create forms, button arrays, and so on.

Finally, this chapter described some of the pane classes provided by the Swing class library. Of particular value, you saw working examples of tabbed panes, scrolling panes, and split panes. Then we delved into the more obscure corners of Swing with a quick overview of layered panes and directory panes. In a later chapter, you will learn about other panes supported by Swing. For example, when we start discussing text management, you will see an example of a special text pane that can be used to view Hypertext Markup Language (HTML) .

Labels
and buttons

4.1   Basic user interface components

The key to every user interface is the ability to inform the user about important pieces of information and to allow him/her to invoke actions through the use of a keyboard, mouse, or other input device. The API must implement a sufficient degree of functionality to allow developers to detect user input and to display or alter program data; however, this functionality should not hinder the user's ability to complete tasks. The software industry has standardized some basic controls—buttons and text labels, for example. These have enabled us to create some slick applications with relative ease.

The designers of Java decided that the language needed a standard interface, so they introduced components which were common to all platforms. In chapter 1, we reviewed AWT and quickly covered the input and display mechanisms it provides. In the previous chapter, you began to see working examples of Java code which created instances of AWT and Swing components, though that chapter offered relatively little information regarding how to create user interface components and how to control them.

Starting with this chapter, we will begin to examine the key user interface classes provided by Swing and, where necessary, to compare them with AWT. In this chapter, we shall begin with the most basic of components: labels, buttons, check boxes, and radio buttons.

Though this book has, to this point, stressed application development, all Swing user interface components are also compatible with applets. So, if you are building applets, you should recognize that all of the information in this chapter regarding applications applies equally to applets. There are some caveats to consider when building applets, and these will be identified whenever possible.

4.2   Labels

Without question, the simplest form of user interface components is the label. Labels are, essentially, just text strings that are used to identify other components. Labels can have their own fonts, foreground and background colors, and can be positioned anywhere within the bounds of their owner.

Versions of Java previous to 1.2 offered only the AWT label class called Label; however, Swing introduces a new JLabel class for the same purpose. JLabel is much more than a simple wrapper around the old AWT label class. Since it is derived from JComponent, JLabel implements all of the Swing component features such as keyboard accelerators, borders, and so on. For the remainder of this section, we will take a look at some of these features, but first you need to know how to create an instance of a JLabel.

GUIDELINE

Use a standard and consistent sans serif font. Users who stare at computer monitors prefer a sans serif font for legibility. Whichever one you choose, be consistent throughout. If you are going below 8 point on any font, it is probably too small. It's best not to apply styles to standard fonts on labels in order to improve legibility. It's probably a good idea to make your label backgrounds transparent to the dialog.

4.2.1 A JLabel sample program

If you compare the list of JLabel constructors to that of the AWT label class, you see that Swing offers a much richer API, allowing many more constructors with abilities not available in AWT. Listing 4.1 is a code fragment that creates JLabel instances using some of the features provided by Swing:

```
class TestFrame
        extends JFrame
{
    public TestFrame()
    {
        setTitle( "JLabel Application" );
        setSize( 300, 200 );
        setBackground( Color.gray );

        JPanel topPanel = new JPanel();
        topPanel.setLayout( new GridLayout( 2, 2 ) );
        getContentPane().add( topPanel );

        JLabel label1 = new JLabel();
        label1.setText( "Label1" );
        topPanel.add( label1 );

        JLabel label2 = new JLabel( "Label2" );
        label2.setFont( new Font( "Helvetica", Font.BOLD, 18 ) );
        topPanel.add( label2 );

        Icon image = new ImageIcon( "screwdriver.gif" );
```

Listing 4.1   JLabel program source code

```
        JLabel label3 = new JLabel( "Label3", image,
                                SwingConstants.CENTER );
        label3.setVerticalTextPosition( SwingConstants.TOP );
        topPanel.add( label3 );

        JLabel label4 = new JLabel( "Label4",
                                SwingConstants.RIGHT );
        topPanel.add( label4 );
    }

    public static void main( String args[] )
    {
        // Create an instance of the Test application
        TestFrame mainFrame = new TestFrame();
        mainFrame.setVisible( true );
    }
}
```

Listing 4.1   JLabel program source code (continued)

The results of this sample program are shown in figure 4.1. Notice that Label2 demonstrates a change in font, and that Label3 includes a graphic. The size of the graphic determines the minimum size for the label.

4.2.2   Setting fonts and colors

As you observed in the previous sample program, the font can be easily changed. Simply create a new font and use the setFont() method in the JLabel class to effect the change. The font can be any of the standard fonts and sizes supported by the JVM. Use a line similar to the following code to control the font used for a label:

```
label.setFont( new Font( "Dialog", Font.PLAIN, 12 ) );
```

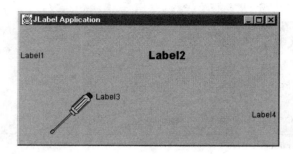

Figure 4.1
JLabel program output

The foreground and background colors of a label can also be changed. To accomplish this, use the setForeground() and setBackground() methods. If you are familiar with AWT, then you probably recognize these methods, and they can be used in exactly the same way with Swing components. Write source code similar to those shown below to set the color attributes of a JLabel instance:

```
label.setBackground( Color.blue );
label.setForeground( Color.yellow );
```

 The color specified in the setForeground() and setBackground() methods can be any of the standard colors identified in the AWT Color or System-Color classes, or may be an RGB value of your own specification.

4.2.3 Text alignment

The example in listing 4.1 included labels with text alignments other than the default. In order to accomplish this task, the constructor referenced the SwingConstants class, which is a class holding constant values for all classes in the Swing library. Five of these constant values are applicable to the JLabel class's text alignment.

Constant Value	Purpose
SwingConstants.LEFT	Left horizontal alignment
SwingConstants.CENTER	Center horizontal or vertical alignment
SwingConstants.RIGHT	Right horizontal alignment
SwingConstants.TOP	Top vertical alignment
SwingConstants.BOTTOM	Bottom vertical alignment

As the example shows, the alignment can be specified in the constructor; however, there are a number of methods implemented by the JLabel class that provide additional control. To change the horizontal alignment, use a line of source code like the following:

```
label.setHorizontalAlignment( SwingConstants.RIGHT );
```

Or for vertical alignment:

```
label.setVerticalAlignment( SwingConstants.BOTTOM );
```

Additional control is provided for labels that include both text and an image. The text can be aligned in the vertical or horizontal aspects, and independently of the image. Use the following code to perform this task:

```
label.setHorizontalTextAlignment( SwingConstants.LEFT );
label.setVerticalTextAlignment( SwingConstants.TOP );
```

Figure 4.2 shows all combinations of vertical and horizontal alignments and the effects they have on the text.

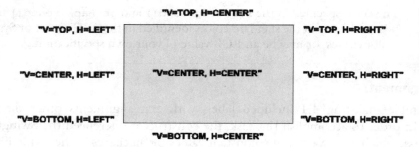

Figure 4.2   JLabel text alignment

4.2.4   Adding an image to a label

The sample code in listing 4.1 included a label with an image of a screwdriver. As we saw, the image can be set during the construction of the object using the following code:

```
Icon image = new ImageIcon( "screwdriver.gif" );
JLabel label3 = new JLabel( "Label3", image,
                        SwingConstants.CENTER );
```

However, the icon can be set at any time using code similar to this:

```
Icon image = new ImageIcon( "screwdriver.gif" );
label2.setIcon( image );
```

Icons are not scaled to fit the label bounds, so once a label has been drawn, adding a large icon may cause clipping to occur. To remove an icon from an existing label, execute the following code:

```
label2.setIcon( null );
```

Finally, JLabel supports the concept of a disabled icon (the image shown when the component is disabled). To set the disabled image, add code similar to this:

```
ImageIcon image = new ImageIcon( "disabled_driver.gif" );
label2.setDisabledIcon( image );
```

FYI Swing has a partially documented class named GrayFilter which can create a disabled image for you automatically. This is how Swing toolbar buttons turn gray when disabled. To create a normal image and a disabled image, you can use code like the following:

```
ImageIcon image = new ImageIcon( "screwdriver.gif" );
ImageIcon DImage = new ImageIcon( GrayFilter
    .createDisabledImage( image.getImage() ) );
```

The results produced by a disabled image are shown in figure 4.3. Note that this disabled image appears automatically if the label is disabled.

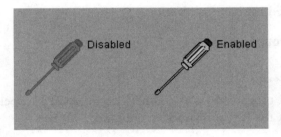

Figure 4.3
Disabled and enabled icons in JLabel

4.2.5 JLabel variables

```
protected Component labelFor
```

This variable holds the instance of the component associated with this label. This part of the accessibility support in Swing can be used to help attach labels (with keyboard accelerators) to the components that they describe.

4.2.6 JLabel constructors

```
JLabel( String text, Icon icon, int horizontalAlignment )
```

This constructor creates a JLabel instance with the specified string, icon, and horizontal alignment.

```
JLabel( String text int horizontalAlignment )
```

This constructor creates a JLabel instance with the specified string and horizontal alignment.

```
JLabel( String text )
```

This constructor creates a JLabel instance with the specified string.

```
JLabel( Icon image, int horizontalAlignment )
```

This constructor creates a JLabel instance with the specified icon and horizontal alignment.

```
JLabel( Icon image )
```

This constructor creates a JLabel instance with the specified icon image.

```
JLabel ()
```

This default constructor creates a JLabel instance with no text or icon. The horizontal alignment is defaulted to right justification.

4.2.7 JLabel significant method groupings

```
public String getText()
public void setText( String text )
```

With exactly the same method prototypes as the Label class in AWT, JLabel provides two methods to get or set the text shown for the instance.

```
public Icon getIcon()
public void setIcon(Icon icon)
public Icon getDisabledIcon()
public void setDisabledIcon(Icon disabledIcon)
public int getIconTextGap()
public void setIconTextGap(int iconTextGap)
```

The methods in this group control the icon images for the JLabel instance for all possible states supported by the label.

```
public void setDisplayedMnemonic(char aKey)
public char getDisplayedMnemonic ()
protected int checkHorizontalKey(int x, String s)
protected int checkVerticalKey(int x, String s)
```

The methods in this group manage any keyboard accelerator keys associated with this JLabel instance.

```
public int getVerticalAlignment()
public void setVerticalAlignment(int alignment)
public int getHorizontalAlignment()
public void setHorizontalAlignment(int alignment)
public int getVerticalTextPosition()
public void setVerticalTextPosition(int textPosition)
public int getHorizontalTextPosition()
public void setHorizontalTextPosition(int textPosition)
```

In some of the previous examples in this section, you were shown the capabilities of JLabel to control the alignment of contained text and graphics. The methods in this group manage these aspects of the JLabel component.

```
public Component getLabelFor()
public void setLabelFor(Component c)}
```

Labels usually describe some other component in the user interface. These methods allow developers to associate the JLabel instance to their related components. This mechanism is closely related to keyboard acceleration. Any accelerator for the label gives the focus to the component with which it is associated.

4.3   AbstractButton

Recalling the class hierarchy of Swing components, you will remember that all UI classes are derived from JComponent. As shown in figure 4.4, one of the child classes included in the JComponent tree is named AbstractButton. This intermediate class subsequently spawns two distinct forms of buttons: JButton and JToggle-Button. You will never use AbstractButton directly, but, inevitably, you will implement an application with some of its children. Since it plays such an important role in the world of Swing buttons, we should examine it more closely.

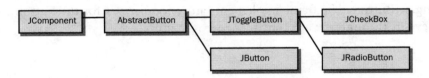

Figure 4.4   AbstractButton class hierarchy

AbstractButton manages most of the functionality of all other Swing button classes shown in figure 4.4. It contains the code responsible for attaching icons to a button face, managing keyboard accelerators, and setting the text alignment, to name of few of its more important functions.

4.3.1 Listening for button events

In some of the previous sample applications in this book, I have shown how to listen for events; however, we haven't really examined the code required to accomplish this. Let's take a closer look at the types of events a button generates and how you can write code to listen for them.

The most frequently used listener for buttons is the ActionListener, which listens for user mouse clicks on buttons' surfaces. To create a listener for actions, you must create a class that implements ActionListener. All this really means is that you need to provide an `actionPerformed()` method.

An action listener class can be created as a separate entity which is independent of the class containing the button instance. This is the most time efficient way to handle button events, and has the added bonus of allowing buttons from several window classes to be managed from a single class. For example, almost all Cancel buttons perform the same task, so a single method can be written to handle this operation for all your application's dialogs.

Having said this, I personally prefer to implement the ActionListener in the class that owns the button instance. This is not as time efficient as using a separate listener class and can require me to write common code in several places; however, I find it much easier to understand the code several months after I've written it. I know that the action event handler for all controls in my window-based class are handled within that class., and I am not forced to hunt through an entire project to find the ActionListener class for a given button. You may notice that most of the examples in this book are written in this fashion, but this is not a requirement, and you are certainly not obligated to follow my lead.

The following sample application, listing 4.2, creates a JFrame instance containing a JButton. The frame implements an action listener for the button to intercept events through the `actionPerformed()` method.

```
import java.awt.*;
import java.awt.event.*;
import com.sun.java.swing.*;

class TestFrame
        extends    JFrame
        implements ActionListener
{
    private     int         iCounter = 0;  // Keep track of button presses
    private     JButton     button = null; // A place to save the button

    public TestFrame()
    {
        setTitle( "ActionListener Application" );
        setBackground( Color.gray );

        JPanel topPanel = new JPanel();
        topPanel.setLayout( new FlowLayout() );
        topPanel.setPreferredSize( new Dimension( 300, 200 ) );
        getContentPane().add( topPanel );

        // Create a button instance and add it to the panel
        button = new JButton( "Press Me" );
        topPanel.add( button );

        // Attach an action listener to the button
        button.addActionListener( this );
    }

    public void actionPerformed( ActionEvent event )
    {
        // Make sure the event is for the button
        if( event.getSource() == button )
        {
            // Increment the button press count
            iCounter++;

            // Change the button text
            button.setText( "Pressed " + iCounter + " times" );
            System.out.println( "Click" );
            pack();
        }
    }

    public static void main( String args[] )
    {
        // Create an instance of the test application
        TestFrame mainFrame = new TestFrame();
```

Listing 4.2   An ActionListener sample

```
        mainFrame.pack();
        mainFrame.setVisible( true );
    }
}
```

Listing 4.2   An ActionListener sample (continued)

IMHO   If you have previously written Java 1.1+ code using AWT, then you will recognize that the technique shown here to listen for button actions is exactly the same. The point of the example in listing 4.2 is to show that Swing and AWT share common roots, so, much of what you already know about AWT is applicable to Swing. Sun's Swing developers understood that many people migrating from AWT would want to bring their existing code with them, so they invested a great deal of time and effort to ensure that AWT code is easy to port. Most of the concepts of AWT still work with Swing.

```
        button.addActionListener( this );
```

The parameter `this` indicates that the instance of the JFrame actually implements the ActionListener by providing the `actionPerformed()` method.

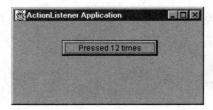

The `actionPerformed()` code determines whether the event was generated by the user as a result of clicking the button. If this is the reason for the event, the action handler increments the internal click counter and modifies the text on the button face. The outcome of this code is a frame similar to the one shown in figure 4.5, containing a JButton instance with dynamically changing button text.

Figure 4.5
ActionListener sample output

4.3.2   Adding icons to buttons

We have already seen an example of a JLabel instance with an attached image. Even though buttons and labels handle images in slightly different ways, the interfaces for each are the same. Since you already know how to add an image to a label, you also know how to perform the same task on a button. Consider modifying the previous example to include an icon image on the button surface, but let's make this simple application a bit more interesting by adding an animated GIF file. Listing 4.3 shows you the code:

```
import java.awt.*;
import java.awt.event.*;
import com.sun.java.swing.*;

class TestFrame
        extends        JFrame
        implements     ActionListener
{
    // Keep track of button presses
    private     int     iCounter    = 0;

    // A place to save the button
    private     JButton     button = null;

    public TestFrame()
    {
        setTitle( "Animated Button Application" );
        setBackground( Color.gray );

        JPanel topPanel = new JPanel();
        topPanel.setLayout( new FlowLayout() );
        getContentPane().add( topPanel );

        // Create a button instance and add it to the panel
        ImageIcon image = new ImageIcon( "earth.gif" );
        button = new JButton( "Press Me", image );
        button.setPreferredSize( new Dimension( 250, 90 ) );
        topPanel.add( button );

        // Attach an action listener to the button
        button.addActionListener( this );
    }

    public void actionPerformed( ActionEvent event )
    {
        // Make sure the event is for the button
        if( event.getSource() == button )
        {
            // Increment the button press count
            iCounter++;
            // Change the button text
            button.setText( "Pressed " + iCounter + " times" );
            System.out.println( "Click" );
            pack();
```

Listing 4.3   An animated button sample

```
        }
    }

    public static void main( String args[] )
    {
        // Create an instance of the test application
        TestFrame mainFrame = new TestFrame();
        mainFrame.pack();
        mainFrame.setVisible( true );
    }
}
```

Listing 4.3   An animated button sample (continued)

This code resembles listing 4.2, but it adds an icon image using code similar to that of the JLabel image example. Like the JLabel example, an image can be applied to a JButton instance either via the constructor or by using the setIcon() method.

Notice that the code in listing 4.3 is required to do nothing to manage the image animation. Behind the scenes, this method is actually starting an internal thread to flip to each frame of the GIF animation. If you run the listing 4.3 code, you will be amazed with the output. This example requires only 21 lines of code!

FYI   If a button contains an image, you can optionally assign individual icons for the normal, selected, pressed, rollover, and disabled states. This allows for total flexibility when creating image-based buttons. See the Swing online documentation for AbstractButton for more detail on the following methods:

```
setIcon()
setDisabledIcon()
setDisabledSelectedIcon()
setPressedIcon()
setRolloverIcon()
setRolloverSelectedIcon()
setSelectedIcon()
```

4.3.3   Enabling and disabling buttons

With the exception of action event handling support, the code most often written to manage buttons is used to enable or disable buttons. In a typical form-based dialog box, for example, it may be desirable to disable the OK button until the user populates any required fields. To disable or enable a button or check box, use the following code:

```
button.setEnabled( bState );
```

where `bState` is either true (to enable) or false (to disable) the component. If disabled, the button frame, its text, and image will all be redrawn in a flatter gray shade to indicate to the user that no action can be performed.

4.3.4 Adding a keyboard mnemonic

A relatively recent addition to Java is the ability to create applications that support mouseless operation (that is, use of the keyboard only). Swing applies this capability to its family of user interface components, allowing the assignment of keyboard mnemonics to any JComponent child, including buttons and check boxes. Figure 4.6 shows a collection of buttons with keyboard mnemonics.

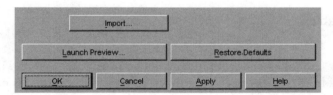

Figure 4.6
Keyboard mnemonics

GUIDELINE

Carefully choose keyboard mnemonics. The generally accepted guidelines for mnemonics for text are in order of precedence:

- Use the first letter unless another letter provides a better association
- Use a distinctive consonant
- Use a vowel

Avoid using thin letters and those with descenders (for example, *q* and *y*) if you can, as they are not easily visible when underlined.

Users in MS-Windows environments might be used to common accelerators such as Enter (for OK), Esc (for Cancel) and F1 (for Help). If in doubt, check the style guide or application exemplars of the target platform.

To add a keyboard mnemonic to a button or check box, use code resembling the following:

```
button.setMnemonic( 'R' );
```

This code assigns the key *R* to the button instance. Note that the first appearance of the assigned accelerator in the button text will be underlined to indicate which key represents the shortcut. Be careful not to duplicate keyboard shortcuts for components sharing the same panel, or you will get unexpected results.

IMHO   If you are building internationalized applications, you will need to specify a mnemonic for each component in each language. Unlike the Microsoft Windows resource style, you cannot add an & character to your strings to identify the short cut character. In my opinion, this inability is a major weakness in Swing.

4.3.5 AbstractButton variables

```
protected ButtonModel model
```

This variable holds the model associated with this button instance. Swing will initially default this variable to an instance of the ButtonModel class, but this can be changed with a call to the setModel() method.

```
protected ChangeListener changeListener
```

This variable contains an instance of the button's model listeners.

```
protected ActionListener actionListener
```

This variable contains an instance of the button's action listeners.

```
protected ItemListener itemListener
```

This variable contains an instance of the button's item listeners.

```
protected transient ChangeEvent changeEvent
```

This variable tracks the change event for the button instance. Only one ChangeEvent is needed per button instance, since the event's only state is the source property. The source of events generated is always the this instance.

4.3.6 AbstractButton significant method groupings

The API for AbstractButton is quite extensive, reflecting its importance. We will examine some of the methods provided in this class, though many are somewhat obscure and I will only gloss over them. The Swing online documentation and examples will assist you in working with some of the less often used methods.

```
public String getText()
public void setText( String text )
```

With exactly the same method prototypes as the Button class in AWT, JLabel provides two methods to get or set the text shown for the instance.

```
public Icon getIcon()
public void setIcon( Icon defaultIcon )
public Icon getPressedIcon()
public void setPressedIcon( Icon pressedIcon )
public Icon getSelectedIcon()
public void setSelectedIcon( Icon selectedIcon )
public Icon getRolloverIcon()
public void setRolloverIcon( Icon rolloverIcon )
public Icon getRolloverSelectedIcon()
public void setRolloverSelectedIcon( Icon rolloverSelectedIcon )
public Icon getDisabledIcon()
public void setDisabledIcon( Icon disabledIcon )
public Icon getDisabledSelectedIcon()
public void setDisabledSelectedIcon( Icon disabledSelectedIcon )
```

The methods in this group manage the icon images associated with each button state. If images are not specified for a given state, AbstractButton will assign a default image based on the default icon.

```
public int getVerticalAlignment()
public void setVerticalAlignment( int alignment )
public int getHorizontalAlignment()
public void setHorizontalAlignment( int alignment )
public int getVerticalTextPosition()
public void setVerticalTextPosition( int textPosition )
public int getHorizontalTextPosition()
public void setHorizontalTextPosition( int textPosition )
protected int checkHorizontalKey( int key, String exception )
protected int checkVerticalKey( int key, String exception )
```

Like the JLabel class, buttons can assign a particular alignment to the text and, independently, to any icon image. The methods in this group manage both the vertical and horizontal alignments.

Even though Swing implements the following old AWT Button APIs for compatibility, they have been deprecated and should not be used in any new code. For example, instead of:

```
String getLabel()
void setLabel( String label )
```

use:

```
String getText()
void setText( String label )
```

4.4   Push buttons

Most of the button examples shown in this chapter used a Swing class called JButton. JButton implements a basic push button, and since we have seen so many examples of it already, I won't bore you with it any further. You will, however, use JButton extensively in GUI applications for common button operations, such as OK and Cancel buttons.

UI
GUIDELINE
Use consistent button size. An example of a standard button size is 100 pixels wide by 25 pixels high. Consider making text more concise in order to minimize the width of buttons. Keep standard button sizes throughout the applications to create more visually appealing dialogs. Wherever possible, avoid placing differently sized buttons in close proximity.

4.4.1   Default buttons

Most graphical user interfaces use a default button. When a dialog box is opened, it is customary to see at least one button component which is the button equivalent to the user pressing the Enter key on the keyboard. This is called the default button.

Swing provides this functionality, not only in dialog boxes, but also in any frame or window. The default button mechanism is accessed through the JRootPane instance. Recall from our discussion of JFrame and JApplet in chapter 3 that the base container object of these components is an instance of the JRootPane class.

If you examine Sun's online documentation for JRootPane, you will notice the method `setDefaultButton()` that accepts a JButton instance as a parameter.

This `setDefaultButton()` method controls the button activated when the user initiates an activation event (usually the Enter key) in the root pane. This action occurs regardless of which component within the root pane currently has the focus. To disassociate the default action and button, pass a null value to the root pane using the same `setDefaultButton()` method.

Since the default button must be a JButton instance, this class provides a method used to determine if the given instance is the current default. The `isDefaultButton()` method in the JButton returns a boolean value indicating whether or not this button instance is activated as a result of the default action.

4.4.2 JButton constructors

```
JButton()
```

This constructor creates an instance of a JButton component with no text or icon image.

```
JButton( Icon icon )
```

This constructor creates an instance of a JButton component with the specified icon image.

```
JButton( String sText )
```

This constructor creates an instance of a JButton component with the specified button text.

```
JButton( String sText,  Icon icon )
```

This constructor creates an instance of a JButton component with the specified button text and icon image.

4.4.3 The JButton API

Recall that JButton extends AbstractButton, which in turn indirectly extends JComponent. As you can see from the online Swing documentation, JButton implements only three methods, all of which have uses associated with the creation of pluggable look-and-feel or accessibility. However, based on its parentage, the JButton class has access to the methods in both AbstractButton and the JComponent class. You can apply any methods from JButton's parents to instances of any button, allowing operations such as color and font changes, border changes, and so on.

4.5   Toggle buttons

Figure 4.7
Toggling buttons

Swing also provides a class named JToggleButton, which presents buttons in much the same way as JButton. The real difference is one of operation. Toggle buttons work like the Caps Lock key on a keyboard, whereas JButton operates in the same manner as the letter or number keys. JToggleButton provides a press-and-hold mechanism, so they are ideal for user interfaces that demand modal operations. See figure 4.7 for an example of an array of toggling buttons.

If you refer back to the class hierarchy for AbstractButton (see figure 4.4), you will notice that JToggleButton is the parent class for JCheckBox and JRadioButton. Since both of these component types exhibit the same toggling behavior, Swing provides these characteristics in JToggleButton. As such, JToggleButton takes on many of the features of its children. For example, consider the following code example in listing 4.4:

```
import java.awt.*;
import java.awt.event.*;
import com.sun.java.swing.*;

class TestFrame
        extends     JFrame
{
    public TestFrame()
    {
        setTitle( "ToggleButton Application" );
        setBackground( Color.gray );

        JPanel topPanel = new JPanel();
        topPanel.setLayout( new FlowLayout() );
        getContentPane().add( topPanel );

        // Create some buttons and add them to the panel
        JToggleButton button1 = new JToggleButton( "Button 1", true );
        topPanel.add( button1 );

        JToggleButton button2 = new JToggleButton( "Button 2", false );
        topPanel.add( button2 );

        JToggleButton button3 = new JToggleButton( "Button 3", false );
        topPanel.add( button3 );
```

Listing 4.4   JToggleButton sample code

```
        // Group the buttons so they interact with each other
        ButtonGroup buttonGroup = new ButtonGroup();
        buttonGroup.add( button1 );
        buttonGroup.add( button2 );
        buttonGroup.add( button3 );
    }

    public static void main( String args[] )
    {
        // Create an instance of the test application
        TestFrame mainFrame = new TestFrame();
        mainFrame.pack();
        mainFrame.setVisible( true );
    }
}
```

Listing 4.4   JToggleButton sample code (continued)

The program first adds the buttons to the panel, which in itself is enough to make the program do something; but suppose that you want to prevent Button 2 and Button 3 from toggling when Button 1 is depressed. If you are familiar with AWT radio buttons, you will recall that you could relate a group of them by creating a CheckboxGroup instance and adding the related radio buttons to it. In Swing, you can group button components other than check boxes, so we use a new class called ButtonGroup, which is functionally equivalent to its AWT counterpart.

Well, it's no big surprise to discover that JToggleButton instances can also be added to a ButtonGroup, and that is what the sample code in listing 4.4 does with the last four lines of code for the constructor. This means that you no longer need to write a lot of code to manually untoggle each button in the array when a new button is pressed.

GUIDELINE

According to Sun, modern user interface design guidelines frown on creating a toggling button array like the one produced by listing 4.4. However, implementing an application exhibiting this behavior is left entirely in the hands of the developer. The point of listing 4.4 is simply to show you that the capability to implement grouped toggle buttons is available, if required.

4.5.1   JToggleButton constructors

```
JToggleButton()
```

This constructor creates an instance of a JToggleButton component with no text or icon image.

```
JToggleButton( Icon icon )
```

This constructor creates an instance of a JToggleButton component with the specified icon image.

```
JToggleButton( Icon icon, boolean bSelected )
```

This constructor creates an instance of a JToggleButton component with the specified icon image. The `bSelected` parameter controls the initial toggle state of the button.

```
JToggleButton( String sText )
```

This constructor creates an instance of a JToggleButton component with the specified button text.

```
JToggleButton( String sText, boolean bSelected )
```

This constructor creates an instance of a JToggleButton component with the specified button text. The `bSelected` parameter controls the initial toggle state of the button.

```
JToggleButton( String sText,  Icon icon )
```

This constructor creates an instance of a JToggleButton component with the specified button text and icon image.

```
JToggleButton( String sText,  Icon icon, boolean bSelected )
```

This constructor creates an instance of a JToggleButton component with the specified button text and icon image. The `bSelected` parameter controls the initial toggle state of the button.

4.6   Check boxes

Swing provides a class, named JCheckBox, that extends JToggleButton to implement a standard check box control. A check box has just two states (checked and unchecked) which are toggled by the user using the mouse or the optional assigned keyboard accelerator. Programmatically, the state of a check box can be determined using code similar to the following fragment:

```
boolean bValue = checkbox.isSelected();
```

To set the state of a check box at run time, use:

```
checkbox.setSelected( bValue );
```

Where `bValue` is true or false, to set or reset the state of the check box.

GUIDELINE

Use check boxes to apply multiple simultaneous states. Check boxes are used to show an on or off state. They can be used most effectively as groups to convey the fact that an object or a view can have multiple states at once and to allow the user to change any one of them without affecting the others. Check boxes can also be used in isolation.

4.6.1 Special layout considerations

Previously, we briefly described some of the new layout managers provided by Swing and focused on the BoxLayout manager; however, at that time we did not delve too deeply into the use of this layout manager. Well, the time has come to take a more practical look at BoxLayout because it greatly simplifies displaying JCheckBox components in a column format (and also the JRadioButton class, which we will look at next).

Though you can apply check boxes or radio buttons using any layout manager, the BoxLayout manager offers the simplest approach. This suggestion to use Box-Layout for check boxes and radio buttons does not, however, mandate that you use this layout manager for all panels that contain these components. If you find yourself in a situation where you need to intermix a group of check boxes with text fields, for example, the easiest solution is to create a subpanel (using JPanel) with box layout for the check box(es) and add it to the main panel at the correct location.

For example, let's assume we want to create a panel that looks like the one shown in figure 4.8. Notice that there is a mix of text fields, labels, and check boxes contained in what appears to be a single panel. In reality, this is a series of panels in which the two check boxes appear in a JPanel (innerPanel) possessing an instance of the BoxLayout manager. This panel is then added to the main panel (topPanel). Listing 4.5 demonstrates the use of BoxLayout to produce the output in figure 4.8.

```
import java.awt.*;
import java.awt.event.*;
```

Listing 4.5   Check box and BoxLayout sample code

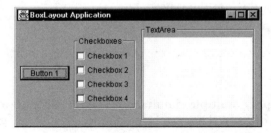

Figure 4.8
A sample panel
with check boxes

```java
import com.sun.java.swing.*;
import com.sun.java.swing.border.*;

class TestFrame
        extends JFrame
{
    public TestFrame()
    {
        setTitle( "BoxLayout Application" );
        setBackground( Color.gray );

        JPanel topPanel = new JPanel();
        topPanel.setLayout( new FlowLayout() );
        getContentPane().add( topPanel );

        // Create some buttons and add them to the panel
        JButton button1 = new JButton( "Button 1" );
        button1.setMaximumSize( new Dimension( 100, 25 ) );
        topPanel.add( button1 );

        // Create a check box array
        JPanel innerPanel = new JPanel();
        innerPanel.setLayout( new BoxLayout( innerPanel,
                            BoxLayout.Y_AXIS ) );
        innerPanel.setPreferredSize( new Dimension( 100, 120 ) );
        innerPanel.setBorder( new TitledBorder(
                            new EtchedBorder(), "Checkboxes" ) );
        topPanel.add( innerPanel );

        JCheckBox check1 = new JCheckBox( "Checkbox 1" );
        innerPanel.add( check1 );
        JCheckBox check2 = new JCheckBox( "Checkbox 2" );
        innerPanel.add( check2 );
        JCheckBox check3 = new JCheckBox( "Checkbox 3" );
        innerPanel.add( check3 );
```

Listing 4.5   Check box and BoxLayout sample code (continued)

```
        JCheckBox check4 = new JCheckBox( "Checkbox 4" );
        innerPanel.add( check4 );

        JPanel textPanel = new JPanel( new BorderLayout() );
        textPanel.setBorder( new TitledBorder(
                        new EtchedBorder(), "TextArea" ) );
        JTextArea area = new JTextArea( "", 10, 30 );
        area.setPreferredSize( new Dimension( 170, 130 ) );
        textPanel.add( area );
        topPanel.add( textPanel );
    }

    public static void main( String args[] )
    {
        // Create an instance of the test application
        TestFrame mainFrame = new TestFrame();
        mainFrame.pack();
        mainFrame.setVisible( true );
    }
}
```

Listing 4.5   Check box and BoxLayout sample code (continued)

4.6.2   JCheckBox constructors

`JCheckBox()`

This constructor creates an instance of a check box with no text or icon image.

`JCheckBox( Icon icon )`

This constructor creates an instance of a check box with the specified icon image.

`JCheckBox( Icon icon, boolean bSelected )`

This constructor creates an instance of a check box with the specified icon image. The `bSelected` parameter controls the initial toggle state of the check box.

`JCheckBox( String sText )`

This constructor creates an instance of a check box with the specified text.

`JCheckBox( String sText, boolean bSelected )`

This constructor creates an instance of a check box with the specified text. The `bSelected` parameter controls the initial toggle state of the check box.

`JCheckBox( String sText, Icon icon )`

This constructor creates an instance of a check box with the specified text and icon image.

```
JCheckBox( String sText, Icon icon, boolean bSelected )
```

This constructor creates an instance of a check box with the specified text and icon image. The `bSelected` parameter controls the initial toggle state of the check box.

4.7 Radio buttons

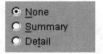

**Figure 4.9
Example of Swing
radio buttons**

Most of the statements made regarding AbstractButton and JCheckBox apply equally to radio buttons. Radio buttons are arrays of buttons used to select the mode of a particular application function, and Swing implements this component in a class called JRadioButton. As with AWT radio buttons, those in Swing are always associated with a ButtonGroup instance, which we reviewed during the discussion of AbstractButton.

GUIDELINE

Use radio buttons to apply mutually exclusive states. Radio buttons are binary, but are never found in isolation. These should only be used to toggle within a group of mutually exclusive states, and they allow the user to select a single state which clears the others.

The suggestions regarding BoxLayout that were highlighted when we talked about JCheckBox apply equally to JRadioButton. It should be noted that, within the same BoxLayout panel, you are free to mix radio buttons, check boxes, and toggle buttons, if appropriate. In fact, BoxLayout is not restricted to these components. BoxLayout fully supports all Swing and AWT components; however, its use will not be appropriate for every application.

4.7.1 JRadioButton constructors

```
JRadioButton()
```

This constructor creates an instance of a radio button with no text or icon image.

```
JRadioButton( Icon icon )
```

This constructor creates an instance of a radio button with the specified icon image.

```
JRadioButton( Icon icon, boolean bSelected )
```

This constructor creates an instance of a radio button with the specified icon image. The `bSelected` parameter controls the initial toggle state of the radio button.

```
JRadioButton( String sText )
```

This constructor creates an instance of a radio button with the specified text.

```
JRadioButton( String sText, boolean bSelected )
```

This constructor creates an instance of a radio button with the specified text. The `bSelected` parameter controls the initial toggle state of the radio button.

```
JRadioButton ( String sText, Icon icon )
```

This constructor creates an instance of a radio button with the specified text and icon image.

```
JRadioButton ( String sText, Icon icon, boolean bSelected )
```

This constructor creates an instance of a radio button with the specified text and icon image. The bSelected parameter controls the initial toggle state of the radio button.

4.8 Chapter summary

In this chapter, we started to examine some actual Swing components and ways in which they could be used to create some simple applications. The first component described was the simple label, which is commonly used to identify the purpose of other components within a panel.

Next, we examined the intricacies of the AbstractButton class. This class contains almost all of the functionality for every button, check box, and radio button in Swing. Then, we learned about more specific types of buttons, starting with the JButton class, and presented techniques used to enable or disable it and to display animated images on a button face.

Finally, we quickly discussed check boxes and radio buttons, which are fundamental for building modal selections into a user interface. These components operate in much the same way as the equivalent AWT components, though, like JButton, images and keyboard accelerators can be applied.

Though I have not relentlessly examined the purpose for every method in the classes identified in this chapter, I have made an effort to highlight their most common features and describe the techniques used to implement applications with them. This effort will continue into the next several chapters, though the complexity and uniqueness of the components will increase. So far, the components we have studied map almost directly onto the equivalent AWT components; however, as we move forward from this chapter, you will see that the more complex and unique aspects of Swing components relate less and less well to those of AWT.

5

Text management

The Swing components we have discussed have required simple input, and have a simple feedback mechanism. For example, a check box or radio button needs only a mouse click to toggle its state, and will display this state in the form of a check mark or a highlighted dot. You have seen examples of components that allow keyboard text input, but you have not yet seen any details about them.

In this chapter, you will begin to see components that allow text input and give you the capability to build something practical with Swing. We will start by examining the JTextComponent class, which provides the basic intelligence found in all derived text components.

Then, we will look at the standard AWT-like text field, which provides an interface to enter a single line of text. We will take a deeper look at the JTextArea component, which you can use to enter and/or display multiple lines of text. These components are as functional as those you may already recognize in AWT, but much more can be accomplished with Swing than with AWT.

As we progress more deeply into text management, we will study the document management capabilities built into Swing text components. We will show you how to easily display HTML and Rich Text Format (RTF) documents, as well as text with a custom document format. By the time you finish this chapter, you will be able to create simple form-based user interfaces built entirely with Swing components, and we will have laid the groundwork for learning about the more advanced components.

Finally, we will examine the combo box (or pull-down list), which is a hybrid of a simple mouse-only component and a text field. The Swing combo box is similar to the Choice control in AWT, but offers additional features, such as an editable selection field.

5.1 JTextComponent

If you have previous experience with AWT, then you know that text support was quite limited. The basic design approach in AWT is to wrap a thin native interface around the plain text support provided by the operating system. This technique provides the benefit of supporting internationalization, but it does not meet the needs of many developers. For example, AWT doesn't support multiple fonts within the same text windows, nor does it allow embedding graphic images in the text.

Due to these limitations, developers requiring special features were forced to write their own text management classes. This can result in unscheduled project delays because of the additional work. More significantly, the classes written to support special features are nonstandard and often incomplete. For instance, many developers either fail to consider or don't need internationalization, so they omit it. If foreign language support becomes important at some point in the future, upgrading the existing code would be a nightmare.

Swing has a solution to AWT's text support problems. The developers of Swing realized the limitations in AWT, and decided on a different approach whereby all text manipulation classes are basically implementations of a text editor, whether they be single line or multiple lines of plain text, HTML, or some custom developer-written format. The result of their efforts is a tiered class hierarchy in which the base text class, JTextComponent, holds all of the knowledge needed to implement a text editor, and its children simply describe a technique to apply this knowledge to a specific task.

Figure 5.1 illustrates the class hierarchy for JTextComponent. Each of the classes will be described in some detail as we progress through this chapter, but, for now, let's concentrate on JTextComponent. The designers of Swing set the following requirements for JTextComponent:

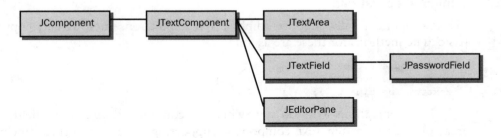

Figure 5.1   JTextComponent class hierarchy

- JTextComponent supports the previous AWT API, as much as possible. This greatly simplifies the conversion process from AWT to Swing. There are some pitfalls when converting, but, in general, converting AWT text controls to Swing is easy.

- JTextComponent provides a rich set of components capable of interacting with the native operating system for operations like direct manipulation (drag and drop) and clipboard operations. This class also lays the foundation to support formats beyond plain text, such as HTML and RTF. It also allows developers to design custom text formats.

- JTextComponent fully supports Swing's pluggable look-and-feel capabilities. In addition to completely replacing the look-and-feel of text components, you can also implement custom text and graphics styles.

In the remainder of this section, we will make a more detailed examination of some features provided in the JTextComponent class.

 The AWT TextEvent and TextListener have been replaced by Document-Event and DocumentListener interfaces in Swing. Though the Document-Event interface provides substantially more information about the nature of a text change, it is incompatible with AWT. If you are converting AWT code which makes use of TextEvent or TextListener, you will have a bit more work to do.

5.1.1 Clipboard operations

JTextComponent fully supports clipboard manipulations such as cut, copy, and paste. The methods for these are as follows:

```
textComponent.copy();
textComponent.cut();
textComponent.paste();
```

These operations work on any Swing text component, be it a text field, a text area, or a user written text component supporting a custom format (including graphics). Because JTextComponent provides the clipboard mechanism for you, a great deal of time can be saved when you write text components with custom text formats.

5.1.2 Saving and loading

You might expect JTextComponent to handle clipboard operations (and it does); however, this class also offers features you might not be expecting. For example, JTextComponent also includes the mechanism to save and load text within the component. This is useful if you are writing something like a text editor application, where you want to interact with the operating system to load or save files. The beauty of the approach provided by JTextComponent is that it is totally system independent, and, in addition, is not restricted to disk files. JTextComponent can save or load any type of stream (a URL, for example). To use these methods, add code like the following:

```
textComponent.read( xcReadStream, "http://www.mysite.com" );
textComponent.read( xcStreamStream );
```

5.1.3 JTextComponent constants

```
public static final String FOCUS_ACCELERATOR_KEY
```

This constant contains the bound property name for the focus accelerator.

5.1.4 JTextComponent constructors

```
JTextComponent()
```

This constructor creates an instance of a text component. Only children of this class will call it.

5.1.5 JTextComponent significant method groupings

```
public void setDocument(Document doc)
public Document getDocument()
```

Every JTextComponent (or derivative) instance has an associated Document. Swing will assign a default which can be retrieved, but the document instance can be changed with the setDocument() method.

```
public void setText(String t)
public String getText()
public String getSelectedText()
public void replaceSelection(String content)
public String getText(int offs, int len)
                    throws BadLocationException
```

Using the same techniques as those in the AWT TextComponent class, the methods in this group manage all text within the component. This group also includes a method to replace the selected text with the specified string.

```
public Caret getCaret()
public void setCaret(Caret c)
public void setCaretPosition(int position)
public int getCaretPosition()
public void moveCaretPosition(int pos)
```

The caret (the blinking cursor), which is used as part of the selection mechanism for a text component, can be controlled with the methods in this group.

```
public Highlighter getHighlighter()
public void setHighlighter(Highlighter h)
```

By default, Swing will assign a highlighter to each text component instance. The methods in this group manage the highlighter, allowing it to be changed to a custom version if desired.

```
public Color getCaretColor()
public void setCaretColor(Color c)
public Color getSelectionColor()
public void setSelectionColor(Color c)
public Color getSelectedTextColor()
public void setSelectedTextColor(Color c)
public Color getDisabledTextColor()
public void setDisabledTextColor(Color c)
```

This group of methods manages the colors of the various attributes of a text component. The color for each text state (normal, disabled, and selected) can be changed.

```
public void cut()
public void copy()
public void paste()
```

Every text component supports clipboard manipulation. This group of methods supports copying and cutting the currently selected text, as well as pasting the contents of the clipboard into the component's document.

```
public void read( Reader in, Object desc ) throws IOException
public void write( Writer out ) throws IOException
```

This group of methods handles loading documents from a stream and saving them back again (unlike AWT's text components).

```
public synchronized int getSelectionStart()
public synchronized void setSelectionStart(int selectionStart)
public synchronized int getSelectionEnd()
public synchronized void setSelectionEnd(int selectionEnd)
public void select(int selectionStart, int selectionEnd)
public synchronized void selectAll()
```

Text selection is a very important feature of the text component class hierarchy. These methods allow developers to programmatically select regions of text within the document.

5.2 Document handling

The previous section contained a note concerning the lack of TextListener and TextEvent in Swing's text component classes. With AWT, these classes are used to determine if the user has changed the contents of a text component, for example. Since Swing does not support this technique, it must offer developers another option. The developers of Swing adopted a much more intelligent approach to handling text changes and formatting, and it does this with a class named Document.

FYI
In the Swing MVC architecture, the Document class serves as a model. It contains no capability for user interface. These functions originate with the users of this class, such as JTextField and JTextArea.

Document is a Swing-based container used to hold text and to provide notification of changes to this text. The Document class also implements support for mark-up (text selection) and includes an internal structure to manage changes to its text. The structure of these elements (see figure 5.2) consists of a base unit of containment called an element, each of which includes an arbitrary set of attributes associated with its text. At the front end, the element structure maps to an instance of a view (described in chapter 3 when we discussed JScrollPane).

Figure 5.2 shows how text and control information is packed into the Document internal element structure. Typically, an instance of Document will contain only a single element structure, but the interface supports building any number of

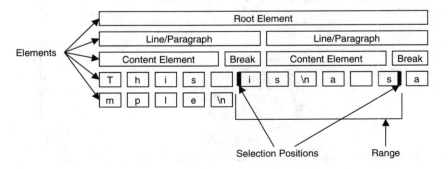

Figure 5.2   Document internal element structure

structural projections over the text element. Also, Document supports multiple root elements and multiple data structures. For example, suppose you need to store modification notes or annotations along with the text. In this case, you need to create an additional data structure associated with the annotations, in addition to the structure that contains the actual text.

Why is the Document class important, and what advantages does it offer over AWT? AWT had only two classes for managing text entry and display: TextField and TextArea. Both classes are limited exclusively to character data. With Swing, and a little creativity, applications (like the one shown in figure 5.3) can be designed with relative ease. Notice that this screen shot shows not only several different font styles and colors, but also includes graphics. Accomplishing the same things with AWT would be quite difficult.

At this time, I won't give you any specific examples for usage of the Document class, since you do not have enough information yet to make such an example prac-

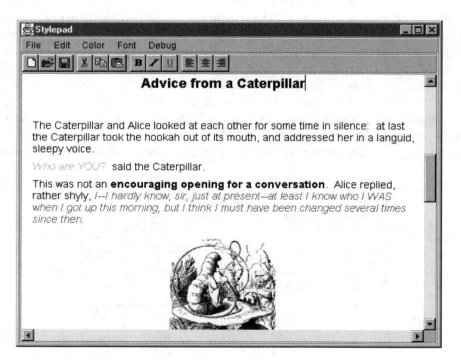

Figure 5.3   Sample application using the Document class

tical. As we progress through the rest of this chapter, you will see samples showing you how to interface to the Document instance associated with the text classes we will discuss.

5.2.1 Document constants

```
public static final String StreamDescriptionProperty
```

This constant contains the property name for the description of the stream used to initialize the document instance. This should be used if you know anything about the stream used to initialize the document.

```
public static final String TitleProperty
```

This constant holds the property name for the title of the document, if there is one.

5.2.2 Document significant method groupings

```
public abstract String getText( int offset, int length)
                          throws BadLocationException
public abstract void getText( int offset, int length, Segment txt )
                          throws BadLocationException
public abstract void insertString(int offset, String str,
                    AttributeSet a) throws BadLocationException
public abstract void remove(int offs,
                int len) throws BadLocationException
```

These methods are used to retrieve, insert, and remove text strings from a document. The specified offset and length determine the location and size of the string being manipulated. All methods throw a `BadLocationException` if the location specified is invalid.

```
public abstract int getLength()
```

This method returns an integer containing the number of characters held by the document.

```
public abstract void addDocumentListener(
                    DocumentListener listener )
public abstract void removeDocumentListener(
                    DocumentListener listener )
```

The Document class supports a DocumentListener which waits for changes to the document (insertion or removal of elements). DocumentListeners can be added or removed with the methods in this group.

```
public abstract Position getStartPosition()
public abstract Position getEndPosition()
public abstract Position createPosition(int offs)
                              throws BadLocationException
```

Each of the methods in this group manages the positions of important parts of the document. The start and end methods return the starting and ending positions of the document, while the `createPosition()` method allows you to create a specific position within the document which tracks as changes are made.

```
public abstract Object getProperty(Object key)
public abstract void putProperty(Object key, Object value)
```

These methods allow properties to be managed. It was previously mentioned that custom properties could be assigned to the document and its elements, and these methods implement this capability.

```
public abstract Element[] getRootElements()
public abstract Element getDefaultRootElement()
```

These methods manage the root element(s) of the document.

```
public abstract void render(Runnable r)
```

This method allows the model to be safely rendered, if the model supports asynchronous updates. The given renderer will be executed in a safe way, preventing changes while it is active.

5.3 Text fields and password fields

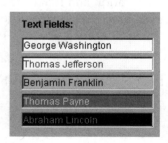

Figure 5.4
Example of Swing text fields

If you have experience with the AWT user interface, you already know about the standard text field. Swing offers a similar class, and we will start our study of text components with this simple data entry object. Text fields are simple entry boxes which allow a single line of text entered with any character from the keyboard. It is important to note that text fields, and Java in general, are UNICODE compliant. This means that any character from any language can be entered and displayed, provided that the operating system supports the character set. See figure 5.4 for examples of some text fields from the SWINGSET demonstration supplied in the Swing example programs.

A text field includes only the editable field itself. Normally, you would associate a JLabel instance with a text field to identify the purpose of the field.

Text fields, having JComponent as their parents, have many of the same capabilities as the JLabel we previously examined. They possess a font, a background color, and a foreground color. They can be associated with a keyboard accelerator (which is our next topic of discussion), and they generate events that can be handled with a listener class. The Swing text field is defined by a class called JTextField, which is derived from JTextComponent. As a result, JTextField exposes all of the functionality of its parent, such as text selection and clipboard operations. The basic construction technique for a text field is as follows:

```
JTextField field = new JTextField( "Sample" );
```

In this example, the word Sample is placed in the edit field once the instance is created and added to a container. Note that it is possible to create instances that are initially empty. See the API at the end of this section for more information regarding constructors for JTextField.

Align and size your text fields consistently. A graphical rule of thumb is to left align any group of text fields on a dialog, and make groups of text fields the same width and height. The same goes for all types of grouped controls.

UI GUIDELINE

5.3.1 Associating keyboard mnemonics

Figure 5.5
Example of keyboard mnemonics

You have seen several references to keyboard support and mnemonics, but have not yet seen an example. Now is the time! If you are familiar with Microsoft Windows, you have seen applications which include label/text field combinations, where the label offers a keyboard mnemonic (see figure 5.5). When the underlined accelerator key is pressed in conjunction with the ALT key, the focus is given to the text field. For example, in figure 5.5, the field associated with the Top label will receive the focus when the ALT+T key combination is pressed.

When building applications with AWT, implementing a keyboard mnemonic for a text field is nearly impossible, though you could accomplish this with a significant amount of additional code. Fortunately, Swing provides this capability for you.

When we examined the JLabel class and its API, you may have noticed a method named setLabelFor() which accepts a single Component parameter. This method causes the association of JLabel instance with whatever component is supplied as a parameter. So, to associate a JLabel with an instance of JTextField, you can add code similar to the following:

```
JTextField field = new JTextField();
JLabel label = new JLabel( "My Label:" );
label.setLabelFor( field );
```

But this only partially addresses the keyboard mnemonics problem—we still need to add a keyboard accelerator to the label and the field. JLabel includes a different method for this, called setDisplayedMnemonic(). To add an accelerator for the previous example, use:

```
label.setDisplayedMnemonic( 'M' );
```

Finally, we need to inform the text component that it now has an accelerator that generates an action when the user selects it. This is accomplished like this:

```
field1.setFocusAccelerator( 'm' );
```

This code generates an action event when the ALT+M key combination is typed by the user, and the action event requires an actionPerformed() implementation in the code to service the request. As a result of the action, the code must change the focus to the correct component. To do this, the example code executes:

```
Component fieldComponent = label.getLabelFor();
fieldComponent.requestFocus();
```

If you add accelerators as shown here, you will not be able to easily create foreign language versions of your application. To create a language independent application which implements accelerators, you will require a Java property file from which accelerator bindings will be loaded. To review the use of a property file, see the Swing Notepad example which ships with JavaSoft's JFC product.

This completes the solution to the problem. Now the M key is attached as an accelerator, and the association between the label and the text field automatically sets the focus to the text field when the accelerator is selected by the user.

5.3.2 Special event handling

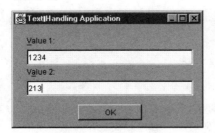

Figure 5.6
Output of the event handling example

As noted previously, classes derived from JText-Component do not support TextListener from the AWT class library. So how does one determine when changes to text contents or some other action occur? Swing offers a technique that is better than the one offered by AWT, because it transparently supports the Document interface. This means that the Document interface supports internationalization and the other significant features offered by this model.

Let's take a closer look at some sample code. In this example, we have two labels, associated text fields, and a single button. This button should be disabled until the first text field contains text, and, as an added requirement, the contents of the text field must be numeric. The user interface layout of the sample should appear as it does in figure 5.6.

FYI Notice that the example also implements keyboard accelerators, as described in the previous section. This was done purely for demonstration purposes, and plays no active part in this application.

As shown in listing 5.1 below, the code to create and lay out this example is straightforward, consisting of bits of code you have seen previously. The TestFrame class, however, implements a DocumentListener which requires three additional methods in order to handle insertions, removals, and changes of the text field.

```
import java.awt.*;
import java.awt.event.*;
import com.sun.java.swing.*;
import com.sun.java.swing.text.*;
```

Listing 5.1   Event handling sample code

```
import com.sun.java.swing.event.*;

class TestFrame
        extends    JFrame
        implements DocumentListener,
                   ActionListener
{
    private JTextField field1;
    private JTextField field2;
    private JButton    button1;
    private JLabel     label1;
    private JLabel     label2;

    public TestFrame()
    {
        // NOTE:  In order to create the desired output, this example
        // uses a NULL layout manager and hard-codes the sizes and
        // positions of components.  This is NOT something you want
        // to do in production code.

        setTitle( "Text Handling Application" );
        setSize( 300, 190 );
        setBackground( Color.gray );

        JPanel topPanel = new JPanel();
        topPanel.setLayout( null );
        getContentPane().add( topPanel );

        // Create afield and label
        field1 = new JTextField();
        field1.setBounds( 20, 40, 260, 25 );
        field1.setFocusAccelerator( 'v' );
        topPanel.add( field1 );

        label1 = new JLabel( "Value 1:" );
        label1.setBounds( 20, 15, 260, 20 );
        label1.setLabelFor( field1 );
        label1.setDisplayedMnemonic( 'V' );
        topPanel.add( label1 );

        // Create a second label and text field
        JTextField field2 = new JTextField();
        field2.setBounds( 20, 90, 260, 25 );
        field2.setFocusAccelerator( 'a' );
        topPanel.add( field2 );

        label2 = new JLabel( "Value 2:" );
        label2.setDisplayedMnemonic( 'a' );
```

Listing 5.1   Event handling sample code (continued)

```
        label2.setBounds( 20, 65, 260, 20 );
        label2.setLabelFor( field2 );
        topPanel.add( label2 );

        // Create a button and add it to the panel
        button1 = new JButton( "OK" );
        button1.setBounds( 100, 130, 100, 25 );
        button1.setEnabled(false );
        topPanel.add( button1 );

        // Add a document listener to the first field
        Document document = field1.getDocument();
        document.addDocumentListener( this );
    }

// Handle keyboard accelerators
public void actionPerformed( ActionEvent e )
{
        // Get the source of the action event
        JLabel label = (JLabel)e.getSource();

        // Give the associated component the focus
        Component fieldComponent = label.getLabelFor();
        fieldComponent.requestFocus();
    }

// Handle insertions into the text field
public void insertUpdate( DocumentEvent event )
{
        String sString = field1.getText();

        try {
            int iValue = Integer.parseInt( sString );
            button1.setEnabled( true );
        }
        catch( NumberFormatException e )
        {
            button1.setEnabled( false );
        }
    }

// Handle deletions from the text field
public void removeUpdate( DocumentEvent event )
{
        // Prevent the user from entering a blank field
        if( field1.getText().length() == 0 )
            button1.setEnabled( false );
```

Listing 5.1   Event handling sample code (continued)

```
        else
        {
            // Do the same error checking as insertUpdate()
            insertUpdate( event );
        }
    }

    // Handle changes to the text field
    public void changedUpdate( DocumentEvent event )
    {
        // Nothing to do here
    }

    // Main() method to get the ball rolling
    public static void main( String args[] )
    {
        // Create an instance of the test application
        TestFrame mainFrame = new TestFrame();
        mainFrame.setVisible( true );
    }
}
```

Listing 5.1   Event handling sample code (continued)

The main points of interest in this sample are the two lines of code that assign the listener to the TestFrame class. These lines, shown below, retrieve the Document instance connected to field1 and add a document listener to it.

```
Document document = field1.getDocument();
document.addDocumentListener( this );
```

From this point on, the application will detect any changes to the first field. This is accomplished by implementing the following abstract method from the DocumentListener class:

```
public void insertUpdate( DocumentEvent event )
public void removeUpdate( DocumentEvent event )
public void changedUpdate( DocumentEvent event )
```

 GUIDELINE **Intelligently grabbing and controlling the focus of text fields.** When entering an editable field into a dialog, the first text field should have the focus. Tabbing should grab the focus of the remaining text fields in the order in which the fields are grouped together. If a dialog contains all text fields, typing in the data on the last field, then pressing enter, should terminate the dialog.

5.3.3 JTextField constructors

`JTextField()`

This constructor creates an instance of a text field with no text.

`JTextField( String text )`

This constructor creates an instance of a text field with the specified text.

`JTextField(int columns)`

This constructor creates an instance of a text field with no text. The field is limited to the selected number of columns.

`JTextField(String text, int columns)`

This constructor creates an instance of a text field with the specified text. The field is limited to the selected number of columns.

`JTextField( Document doc, String text, int columns)`

This constructor creates an instance of a text field with the specified text and implements the chosen document model. The field is limited to the selected number of columns.

FYI Swing also implements a JPasswordField which acts much like JTextField, except that the output is hidden from the user. This is used for entry of confidential input ,such as passwords.

JPasswordField constructors

`JPasswordField()`

This constructor creates an instance of a password field with no text.

`JPasswordField( String text )`

This constructor creates an instance of a password field with the specified text.

`JPasswordField(int columns)`

This constructor creates an instance of a password field with no text. The field is limited to the selected number of columns.

`JPasswordField(String text, int columns)`

This constructor creates an instance of a password field with the specified text. The field is limited to the selected number of columns.

```
JPasswordField( Document doc, String text, int columns)
```

This constructor creates an instance of a password field with the specified text, implementing the chosen document model. The field is limited to the selected number of columns.

5.3.4 JPasswordField significant method groupings

```
public char getEchoChar()
public void setEchoChar(char c)
public boolean echoCharIsSet()
```

The JPasswordField class prevents unmasked output from appearing in the field. The character that is echoed to the field is defaulted to an asterisk (*), but it can be changed by the methods in this group.

5.4 Text areas

Though text fields offer answers to many implementation questions, they fall short in some situations. Often, as a developer, you need to present a text component to the user which will accept more than one line of text. The text component which allows this is called a text area, and it is characterized by its ability to accept entry or display many lines of text simultaneously.

Like the text field in the last section, the text area has its origins in AWT (in the TextArea class). TextArea supports internationalization, albeit in a limited manner, and automatically provides horizontal and vertical scroll bars if the text buffer is larger than the presentation space. The AWT TextArea class does have some limitations, but, in general, offers most of the functionality required; however, for consistency, the Swing development team designed a new class called JTextArea (see figure 5.7). Since JTextArea is derived from JTextComponent, it inherently supports the capability to save or load the contents of the text area both to and from a stream.

The screen capture in figure 5.7 contains some source code loaded into the JTextArea instance by using the read() method in its JTextComponent parent. The source code to produce this output is show in listing 5.2. We can accomplish these results with just 27 lines of code!

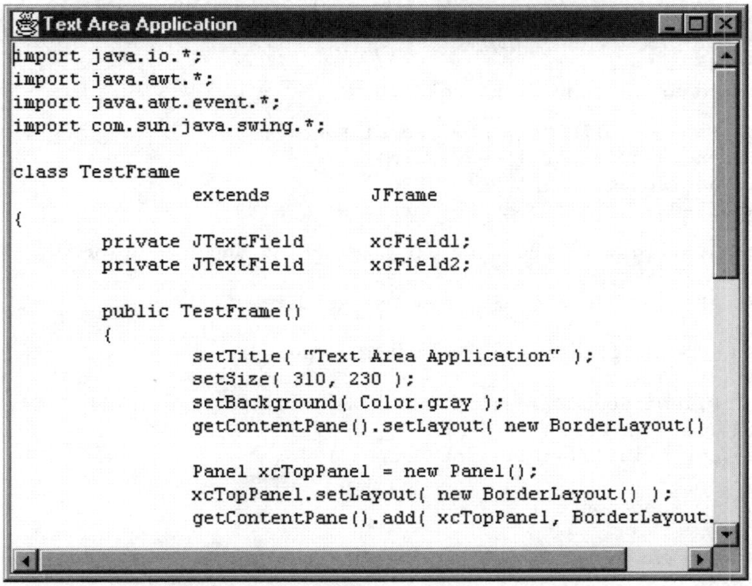

```
Text Area Application                        _ □ ×
import java.io.*;
import java.awt.*;
import java.awt.event.*;
import com.sun.java.swing.*;

class TestFrame
            extends          JFrame
{
        private JTextField      xcField1;
        private JTextField      xcField2;

        public TestFrame()
        {
                setTitle( "Text Area Application" );
                setSize( 310, 230 );
                setBackground( Color.gray );
                getContentPane().setLayout( new BorderLayout()

                Panel xcTopPanel = new Panel();
                xcTopPanel.setLayout( new BorderLayout() );
                getContentPane().add( xcTopPanel, BorderLayout.
```

Figure 5.7   An example of JTextArea

```java
import java.io.*;
import java.awt.*;
import java.awt.event.*;
import com.sun.java.swing.*;

class TestFrame
        extends    JFrame
{
    public TestFrame()
    {
        setTitle( "Text Area Application" );
        setSize( 310, 230 );
        setBackground( Color.gray );
        getContentPane().setLayout( new BorderLayout() );

        JPanel topPanel = new JPanel();
        topPanel.setLayout( new BorderLayout() );
```

Listing 5.2   JTextArea sample

```
        getContentPane().add( topPanel, BorderLayout.CENTER );

        // Create a text area
        JTextArea area = new JTextArea();

        JScrollPane scrollPane = new JScrollPane();
        scrollPane.getViewport().add( area );
        scrollPane.setBounds( 10, 10, 280, 180 );
        topPanel.add( scrollPane, BorderLayout.CENTER );

        // Load a file into the text area, catching any exceptions
        try {
            FileReader fileStream = new FileReader(
                                    "TestFrame.java" );
            area.read( fileStream, "TestFrame.java" );
        }
        catch( FileNotFoundException e )
        {
        System.out.println( "File not found" );
        }
        catch( IOException e )
        {
            System.out.println( "IOException occurred" );
        }
    }

    public static void main( String args[] )
    {
        // Create an instance of the test application
        TestFrame mainFrame = new TestFrame();
        mainFrame.setVisible( true );
    }
}
```

Listing 5.2   JTextArea sample (continued)

 Notice that the sample code in listing 5.2 creates an instance of a JscrollPane, and inserts the JTextArea into it. JTextArea does not provide scrolling capability, so you must use this technique to implement the ability to scroll.

This completes our look at basic text components. The examples shown so far in this chapter have been simple, but components based on the JTextComponent class can become quite complex. If you are interested in a more detailed sample of text components, study the STYLEPAD example provided with the Swing package.

5.4.1 JTextArea constructors

```
JTextArea()
```

This constructor creates an instance of a text area with no text.

```
JTextArea( String text )
```

This constructor creates an instance of a text area with the specified text.

```
JTextArea( int rows, int columns )
```

This constructor creates an instance of a text field with the specified number of rows and columns, and having no text.

```
JTextArea(String text, int rows, int columns)
```

This constructor creates an instance of a text field with the specified number of rows and columns, and having the specified text.

```
JTextArea(Document doc)
```

This constructor creates an instance of a text field implementing the specified Document model, and having no text.

```
JTextArea(Document doc, String text, int rows, int columns)
```

This constructor creates an instance of a text field populated using the specified Document model. It contains the supplied text, formatted with the desired number of rows and columns.

5.4.2 JTextArea significant method groupings

```
public void insert(String str, int pos)
public void append(String str)
public void replaceRange(String str,
                    int start, int end)
```

Like the AWT TextArea class, JTextArea implements methods to insert and append text into the component's document. To facilitate porting, the methods in the Swing class are compatible with their AWT cousin.

```
public void setTabSize(int size)
public int getTabSize()
```

The text area will pad tab characters with a specified number of spaces. The methods in this group allow the tab size to be changed or retrieved. This is useful if you want to present some custom display format.

5.5 Combo boxes

All of the components we have examined in this chapter have been derived from JTextComponent; however, there are other components in Swing which handle text. Though these components are generally not parented by JTextComponent, they are usually composed of at least one JTextComponent child with the addition of some other functionality.

Our first example of this type of class is the combo box (also known as a pull-down list). A combo box is the combination of a text field, a button, and a list—all in a single component. By default, the selected text is displayed in the text field, which acts as the current selection box. The button to the right of the text field controls the display of the list box, and is used to select an item from a preconfigured list of items. In AWT, this was as much capability as a combo box could offer. In Swing, the combo box has been improved with the addition of editing capability in the selection text field, and with the ability to display icons along with, or in place of, the items' text. Figure 5.8 shows some sample combo boxes created with Swing. Notice the presence of icons in the pull-down list and selection fields.

In Swing, the combo box class is named JComboBox, and its API is typically a super-set of AWT's Choice class. This helps to make conversions from AWT to Swing much easier.

UI GUIDELINE

Use combo boxes to conserve real estate. Combo boxes are ideal for allowing the user to choose a single item from a long list of options, without consuming a lot of dialog real estate. If you are running out of room in a dialog, and you need a UI that allows for either selecting from a list of choices or typing in place, use a combo box. Consider deploying the scroll bar when the item list reaches ten items, or if you need to display a hierarchy. The Swing JComboBox will automatically add scroll bars after approximately seven items, but you can change this by setting the preferred size of the instance.

Listing 5.3 contains sample code to create a Swing-based combo box and populate it with the names of some countries. This sample does not support graphical images, but we will look at this in chapter 9 when we discuss list boxes (which are implemented with the same technique). If you wish to preview list boxes, you can study the SWINGSET code that ships with the JFC product—and specifically, the ComboBoxPanel.java file.

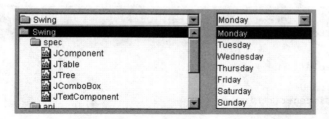

Figure 5.8
Some examples of combo boxes

```
import java.awt.*;
import java.awt.event.*;
import com.sun.java.swing.*;
import com.sun.java.swing.event.*;

class TestFrame
        extends    JFrame
        implements ItemListener
{
    private    JComboBox  combo;

    final   String[]    sList =
                        {
                            "Canada",
                            "USA",
                            "Australia",
                            "Bolivia",
                            "Denmark",
                            "Japan"
                        };
    public TestFrame()
    {
        setTitle( "ComboBox Application" );
        setSize( 300, 80 );
        setBackground( Color.gray );

        JPanel topPanel = new JPanel();
        topPanel.setLayout( null );
        getContentPane().add( topPanel );

        // Create a combo box
        combo = new JComboBox();
        combo.setBounds( 20, 15, 260, 20 );
        topPanel.add( combo );

        // Populate the combo box list
```

Listing 5.3 JComboBox sample code

```
        for( int iCtr = 0; iCtr < sList.length; iCtr++ )
            combo.addItem( sList[iCtr] );

        // Allow edits
        combo.setEditable( true );

        // Watch for changes
        combo.addItemListener( this );
    }

    public void itemStateChanged( ItemEvent event )
    {
        if( event.getSource() == combo
                && event.getStateChange() == ItemEvent.SELECTED )
        {
            System.out.println( "Change:"
                            + combo.getSelectedItem() );
        }
    }

    public static void main( String args[] )
    {
        // Create an instance of the Test application
        TestFrame mainFrame = new TestFrame();
        mainFrame.setVisible( true );
    }
}
```

Listing 5.3   JComboBox sample code (continued)

5.5.1   Adding and removing list items

Listing 5.3 adds items to the combo box instance by using the following code:

```
// Populate the combo box list
for( int iCtr = 0; iCtr < sList.length; iCtr++ )
    combo.addItem( sList[iCtr] );
```

This addItem() method accepts a string, and places it in the combo box list at the end of the list. To remove items, Swing implements three methods. The first removes the item specified in the parameter list, while the second removes a specified item from the list according to the supplied index. The third technique removes all items from the list portion of the combo box. Examples of these methods, in the order given, are as follows:

```
comboBox.removeItem( (String)"Canada" );
comboBox.removeItemAt( 3 );
comboBox.removeAllItems();
```

List indices begin at zero , and count upward. There is a theoretical limit of 2^{32} items in any list; however, the practical limit should be less than twenty. Swing will apply scroll bars to the list if required.

When using the `removeItem()` method to remove items by string, make sure you use the (String) cast. `removeItem()` assumes an Object data type by default, and failing to cast will result in a compiler error.

5.5.2 Selecting items

There are two ways to select an item in a combo box. The first, and easier, is to have the user select an item via a mouse click. The second is to perform the selection operation programmatically using code like this:

```
comboBox.setSelectedItem( (String)"Canada" );
```

or

```
comboBox.setSelectedIndex( 4 );
```

Similarly, you can determine which item is selected, by using the following code:

```
String sString = comboBox.getSelectedItem();
```

Or, to determine the selected index number, use:

```
int iIndex = comboBox.getSelectedIndex();
```

5.5.3 Allowing field editing

With the AWT combo boxes, you loaded the list, and the user took what was available. The AWT component totally lacks the capability to allow user editing, even when the available options are unsuitable. The Swing JComboBox component allows editing of the selection field with the addition of one simple line of code. To enable or disable editing, use code such as this:

```
comboBox.setEditable( true );
```

If you run the sample code in listing 5.3, you will notice that the combo field is editable. If the user changes the selection field by typing new text with the keyboard, followed by an Enter key, the combo box will generate an item change event. Since the sample program includes an ItemListener, you should see a console message indicating the selection text.

5.5.4 Other combo box tricks

There are other features of the JComboBox control. For instance, the display of the pop-up list can be controlled programmatically using the following methods:

```
showPopup();// Displays the pop-up list
hidePopup();// Hides the pop-up list
```

Another useful method is the getItemCount() which returns the number of items in the list. Also, you can retrieve any item using the getItemAt() method. For additional features of the JComboBox component, study the API by checking the online documentation provided with Swing.

5.5.5 JComboBox constructors

```
JComboBox()
```

This constructor creates an instance of a combo box with a default data model.

```
JComboBox( ComboBoxModel aModel )
```

This constructor creates an instance of a combo box with a specified data model.

5.5.6 JComboBox significant method groupings

```
public void addItem(Object anObject)
public void insertItemAt(Object anObject, int index)
public void removeItem(Object anObject)
public void removeItemAt(int anIndex)
public void removeAllItems()
```

Combo box items can be added or removed with the methods in this group. For portability, these methods are generally compatible with those of their cousins in the AWT Choice component.

```
public void setSelectedItem(Object anObject)
public Object getSelectedItem()
public Object[] getSelectedObjects()
public void setSelectedIndex(int anIndex)
public int getSelectedIndex()
public int getItemCount()
public Object getItemAt(int index)
```

Methods in this group manage the selected item and index references for the list. This includes methods to determine the list size, and the currently selected item or index.

```
public void showPopup()
public void hidePopup()
```

These methods control the presence of the selection list on the screen.

```
public void setModel(ComboBoxModel aModel)
public ComboBoxModel getModel()
```

These methods manage the model used by the combo box instance. By default, JComboBox will assign a default model, but custom models can be created and added to the instance.

```
public void setRenderer(ListCellRenderer aRenderer)
public ListCellRenderer getRenderer()
public void setEditor(ComboBoxEditor anEditor)
public ComboBoxEditor getEditor()
public void configureEditor(ComboBoxEditor anEditor,
                            Object anItem)
```

JComboBox supports the ability to custom render the list items and current selection. Additionally, the field can have a custom editor applied in order to achieve some desired special effect. These methods manage the editor and the renderer used for the combo box instance.

```
public void addItemListener(ItemListener aListener)
public void removeItemListener(ItemListener aListener)
public void addActionListener(ActionListener l)
public void removeActionListener(ActionListener l)
```

These methods regulate the presence of listeners for the combo box instance. Combo boxes support two types of events: action events and item selection events.

5.6   Viewing HTML and other content types

In chapter 3, we examined several of the pane classes provided in the Swing class library, but you were warned that we would see more. Now we will look at a new type of pane—one that you will probably find an unexpected and pleasant surprise. In this section, we will discuss the JEditorPane class, which is capable of displaying HTML text. Figure 5.9 shows a sample of the features this class provides. In this

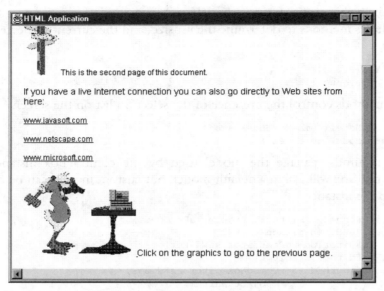

Figure 5.9   An example of a text pane containing HTML

example, the HTML viewer has loaded a sample page from a file, but it can just as easily pull web pages from live Internet sites.

FYI   JEditorPane is not limited to displaying HTML content. Within each JEditorPane instance is an assigned EditorKit which controls the policy of a specific MIME content type. If you load the editor pane from a URL, the instance will automatically determine the content type, and display data in the correct format.

With the JEditorPane class, you can quickly and easily create HTML viewers for online help files, or for simply integrating Internet capability into your applications. As you will see, JEditorPane supports a listener that can be used to detect hyperlink changes. This offers you the option of tracking URL changes in the control that you can utilize to build a simple web browser. Let's take a look at an example.

Listing 5.4 contains a great deal of useful information, and we will examine some of this information in the following section. The basic construction and

```
import java.io.*;
import java.net.*;
import java.awt.*;
import java.awt.event.*;
import com.sun.java.swing.*;
import com.sun.java.swing.event.*;

class TestFrame
        extends    JFrame
        implements HyperlinkListener
{
    private   JEditorPane    html;
    private   String         sPath = System.getProperty( "user.dir" ) + "/";

    public TestFrame()
    {
        setTitle( "HTML Application" );
        setSize( 400, 300 );
        setBackground( Color.gray );
        getContentPane().setLayout( new BorderLayout() );

        JPanel topPanel = new JPanel();
        topPanel.setLayout( new BorderLayout() );
        getContentPane().add( topPanel, BorderLayout.CENTER );

        try {
            // Load the URL we want to display
            URL url = new URL( "file:///" + sPath + "Main.htm" );

            // Create an HTML viewer to display the URL
            html = new JEditorPane( url );
            html.setEditable( false );

            JScrollPane scrollPane = new JScrollPane();
            scrollPane.getViewport().add( html, BorderLayout.CENTER );

            topPanel.add( scrollPane, BorderLayout.CENTER );

            html.addHyperlinkListener( this );
        }
        catch( MalformedURLException e )
        {
            System.out.println( "Malformed URL: " + e );
        }
        catch( IOException e )
        {
            System.out.println( "IOException: " + e );
        }
```

Listing 5.4   HTML viewer sample code

```
    }

    public void hyperlinkUpdate( HyperlinkEvent event )
    {
        if( event.getEventType() ==
                        HyperlinkEvent.EventType.ACTIVATED )
        {
            // Load some cursors
            Cursor cursor = html.getCursor();
            Cursor waitCursor = Cursor.getPredefinedCursor(
                                        Cursor.WAIT_CURSOR );
            html.setCursor( waitCursor );

            // Handle the hyperlink change
            SwingUtilities.invokeLater( new PageLoader( html,
                        event.getURL(), cursor ) );
        }
    }

    public static void main( String args[] )
    {
        // Create an instance of the test application
        TestFrame mainFrame = new TestFrame();
        mainFrame.setVisible( true );
    }
}
```

Listing 5.4   HTML viewer sample code (continued)

layout code in this listing is straightforward, since we created only a single component. Note, however, that like the JTextArea component, JEditorPane must be
placed within a scrolling pane in order to support scroll bars.

5.6.1   Listening for hyperlink changes

Listing 5.3 contains some particularly interesting code. First, it associates a hyperlink listener with the instance of the JEditorPane. This allows us to detect and manage changes when the user follows a hyperlink on an HTML page. The listener is
attached with the following code:

```
html.addHyperlinkListener( this );
```

In the case of our sample application, the listener is the TestFrame class, so we
are required to implement the hyperlinkUpdate() method. This method has the
following format:

```
public void hyperlinkUpdate( HyperlinkEvent event )
```

The HyperlinkEvent which is received contains all the information needed to determine the new URL. In our example, the new URL is passed to another class to load the web page into the viewer, using the following line of code:

```
SwingUtilities.invokeLater( new PageLoader( html,
                         event.getURL(), cursor ) );
```

There are a couple of points to make about this line. First, the PageLoader class is a class built into the listing 5.3 application. The source code for this class is contained in an online source code package for this book. I haven't shown it here, because it is essentially a duplicate of the code from the SWINGSET sample application which is included with JFC.

The second point of interest in this line of source code is the call to `Swing-Utilities.invokeLater()`. This is a special method, supported by Swing, to cause some processing to occur at a later time. You cannot interact with Swing components within a thread, so Swing provides the `invokeLater()` method. This method accepts a task (in our case, the creation of a new class instance), and places it on Swing's internal task queue for execution whenever it becomes possible.

 In the final chapter of this book we will discuss the use of this method, and situations in which `SwingUtilities.invokeLater()` can be utilized to make your applications perform better.

5.6.2 JEditorPane constructors

```
JEditorPane()
```

This constructor creates an instance of an editor pane with no associated URL.

```
JEditorPane( URL initialPage )
```

This constructor creates an instance of an editor pane with an associated URL.

```
JEditorPane( String url )
```

This constructor creates an instance of an editor pane with the associated string containing a URL specification.

5.6.3 JEditorPane significant method groupings

```
public synchronized void addHyperlinkListener(
                        HyperlinkListener listener )
public synchronized void removeHyperlinkListener(
                        HyperlinkListener listener )
```

These methods control the presence of hyperlink listeners. These listeners detect changes invoked by the user when an HTML hyperlink is selected.

```
public void fireHyperlinkUpdate( HyperlinkEvent e )
```

This method notifies all registered hyperlink listeners that a new hyperlink has been selected. The hyperlink is passed as a parameter to this method. This method is normally called by the currently installed EditorKit when there is hyperlink activity.

```
public final EditorKit getEditorKit()
public final void setEditorKit(EditorKit kit)
public EditorKit getEditorKitForContentType(String type)
public void setEditorKitForContentType(
                        String type, EditorKit k)
public static EditorKit createEditorKitForContentType(
                        String type)
public static void registerEditorKitForContentType(
                        String type, String classname )
```

These methods manage the editor kit used by the JEditorPane instance. An editor kit is a policy keeper for a specific content type. For example, HTML has a specific editor kit which is the default for JEditorPane; however, other editor kits could be implemented for other document formats. For example, an editor kit for RTF could be loaded into the editor instance.

```
public void setPage( URL page ) throws IOException
public void setPage(String url) throws IOException
public URL getPage()
```

The methods in this group manage the page currently loaded into the control. The setPage() methods allow new pages to be loaded into memory.

```
public final String getContentType()
public final void setContentType(String type)
```

These methods determine and assign the content type for the editor pane.

5.7 Viewing RTF format

In the previous section, we examined ways to view HTML text using Swing's JEditorPane class. JEditorPane creates an instance of an EditorKit class to help manage the format of the text in the view. In the case of HTML text, JEditorPane uses the HTMLEditorKit. In the previous example, HTML text was handled automatically, based on the content type of the URL we provided.

Swing not only allows you to create your own custom editor kits, but also provides an important, second kit, called RTFEditorKit. The RTFEditorKit class handles reading and parsing of RTF files, including all character attributes and text styles. RTF files can be produced by most word processors, or by the WORDPAD application in Microsoft Windows.

FYI The current RTFEditorKit class will not handle graphical images embedded in the RTF file. If graphics do exist, the RTF parser will simply ignore them.

The best way to demonstrate the Swing mechanism for viewing RTF is with an example. Listing 5.5 contains code to create a JEditorPane, and apply an instance of RTFEditorKit to it. Unlike the HTML example, we load sample RTF from a file, rather than from a URL, so we need to identify the document format manually. This is done with a call to the `setEditorKit()` method, providing it with our instance of the RTFEditorKit. Once the editor pane has been correctly configured, the sample code uses the `read()` method in the editor kit to load a sample RTF file (TEST.RTF) into the document handler.

```java
import java.awt.*;
import java.io.*;
import com.sun.java.swing.*;
import com.sun.java.swing.text.*;
import com.sun.java.swing.text.rtf.*;

class TestFrame
        extends      JFrame
{
    public TestFrame()
    {
```

Listing 5.5   RTF viewer sample code

```
        setTitle( "RTF Text Application" );
        setSize( 400, 240 );
        setBackground( Color.gray );
        getContentPane().setLayout( new BorderLayout() );

        JPanel topPanel = new JPanel();
        topPanel.setLayout( new BorderLayout() );
        getContentPane().add( topPanel, BorderLayout.CENTER );

        // Create an RTF editor window
        RTFEditorKit rtf = new RTFEditorKit();
        JEditorPane editor = new JEditorPane();
        editor.setEditorKit( rtf );
        editor.setBackground( Color.white );

        // This text could be big, so add a scroll pane
        JScrollPane scroller = new JScrollPane();
        scroller.getViewport().add( editor );
        topPanel.add( scroller, BorderLayout.CENTER );

        // Load an RTF file into the editor
        try {
            FileInputStream fi = new FileInputStream( "test.rtf" );
            rtf.read( fi, editor.getDocument(), 0 );
        }
        catch( FileNotFoundException e )
        {
            System.out.println( "File not found" );
        }
        catch( IOException e )
        {
            System.out.println( "I/O error" );
        }
        catch( BadLocationException e )
        {
        }
    }

    public static void main( String args[] )
    {
        // Create an instance of the test application
        TestFrame mainFrame = new TestFrame();
        mainFrame.setVisible( true );
    }
}
```

Listing 5.5   RTF viewer sample code (continued)

The result of this listing is shown in figure 5.10. The editor pane receives the TEST.RTF sample, which was created using Microsoft Word on the Windows platform. The pane supports varying fonts, font sizes, and attributes (such as underlining and italics). We can even accurately reproduce changes to the color of a font.

FYI The current RTFEditorKit class will not handle tables produced by Microsoft Word. Rendering RTF containing these tables will result in inaccurate document formatting.

5.8 Simple document processing

Before we leave text management, we should develop a simple example to demonstrate some of the features that we have not yet covered. We have seen how the JEditorPane class works to display HTML text and other formats, but in most text-based applications, HTML is of little value. We need to find a class in Swing which will provide the capability to display several different text styles in a format of our own choosing.

Swing offers a class named JTextPane, which extends JEditorPane to allow support for character and text attributes. Like the JTextArea class, JTextPane allows the user to enter and edit text from the keyboard; however, JTextPane also supports the display of an infinite number of configurable text styles. Using a very simple word processing example, we will examine how this simple, powerful class can be integrated into our own code.

This example offers text style changes similar to the STYLEPAD application which ships with JFC; however, in our example, the code has been greatly reduced

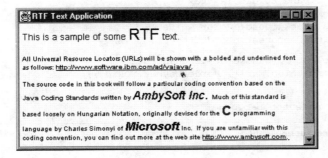

Figure 5.10
RTF viewer application output

in order to focus on how text style changes work within the JTextPane class. So, the example shows only how the text style mechanism works, but the code does not support file management, or most of the other features of a complete word processor.

The code shown in listing 5.6 creates an application window with an instance of a JTextPane, and a simple toolbar containing only a combo box. We will also create several different text styles which we can apply to any text we enter into the editor. Each of the styles we create is added to an instance of a hash table, so we can support a number of different styles in our editor. The createStyles() method builds each text style, and inserts them into the hash table for later reference when the user chooses a text style from the combo box.

```java
class TestFrame
        extends        JFrame
        implements     ActionListener
{
    private Hashtable              attributes;
    private     JComboBox          styleCombo;
    private     DefaultStyledDocument doc;
    private     JTextPane          textComponent;

    public TestFrame()
    {
        setTitle( "Document Handling Application" );
        setSize( 300, 190 );
        setBackground( Color.gray );

        JPanel topPanel = new JPanel( new BorderLayout() );
        getContentPane().add( topPanel );

        // Create styles for the document
        StyleContext sc = new StyleContext();
        doc = new DefaultStyledDocument( sc );
        createStyles( sc );

        // Create a text pane to display text
        textComponent = new JTextPane( doc );
        textComponent.setBackground( Color.white );
        topPanel.add( textComponent, BorderLayout.CENTER );

        // Create a toolbar to handle style changes
        topPanel.add( createToolBar(), BorderLayout.NORTH );
    }

    // Create a VERY simple toolbar panel
```

Listing 5.6   Simple word processor application

```java
public JPanel createToolBar()
{
    JPanel panel = new JPanel( new FlowLayout() );

    styleCombo = new JComboBox();
    styleCombo.addActionListener( this );
    panel.add( styleCombo );

    // Add each style to the combo box
    for( Enumeration e = attributes.keys(); e.hasMoreElements(); )
        styleCombo.addItem( e.nextElement().toString() );

    return panel;
}

// Handle changes to the combo box (style changes)
public void actionPerformed( ActionEvent e )
{
    if( e.getSource() == styleCombo )
    {
        try {
            // Determine the new style
            Style s = (Style)attributes.get(
                        styleCombo.getSelectedItem() );

            // Set the style from the current caret location
            doc.insertString( textComponent.getCaret().getDot(),
                                " ", s );

            // Return to the editor window
            textComponent.grabFocus();
        }
        catch( BadLocationException exception )
        {
        }
    }
}

// Create some different font styles
public void createStyles( StyleContext sc )
{
    Style   myStyle;

    // Allocate a hash table for our styles
    attributes = new Hashtable();

    // No style
    myStyle = sc.addStyle( null, null );
    attributes.put( "none", myStyle );
```

Listing 5.6 Simple word processor application (continued)

```
        // Normal
        myStyle = sc.addStyle( null, null );
        StyleConstants.setLeftIndent( myStyle, 10 );
        StyleConstants.setRightIndent( myStyle, 10 );
        StyleConstants.setFontFamily( myStyle, "Helvetica" );
        StyleConstants.setFontSize( myStyle, 14 );
        StyleConstants.setSpaceAbove( myStyle, 4 );
        StyleConstants.setSpaceBelow( myStyle, 4 );
        attributes.put( "normal", myStyle );

        // Big
        myStyle = sc.addStyle( null, null );
        StyleConstants.setFontFamily( myStyle, "Dialog" );
        StyleConstants.setFontSize( myStyle, 28 );
        attributes.put( "big", myStyle );

        // Bold
        myStyle = sc.addStyle( null, null );
        StyleConstants.setBold( myStyle, true );
        attributes.put( "bold", myStyle );
    }

    // Main() method to get the ball rolling
    public static void main( String args[] )
    {
        // Create an instance of the test application
        TestFrame mainFrame = new TestFrame();
        mainFrame.setVisible( true );
    }
}
```

Listing 5.6   Simple word processor application (continued)

The result of executing the code in this application is illustrated in figure 5.11. Notice how easily styles can be mixed within the display. By selecting a choice from the toolbar combo box, the user can easily change to one of the four preconfigured text styles, and then continue typing. This program isn't a threat to Microsoft Word, but, as you can see, the effort needed to support similar font style capabilities is relatively simple.

One other point we should make, before leaving this example, is that we are not limited to displaying only text. Unlike the JTextArea component we saw earlier, JTextPane also supports graphical content. The STYLEPAD application in the Swing package includes a good example of how this can be accomplished.

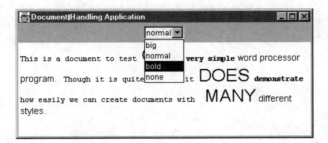

Figure 5.11
Word processor
application output

5.9 Chapter summary

This chapter has covered the basics of text management, and the text components provided by Swing. We started by discussing the JTextComponent class, which is the parent of most text-based controls in Swing. Then, we got a bit more specific by examining the capabilities of the JTextField component. This class allows the user to input a single line of text.

Next, we made a detailed study of some of the multiline text controls supported by Swing, starting with the simple text area. You also saw an example of a Swing technique which you can use to load a text file into a text component and which (unlike the older AWT component) doesn't require dozens of line of code.

Then, you saw the powerful JEditorPane class, which allows you to embed a viewer for HTML into your applications. With a few lines of code, we created a sample which opened and displayed a file-based HTML document, and also provided hyperlinks to several external Internet sites. With the addition of a few more lines of code, you could implement a complete, but limited, web browser.

Next, we discussed the Swing combo box control. Though it visually resembles its AWT cousin, the Swing component allows user editing and graphical display. When we look at list boxes in chapter 9, you will see how to render the list portion to include these graphics, and more.

Finally, we examined the JTextPane class as a tool for displaying mixed text styles and graphics. The capability of this class lies between the text area and the JEditorPane components, allowing custom text styles defined by the developer.

Progress bars, scroll bars, and sliders

6

In this chapter

- Using progress bars
- Using scroll bars
- Using sliders

In the previous two chapters, we began a study of the most common components in Swing, most of which also existed in some form in AWT. User interaction with these components is generally simple, involving only a mouse click or keyboard entry, though some features, such as clipboard manipulation, do have some hidden complexity.

In this chapter, we will examine some of the components which require much more user interaction than those we have previously seen. Some of these components require the user to drag the mouse or click the mouse on one or more hot spots within the control. None of these operations will stress a user's abilities, but, beneath the surface, these components are much more complex than the ones we have previously used.

However, the first class we will look at, the progress bar, may be the simplest in this book—at least, from a user perspective. The progress bar requires no user interaction, but it does blend nicely with the second component we will discuss, the scroll bar. As we have seen, the scroll bar is a frequent participant in text areas and other components using scrolling panes, but scroll bars can also appear as independent components within your user interface.

Finally, we will study the Swing slider class. The slider component acts like the sliding volume control on a stereo system. The user can change a value by dragging the mouse to slide a control bar in the slider from one end to the other, changing the value.

6.1   Progress bars

In typical applications, there will inevitably be places where a time consuming task occurs which requires the user to wait. In the past, you could address this situation in one of two ways when building Java applications. If you were writing with Java 1.0, you could either do nothing, or you could display a text message somewhere in your user interface indicating that a time intensive task was occurring. With Java 1.1, Sun introduced the capability to change the cursor to an hourglass (oooh!).

GUIDELINE **Use a progress bar every chance you get.** Feedback is essential to the user for any action which is not immediate. If you know approximately how long the task will take, use a progress bar, even if it displays only momentarily. For longer tasks, consider that even a mock progress meter which flows back and forth is better than no feedback at all.

Neither of these alternatives is particularly effective from a user's perspective, since neither really tells the user how long the wait will be. Swing addresses this problem by providing developers with a new component, called a progress bar, to provide capability that has been available in other graphical user interfaces for several years. The progress bar class, JProgressBar, presents the user with a segmented bar graph much like the LED audio meters which are common on stereo cassette recorders. This component indicates, in real-time, the progress that a lengthy task is making, and offers a viewable status for your users. It lets the user know that the program and the computer have not crashed.

Because they are all closely related, examining the components in this chapter will involve concepts that have already been presented. Progress bars are much like scroll bars and sliders, and, in fact, all of these components use the same data model. A progress bar can be thought of as a read-only slider control, capable only of indicating the current position within the total range.

Figure 6.1 shows a typical progress bar from the SWINGSET sample application which ships with Swing. If you have run the SWINGSET sample, you will recognize this as the first screen the application displays. Since the application loads all of its panels at startup, the user must wait quite a while before he or she can start using the components. To eliminate this problem, we need to create an initial dialog with a progress bar indicating in real-time the status of the initialization process.

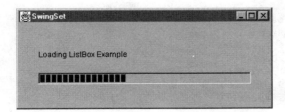

Figure 6.1
Example of a progress bar

The technique used to accomplish this feat is actually quite simple, requiring only a few lines of additional source code. Let's take a look at a small sample application which you can adapt to any time demanding process of your own. The code in listing 6.1 implements a simple panel containing a progress bar, a label, and a button. When the Start button is pressed, the application simulates some time consuming task. At the completion of each task, the program updates its progress bar, showing the user the relative time remaining for the process to complete. Notice that the code responsible for creating the progress bar is only seven lines long.

```java
import java.util.*;
import java.awt.*;
import java.awt.event.*;
import com.sun.java.swing.*;
import com.sun.java.swing.event.*;

class TestFrame
       extends    JFrame
       implements ActionListener
{
    private    JProgressBar    progress;
    private    JButton         button;
    private    JLabel          label1;
    private    JPanel          topPanel;

    public TestFrame()
    {
        setTitle( "Progress Bar Application" );
        setSize( 310, 130 );
        setBackground( Color.gray );

        topPanel = new JPanel();
        topPanel.setPreferredSize( new Dimension( 310, 130 ) );
        getContentPane().add( topPanel );

        // Create a label and progress bar
        label1 = new JLabel( "Waiting to start tasks..." );
        label1.setPreferredSize( new Dimension( 280, 24 ) );
        topPanel.add( label1 );

        progress = new JProgressBar();
        progress.setPreferredSize( new Dimension( 300, 20 ) );
        progress.setMinimum( 0 );
        progress.setMaximum( 20 );
        progress.setValue( 0 );
        progress.setBounds( 20, 35, 260, 20 );
        topPanel.add( progress );

        button = new JButton( "Start" );
        topPanel.add( button );
        button.addActionListener( this );
    }

    public void actionPerformed( ActionEvent event )
    {
        if( event.getSource() == button )
        {
            // Prevent more button presses
```

Listing 6.1   Sample code for a progress indicator

```
                button.setEnabled( false );

            // Perform all of our bogus tasks
            for( int iCtr = 1; iCtr < 21; iCtr++ )
            {
                // Do some sort of simulated task
                DoBogusTask( iCtr );

                // Update the progress indicator and label
                label1.setText( "Performing task " + iCtr + " of 20" );
                Rectangle labelRect = label1.getBounds();
                labelRect.x = 0;
                labelRect.y = 0;
                label1.paintImmediately( labelRect );

                progress.setValue( iCtr );
                Rectangle progressRect = progress.getBounds();
                progressRect.x = 0;
                progressRect.y = 0;
                progress.paintImmediately( progressRect );
            }
        }
    }

    public void DoBogusTask( int iCtr )
    {
        Random random = new Random( iCtr );

        // Waste some time
        for( int iValue = 0;
                iValue < random.nextFloat() * 10000; iValue++ )
        {
            System.out.println( "iValue=" + iValue );
        }
    }

    public static void main( String args[] )
    {
        // Create an instance of the test application
        TestFrame mainFrame    = new TestFrame();
        mainFrame.setVisible( true );
        mainFrame.pack();
    }
}
```

Listing 6.1 Sample code for a progress indicator (continued)

The action handler code does something a bit peculiar which I need to clarify for you. After the value of the label and progress indicator are changed, the application executes these four lines of code:

```
Rectangle progressRect = progress.getBounds();
progressRect.x = 0;
progressRect.y = 0;
progress.paintImmediately( progressRect );
```

Since the release of Java 1.1.3, Sun changed the way that the painting of components is handled. In these later versions of the language specification, paint messages are queued into a single repaint to help improve performance. Unfortunately, this can cause problems in situations where it is desirable to force a component repaint. To work around this new problem, the Swing architects added a `paintImmediately()` method. This method requires a rectangle, so, in our example, we determine the rectangle for the progress bar and call the `paintImmediately()` method to refresh the component after its value is changed. Without these lines of code, the progress bar would repaint only after all of our time consuming tasks have finished because it would receive only a single cached paint message.

Another technique to solve this problem would be to start a thread to execute our time consuming tasks. This frees up execution time on the main thread, but Swing components cannot be accessed reliably on the secondary thread. If component access is a requirement, then you will have to use a procedure similar to the one shown in listing 6.1.

GUIDELINE Integrate the progress bar as part of the overall feedback to the user. The progress bar can be part of a dialog which tells the user that a normal, time consuming event is still ongoing. Explanatory text should always be given, and a Cancel button should be provided, whenever possible. The progress bar gives the user an estimate of the time necessary for completion of the task, but other feedback elements (such as animation or a sequence of timely visuals) may be in order, particularly for longer tasks.

6.1.1 JProgressBar variables

```
protected int orientation
```

This variable contains the orientation (HORIZONTAL or VERTICAL) for the progress bar.

```
protected boolean paintBorder
```

This boolean value is set if the border of the progress bar border is to be repainted when repaint events are received.

```
protected BoundedRangeModel barModel
```

This variable contains the instance of the current progress bar model. This is defaulted at object creation time, but can be changed to a custom model if desired.

```
protected transient ChangeEvent changeEvent
```

This variable holds the change event for this instance. Only one `ChangeEvent` is needed per instance, since the event's only interesting property is the immutable source—the progress bar.

```
protected ChangeListener changeListener
```

This variable contains the current change listener for this instance.

6.1.2 JProgressBar constructors

```
JProgressBar()
```

This constructor creates an instance of a JProgressBar.

6.1.3 JProgressBar significant method groupings

```
public int getValue()
public int getMinimum()
public int getMaximum()
public void setValue(int n)
public void setMinimum(int n)
public void setMaximum(int n)
```

The methods in this group control the minimum, maximum, and current values of the progress bar.

```
protected ChangeListener createChangeListener()
public void addChangeListener(ChangeListener l)
public void removeChangeListener(ChangeListener l)
```

These methods manage the change listener used by the progress bar. A change event can optionally be generated each time the progress bar value changes.

```
public BoundedRangeModel getModel()
public void setModel(BoundedRangeModel newModel)
```

These methods manage the model used by the progress bar instance. By default, JProgressBar will assign a default model, but custom models can be created and added to the instance, if desired.

6.2 Scroll bars

Scroll bars have become a common element in all graphical user interfaces. In most applications, they are used as an indicator to the user that there is more data to see than can currently be displayed. The most typical use of scroll bars is for scrolling panes; however, as you will see, scroll bars can be used for other applications as well.

AWT provides an adequate scroll bar component, but it does not support the pluggable look-and-feel capabilities of Swing, so the designers at Sun implemented a new class to replace the old one in AWT. This class, named JScrollBar, supports an API virtually identical to its AWT predecessor, but which includes the extensions necessary to function in the Swing world.

IMHO If you require a scale associated with the scroll bar, then you probably want to use a slider control instead of a scroll bar. See the next section for details on sliders. Scroll bars do not include a scale, so you need to implement this yourself, if required.

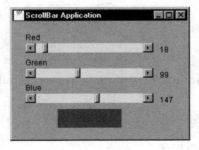

Figure 6.2
An example of scroll bars

The screen capture in figure 6.2 shows an example of some scroll bars at work in an application other than a scrolling pane. This application is somewhat obsolete with Swing, since a better solution would be to use slider component instances (which we will look at in the next section), but it suits our needs for the purposes of demonstration.

This screen was generated with the code shown in listing 6.2. This simple application creates a scroll bar for each of the primary system colors (red, green, and blue), and allows the user to manipulate these scrollers to control the color of the sample chip at the bottom of the window.

Notice that the sample code implements an `AdjustmentListener` to watch for changes to any of the scrollers. If the values of any of the scroll bars change, the `adjustmentValueChanged()` method retrieves the scroll values and changes the labels for each color, then adjusts the color of the sample.

 The orientation field in the scroll bar accepts a value of `SwingConstants.HORIZONTAL` or `SwingConstants.VERTICAL` to set the scroll bar horizontally or vertically. See the SwingConstants class in the online Swing documentation for more details.

```java
import java.util.*;
import java.awt.*;
import java.awt.event.*;
import com.sun.java.swing.*;

class TestFrame
      extends      JFrame
      implements AdjustmentListener
{
    private      JScrollBar      scrollerR;
    private      JScrollBar      scrollerG;
    private      JScrollBar      scrollerB;
    private      JLabel          fieldR;
    private      JLabel          fieldG;
    private      JLabel          fieldB;
    private      JLabel          labelR;
    private      JLabel          labelG;
    private      JLabel          labelB;
    private      JPanel          labelColor;
    private      JPanel          topPanel;

public TestFrame()
    {
        setTitle( "ScrollBar Application" );
        setBackground( Color.gray );

        topPanel = new JPanel();
        topPanel.setPreferredSize( new Dimension( 300, 220 ) );
        getContentPane().add( topPanel );

        // Create the labels
```

Listing 6.2   Sample code for a JScrollBar

```
        labelR = new JLabel( "Red" );
        labelR.setPreferredSize( new Dimension( 300, 24 ) );
        topPanel.add( labelR );

        // Create the scroll bars
        scrollerR = new JScrollBar( SwingConstants.HORIZONTAL,
                                    0, 0, 0, 255 );
        scrollerR.setPreferredSize( new Dimension( 200, 15 ) );
        scrollerR.addAdjustmentListener( this );
        topPanel.add( scrollerR );

        fieldR = new JLabel( "0" );
        fieldR.setPreferredSize( new Dimension( 50, 20 ) );
        topPanel.add( fieldR );

        labelG = new JLabel( "Green" );
        labelG.setPreferredSize( new Dimension( 300, 24 ) );
        topPanel.add( labelG );

        scrollerG = new JScrollBar( SwingConstants.HORIZONTAL,
                                    0, 0, 0, 255 );
        scrollerG.setPreferredSize( new Dimension( 200, 15 ) );
        scrollerG.addAdjustmentListener( this );
        topPanel.add( scrollerG );

        fieldG = new JLabel( "0" );
        fieldG.setPreferredSize( new Dimension( 50, 20 ) );
        topPanel.add( fieldG );

        labelB = new JLabel( "Blue" );
        labelB.setPreferredSize( new Dimension( 300, 24 ) );
        topPanel.add( labelB );

        scrollerB = new JScrollBar( SwingConstants.HORIZONTAL,
                                    0, 0, 0, 255 );
        scrollerB.setPreferredSize( new Dimension( 200, 15 ) );
        scrollerB.addAdjustmentListener( this );
        topPanel.add( scrollerB );

        fieldB = new JLabel( "0" );
        fieldB.setPreferredSize( new Dimension( 50, 20 ) );
        topPanel.add( fieldB );

        labelColor = new JPanel();
        labelColor.setPreferredSize( new Dimension( 100, 40 ) );
        labelColor.setBackground( new Color( 0, 0, 0 ) );
        topPanel.add( labelColor );
    }
```

Listing 6.2 Sample code for a JScrollBar (continued)

```
    // Watch for scroll bar adjustments
    public void adjustmentValueChanged( AdjustmentEvent event )
    {
        // The event came from our scrollers, handle it.
        if( event.getSource() == scrollerR ||
            event.getSource() == scrollerG ||
            event.getSource() == scrollerB )
        {
            // Get the current color settings
            int iRed = scrollerR.getValue();
            int iGreen = scrollerG.getValue();
            int iBlue = scrollerB.getValue();

            // Set the value labels
            fieldR.setText( "" + iRed );
            fieldG.setText( "" + iGreen );
            fieldB.setText( "" + iBlue );

            // Update the color chip
            labelColor.setBackground(
                        new Color( iRed, iGreen, iBlue ) );
            labelColor.repaint();
        }
    }

    public static void main( String args[] )
    {
        // Create an instance of the test application
        TestFrame mainFrame = new TestFrame();
        mainFrame.setVisible( true );
        mainFrame.pack();
    }
}
```

Listing 6.2 Sample code for a JScrollBar (continued)

GUIDELINE

Use a scroll bar to specify ranged values in proportional terms. Although much more frequently used as part of a scrolling area, scroll bars can also allow the user to select imprecise numeric or qualitative data which lie on a continuum. Consider using different components for discrete numeric or text selections.

6.2.1 JScrollBar variables

```
protected int orientation
```

This variable contains the orientation (HORIZONTAL or VERTICAL) for the progress bar.

```
protected BoundedRangeModel model
```

This variable contains the instance of the current scroll bar model. This is defaulted at object creation time, but can be changed to a custom model if desired.

```
protected int unitIncrement
```

This variable contains the size of the increment or decrement used for unit changes. A unit change occurs when the user clicks the up or down arrow buttons in the scroll bar.

```
protected int blockIncrement
```

This variable contains the size of the increment used for block changes. A block change occurs when the user clicks the mouse button in the gray area above and below the slider button in the scroll bar.

6.2.2 JScrollBar constructors

```
JScrollBar()
```

This constructor creates an instance of a JScrollBar.

```
JScrollBar( int orientation, int value,
            int extent, int minimum, int maximum )
```

This constructor creates an instance of a JScrollBar with the specified orientation (HORIZONTAL or VERTICAL) and assigns minimum, maximum, and current values.

6.2.3 JScrollBar significant method groupings

```
public int getValue()
public int getMinimum()
public int getMaximum()
public void setValue(int n)
public void setMinimum(int n)
public void setMaximum(int n)
```

The methods in this group control the minimum, maximum, and current values of the scroll bar.

```
protected ChangeListener createChangeListener()
public void addChangeListener(ChangeListener l)
public void removeChangeListener(ChangeListener l)
```

These methods manage the change listener used by the scroll bar. A change event can optionally be generated each time the scroll bar value changes (usually, through some user interaction).

```
public BoundedRangeModel getModel()
public void setModel(BoundedRangeModel newModel)
```

These methods manage the model used by the scroll bar instance. By default, JScrollBar will assign a default model, but custom models can be created and added to the instance if desired.

6.3 Sliders

Typically, when building applications with AWT, scroll bars were used to get user input for ranged values. The scroll bar application created in the previous section is a classic example of this technique. Unfortunately, as shown in figure 6.2, this requires the addition of a label to indicate the current value of the scroll bar, requiring the additional burden of code to update this label when the scroll bar value changes. This results in a crude user interface when compared to more advanced interfaces, such as Windows 95.

Fortunately, JavaSoft recognized this limitation and devised a new control which Windows developers will immediately recognize. The slider control, though similar in nature to the scroll bar, presents a much cleaner user interface. Additionally, sliders can include a value scale, which offers immediate value feedback to the user and reduces the amount of code needed to support the interface.

GUIDELINE

Use a slider to specify ranged values in discrete terms. Sliders allow the user to select a fixed number of numeric or text values within a range of values. This is particularly true if the tick marks accurately represent the ratios of change within the range, but this does not necessarily have to be the case. For example, a text label could be used in conjunction with a slider to allow selection of qualitative items. If the real estate is limited, transfer the contents to a combo box. For more precise numeric input, create a spin control.

In Swing, the slider class is called JSlider, and has no equivalent in AWT. Figure 6.3 shows several examples of the JSlider control showing the variations on orientation and scale which are supported.

FYI If you are porting AWT applications containing interfaces like the one shown in figure 6.2, you will need to rewrite some portions of your code. Fortunately, the API for JSlider is almost identical to that of the AWT ScrollBar component.

Listing 6.3 duplicates the color selector you saw in the previous section. The difference is the use of the Swing JSlider controls, rather than scroll bars. As you can see from the sample output in figure 6.4, the user interface is cleaner than the scroll bar example.

```
import java.util.*;
import java.awt.*;
import java.awt.event.*;
import com.sun.java.swing.*;
import com.sun.java.swing.event.*;
```

Listing 6.3   Sample code for a JSlider

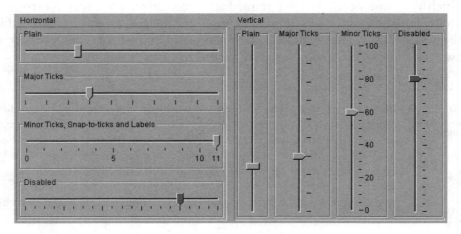

Figure 6.3   Example of sliders using tick marks and text labels

```
class TestFrame
        extends    JFrame
        implements ChangeListener
{
    private    JSlider    scrollerR;
    private    JSlider    scrollerG;
    private    JSlider    scrollerB;
    private    JLabel     labelR;
    private    JLabel     labelG;
    private    JLabel     labelB;
    private    Label      labelColor;
    private    JPanel     topPanel;

    public TestFrame()
    {
        setTitle( "Slider Application" );
        setSize( 330, 280 );
        setBackground( Color.gray );

        topPanel = new JPanel();
        topPanel.setLayout( null );
        topPanel.setDoubleBuffered( false );
        getContentPane().add( topPanel );

        // Create the labels
        labelR = new JLabel( "Red" );
        labelR.setBounds( 20, 15, 250, 20 );
        topPanel.add( labelR );

        labelG = new JLabel( "Green" );
        labelG.setBounds( 20, 75, 250, 20 );
```

Listing 6.3   Sample code for a JSlider (continued)

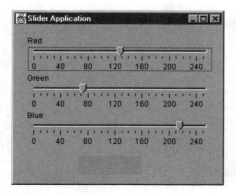

Figure 6.4
Output of slider sample application

```
      topPanel.add( labelG );

      labelB = new JLabel( "Blue" );
      labelB.setBounds( 20, 135, 250, 20 );
      topPanel.add( labelB );

      labelColor = new Label();
      labelColor.setBounds( 100, 210, 100, 30 );
      labelColor.setBackground( new Color( 0, 0, 0 ) );
      topPanel.add( labelColor );

      // Create the sliders
      scrollerR = new JSlider( SwingConstants.HORIZONTAL,
                                        0, 255, 0 );
      scrollerR.setBounds( 20, 35, 290, 40 );
      scrollerR.setMajorTickSpacing( 40 );
      scrollerR.setMinorTickSpacing( 10 );
      scrollerR.setPaintTicks( true );
      scrollerR.setPaintLabels( true );
      scrollerR.addChangeListener( this );
      topPanel.add( scrollerR );

      scrollerG = new JSlider( SwingConstants.HORIZONTAL,
                                        0, 255, 0 );
      scrollerG.setBounds( 20, 95, 290, 40 );
      scrollerG.setMajorTickSpacing( 40 );
      scrollerG.setMinorTickSpacing( 10 );
      scrollerG.setPaintTicks( true );
      scrollerG.setPaintLabels( true );
      scrollerG.addChangeListener( this );
      topPanel.add( scrollerG );

      scrollerB = new JSlider( SwingConstants.HORIZONTAL,
                                        0, 255, 0 );
      scrollerB.setBounds( 20, 155, 290, 40 );
      scrollerB.setMajorTickSpacing( 40 );
      scrollerB.setMinorTickSpacing( 10 );
      scrollerB.setPaintTicks( true );
      scrollerB.setPaintLabels( true );
      scrollerB.addChangeListener( this );
      topPanel.add( scrollerB );
   }

   // Watch for scroll bar adjustments
   public void stateChanged( ChangeEvent event )
   {
      // The event came from our scrollers, handle it.
```

Listing 6.3   Sample code for a JSlider (continued)

```
          if( event.getSource() == scrollerR ||
              event.getSource() == scrollerG ||
              event.getSource() == scrollerB )
          {
              // Get the current color settings
              int iRed = scrollerR.getValue();
              int iGreen = scrollerG.getValue();
              int iBlue = scrollerB.getValue();

              // Update the color chip
              labelColor.setBackground(
                      new Color( iRed, iGreen, iBlue ) );
          }
      }
      public static void main( String args[] )
      {
          // Create an instance of the test application
          TestFrame mainFrame = new TestFrame();
          mainFrame.setVisible( true );
      }
  }
```

Listing 6.3   Sample code for a JSlider (continued)

6.3.1 Listening for slider activity

Comparing the slider code in listing 6.3 to the scroll bar code in listing 6.2, you should recognize that there are many similarities, but there are also some significant differences. The most noticeable of these is the way the code listens for changes. The slider example implements a ChangeListener, requiring the implementation of a `stateChanged()` method. Each of the sliders then adds a change listener using the following lines of code:

```
  scrollerR.addChangeListener( this );
  scrollerG.addChangeListener( this );
  scrollerB.addChangeListener( this );
```

The `stateChanged()` method is almost identical to the listener implemented for the scroll bar example. Since we no longer need the fields to show the values of the scrollers, the lines of code to control them have been deleted from the listener.

6.3.2 JSlider variables

```
  protected int orientation
```

This variable contains the orientation (HORIZONTAL or VERTICAL) for the slider component.

```
protected BoundedRangeModel sliderModel
```

This variable contains the instance of the current slider model. This is defaulted at object creation time, but can be changed to a custom model if desired.

```
protected transient ChangeEvent changeEvent
```

This variable holds the change event for this instance. Only one ChangeEvent is needed per instance since the event's only interesting property is the immutable source—the slider.

```
protected ChangeListener changeListener
```

This variable contains the current change listener for this instance.

```
protected int majorTickSpacing
protected int minorTickSpacing
```

These variables control the size of major and minor tick mark spacing within the slider instance.

```
protected boolean snapToTicks
```

This boolean value is set to "true" if the slider control will automatically snap to the tick marks on the control's scale.

6.3.3   JSlider constructors

```
JSlider()
```

This constructor creates an instance of a JSlider.

```
JSlider( int orientation, int value, int minimum, int maximum )
```

This constructor creates an instance of a JSlider with the specified orientation (HORIZONTAL or VERTICAL) and the assign minimum, maximum, and current values.

6.3.4   JSlider significant method groupings

```
public int getValue()
public int getExtent()
public int getMinimum()
public int getMaximum()
public void setValue(int n)
```

```
public void setExtent(int n)
public void setMinimum(int n)
public void setMaximum(int n)
```

The methods in this group control the extent, minimum, maximum, and current values of the slider.

```
protected ChangeListener createChangeListener()
public void addChangeListener(ChangeListener l)
public void removeChangeListener(ChangeListener l)
```

These methods manage the change listener used by the slider. A change event can optionally be generated each time the slider value changes (usually through some user interaction).

```
public BoundedRangeModel getModel()
public void setModel(BoundedRangeModel newModel)
```

These methods manage the model used by the slider instance. By default JSlider will assign a default model, but custom models can be created and added to the instance, if desired.

```
public int getMajorTickSpacing()
public int getMinorTickSpacing()
public boolean getSnapToTicks()
public void setMajorTickSpacing(int n)
public void setMinorTickSpacing(int n)
public void setSnapToTicks(boolean b)
```

These methods manage the characteristics of the major and minor tick marks displayed on the scale when the slider is drawn.

```
public void setLabelTable(Dictionary labels)
public Dictionary getLabelTable()
protected void updateLabelUIs()
public Hashtable createStandardLabels(int increment, int start)
```

The methods in this group manage the labels drawn on the slider scale. JSlider offers full control of the mechanism used to draw each of the value labels on the scale.

6.4   Chapter summary

This chapter covered the dragging controls provided by the Swing class library. First, we examined the JProgressBar class, which implements a read-only scroller that can be utilized in applications where time intensive tasks occur.

Then, the Swing JScrollBar class was presented. This class is used primarily to create scrolling panes, but it is also appropriate for some types of user input, such as the color selection application presented in this chapter.

Finally, we studied a new user interface class, called a slider. The Swing JSlider control is more appropriate than the scroll bar for collecting most ranged user input. The color selection application was rewritten with the slider, which presented a much cleaner interface than the example that used scroll bars.

This concludes our examination of the basic components provided by Swing. In the coming chapters, we will start discussing classes which are either enhanced versions of AWT counterparts, or are completely unique to Swing; however, you should now have enough knowledge to build many complex applications and applets.

7

Menus and toolbars

In this chapter

- Creating and using application menus
- Creating and using pop-up menus
- Creating and using toolbars

When Xerox, Apple, Sun, and Microsoft introduced graphical user interfaces several years ago, they all implemented menu capabilities. Previous to this, older text interfaces either offered nothing comparable, or presented a menu-like hodgepodge of text elements restricted by the limitations of a text-based interface. Menus were a godsend to many people intimidated by computers, because they were finally able to understand the functionality of the applications they were using.

Today, the implementation of menus has become a requirement of any commercial application—you are not likely to see a product without some form of menu. The reason for this is obvious—all of the graphical user interface platforms available today simplify the use of menus to the point where it is more difficult to build an application without a menu than it is to simply support one.

Since all GUIs provide at least basic menuing capability, Sun added support for menus into Java. This feature has been available in some form in all versions of Java since version 1.0. In version 1.1, Sun improved menu support by adding keyboard accelerators and pop-up menus, but, for the most part, menuing support in Java has remained unchanged—at least, until the release of Swing.

I should begin by defining exactly what a menu is. This may seem obvious to an application user, since it is simply the typical interface he or she will use to interface to program options and features. To a developer, a menu is a much more complex piece of technology than a simple group of options. Menus are objects attached to an application, and they are made up of many smaller components, including panels, pull-down lists, and, possibly, even tool tips and graphics. In Java, the menu instance manages its own mouse events and, usually, also handles keyboard events stimulated by some user interaction.

UI
GUIDELINE

Provide all of the functionality via menus. All of the software's functionality should be provided via the menu, along with any accelerators which have been assigned. Menus are designed for the novice user, and they present a precise description of the intended action. In addition, they teach the novice about the functionality of an application and lead the novice toward shortcuts which make tasks more efficient.

Back in chapter 3, I mentioned that Swing's JFrame and JApplet instances could have menus attached to them; however, so far in this book you haven't seen an example code to create a menu. In this chapter, we will discuss the menu support provided by Swing, and I will present several examples illustrating many of the key features of menus. By the end of this chapter, you should be able to create complete applications with capabilities comparable to applications you may have previously created with AWT.

We will identify and learn about all of the classes in the Swing menu hierarchy (see figure 7.1). Each class will be examined in detail, and an example will be presented to illustrate its use. You will also find details regarding the toolbar support implemented in the Swing class library. Toolbars and menus typically go hand-in-hand, so it is convenient to discuss them at the same time.

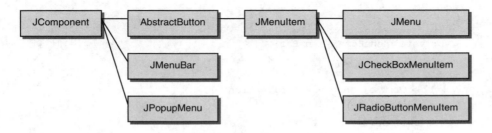

Figure 7.1   Swing menu class hierarchy

7.1   Menu bars

Most applications include some form of menu to allow the user to select functions provided the program. Commonly, menu options are listed in a row at the top of the application window. This row is known as a menu bar.

Menu bars in Java programs are typically shown in the same orientation and position as they are for any other application on the operating system platform. Under Microsoft Windows, this means that the menu bar is a horizontal list of pull-down menus appearing at the top of the application window. With AWT, the menu bar could appear only in this position and could be applied only to an application because AWT applets do not support menu bars.

Swing implements a JMenuBar class which, for compatibility, fully supports the AWT API for menu bars; however, this class offers some features not found in AWT. For example, Swing menu bars can be placed anywhere within the application window, and JMenuBar instances can be applied to applets, as well.

7.1.1 Creating application menus

The easiest way to show you how an application menu can be created is with an example. Listing 7.1 shows sample code which implements only the menu bar itself. Later, we will extend this example with more complex functionality.

```java
import java.awt.*;
import java.awt.event.*;
import com.sun.java.swing.*;

class TestFrame
        extends JFrame
{
    private JPanel      topPanel;
    private JMenuBar    menuBar;

    public TestFrame()
    {
        setTitle( "MenuBar Application" );
        setSize( 310, 130 );

        topPanel = new JPanel();
        topPanel.setLayout( new BorderLayout() );
        getContentPane().add( topPanel );

        // Create the menu bar
        menuBar = new JMenuBar();

        // Set this instance as the application's menu bar
        setJMenuBar( menuBar );

        menuBar.add( new JMenu( "Test" ) );
    }
    public static void main( String args[] )
    {
        // Create an instance of the test application
        TestFrame mainFrame = new TestFrame();
        mainFrame.setVisible( true );
    }
}
```

Listing 7.1   Simple JMenuBar code

Figure 7.2 illustrates the output resulting from executing the code in listing 7.1. It isn't a particularly inspiring application. In fact, if we omitted the last line of the constructor, the program would output nothing at all. We will talk about the purpose of this last line in the next section.

Figure 7.2
Simple JMenuBar example

There is one final point to make. The line:

```
setJMenuBar( menuBar );
```

is a special method call to assign the menu bar to the JFrame instance. This method is really a convenience for AWT developers, but you can use it to add a menu bar to the upper part of any frame. Menu bars, in Swing, are not limited to the traditional location, however. Since JMenuBar instances are derived from JComponent, you can add them to any location you choose. Try replacing the `setJMenuBar()` call in listing 7.1 with this line:

```
topPanel.add( menuBar, BorderLayout.SOUTH );
```

 Using this technique, you can also add menus to a JApplet instance. Unlike the AWT Applet class, JApplet does provide a `setJMenuBar()` method.

7.1.2 JMenuBar constructors

```
public JMenuBar()
```

This constructor creates a new instance of a JMenuBar. The menu bar can be added to a JFrame or JApplet instance. Note that the ability to add menu bars to applets is unique to Swing and is not possible with AWT.

7.1.3 JMenuBar significant method groupings

```
public void setSelected(Component sel)
public boolean isSelected()
```

These methods manage the selection state of the JMenuBar component. Any menu object can be disabled, which also disables all of its child menu items.

```
public SingleSelectionModel getSelectionModel()
```

```
public void setSelectionModel(SingleSelectionModel model)
```

These methods manage the selection model used by the menu bar. Swing will assign a default selection model, but you can create and specify a new selection model, if desired.

```
public JMenu add(JMenu c)
public void remove(int index)
public JMenu getMenu(int index)
public int getMenuCount()
```

The methods in this group are responsible for adding and removing menu instances from the menu bar. Additionally, you can obtain a count containing the number of menu instances contained by the menu bar. Individual menu instances can be retrieved with the getMenu() method.

```
public void setHelpMenu(JMenu menu)
public JMenu getHelpMenu()
```

Like AWT menus, you can identify a menu instance in the menu bar as the Help menu for the application. The Help menu is invoked when the F1 accelerator key is pressed.

7.2   Menus

In the last section, we developed an example program showing a menu bar. This example included a line of source code like the one shown below. This line created a menu instance labeled "Test."

```
menuBar.add( new JMenu( "Test" ) );
```

A menu implemented in Swing with the JMenu class contains instances of menu items or separators. If you examine any application containing a menu bar, you will notice that the menu bar contains pull-down menu objects which you can select with a mouse-click or, quite often, a keyboard accelerator. In this section, we will examine menu implementation, and we will extend our sample application from listing 7.1 to include some standard pull-down menu instances. To address portability concerns, menu creation in Swing closely resembles that of AWT—a JMenu instance is created and inserted into the menu bar using the add() method.

User interface guidelines recommend that menus appear in a standard format. Typically, the first menu on the menu bar is the File menu, which contains options for file related operations. The second object in the menu bar is usually the Edit menu, which holds options for editing information in the program. This usually includes options for clipboard manipulation, such as copy, cut, and paste operations.

7.2.1 Creating cascading menus

As you know from using most graphical applications, menus include items which link to internal functionality in the program; however, not all objects in a menu are items which perform a program task. Some objects found in a menu are actually submenus, which implement more specific items. This technique is known as menu cascading.

Cascading menus (menus added to menus) provide a mechanism to reduce the number of top level menus required in an application, thereby reducing the overall complexity of the user interface. For example, suppose your application supports configuration of several types of properties (for example, system properties, editor properties, display properties, and so on). You could add each of these options to a menu using a menu separator as a way to group them (see figure 7.3); however, a better approach is to create a new JMenu instance containing only the property items, then add this instance to the parent menu. Figure 7.4 shows the improved interface using cascading menus.

Listing 7.2 shows an enhanced menu application, including menu objects attached to the menu bar and some cascading menus added to the File menu. The additional code is highlighted to show you what has been added in this section.

The output of this program is shown in figure 7.5. Notice that the File menu includes a Properties submenu which we will populate in the next section. If you examine the output closely, you will also see that above and below the Properties

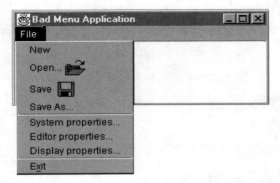

Figure 7.3
Possible menu layout
(a bad approach)

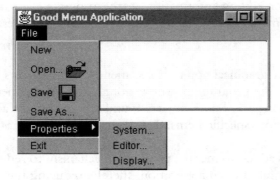

Figure 7.4
Cascading menu layout
(a better approach)

```
import java.awt.*;
import java.awt.event.*;
import com.sun.java.swing.*;

class TestFrame
      extends JFrame
{
    private JPanel        topPanel;
    private JMenuBar      menuBar;
    private JMenu         menuFile;
    private JMenu         menuEdit;
    private JMenu         menuProperty;

    public TestFrame()
    {
        setTitle( "Menu Application" );
        setSize( 310, 130 );

        topPanel = new JPanel();
```

Listing 7.2   Sample JMenu code

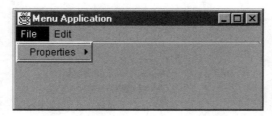

Figure 7.5
JMenu application output

```
        topPanel.setLayout( new BorderLayout() );
        getContentPane().add( topPanel );

        // Create the menu bar
        menuBar = new JMenuBar();

        // Set this instance as the application's menu bar
        setJMenuBar( menuBar );

        // Build the property submenu
        menuProperty = new JMenu( "Properties" );

        // Create the file menu
        menuFile = new JMenu( "File" );
        menuBar.add( menuFile );

        // Add the property menu
        menuFile.addSeparator();
        menuFile.add( menuProperty );
        menuFile.addSeparator();

        // Create the file menu
        menuEdit = new JMenu( "Edit" );
        menuBar.add( menuEdit );
    }

    public static void main( String args[] )
    {
        // Create an instance of the test application
        TestFrame mainFrame = new TestFrame();
        mainFrame.setVisible( true );
    }
}
```

Listing 7.2   Sample JMenu code (continued)

menu, horizontal lines have been drawn. These lines are known as separators and were created by executing the following line of code:

```
        menuFile.addSeparator();
```

Any time you need to logically divide menus and menu items you can insert a separator. This helps clarify blocks of options within your menus, making it easier to use your program.

7.2.2   JMenu variables

```
protected MenuUI ui
```

This variable contains an instance of the user interface component loaded by the pluggable look-and-feel controller.

```
protected JMenu.WinListener popupListener
```

This variable holds an instance of the listener responsible for pop-up menus.

7.2.3 JMenu constructors

```
public JMenu()
```

This constructor creates a new instance of a JMenu object with no text label.

```
public JMenu(String s)
```

This constructor creates a new instance of a JMenu object with the specified text label.

```
public JMenu(String s, boolean b)
```

This constructor creates a new instance of a JMenu object with the specified text label. The boolean parameter value controls the enabled/disabled state of the menu instance.

7.2.4 JMenu significant method groupings

```
public boolean isSelected()
public void setSelected(boolean b)
```

These methods manage the selection state of the JMenu component. Any menu object can be disabled, which also disables all of its child menu items.

```
public JPopupMenu getPopupMenu()
public boolean isPopupMenuVisible()
public void setPopupMenuVisible(boolean b)
```

These methods control the visibility of the pop-up menu associated with this JMenu instance. Each submenu is shown as a pop-up menu instance, and its visibility is managed by these methods.

```
public int getDelay()
public void setDelay(int d)
```

The methods in this group control the time which elapses before a menu Tool-Tip appears in conjunction with the menu instance.

```
public JMenuItem add(JMenuItem menuItem)
public Component add(Component c)
```

```
public void add(String s)
public JMenuItem add(Action a)
public void addSeparator()
public void insert(String s, int pos)
public JMenuItem insert(JMenuItem mi, int pos)
public JMenuItem insert(Action a, int pos)
public void insertSeparator(int index)
```

The methods in this group are responsible for adding and inserting new menu items into the menu instance. Additionally, menu separators can be added using the addSeparator() or insertSeparator() methods.

```
public void remove(JMenuItem item)
public void remove(Action a)
public void remove(int pos)
public void removeAll()
```

This method group is used to remove items from a menu instance. Items can be removed by specifying their instance, index position, or associated action.

```
public JMenuItem getItem(int pos)
public int getItemCount()
public Component getMenuComponent(int n)
public Component[] getMenuComponents()
public boolean isMenuComponent(Component c)
public int getMenuComponentCount()
```

These methods return menu components and counts. Of these methods, get-ItemCount() will be most often used, since it returns the number of items associated with the menu instance.

```
public void addMenuListener(MenuListener l)
public void removeMenuListener(MenuListener l)
```

This method group manages the menu and window listeners which can be attached to a JMenu instance. The menu listener is responsible for detecting changes to the enabled or disabled state of the menu instance.

7.3   Menu items

So far in this chapter, we have created a simple application with a menu bar and extended it by adding some pull-down menus, but we have not yet provided any way for a user to invoke any program functionality. Before we can complete our application menu, we need to understand a few things about menu items.

A menu item is a member of a group of options associated with a menu instance, like those shown in the previous section. Menu items include associated text to distinguish them from other options and may also include a graphical image. Menu items typically have an optional shortcut key to help users accelerate through menus using only the keyboard. The shortcut activates a predefined action event normally intercepted by the application's code in order to initiate some program function.

Swing has a complete set of classes for creating menu items. In this section, we will limit ourselves to the standard text menu item so we can become familiar with simple application menuing. In subsequent sections, we will discuss more advanced types of menu items.

If you are experienced with the AWT menuing mechanism, you need to know that menuing in JFC is not necessarily backward compatible with older AWT techniques. Pay attention to the class names, particularly if you are porting AWT code to Swing, and do not mix AWT menu objects with any provided by Swing. In Swing, a menu item is represented by the JMenuItem class, which, for upward compatibility, functions the same as its AWT counterpart. In this section, we will examine all aspects of the JMenuItem class and how it fits into the menuing environment supported by JFC.

Though JMenuItem supports several constructors, the most frequently used form looks like this:

```
JMenuItem menuItem = new JMenuItem( "Sample" );
```

Another common form of constructor is:

```
JMenuItem menuItem = new JMenuItem();
    .
    .
    .
menuItem.setText( "Sample" );
```

You might question the efficiency of this second form; however, it is useful if you write your code such that menus are constructed in one part of the code, while menu text is added in another. If you are writing code to support several languages, you may have a menu population method for each language. Each of these methods consists of a list of setText() method calls for each menu item.

Let's take a look at an expanded version of the application we have been building in this chapter. Listing 7.3 extends the pull-down menus to include some of the menu items you would typically see in the File and Edit menus of most applications.

The code creates New, Open..., Save, Save as..., and Exit menu items using the JMenuItem class. It also populates the Properties submenu, so you can appreciate the effects of cascading menus. Listing 7.3 shows the entire example, with high-lighting on the source code added in this section.

```java
import java.awt.*;
import java.awt.event.*;
import com.sun.java.swing.*;

class TestFrame
        extends     JFrame
        implements ActionListener
{
    private final int     ITEM_PLAIN =   0;  // Item types
    private final int     ITEM_CHECK =   1;
    private final int     ITEM_RADIO =   2;

    private   JPanel      topPanel;
    private   JMenuBar    menuBar;
    private   JMenu       menuFile;
    private   JMenu       menuEdit;
    private   JMenu       menuProperty;
    private   JMenuItem   menuPropertySystem;
    private   JMenuItem   menuPropertyEditor;
    private   JMenuItem   menuPropertyDisplay;
    private   JMenuItem   menuFileNew;
    private   JMenuItem   menuFileOpen;
    private   JMenuItem   menuFileSave;
    private   JMenuItem   menuFileSaveAs;
    private   JMenuItem   menuFileExit;
    private   JMenuItem   menuEditCopy;
    private   JMenuItem   menuEditCut;
    private   JMenuItem   menuEditPaste;

    public TestFrame()
    {
        setTitle( "Complete Menu Application" );
        setSize( 310, 130 );

        topPanel = new JPanel();
        topPanel.setLayout( new BorderLayout() );
        getContentPane().add( topPanel );

        // Create the menu bar
        menuBar = new JMenuBar();
```

Listing 7.3   Sample code for JMenuItem

```
        // Set this instance as the application's menu bar
        setJMenuBar( menuBar );

        // Build the property submenu
        menuProperty = new JMenu( "Properties" );
        menuProperty.setMnemonic( 'P' );

        // Create property items
        menuPropertySystem = CreateMenuItem( menuProperty, ITEM_PLAIN,
                            "System...", null, 'S', null );
        menuPropertyEditor = CreateMenuItem( menuProperty, ITEM_PLAIN,
                            "Editor...", null, 'E', null );
        menuPropertyDisplay = CreateMenuItem( menuProperty, ITEM_PLAIN,
                            "Display...", null, 'D', null );

        // Create the file menu
        menuFile = new JMenu( "File" );
        menuFile.setMnemonic( 'F' );
        menuBar.add( menuFile );

        // Build a file menu items
        menuFileNew = CreateMenuItem( menuFile, ITEM_PLAIN,
                            "New", null, 'N', null );
        menuFileOpen = CreateMenuItem( menuFile, ITEM_PLAIN, "Open...",
                            new ImageIcon( "open.gif" ), 'O',
                            "Open a new file" );
        menuFileSave = CreateMenuItem( menuFile, ITEM_PLAIN, "Save",
                            new ImageIcon( "save.gif" ), 'S',
                            " Save this file" );
        menuFileSaveAs = CreateMenuItem( menuFile, ITEM_PLAIN,
                            "Save As...", null, 'A',
                            "Save this data to a new file" );

        // Add the property menu
        menuFile.addSeparator();
        menuFile.add( menuProperty );
        menuFile.addSeparator();
        menuFileExit = CreateMenuItem( menuFile, ITEM_PLAIN,
                            "Exit", null, 'x',
                            "Exit the program" );

        // Create the file menu
        menuEdit = new JMenu( "Edit" );
        menuEdit.setMnemonic( 'E' );
        menuBar.add( menuEdit );

        // Create edit menu options
```

Listing 7.3   Sample code for JMenuItem (continued)

```
       menuEditCut = CreateMenuItem( menuEdit, ITEM_PLAIN,
                           "Cut", null, 't',
                           "Cut data to the clipboard" );
       menuEditCopy = CreateMenuItem( menuEdit, ITEM_PLAIN,
                           "Copy", null, 'C',
                           "Copy data to the clipboard" );
       menuEditPaste = CreateMenuItem( menuEdit, ITEM_PLAIN,
                           "Paste", null, 'P',
                           "Paste data from the clipboard" );
}

public JMenuItem CreateMenuItem( JMenu menu, int iType,
             String sText, ImageIcon image,
                 int acceleratorKey, String sToolTip )
{
    // Create the item
    JMenuItem menuItem;

    switch( iType )
    {
        case ITEM_RADIO:
            menuItem = new JRadioButtonMenuItem();
            break;

        case ITEM_CHECK:
            menuItem = new JCheckBoxMenuItem();
            break;

        default:
            menuItem = new JMenuItem();
            break;
    }

    // Add the item test
    menuItem.setText( sText );

    // Add the optional icon
    if( image != null )
       menuItem.setIcon( image );

    // Add the accelerator key
    if( acceleratorKey > 0 )
       menuItem.setMnemonic( acceleratorKey );

    // Add the optional tool tip text
    if( sToolTip != null )
       menuItem.setToolTipText( sToolTip );
```

Listing 7.3   Sample code for JMenuItem (continued)

```
        // Add an action handler to this menu item
        menuItem.addActionListener( this );

        menu.add( menuItem );

        return menuItem;
    }

    public void actionPerformed( ActionEvent event )
    {
        System.out.println( event );
    }

    public static void main( String args[] )
    {
        // Create an instance of the test application
        TestFrame mainFrame = new TestFrame();
        mainFrame.setVisible( true );
    }
}
```

Listing 7.3 Sample code for JMenuItem (continued)

Figure 7.6 shows the File menu produced by this example. Note the presence of keyboard mnemonics and graphics in this screen capture. We will examine these in more detail in the remainder of this section.

The key to this example is the `CreateMenuItem()` method, which is a helper to eliminate duplicate code for each of the menu items. The rest of this section will describe the details of this important method. If you wish, you can add this method to your own applications, modifying it to suit your own specific needs.

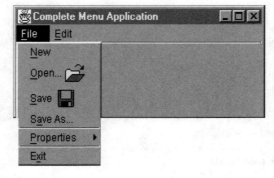

Figure 7.6
Complete menu application

7.3.1 Adding graphics to menu items

If you examine figure 7.6, you will notice that the menu options Open and Save appear a bit different than the others because they include graphics. Each item rendered in a menu pull-down is really just an extended instance of `AbstractButton`, which, as we know from chapter 4, can include an ImageIcon in addition to text information. To accomplish this in the `CreateMenuItem()` method, we implement the following code:

```
// Add the optional icon
if( image != null )
    menuItem.setIcon( image );
```

This image variable is a handle to an instance of a GIF file loaded from a disk. You can even add animated images to a menu item using the same technique, and Swing will manage all the resources required to handle the animated GIF file.

GUIDELINE

Place graphics, check boxes, and accelerators inside menus. Any graphics and check boxes for menu items should be placed to the left of menu items, and shortcut descriptions should be placed to the right. The trend is to duplicate the toolbar icon of a feature beside the associated menu item as a mnemonic. There are existing guidelines for mnemonics for different platforms, so you might want to consult a style guide.

7.3.2 Adding ToolTips

Run the code shown in listing 7.3, and place the mouse pointer on the Save menu item. If you leave the pointer still for a second, you will see a pop-up line showing a brief description of the item's function. Look at the `CreateMenuItem()` method, and you will see the code to do this:

```
// Add the optional tool tip text
if( sToolTip != null )
    menuItem.setToolTipText( sToolTip );
```

This line of code sets the ToolTip text displayed for a menu item based on text supplied by the calling method. Tool tips were originally introduced in chapter 3, but, until now, you have not seen any practical examples.

Though you will see tool tips in listing 7.3, it is important to note that they are associated with the JComponent portion of the menu item. As such, you can use exactly the same code to apply tool tips to buttons, text fields, or any other Swing user interface component described in this book.

7.3.3 Menu item keyboard mnemonics

There is one other oddity in the `CreateMenuItem()` method of listing 7.3. The line which is shown as

```
// Add the accelerator key
if( acceleratorKey > 0 )
    menuItem.setMnemonic( acceleratorKey );
```

is something you may not have seen before. This line assigns a keyboard accelerator, or shortcut key, to the JMenuItem instance. The `setMnemonic()` method accepts a character (the actual shortcut character) and scans the menu item string for the first instance of it. If you observe the Exit menu item in figure 7.6, you will see that the *x* is underlined, indicating that the *x* key is the shortcut.

 Make sure that you do not use the same shortcut key for more than one menu item within the same menu, otherwise, you may experience some unpredictable results when the keyboard accelerator is invoked.

The implementation of menus with keyboard accelerators is now commonplace in applications, and I urge you to add them to the programs you write. Though user interface standards and guidelines are far beyond the scope of this book, you should pay attention to the accelerators you select as well as to the layout of your menus. Unless you are a user interface designer, you will probably lack the knowledge and experience needed to comply with all the rules. So, your best option is to examine the multitude of commercial products to see what accelerators they use and how their menus are formatted. For example, the File menu is universally accepted as the first menu in the menu bar, and, almost exclusively, its shortcut key is *F*.

7.3.4 Responding to a menu selection

Menu items selected by the user generate action events which can be intercepted by the application. To accomplish this, simply add an action listener to the item as you would for a button. For example, consider the following code:

```
JMenuItem menuFileSave = new JMenuItem( "Save" );
MenuFileSave.addActionListener( myMenuListener );
```

The listener's `actionPerformed()` method looks something like this:

```
public void actionPerformed( ActionEvent event )
{
   if( event.getSource() == menuFileSave )
   {
       // Handle this menu selection
   }
}
```

7.3.5 JMenuItem constructors

```
public JMenuItem()
```

This constructor creates a default menu item instance with no set text or icon.

```
public JMenuItem(Icon icon)
```

This constructor creates a default menu item instance with the specified icon image.

```
public JMenuItem(String text)
```

This constructor creates a default menu item instance with the specified text.

```
public JMenuItem(String text, Icon icon)
```

This constructor creates a default menu item instance with the specified text and icon image.

```
public JMenuItem(String text, MenuShortcut shortcut)
```

This constructor creates a default menu item instance with the specified text. The supplied AWT `MenuShortcut` parameter contains the keyboard accelerator used to invoke this menu option.

7.3.6 JMenuItem significant method groupings

```
public void setArmed(boolean b)
public boolean isArmed()
```

The methods in this group manage the armed state of the menu item. If the item is armed and the mouse button is released while the mouse pointer is over the item, that menu will fire an action event. If the mouse pointer is not over the item when the button is released, no action event will be fired and the item will be disarmed.

```
public void setEnabled(boolean b)
```

This method accepts a boolean value used to control the enabled or disabled state of the menu item.

```
public void setAccelerator(KeyStroke keyStroke)
public KeyStroke getAccelerator()
```

This method group controls the keyboard accelerator for the menu item.

7.4   Check box menu items

In addition to the standard menu item, Swing (and AWT) offers a second, and more interactive, menu item. The check box menu item offers modal operation within a menu, in that the option can be checked or unchecked. This is quite useful when you require menu options which control the on/off state of a particular feature in your code. The use of check box menu items has the added effect of eliminating the need for an additional dialog box to control application parameters, usually resulting in smaller, cleaner code.

In Swing, the check box menu item is implemented in a class called JCheck-BoxMenuItem, which deliberately mimics the capability and API of its AWT cousin. The components can be freely mixed with other menu items, and, like the JMenuItem component, can support text or graphic images (even those with animation). The object construction process is essentially the same as for JMenuItem, except for the ability to set the initial checked/unchecked state of the instance. Listing 7.4 shows a code sample implementing several instances of JCheckBox-MenuItem.

```
import java.awt.*;
import com.sun.java.swing.*;

class TestFrame
      extends JFrame
  {
```

Listing 7.4   Sample code for JCheckBoxMenuItem

```
    private JPanel  topPanel;

    public TestFrame()
    {
        setTitle( "Menu Application #2" );
        setSize( 310, 130 );
        setBackground( Color.gray );

        topPanel = new JPanel();
        topPanel.setLayout( new BorderLayout() );
        getContentPane().add( topPanel );

        JMenuBar menuBar = new JMenuBar();
        setJMenuBar( menuBar );

        JMenu optionMenu = new JMenu( "Menu" );
        menuBar.add( optionMenu );

        // Create the check box menu items
        JCheckBoxMenuItem menuEditInsert
                    = new JCheckBoxMenuItem( "Insert" );
        optionMenu.add( menuEditInsert );
        JCheckBoxMenuItem menuEditWrap
                    = new JCheckBoxMenuItem( "Wrap lines" );
        optionMenu.add( menuEditWrap );
        JCheckBoxMenuItem menuEditCaps
                    = new JCheckBoxMenuItem( "Caps Lock" );
        optionMenu.add( menuEditCaps );
    }

    public static void main( String args[] )
    {
        // Create an instance of the test application
        TestFrame mainFrame = new TestFrame();
        mainFrame.setVisible( true );
    }
}
```

Listing 7.4   Sample code for JCheckBoxMenuItem (continued)

The screen capture in figure 7.7 shows the result of executing this application. Though we did not implement an action listener in this sample, the menu items can be checked and unchecked. This functionality comes automatically when using a JCheckBoxMenuItem. Notice in this figure that two of the three menu options include a checkmark in the left-hand margin indicating that the state for these is "true".

Figure 7.7
JCheckBoxMenuItem sample

7.4.1 Managing check box state

Each JCheckBoxMenuItem instance contains a state attribute containing a boolean "true" value if the item is checked and a "false" value if it is not. This checked state of the item can be controlled in one of two ways: the user can select the menu item to toggle the state, or the developer can control the state programmatically. To change the checked state of a check box menu item or to monitor its value, use lines of code like the two shown below:

```
// Set the checked menu item
menuCheckItem.setState( true );

// Get the state of the item
boolean bState = menuCheckItem.getState();
```

7.4.2 JCheckBoxMenuItem variables

```
protected Action action
```

This variable contains the instance of the action invoked when an action event occurs.

7.4.3 JCheckBoxMenuItem constructors

```
public JCheckBoxMenuItem()
```

This first constructor creates an initially unselected JCheckBoxMenuItem with no set text or icon.

```
public JCheckBoxMenuItem(Icon icon)
```

This constructor creates an initially unselected JCheckBoxMenuItem with the specified icon.

```
public JCheckBoxMenuItem(String text)
```

This constructor creates an initially unselected JCheckBoxMenuItem with the specified text identifier.

```
public JCheckBoxMenuItem(String text, Icon icon)
```

This first constructor creates an initially unselected JCheckBoxMenuItem with the specified text and icon image.

```
public JCheckBoxMenuItem(String text, boolean b)
```

This first constructor creates a JCheckBoxMenuItem initially set to the supplied selection state in the b parameter. The component is constructed with the specified text.

```
public JCheckBoxMenuItem(String text, Icon icon, boolean b)
```

This first constructor creates a JCheckBoxMenuItem initially set to the supplied selection state in the *b* parameter. The component is constructed with the specified text and icon image.

7.4.4 JCheckBoxMenuItem significant method groupings

```
public synchronized void setState(boolean b)
public boolean getState()
```

These methods manage the current selection state of the JCheckBoxMenuItem instance.

```
public synchronized Object[] getSelectedObjects()
```

This method returns an array of objects based on the selections currently chosen by the user.

7.5 Radio button menu items

The menu items shown so far in this chapter relate directly to comparable classes in AWT, but Swing also provides a third menu item type not found in AWT. Resembling the check box menu item shown in the previous section, the radio button menu item, provides the capability to implement arrays of radio buttons within a menu.

Swing provides the JRadioButtonMenuItem class, which exhibits the combined characteristics of the JMenuItem and JRadioButton classes, allowing the presence of this functionality within an application menu. A product of this class is shown in figure 7.8, where you will see three menu items grouped as a set of radio buttons, with the Medium Cursor item selected.

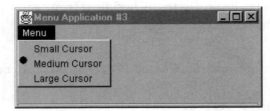

Figure 7.8
JRadioButtonMenuItem sample

Listing 7.5 shows the code used to create this menu; however, as with the previous examples in this chapter, executing this code will not yet produce the expected results. This example should be straightforward, but one point should be made in its regard. In chapter 4, when we discussed JRadioButton, you saw an example of the ButtonGroup class, which is used to link the components into a single user interface entity. Since JRadioButtonMenuItem instances are a type of radio button, you also need to relate these components with a ButtonGroup instance.

```
import java.awt.*;
import com.sun.java.swing.*;

class TestFrame
        extends     JFrame
{
    private     JPanel topPanel;

    public TestFrame()
    {
        setTitle( "Menu Application #3" );
        setSize( 310, 130 );

        topPanel = new JPanel();
        getContentPane().add( topPanel );

        JMenuBar menuBar = new JMenuBar();
        setJMenuBar( menuBar );

        JMenu optionMenu = new JMenu( "Menu" );
        menuBar.add( optionMenu );

        JRadioButtonMenuItem menuCursorSmall =
                new JRadioButtonMenuItem( "Small Cursor" );
        optionMenu.add( menuCursorSmall );
        JRadioButtonMenuItem menuCursorMedium =
```

Listing 7.5   Sample code for JRadioButtonMenuItem

```
                  new JRadioButtonMenuItem( "Medium Cursor" );
        optionMenu.add( menuCursorMedium );
        JRadioButtonMenuItem menuCursorLarge =
                  new JRadioButtonMenuItem( "Large Cursor" );
        optionMenu.add( menuCursorLarge );

        ButtonGroup cursorGroup = new ButtonGroup();
        cursorGroup.add( menuCursorSmall );
        cursorGroup.add( menuCursorMedium );
        cursorGroup.add( menuCursorLarge );
    }

    public static void main( String args[] )
    {
        // Create an instance of the test application
        TestFrame mainFrame = new TestFrame();
        mainFrame.setVisible( true );
    }
}
```

Listing 7.5   Sample code for JRadioButtonMenuItem (continued)

7.5.1   JRadioButtonMenuItem variables

`protected Action action`

This variable contains the instance of the action invoked when an action event occurs.

7.5.2   JRadioButtonMenuItem constructors

`public JRadioButtonMenuItem()`

This constructor creates an initially unselected JRadioButtonMenuItem with no set text or icon.

`public JRadioButtonMenuItem(Icon icon)`

This constructor creates an initially unselected JRadioButtonMenuItem with the specified icon.

`public JRadioButtonMenuItem(String text)`

This constructor creates an initially unselected JRadioButtonMenuItem with the specified text identifier.

`public JRadioButtonMenuItem(String text, Icon icon)`

This constructor creates an initially unselected JRadioButtonMenuItem with the specified text and icon image.

7.6   Pop-up menus

Menu bars in conjunction with menus do not address all of the issues associated with menus in applications and applets. A second type of menu exists in Swing (and AWT) which provides additional utility in Java programs.

The pop-up menu (sometimes referred to as a context menu) gets its name from the way it "pops" up when you click the correct mouse button (sometimes with the inclusion of a key press, on some platforms). This type of menu is used most often for quick access to context-sensitive options for a given task. For example, in an application like the Microsoft Word word processor on the Windows platform, you can click the right mouse button in the document window to display options appropriate to document editing (such as clipboard operations, font selection, and paragraph formatting).

Think about the user's task when designing pop-up menus. Pop-up menus are context sensitive to the area in which they are invoked, thus, the most frequently used features for any given area must be determined beforehand to populate these effectively. Pop-up menus should not be a substitute for other portions of a UI, but rather, they are a redundant method of invoking a subset of the features when the user needs them. If targeting Macintosh users, keep in mind that their mouse interactions primary involve single clicks with one mouse button.

The final Swing menu class we will examine in this chapter is the JPopupMenu class. It provides platform independent pop-up menuing which can be attached to any other component (for example, a text field or text area). The basic construction process for a JPopupMenu instance uses code similar to the following:

```
// Create the submenu items
JMenuItem menuItem1 = new JMenuItem( "Copy" );
JMenuItem menuItem2 = new JMenuItem( "Cut" );
JMenuItem menuItem3 = new JMenuItem( "Paste" );

// Construct the pop-up menu
JPopupMenu popupMenu = new JPopupMenu();
popupMenu.add( menuItem1 );
```

```
popupMenu.add( menuItem2 );
popupMenu.add( menuItem3 );
```

Let's take a look at a complete example. The code in listing 7.5 creates a basic JFrame instance and adds a pop-up menu to it. The menu contains some standard Swing menu items without graphics, though you could also add radio button and check box menu items, as well as graphical images.

Each of the menu items supports an action listener which is intercepted by the frame through the `actionPerformed()` method. Mouse operations are examined in the `processMouseEvent()` method in order to detect context menu triggering. All mouse events are then subsequently sent to the parent class for possible further processing.

```java
import java.awt.*;
import java.awt.event.*;
import com.sun.java.swing.*;

class TestFrame
        extends    JFrame
        implements ActionListener
{
    private    JPanel      topPanel;
    private    JPopupMenu  popupMenu;

    public TestFrame()
    {
        setTitle( "Popup Menu Application" );
        setSize( 310, 130 );
        setBackground( Color.gray );

        topPanel = new JPanel();
        topPanel.setLayout( null );
        getContentPane().add( topPanel );

        // Create some menu items for the pop-up
        JMenuItem menuFileNew = new JMenuItem( "New" );
        JMenuItem menuFileOpen = new JMenuItem( "Open..." );
        JMenuItem menuFileSave = new JMenuItem( "Save" );
        JMenuItem menuFileSaveAs = new JMenuItem( "Save As..." );
        JMenuItem menuFileExit = new JMenuItem( "Exit" );

        // Create a pop-up menu
        popupMenu = new JPopupMenu( "Menu" );
        popupMenu.add( menuFileNew );
        popupMenu.add( menuFileOpen );
```

Listing 7.6   Sample code for JPopupMenu

```
        popupMenu.add( menuFileSave );
        popupMenu.add( menuFileSaveAs );
        popupMenu.add( menuFileExit );

        topPanel.add( popupMenu );
        // Action and mouse listener support
        enableEvents( AWTEvent.MOUSE_EVENT_MASK );
        menuFileNew.addActionListener( this );
        menuFileOpen.addActionListener( this );
        menuFileSave.addActionListener( this );
        menuFileSaveAs.addActionListener( this );
        menuFileExit.addActionListener( this );
    }

    public void processMouseEvent( MouseEvent event )
    {
        if( event.isPopupTrigger() )
        {
            popupMenu.show( event.getComponent(),
                            event.getX(), event.getY() );
        }

        super.processMouseEvent( event );
    }

    public void actionPerformed( ActionEvent event )
    {
        // Add action handling code here
        System.out.println( event );
    }

    public static void main( String args[] )
    {
        // Create an instance of the test application
        TestFrame mainFrame = new TestFrame();
        mainFrame.setVisible( true );
    }
}
```

Listing 7.6   Sample code for JPopupMenu (continued)

Listing 7.6 contains the source code for a complete application. You can compile and execute this code to produce the results shown in figure 7.9. Note that, although the frame in figure 7.8 contains no components, you can easily add them, and then create a different pop-up context menu for each. The parameter supplied in the JPopupMenu constructor controls which user interface component owns the pop-up menu.

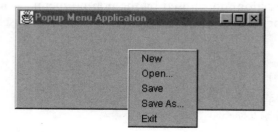

Figure 7.9
JPopupMenu sample

FYI If you are mixing heavyweight AWT components and lightweight Swing components in the same application, you may experience some problems relating to pop-up menus. Since heavyweight components are always drawn on top of lightweights, it is possible to have the pop-up menu appear underneath a component. To solve this problem, add the following line of code to the pop-up menu code:

```
setLightWeightPopupEnabled( false );
```

This code forces the pop-up menu to be shown as a heavyweight component, drawing it on top of all other components

---

7.6.1 JPopupMenu constructors

```
public JPopupMenu()
```

This constructor creates a new instance of a JPopupMenu initially containing no menu items.

```
public JPopupMenu( String label )
```

This constructor creates a new instance of a JPopupMenu initially containing no menu items. The String parameter associates a pop-up menu with a named label for the pop-up menu.

7.6.2 JPopupMenu significant method groupings

```
public SingleSelectionModel getSelectionModel()
public void setSelectionModel(SingleSelectionModel model)
```

These methods manage the selection model used by the pop-up menu. Swing will assign a default selection model, but you can create and specify a new selection model, if desired.

```
public JMenuItem add(JMenuItem menuItem)
public JMenuItem add(Action a)
public void addSeparator()
public void insert(Action a, int index)
public void insert(Component component, int index)
```

The methods in this group are responsible for adding and inserting new menu items into the pop-up menu instance. Additionally, menu separators can be added using the addSeparator() methods.

```
public void addPopupMenuListener(PopupMenuListener l)
public void removePopupMenuListener(PopupMenuListener l)
```

These methods manage the presence of pop-up listeners for the menu. With a pop-up menu listener, you can detect if the menu is about to appear or disappear, or if the menu has been canceled.

```
public void setVisible(boolean b)
public boolean isVisible()
```

The two methods shown in this group manage the visibility of the pop-up menu. A "true" value passed to the setVisible() method causes the pop-up to be drawn.

```
public void setLocation(int x, int y)
public void setPopupSize(Dimension d)
public void setPopupSize(int width, int height)
public void show(Component invoker, int x,  int y)
```

This method group controls the size and location of the pop-up menu instance.

7.7 Toolbars

One of the most recognizable features of applications today is the toolbar. Toolbars allow users to quickly invoke the most common program features without forcing them to sift through menus. The addition of toolbars can significantly improve the user interface of a typical application, and toolbars can add a certain aesthetic polish which users appreciate. Since we talked about menus in the previous sections, and toolbars are closely related, a discussion of toolbars is a natural progression.

Previous to the introduction of Swing, if you wanted to add toolbar support to a Java application, you were pretty much on your own. AWT offers no capability for toolbars, so the only recourse, in the past, was to implement a set of buttons in its own panel; however, the lack of support for images in the AWT Button class results in an archaic user interface.

GUIDELINE

Provide frequently used functions with toolbars. The toolbar should contain only the most frequently used features. Toolbars are targeted more towards experienced users in order to give them fast access to common actions. Group toolbar buttons together by similar functionality, and tile them by order of frequency of use and importance, from left to right.

The developers of Swing appreciated that the current direction of user interface design demanded that they implement a toolbar class capable of the latest features, including graphical buttons, fly-over tool tips, and the ability to dock and undock the toolbar. The result of their efforts is a toolbar which easily supports all of these abilities and also allows for non-button components such as images, combo boxes, and so on.

Now, we will examine many of the aspects and nuances of the Swing toolbar class. This class, JToolBar, (like all Swing classes) is rooted from JComponent, so it supports all of the features we have been discussing so far in this book. Since JToolBar is a Swing component (and hence a container), instances of this class can hold any other Swing or AWT user interface component.

7.7.1 Toolbar basics

In this section, we will examine the details of the Swing JToolBar class, and you will be presented with some examples demonstrating the most important concepts. As you will come to appreciate, implementing toolbars in your programs is simple.

We will just dive right into Swing toolbars by presenting an example of a simple toolbar. Listing 7.7 creates a frame which offers the user a toolbar with several buttons. Each of the buttons generates an event which is handled by the `action-Performed()` method, though, in this example, the result of each toolbar action is simply a string written to the console.

GUIDELINE

Graphics and toolbar button details. Typical toolbar button sizes include 24 by 22 pixels for small, and 32 by 30 pixels for large buttons (including the bevel); and you may place, respectively, 16 by 16 and 24 by 24 pixel graphics on these buttons. When using GIF images to place onto graphics, make the graphics backgrounds transparent so that they bleed into the toolbar. GIF images should ideally use a Web-safe 216-color palette. There is a trend towards coolbars, a term denoting multiple state toolbar buttons with a flat appearance which pop out on mouseovers (as in, when the user places the mouse pointer on something).

```java
import java.awt.*;
import java.awt.event.*;
import com.sun.java.swing.*;

class TestFrame
        extends     JFrame
        implements ActionListener
{
    private   JPanel     topPanel;
    private   JButton    buttonNew;
    private   JButton    buttonOpen;
    private   JButton    buttonSave;
    private   JButton    buttonCopy;
    private   JButton    buttonCut;
    private   JButton    buttonPaste;

    public TestFrame()
    {
        setTitle( "Basic Toolbar Application" );
        setSize( 310, 130 );
        setBackground( Color.gray );

        topPanel = new JPanel();
        topPanel.setLayout( new BorderLayout() );
        getContentPane().add( topPanel );

        // Create a new toolbar
        JToolBar myToolbar = new JToolBar();
        topPanel.add( myToolbar, BorderLayout.NORTH );

        // Add some buttons to the toolbar
        buttonNew = addToolbarButton( myToolbar, false, "New",
```

Listing 7.7 JToolBar sample

```
                           "new", "Create a new document" );
    buttonOpen = addToolbarButton( myToolbar, true, "Open",
                  "open", "Open an existing document" );
    buttonSave = addToolbarButton( myToolbar, true, "Save",
                  "save", "Open an existing document" );
    myToolbar.addSeparator();
    buttonCopy = addToolbarButton( myToolbar, true, null,
                  "copy", "Copy selection to the clipboard" );
    buttonCut = addToolbarButton( myToolbar, true, null,
                  "cut", "Cut selection to the clipboard" );
    buttonPaste = addToolbarButton( myToolbar, true, null,
                  "paste", "Paste selection from the clipboard" );

    // Add a text area just to fill up the space
    JTextArea textArea = new JTextArea();
    topPanel.add( textArea, BorderLayout.CENTER );
}

// Helper method to create new toolbar buttons
public JButton addToolbarButton( JToolBar toolBar,
                   boolean bUseImage, String sButtonText,
                     String sButton, String sToolHelp )
{
    JButton b;

    // Create a new button
    if( bUseImage )
        b = new JButton( new ImageIcon( sButton + ".gif" ) );
    else
        b = (JButton)toolBar.add( new JButton() );

    // Add the button to the toolbar
    toolBar.add( b );

    // Add optional button text
    if( sButtonText != null )
        b.setText( sButtonText );
    else
    {
        // Only a graphic, so make the button smaller
        b.setMargin( new Insets( 0, 0, 0, 0 ) );
    }

    // Add optional tool tip help
    if( sToolHelp != null )
        b.setToolTipText( sToolHelp );

    // Make sure this button sends a message when the user
```

Listing 7.7   JToolBar sample (continued)

```
        // clicks it
        b.setActionCommand( "Toolbar:" + sButton );
        b.addActionListener( this );

        return b;
    }

    public void actionPerformed( ActionEvent event )
    {
        // Add action handling code here
        System.out.println( event );
    }

    public static void main( String args[] )
    {
        // Create an instance of the test application
        TestFrame mainFrame = new TestFrame();
        mainFrame.setVisible( true );
    }
}
```

Listing 7.7   JToolBar sample (continued)

The results produced by executing listing 7.7 are shown in figure 7.10. Notice that the example implements several different styles of buttons ranging from a simple, unadorned button, to those including graphics and text, and those with only a graphic. As an added feature, each button on the toolbar includes fly-over help to indicate its function more clearly.

7.7.2 A toolbar with many faces

There is a more subtle feature of toolbars which is not shown in figure 7.10—the ability to undock the toolbar and move it someplace else. When the mouse is posi-

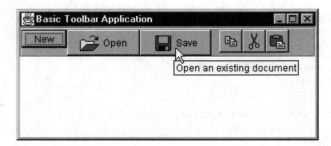

Figure 7.10
Toolbar program output

tioned over the gray area of the toolbar, press and hold the mouse button and drag the toolbar out of the application window. Note the effect this has—the toolbar appears within its own frame on the desktop (see figure 7.11). This is functionality which our application provided with no additional development.

Dragging the menu back onto the application frame can restore an undocked toolbar. If you try this with the example in listing 7.6, you may notice something interesting. Not only can the toolbar be dropped in its original location, but you can also orient it vertically along either side of the frame, or horizontally at the bottom.

7.7.3 Docking and undocking toolbars

As you now know, the toolbar class supports docking and undocking with simple mouse drag operations; however, in some situations this feature is undesirable. The following line of code disables toolbar docking regardless of the look-and-feel library in use:

```
myToolbar.setFloatable( false );
```

If you are creating a program to run on several platforms, a dockable toolbar may be inappropriate in some situations. For example, in the Microsoft Windows environment, many applications support this feature, but let's assume that you do not want this functionality to appear when your application is executed on a UNIX platform. When using the Swing toolbar class, it is also possible to disable toolbar docking for a specific look-and-feel, while letting this capability remain in the look-and-feel of other toolbars. To accomplish this, the code needs to access the ComponentUI class for the toolbar, since the docking feature is UI model specific. The fol-

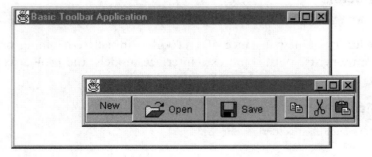

Figure 7.11   Toolbar program output

lowing code disables toolbar docking and undocking only on the Motif platform, while the Windows version of the program would allow this feature.

```
// Make sure the toolbar doesn't float
ToolBarUI ui = myToolBar.getUI();
if( ui instanceof MotifToolBarUI )
{
    MotifToolBarUI toolbarUI = (MotifToolBarUI)ui;
    toolbarUI.setFloatable( false );
}
```

Be careful about implementing undocking toolbars. While this feature is quite slick and tempting to use, some users have problems with accidentally undocking toolbars, redocking the toolbars, or losing toolbars once undocked. Should there be a need to undock toolbars, make every attempt to ensure that any undocked toolbars do not ever disappear when undocked in a multiple window environment.

7.7.4 Adding other components to a toolbar

A JToolBar instance is not limited to the inclusion of buttons. Remember that the JToolBar class is derived from JComponent, so, by definition, it is a container which can hold any Swing or AWT component. For example, the following code adds a checkbox and an image to a toolbar instance.

```
myToolbar.add( new JCheckBox( "Click here" ) );
myToolbar.add( new JLabel( new ImageIcon( "save.gif" ) ) );
```

7.7.5 JToolBar constructors

```
public JToolBar()
```

This constructor creates a new instance of a JToolBar initially containing no buttons or other components. With some user interface models, the toolbar is floatable, by default.

7.7.6 JToolBar significant method groupings

```
public int getComponentIndex(Component c)
public Component getComponentAtIndex(int i)
```

This pair of methods returns information about the components contained within the toolbar. Each component has an associated index. Given the index, the component can be retrieved, and, by specifying a component, the index can be found.

```
public void addSeparator()
```

This method adds a new separator to the toolbar at the current index location. This is used to leaves gaps in the layout to improve component grouping within the toolbar.

```
public JButton add(Action a)
```

This method is unique in that you can have the toolbar instance automatically create a JButton instance simply by adding a new action. Actions can be jointly associated with menu operations and toolbar buttons.

7.8   Chapter summary

In this chapter, we have examined much of the material required to support menus within your Swing-based applications and applets. We started by implementing a basic menu bar using the JFC JMenuBar class. Then, we discussed the JMenu class and used it to add pull-down menus to our sample code. You now know that menus can be easily applied to Java applications. In addition, this chapter pointed out that Swing menus could be applied to applets, too. This is a new Swing feature with which AWT applet developers will immediately identify and appreciate.

This chapter identified the three basic types of menu items which are supported by swing menus, including the standard JMenuItem as well as menu items which implement check boxes and grouped radio buttons.

As a final examination of menu support in Swing, we examined the JPopupMenu class, which Swing provides to support context menus (the menu that appears when you click the secondary mouse button on something). This class is essentially a clone of AWT's PopupMenu class, so developers familiar with that API can quickly convert their existing applications.

Finally, this chapter described the JToolBar class which Swing uses to implement and support toolbars within an application or applet. We saw how toolbars can be undocked from their owner frame and how to prevent this from occurring. Also, this section described how to add other components to a toolbar to meet your specific needs.

This chapter marks the end of AWT compatibility in this book, and with the presentation of JToolBar, we have seen the last of our old friend, AWT. Though comparisons to AWT may still be drawn occasionally, the remaining chapters in this book discuss features found only in Swing.

Dialogs and
internal frames

8

In this chapter

- Basic dialog creation with Swing
- Using chooser dialogs
- Internal frames

We have already examined several ways that a Swing application can obtain input from the user; but, in the examples presented so far, all user input came from components created within a main application frame. In most cases, the main window of an application holds the primary content of the program, and it is not possible for the user to accomplish all of their tasks from the main window. For example, in a word processor or text editor, the user must have some mechanism for saving and loading files into the application. Some of these needs can be met with additional toolbar and menu options, but, in most situations, this is impractical.

To address this problem, the architects of early graphical user interfaces adopted an approach allowing secondary application windows to appear within the interface. These extra windows permitted the user to briefly divert from normal program procedures to carry on a separate conversation with the application in a separate window. These separate windows became known as dialog boxes (or dialogs), and they have been implemented in every GUI available today, including Java.

GUIDELINE

Use dialogs only for actions that deviate from the primary task flow. Any dialog pauses the interaction of an application with the user. Dialogs should *ideally* be designed such that they could be ignored altogether, without disrupting the user's ability to complete their job. This implies that it is best to minimize the use of dialogs and emphasize direct manipulation within the UI design.

Dialog box implementation with AWT is limited to creating a simple window which presents a blank panel on which the developer must construct the desired components. Where possible, AWT also provides peer classes to map operating-system-specific operations onto a Java class. For example, on the Windows platform, Java provides a FileDialog class supplying a link to the standard native file dialog. Though AWT's support of dialogs is adequate for most purposes, it lacks the completeness demanded by many developers.

In this chapter, we will examine the dialog support implemented by Swing. Some of these classes will overlap those currently available in AWT, but Swing improves on these and provides many prewritten specialty dialogs that you can reuse in your own applications. Figure 8.1 shows the set of Swing classes that we will discuss in this chapter.

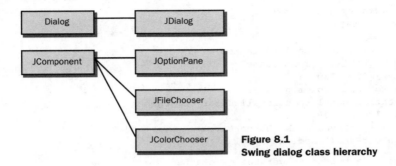

Figure 8.1
Swing dialog class hierarchy

8.1 Simple dialogs

The first class we will examine is the one used to create simple dialogs. The JDialog component operates much like JFrame—it creates a window possessing a title bar, control menu, and other embellishments familiar to most users. Like JFrame, JDialog also implements an instance of JContentPane on which other components and panels are added (as well as the other specialized panes described in our coverage of JFrame, for example, JRootPane, JGlassPane, JLayeredPane, and so on).

Let's start by taking a look at a basic JDialog example. In this example, we will create an application frame containing a single button which, when clicked, creates a new instance of a JDialog-based dialog box. Listing 8.1A contains the source code for the main frame, and it is the same code that will be implemented in each of the examples in this chapter.

```
// Imports
import java.awt.*;
import java.awt.event.*;
import com.sun.java.swing.*;

class TestFrame
        extends          JFrame
        implements       ActionListener
{
    // Instance attributes used in this example
    private JPanel  topPanel;
    private JButton buttonDialog;
```

Listing 8.1A   Main application frame source code

```java
// Constructor of main frame
public TestFrame()
{
    // Set the frame characteristics
    setTitle( "Dialog Test Frame" );
    setSize( 310, 130 );
    setBackground( Color.gray );
    // Create a panel to hold all other components
    topPanel = new JPanel();
    topPanel.setLayout( new BorderLayout() );
    getContentPane().add( topPanel );

    // Create a button to get things started
    buttonDialog = new JButton( "Open Dialog" );
    topPanel.add( buttonDialog, BorderLayout.CENTER );

    // Add an action listener to listen for button clicks
    buttonDialog.addActionListener( this );
}

// ActionListener handler to listen for button clicks
// within this application frame
public void actionPerformed( ActionEvent event )
{
    // Display a message on the console
    System.out.println( event );

    // Create an instance of the test dialog
    TestDialog testDialog = new TestDialog( this );
    testDialog.setVisible( true );
}

// Main entry point for this example
public static void main( String args[] )
{
    // Create an instance of the test application
    TestFrame mainFrame = new TestFrame();
    mainFrame.setVisible( true );
}
}
```

Listing 8.1A   Main application frame source code (continued)

Listing 8.1B contains the code that implements that actual dialog box. It creates a new class, TestDialog, derived from the Swing JDialog class, and it only implements a scrollable text area loaded with a source file. Notice that the dialog contains its own title and can be resized and repositioned independently of its parent frame.

```java
// Imports
import java.io.*;
import java.awt.*;
import java.awt.event.*;
import com.sun.java.swing.*;

class TestDialog
      extends JDialog
  {
    // Instance attributes used in this dialog
    private JFrame        parentFrame;
    private JScrollPane   scrollPane1;

    // Dialog constructor
    public TestDialog( JFrame parentFrame )
    {
        // Make sure we call the parent
        super( parentFrame );
        // Save the owner frame in case we need it later
        this.parentFrame = parentFrame;

        // Set the characteristics for this dialog instance
        setTitle( "Test Dialog" );
        setSize( 200, 200 );
        setDefaultCloseOperation( DISPOSE_ON_CLOSE );

        // Create a panel for the components
        JPanel topPanel = new JPanel();
        topPanel.setLayout( new BorderLayout() );
        getContentPane().add( topPanel );

        // Populate the panel with something the user
        // can play with
        CreateTopPane( topPanel );
    }

    private void CreateTopPane( JPanel topPanel )
    {
        // Create a text area
        JTextArea area = new JTextArea();

        // Load a file into the text area, catching any exceptions
        try {
            FileReader fileStream = new FileReader( "TestFrame.java" );
            area.read( fileStream, "TestFrame.java" );
        }
        catch( FileNotFoundException e )
```

Listing 8.1B   Simple dialog source code

```
        {
            System.out.println( "File not found" );
        }
        catch( IOException e )
        {
            System.out.println( "IOException occurred" );
        }

        // Create the scrolling pane for the text area
        scrollPane1 = new JScrollPane();
        scrollPane1.getViewport().add( area );
        topPanel.add( scrollPane1, BorderLayout.CENTER );
    }
}
```

Listing 8.1B   Simple dialog source code (continued)

When you execute the examples in listings 8.1A and 8.1B, you will be presented with the basic frame containing the Open Dialog button. If you click this button, a new instance of the TestDialog class is created and displayed. There is a subtlety in this example, however.

Click the main frame's button two or three times and note the effect—each time the button is pressed, a new, independent dialog instance appears. The main frame still responds to each user input, as do each of the dialog instances that have been created. The result of this example is shown in figure 8.2.

8.1.1   Handling the close operation

Listing 8.1B contains one line of code that you may not have seen before, so it deserves a bit of explanation:

```
setDefaultCloseOperation( DISPOSE_ON_CLOSE );
```

This line of code controls how the window reacts to the user's request to close it. By default, the window will be hidden if the user closes it, which is unacceptable in our example; so, by using the setDefaultCloseOperation() method, the code notifies the dialog that the dialog will be discarded by calling its dispose() method. We could also configure the dialog to do nothing on close, in which case, we would need to supply a WindowListener within our source code. See the description of the class WindowConstants in the online Swing documentation for more details on the closure options supported.

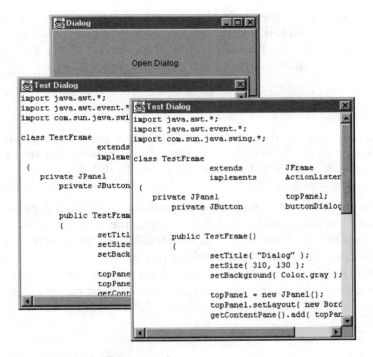

Figure 8.2 Simple dialog example

8.1.2 Modal vs. nonmodal dialogs

The simple example shown in figure 8.2 allowed the user to create an unlimited number of dialogs, while still providing independent control of the main frame of the application. This type of dialog box is referred to as *nonmodal* because each instance operates on its own, disregarding anything else that the user might be doing to the application.

GUIDELINE

Use modal dialogs to stop the application until the user decides to either choose an action or cancel the dialog.

Use nonmodal dialogs to allow for continuing actions to the application while the dialog waits for user input.

The JDialog class also supports modal operation, whereby only a single dialog box instance can be created, and, while it is active, its parent (TestFrame in our case) ignores further input from the user. To control the modality of the dialog, Swing supplies the `setModal()` method, which can be used as follows:

```
TestDialog.setModal( true );
```

 You can also assign the modality of a dialog box while it is being constructed, eliminating one line of source code from your application. See the list of constructors for more detail on constructing modal dialogs.

Whether you implement a dialog box as modal or nonmodal depends on the specific situation in which it will be used. For example, there would be no benefit in implementing your file save/load dialogs as nonmodal, since this would greatly confuse the user (because he or she could continue to make changes to the data being saved while the dialog box is active). However, there may be some merit to implementing a dialog box to perform string searches as nonmodal because it allows the user to search for multiple strings simultaneously.

 GUIDELINE Use appropriate terminating buttons and proper terminology in modal dialogs. Always place both OK and Cancel functionality on modal dialogs. The former confirms the action specified in the dialog, and the second cancels the action in the dialog; both actions terminate the dialog. Try to use affirmative terms in modal dialogs and avoid the word Cancel in a modal dialog as the OK and Cancel buttons now become ambiguous.

8.1.3 A more advanced JDialog example

The example shown in listing 8.1A and 8.1B helps to demonstrate the use of a JDialog instance, but it is quite impractical, so, we should take a little time to examine something a bit more advanced. In this example, we will create a dialog box which implements a tabbed pane with three pages, and, for effect, we will also add a toolbar. Note that none of these user interface components is actually active because this example does not provide any action listeners to handle UI events.

Though I told you this would be a more advanced example of a dialog, it is really more an example of enhanced Swing features. The JDialog class is purposely simple to use, so, instead of attempting to complicate JDialog, I opted to demonstrate the flexibility of Swing dialog boxes. Listing 8.2 contains source code that has been reused from previous examples in this book, but using the code within an instance of JDialog, instead of JFrame.

```java
// Imports
import java.io.*;
import java.awt.*;
import java.awt.event.*;
import com.sun.java.swing.*;

class TestDialog
        extends     JDialog
        implements ActionListener
{
    // Instance attributes used in this dialog
    private JFrame          parentFrame;
    private JButton         buttonCopy;
    private JButton         buttonCut;
    private JButton         buttonPaste;
    private JTabbedPane     tabbedPane;
    private JPanel          panel1;
    private JPanel          panel2;
    private JPanel          panel3;

    // Dialog constructor
    public TestDialog( JFrame parentFrame )
    {
        // Make sure we call the parent
        super( parentFrame, true );

        // Save the owner frame in case we need it later
        this.parentFrame = parentFrame;

        // Set the characteristics for this dialog instance
        setTitle( "Advanced Test Dialog" );
        setSize( 400, 300 );
        setDefaultCloseOperation( DISPOSE_ON_CLOSE );

        // Create a panel for the components
        JPanel topPanel = new JPanel();
        topPanel.setLayout( new BorderLayout() );
        getContentPane().add( topPanel );

        // Create an instance of a toolbar
        CreateToolbar( topPanel );
```

Listing 8.2   Advanced dialog source code

```
        // Create a tabbed pane containing some pages
        CreateTabbedPane( topPanel );
    }

    // This method creates a toolbar for the dialog panel
    private void CreateToolbar( JPanel topPanel )
    {
        // Create a new toolbar
        JToolBar myToolbar = new JToolBar();
        topPanel.add( myToolbar, BorderLayout.NORTH );

        // Add some buttons to the toolbar
        buttonCopy = addToolbarButton( myToolbar, true, null,
                    "copy", "Copy selection to the clipboard" );
        buttonCut = addToolbarButton( myToolbar, true, null,
                    "cut", "Cut selection to the clipboard" );
        buttonPaste = addToolbarButton( myToolbar, true, null,
                    "paste", "Paste selection from the clipboard" );
    }

    // This method creates a tabbed pane with three pages
    private void CreateTabbedPane( JPanel topPanel )
    {
        // Create the tab pages
        CreatePage1();
        CreatePage2();
        CreatePage3();

        // Create a tabbed pane
        tabbedPane = new JTabbedPane();
        tabbedPane.addTab( "Page 1", panel1 );
        tabbedPane.addTab( "Page 2", panel2 );
        tabbedPane.addTab( "Page 3", panel3 );
        topPanel.add( tabbedPane, BorderLayout.CENTER );
    }

    public void CreatePage1()
    {
        panel1 = new JPanel();
        panel1.setLayout( null );

        JLabel label1 = new JLabel( "Username:" );
        label1.setBounds( 10, 15, 150, 20 );
        panel1.add( label1 );

        JTextField field = new JTextField();
        field.setBounds( 10, 35, 150, 20 );
        panel1.add( field );
```

Listing 8.2   Advanced dialog source code (continued)

```
        JLabel label2 = new JLabel( "Password:" );
        label2.setBounds( 10, 60, 150, 20 );
        panel1.add( label2 );

        JPasswordField fieldPass = new JPasswordField();
        fieldPass.setBounds( 10, 80, 150, 20 );
        panel1.add( fieldPass );
    }

    public void CreatePage2()
    {
        panel2 = new JPanel();
        panel2.setLayout( new BorderLayout() );

        panel2.add( new JButton( "North" ), BorderLayout.NORTH );
        panel2.add( new JButton( "South" ), BorderLayout.SOUTH );
        panel2.add( new JButton( "East" ), BorderLayout.EAST );
        panel2.add( new JButton( "West" ), BorderLayout.WEST );
        panel2.add( new JButton( "Center" ), BorderLayout.CENTER );
    }

    public void CreatePage3()
    {
        panel3 = new JPanel();
        panel3.setLayout( new GridLayout( 3, 2 ) );
        panel3.add( new JLabel( "Field 1:" ) );
        panel3.add( new TextArea() );
        panel3.add( new JLabel( "Field 2:" ) );
        panel3.add( new TextArea() );
        panel3.add( new JLabel( "Field 3:" ) );
        panel3.add( new TextArea() );
    }

    // Helper method to create new toolbar buttons
    public JButton addToolbarButton( JToolBar toolBar,
                        boolean bUseImage, String sButtonText,
                                String sButton, String sToolHelp )
    {
        JButton b;

        // Create a new button
        if( bUseImage )
            b = new JButton( new ImageIcon( sButton + ".gif" ) );
        else
            b = (JButton)toolBar.add( new JButton() );

        // Add the button to the toolbar
        toolBar.add( b );
```

Listing 8.2 Advanced dialog source code (continued)

```
        // Add optional button text
    if( sButtonText != null )
        b.setText( sButtonText );
    else
    {
        // Only a graphic, so make the button smaller
        b.setMargin( new Insets( 0, 0, 0, 0 ) );
    }

    // Add optional tool tip help
    if( sToolHelp != null )
        b.setToolTipText( sToolHelp );

    // Make sure this button sends a message when the
    // user clicks it
    b.setActionCommand( "Toolbar:" + sButton );
    b.addActionListener( this );

    return b;
}

public void actionPerformed( ActionEvent event )
{
    // Add action handling code here
    System.out.println( event );
}
}
```

Listing 8.2   Advanced dialog source code (continued)

GUIDELINE **Use appropriate terminating buttons and multiple Undos for nonmodal dialogs.** Non-modal dialogs are less frequently used than modal dialogs, but do serve a purpose because they allow the application to regain focus without forcing the user to terminate the dialog. Since actions on nonmodal dialogs are immediate, the terminating buttons should have OK and Close functionality. This will distinguish them from the meaning of a Cancel when multiple action have already been applied. If you can, also offer multiple Undo features somewhere in the application. Consider visually differentiating the nonmodal dialog from its modal counterparts, since the user can easily confuse them with one another.

Figure 8.3 shows the output of our advanced sample. Notice that this dialog contains a toolbar, which may be an attribute you were not expecting. We could just

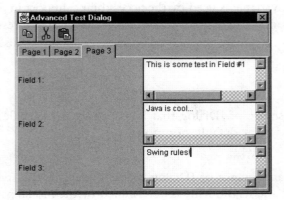

Figure 8.3
Advanced dialog output

as easily attach a menu to the dialog, a feature that might amaze some AWT developers. The example also provides a tabbed pane containing three pages using the same code as listing 3.3 from chapter 3.

GUIDELINE

When you can, avoid cascading modal dialogs. Rather than forcing the user to respond to many modal dialogs before continuing with their task, consider placing the UI on a single modal dialog (if real estate permits). Advanced functions, infrequently used features, or critical confirmations are the exceptions to this suggestion. Use ellipses to indicate any text-based control that invokes a modal dialog (for example, "Advanced...").

8.1.4 JDialog variables

```
protected boolean realModal
```

This variable contains the current modality flag for the dialog. This is independent of any similar support in its parent, the AWT Dialog class.

```
protected JRootPane rootPane
```

This variable contains a reference to the root pane of the dialog. Each dialog instance supports a single component (and an instance of JRootPane) into which all other components are added.

```
protected AccessibleContext accessibleContext
```

The `accessibleContext` variable is used by the accessibility support in Swing. It contains a handle to the context that holds information about the access supported by this instance.

8.1.5 JDialog constructors

```
public JDialog(Frame parent)
```

This constructor creates an instance of JDialog that is owned by the specified parent. The dialog has no title and is, by default, nonmodal.

```
public JDialog( Frame parent, boolean modal )
```

This constructor creates an instance of JDialog that is owned by the specified parent. The dialog has no title, and its modality is determined by the modal parameter supplied by the caller.

```
public JDialog( Frame parent, String title )
```

This constructor creates an instance of JDialog that is owned by the specified parent instance and has the title supplied by the caller.

```
public JDialog( Frame parent, String title, boolean modal )
```

This constructor creates an instance of JDialog that is owned by the specified parent instance and has the title supplied by the caller. The modality of the instance is controlled by the specified modal value.

8.1.6 JDialog significant method groupings

```
public void setModal(boolean newValue)
public boolean isModal()
```

This group of methods controls and determines the current modality of the dialog box instance. These methods override methods of the same name within the AWT Dialog class.

```
public void setContentPane(Container content)
public Container getContentPane()
public void setLayeredPane(JLayeredPane layered)
public JLayeredPane getLayeredPane()
public void setGlassPane(Component glass)
public Component getGlassPane()
protected void setRootPane(JRootPane root)
public JRootPane getRootPane()
```

This group of methods manages all of the predefined panes associated with the dialog instance. All components added to a dialog are actually added to the content pane, which differs from the way AWT manages dialog components.

```
public void setDefaultCloseOperation(int operation)
public int getDefaultCloseOperation()
```

This method group determines the reaction the dialog instance has to a user request to close. The following list describes the options available:

- DO_NOTHING_ON_CLOSE This requires the dialog to provide a `Window-`
  `dowListener` to handle the `windowClosing()` operation.
- HIDE_ON_CLOSE   The dialog is automatically hidden during a close operation.
- DISPOSE_ON_CLOSE   The dialog is automatically hidden and disposed of during a close operation.

8.2   Option dialogs

One of the biggest disadvantages of Java, from a Microsoft Windows developer's perspective, has been the absence of a dialog box that can be used to display generic messages. Windows programmers have grown accustomed to the `Message-` `Box` API to quickly display simple feedback to the user. With standard Java and AWT, creating a component as simple as a `MessageBox` involves a significant amount of coding effort.

Fortunately, Swing now offers Java user interface developers an alternative to address this problem. The JOptionPane class is designed to simplify the process of popping up information to the user, and, in fact, this component goes beyond what the `MessageBox` API offers Windows developers. At first, this class appears quite complex (due to the number of methods it provides), so, we will examine it more closely in this section. As you will see, the JOptionPane class is both invaluable and easy to use.

The basic appearance of a JOptionPane dialog is fairly consistent, though, ultimately, the look-and-feel is responsible for the results displayed. Figure 8.4 illustrates the standard appearance of an option pane, showing its four basic components.

The icon area displays an icon, which is completely under programmer control. A default platform-dependent icon is assigned, depending on the type of message being displayed. Similarly, the button area is populated with one or more

Figure 8.4
Anatomy of a JOptionPane dialog

buttons (Yes, No, OK, Cancel, and so on) according to an option type specified by the developer the option type of the dialog controls which buttons are displayed in the button area. The message area within the JOptionPane instance shows a simple text string, which is usually some form of warning or error message. Finally, the input area content is controlled by the setWantsInput() method within JOption-Pane, allowing the presence of a data entry field that requires the user to enter some text.

This is enough information to start examining some sample code for JOption-Pane. This example, with source code shown in listing 8.3, creates a set of JOption-Pane instances for the predefined message types.

```
// Imports
import java.awt.*;
import java.awt.event.*;
import com.sun.java.swing.*;

class TestFrame
        extends        JFrame
        implements     ActionListener
{
    // Instance attributes used in this example
    private JPanel      topPanel;
    private JButton     buttonError;
    private JButton     buttonWarning;
    private JButton     buttonInfo;
    private JButton     buttonQuestion;
    private JButton     buttonPlain;
```

Listing 8.3   JOptionPane sample source code

```
    // Constructor of main frame
    public TestFrame()
    {
        // Set the frame characteristics
        setTitle( "Dialog Test Frame" );
        setSize( 310, 130 );
        setBackground( Color.gray );

        // Create a panel to hold all other components
        topPanel = new JPanel();
        topPanel.setLayout( new FlowLayout() );
        getContentPane().add( topPanel );

        // Create a button for each message type
        buttonError = new JButton( "Error" );
        topPanel.add( buttonError );
        buttonWarning = new JButton( "Warning" );
        topPanel.add( buttonWarning );
        buttonInfo = new JButton( "Informational" );
        topPanel.add( buttonInfo );
        buttonQuestion = new JButton( "Question" );
        topPanel.add( buttonQuestion );
        buttonPlain = new JButton( "Plain" );
        topPanel.add( buttonPlain );

        // Add an action listener to listen for button clicks
        buttonError.addActionListener( this );
        buttonWarning.addActionListener( this );
        buttonInfo.addActionListener( this );
        buttonQuestion.addActionListener( this );
        buttonPlain.addActionListener( this );
    }

    // ActionListener handler to listen for button clicks
    // within this application frame
    public void actionPerformed( ActionEvent event )
    {
        // Display a message on the console
        System.out.println( event );

        if( event.getSource() == buttonError )
        {
            JOptionPane dialog = new JOptionPane();
            dialog.showMessageDialog( this, "This is an error",
                    "Error", JOptionPane.ERROR_MESSAGE );
        }
```

Listing 8.3   JOptionPane sample source code (continued)

```
        else if( event.getSource() == buttonWarning )
        {
            Object[] possibleValues = { "First", "Second", "Third" };
            JOptionPane dialog = new JOptionPane();
            Object selectedValue = dialog.showInputDialog( this,
                    "This is a warning",
                    "Warning", JOptionPane.WARNING_MESSAGE,
                    null, possibleValues, possibleValues[0] );
        }
        else if( event.getSource() == buttonInfo )
        {
            JOptionPane dialog = new JOptionPane();
            dialog.showConfirmDialog( this,
                    "This is an informational message",
                    "Information", JOptionPane.CANCEL_OPTION,
                    JOptionPane.INFORMATION_MESSAGE, null );
        }
        else if( event.getSource() == buttonQuestion )
        {
            JOptionPane dialog = new JOptionPane();
            dialog.showConfirmDialog( this, "Is this a question?",
                    "Question", JOptionPane.YES_NO_OPTION,
                    JOptionPane.QUESTION_MESSAGE, null );
        }
        else if( event.getSource() == buttonPlain )
        {
            JOptionPane dialog = new JOptionPane();
            dialog.showConfirmDialog( this, "This is a plain message",
                    "Plain", JOptionPane.DEFAULT_OPTION,
                    JOptionPane.PLAIN_MESSAGE, null );
        }
    }

    // Main entry point for this example
    public static void main( String args[] )
    {
        // Create an instance of the test application
        TestFrame mainFrame = new TestFrame();
        mainFrame.setVisible( true );
    }
}
```

Listing 8.3   JOptionPane sample source code (continued)

If the code from listing 8.3 is compiled and executed, you will see results resembling those shown in figure 8.5, which shows various types of option panes

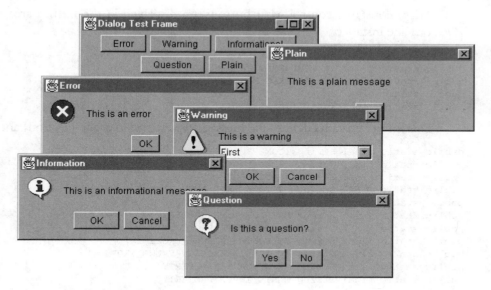

Figure 8.5   JOptionPane sample output

available. Notice the warning option pane containing a combo box control that allows the user to select information and return this information to the owner of the option pane instance.

8.2.1   JOptionPane constants

```
public static final Object UNINITIALIZED_VALUE
```

This constant contains an uninitialized value used as the initial value returned from the input field if the user has not yet made a selection.

```
public static final int DEFAULT_OPTION
public static final int YES_NO_OPTION
public static final int YES_NO_CANCEL_OPTION
public static final int OK_CANCEL_OPTION
public static final int YES_OPTION
public static final int NO_OPTION
public static final int CANCEL_OPTION
public static final int OK_OPTION
public static final int CLOSED_OPTION
```

These constants control what buttons are displayed in the button area of the JOptionPane instance.

```
public static final int ERROR_MESSAGE
public static final int INFORMATION_MESSAGE
public static final int WARNING_MESSAGE
public static final int QUESTION_MESSAGE
public static final int PLAIN_MESSAGE
```

This list of constants defines the message type support by the JOptionPane class.

```
public static final String ICON_PROPERTY
public static final String MESSAGE_PROPERTY
public static final String VALUE_PROPERTY
public static final String OPTIONS_PROPERTY
public static final String INITIAL_VALUE_PROPERTY
public static final String MESSAGE_TYPE_PROPERTY
public static final String OPTION_TYPE_PROPERTY
public static final String SELECTION_VALUES_PROPERTY
public static final String INITIAL_SELECTION_VALUE_PROPERTY
public static final String INPUT_VALUE_PROPERTY
public static final String WANTS_INPUT_PROPERTY
```

These constants hold property name strings for the properties of the JOption-Pane instance. These values are used to reference specific option pane properties.

8.2.2 JOptionPane variables

```
protected static Frame sharedFrame
```

This variable is used to simplify access to static methods while creating a frame.

```
protected transient Icon icon
```

This transient variable holds an instance of the icon displayed within the option pane.

```
protected transient Object message
```

This message variable contains the message that is displayed in the message area of the option pane. This is usually a string type, but this variable can contain other data types, as well.

```
protected transient Object options[]
```

This variable contains an array of objects used in the optional selection list (combo box) in the input area of the option pane.

```
protected transient Object initialValue
```

This variable holds the initial value selected in the selection list within the option pane. If unspecified, this variable has the value UNINITIALIZED_VALUE.

```
protected int messageType
```

This variable holds the message type specified for the option pane. See the list of message types shown in the section on JOptionPane Constants.

```
protected int optionType
```

The `optionType` variable contains the option value specified for this option pane instance. See the list of predefined option types shown in the section on JOptionPane Constants.

```
protected transient Object value
```

This variable holds the value of the item currently selected in the option pane's selection list. It will contain either a valid option, UNINITIALIZED_VALUE, or a null value.

```
protected transient Object selectionValues[]
```

This array of objects contains the values that the user can choose from within the selection list. The current look-and-feel will provide the UI component from which the values can be chosen.

```
protected transient Object inputValue
```

This variable contains the value that the user has input in the input area of the option pane.

```
protected transient Object initialSelectionValue
```

The `initialSelectionValue` variable contains the initial value to select from the `selectionValues[]` array.

```
protected boolean wantsInput
```

If this boolean value is true, a UI component will be provided to allow the user to supply input.

8.2.3 JOptionPane constructors

```
public JOptionPane()
```

This constructor creates a simple instance of JOptionPane.

```
public JOptionPane( Object message )
```

This constructor creates a simple instance of JOptionPane containing the specified message within its message area.

```
public JOptionPane( Object message, int messageType )
```

This constructor creates a simple instance of JOptionPane containing the specified message within its message area, and implementing the supplied message type.

```
public JOptionPane( Object message, int messageType, int optionType )
```

This constructor creates a simple instance of JOptionPane containing the specified message within its message area and implementing the supplied message and option types.

```
public JOptionPane( Object message, int messageType,
                    int optionType, Icon icon )
```

This constructor creates a simple instance of JOptionPane containing the specified message within its message area, and implementing the supplied message and option types. The icon's parameter provides a programmer specified icon image to be displayed within the option pane.

```
public JOptionPane( Object message, int messageType, int optionType,
                    Icon icon, Object options[] )
```

This constructor creates a simple instance of JOptionPane containing the specified message within its message area and implementing the supplied message and option types. The icon's parameter provides a programmer specified icon image to be displayed within the option pane. The options array holds a list of options that will be inserted into the instance's input area.

```
public JOptionPane( Object message, int messageType, int optionType,
                    Icon icon, Object options[], Object initialValue )
```

This constructor creates a simple instance of JOptionPane containing the specified message within its message area, and implementing the supplied message and option types. The icon's parameter provides a programmer specified icon image to be displayed within the option pane. The options array holds a list of options that will be inserted into the instance's input area, and the supplied `initialValue` determines the list item initially selected.

8.2.4 JOptionPane significant method groupings

```
public static String showInputDialog( Object message )
public static String showInputDialog( Component parentComponent,
```

```
                              Object message )
public static String showInputDialog( Component parentComponent,
            Object message, String title, int messageType )
public static Object showInputDialog( Component parentComponent,
            Object message, String title, int messageType,
            Icon icon, Object selectionValues[],
            Object initialSelectionValue )
public static String showInternalInputDialog(
            Component parentComponent, Object message )
public static String showInternalInputDialog(
            Component parentComponent, Object message,
            String title, int messageType)
public static Object showInternalInputDialog(
            Component parentComponent, Object message,
            String title, int messageType,
            Icon icon, Object selectionValues[],
            Object initialSelectionValue )
```

The methods in this group create and display an option pane instance that accepts input from the user. Input can come from a default input component, such as a text field, or from a combo box.

```
public static void showMessageDialog( Component parentComponent,
                            Object message )
public static void showMessageDialog( Component parentComponent,
            Object message, String title, int messageType )
public static void showMessageDialog(Component parentComponent,
            Object message, String title, int messageType,
                        Icon icon)
public static void showInternalMessageDialog(
                Component parentComponent, Object message )
public static void showInternalMessageDialog(
                Component parentComponent, Object message,
                        String title, int messageType )
public static void showInternalMessageDialog(
                Component parentComponent, Object message,
                String title, int messageType, Icon icon )
```

This group of methods displays instances of simple message dialog boxes. They can contain an icon and message text, but do not accept input from the user. This type of option pane is typically used to display status information to the user, usually requiring only an OK acknowledgement.

```
public static int showConfirmDialog( Component parentComponent,
                            Object message )
public static int showConfirmDialog( Component parentComponent,
            Object message, String title, int optionType )
```

```
public static int showConfirmDialog( Component parentComponent,
                Object message, String title, int optionType,
                            int messageType )
public static int showConfirmDialog( Component parentComponent,
                Object message, String title, int optionType,
                            int messageType, Icon icon )
public static int showInternalConfirmDialog(
                Component parentComponent, Object message )
public static int showInternalConfirmDialog(
                Component parentComponent, Object message,
                String title, int optionType )
public static int showInternalConfirmDialog(
                Component parentComponent, Object message,
                String title, int optionType, int messageType )
public static int showInternalConfirmDialog(
                Component parentComponent, Object message,
                String title, int optionType, int messageType,
                Icon icon )
```

The methods in this group create and display instances of a JOptionPane to confirm user selections. This type of option pane is generally used to prompt the user to answer a Yes or No type question (also, OK or Cancel).

```
public static int showOptionDialog( Component parentComponent,
                Object message, String title, int optionType,
                int messageType, Icon icon, Object options[],
                            Object initialValue )
public static int showInternalOptionDialog(
                Component parentComponent, Object message,
                String title, int optionType, int messageType,
                Icon icon, Object options[],
                Object initialValue )
```

The two methods in this group display option panes containing user selectable options. This is typically useful in situations where the user will select one of several options from a combo box.

```
public JDialog createDialog( Component parentComponent, String title )
```

This method creates an instance of a JDialog that wraps the current option pane instance and positions the dialog such that it is centered on the specified component.

```
public JInternalFrame createInternalFrame(
                Component parentComponent, String title )
public static Frame getFrameForComponent( Component parentComponent )
public static JDesktopPane getDesktopPaneForComponent(
```

```
                         Component parentComponent )
public static void setRootFrame( Frame newRootFrame )
public static Frame getRootFrame()
```

This group of methods handles access to frames supporting the JOptionPane instance. They can be used to determine the owner frame, as well as the desktop positioning for the component that owns this option pane instance.

```
public void setMessage( Object newMessage )
public Object getMessage()
public void setIcon( Icon newIcon )
public Icon getIcon()
public void setValue( Object newValue )
public Object getValue()
public void setOptions( Object newOptions[] )
public Object[] getOptions()
public void setInitialValue( Object newInitialValue )
public Object getInitialValue()
public void setMessageType( int newType )
public int getMessageType()
public void setOptionType( int newType )
public int getOptionType()
public void setSelectionValues( Object newValues[] )
public Object[] getSelectionValues()
public void setInitialSelectionValue( Object newValue )
public Object getInitialSelectionValue()
public void setInputValue( Object newValue )
public Object getInputValue()
public void selectInitialValue()
```

This group of methods is used to control and access the various component areas within the option pane. For example, the icon can be controlled, or option values can be loaded into the input area, and subsequent selections by the user can be detected and returned.

```
public void setWantsInput( boolean newValue )
public boolean getWantsInput()
```

These methods control and determine whether the user needs to input some information. If so, the option pane will provide a component into which the user can either type text, or from which he or she can select one of several options.

8.3   The color chooser

In an effort to standardize the general feel of Java applications, the folks at Sun added some common dialog classes to Swing. Not only are these classes easy to use, they can significantly improve the appearance of your applications and, further, provide a standard user interface across all operating system platforms that support Java language. The result of Sun's effort is a collection of software components that you can plug into an application with a minimum of coding effort and time.

The first of the common dialogs that we will examine is the color chooser, implemented in Swing as the JColorChooser class. This class offers two typical modes of operation. First, it can be used as an independent dialog, returning the user's color selection to the caller. The second, and most distinguishing aspect, is its ability to operate as a complex component which can be added to a frame that already exists. In this section, we will examine both of these techniques.

8.3.1   The JColorChooser dialog

The simpler form of JColorChooser implementation is that of an independent dialog. In this configuration, the color chooser creates its own independent dialog box, which minimizes the work required on your part. With just a few lines of code, you can implement color selection and quickly attach it to your application.

```
// Imports
import java.awt.*;
import java.awt.event.*;
import com.sun.java.swing.*;
import com.sun.java.swing.preview.*;

class TestFrame
       extends        JFrame
       implements     ActionListener
{
    // Instance attributes used in this example
    private JPanel     topPanel;
    private JButton    buttonFile;

    // Constructor of main frame
    public TestFrame()
    {
        // Set the frame characteristics
```

Listing 8.4   JColorChooser dialog source code

```
        setTitle( "Color Chooser Dialog Example" );
        setSize( 380, 120 );
        setBackground( Color.gray );

        // Create a panel to hold all other components
        topPanel = new JPanel();
        topPanel.setLayout( new FlowLayout() );
        getContentPane().add( topPanel );

        // Create a button for each message type
        buttonFile = new JButton( "Select Color" );
        topPanel.add( buttonFile );
        // add an action listener to listen for button clicks
        buttonFile.addActionListener( this );
    }

    // ActionListener handler to listen for button clicks
    // within this application frame
    public void actionPerformed( ActionEvent event )
    {
        // Display a message on the console
        System.out.println( event );

        if( event.getSource() == buttonFile )
        {
            // Open a color chooser dialog and retrieve the color
            Color color = JColorChooser.showDialog( this,
                            "Select Color", Color.white );
        }
    }

    // Main entry point for this example
    public static void main( String args[] )
    {
        // Create an instance of the test application
        TestFrame mainFrame = new TestFrame();
        mainFrame.setVisible( true );
    }
}
```

Listing 8.4   JColorChooser dialog source code (continued)

Listing 8.4 shows the source code required to display a JColorChooser dialog and retrieve the user selected color values. Notice that most of the code in this application is simply there to support the application itself (such as, create the frame and button, intercept button events, and so on) The actual code we are interested in is limited to a single line of code:

```
// Open a color chooser dialog and retrieve the color
Color color = JColorChooser.showDialog( this,
                     "Select Color", Color.white );
```

Note that the `showDialog()` method in JColorChooser is static, so a formal instantiation of an object is not required—we can simply use the method, and Swing manages the object construction for us. The results of the simple application in listing 8.4 are shown in figure 8.6. Notice that the entire dialog box, including the buttons and their control logic, has been created automatically for us by Swing.

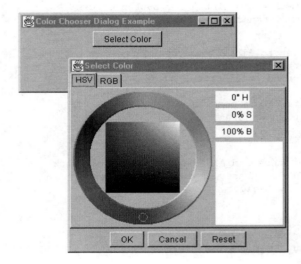

Figure 8.6
JColorChooser dialog output

FYI   The JColorChooser, when implemented as a dialog, creates three buttons: OK, Cancel, and Reset. Currently, there is no way to change the text on these buttons. If you are building internationalized applications, this can be a serious limitation because the color chooser buttons will display English text regardless of the locale or country code of the target platform. You will need to create your own JDialog instance, add JColorChooser as a component, and manage your own control buttons to allow localization of the button text. Note, however, that the HSB and RGB tags shown on the tabbed pane pages cannot be modified.

8.3.2 JColorChooser as a component

As noted in the introduction to this section, you are not limited to a self-contained dialog box to implement a JColorChooser. The JColorChooser can also be used in a complex component added to a dialog. For example, if you are a Microsoft Windows user, you will undoubtedly know about the Windows Color Chooser, which allows not only color-wheel selection, but also permits you to choose from one of a number of preconfigured color choices. The Swing JColorChooser class, as you now know, offers no such capability, but that does not prevent us from implementing a similar capability in a Java application.

So, here's an example that uses an instance of JColorChooser in conjunction with other Swing components in order to allow color selection from the pinwheel or from one of several hard coded color choices. Listing 8.5 contains all of the source code required to implement a JColorChooser component and several standard JButton instances for each of the preconfigured color choices. The JButton instances tap into the color chooser to set their specified color into the space allotted for the current color selection.

```
// Imports
import java.awt.*;
import java.awt.event.*;
import com.sun.java.swing.*;
import com.sun.java.swing.preview.*;

class TestFrame
        extends      JFrame
        implements ActionListener
{
    // Instance attributes used in this example
    private JPanel         topPanel;
    private JPanel         buttonPanel;
    private JColorChooser   chooser;
    private Button         buttonColor[];

    // Pre-configured colors for each button
    private int colors[][] =
    {
        { 255, 255, 255 },
        { 255, 0, 0 },
        { 0, 255, 0 },
        { 0, 0, 255 },
```

Listing 8.5 JColorChooser advanced example

```
            { 192, 192, 192 },
            { 128, 128, 128 },
            { 0, 0, 128 },
            { 0, 0, 0 }
    };

    // Constructor of main frame
    public TestFrame()
    {
        // Set the frame characteristics
        setTitle( "Advanced Color Chooser" );
        setSize( 380, 260 );
        setBackground( Color.gray );

        // Create a panel to hold all other components
        topPanel = new JPanel();
        topPanel.setLayout( new BorderLayout() );
        getContentPane().add( topPanel );

        // Create a color chooser component and add it
        // to the top panel
        chooser = new JColorChooser();
        topPanel.add( chooser, BorderLayout.CENTER );

        // Create a panel to hold color buttons
        buttonPanel = new JPanel();
        buttonPanel.setLayout( new GridLayout( 4, 2 ) );
        buttonPanel.setPreferredSize( new Dimension( 70, 180 ) );
        topPanel.add( buttonPanel, BorderLayout.WEST );

        // Create a button for each color
        buttonColor = new Button[8];
        for( int iCtr = 0; iCtr < 8; iCtr++ )
        {
            buttonColor[iCtr] = new Button();
            buttonColor[iCtr].setBackground( new Color(
                    colors[iCtr][0], colors[iCtr][1],
                    colors[iCtr][2] ) );
            buttonPanel.add( buttonColor[iCtr] );

            // Add an action listener to listen for button clicks
            buttonColor[iCtr].addActionListener( this );
        }
    }

    // ActionListener handler to listen for button clicks
    // within this application frame
```

Listing 8.5   JColorChooser advanced example (continued)

```
    public void actionPerformed( ActionEvent event )
    {
        // Display a message on the console
        System.out.println( event + ":" + chooser.COLOR_PROPERTY );

        // NOTE: This action handler will only receive events
        // from the color selection buttons. If other events
        // must be handled, the events will need to be fully
        // decoded.

        // Get the button instance that caused the event
        JButton button = (JButton)event.getSource();
        Color newColor = button.getBackground();

        // Set the current color selection in the chooser
        chooser.setColor( newColor );
    }

    // Main entry point for this example
    public static void main( String args[] )
    {
        // Create an instance of the test application
        TestFrame mainFrame = new TestFrame();
        mainFrame.setVisible( true );
    }
}
```

Listing 8.5   JColorChooser advanced example (continued)

First, the code in listing 8.5 creates an instance of JColorChooser, which is a complex Swing component. Then, the program creates an array of buttons, each with a specific preset background color. When a button is clicked, the action handler retrieves the button's background color and sends it to the color chooser, which, in turn, changes the current color selection.

The output of this code is shown in figure 8.7. The program creates a frame rather than a dialog, so there are no OK or Cancel buttons shown. You can easily modify this code to extend a JDialog instead, then add some buttons to create a complete color chooser dialog.

8.3.3   JColorChooser constants

```
public static final String COLOR_PROPERTY
```

This constant is of little use to most developers. It contains a string holding the color property name (the string "color").

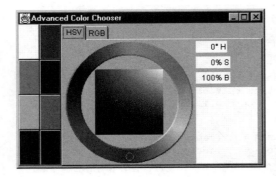

Figure 8.7
JColorChooser advanced program output

8.3.4 JColorChooser constructors

```
public JColorChooser()
```

This constructor creates an instance of a JColorChooser object. By default, the initial color selection value is white.

```
public JColorChooser( Color initialColor )
```

This constructor creates an instance of a JColorChooser object and sets the initial color selection to the specified `initialColor` value.

8.3.5 JColorChooser significant method groupings

```
public static Color showDialog( Component component,
                   String title, Color initialColor )
```

This method creates a modal dialog box containing an instance of a color chooser object. In addition, the dialog contains and supports an OK button to accept the current color selection, and a Cancel button to abort the selection. Finally, the dialog contains a reset button that will restore the current color selection to the value it had when the chooser object was created.

```
public static JDialog createDialog( Component c, String title,
        boolean modal, JColorChooser chooserPane,
        ActionListener okListener,
            ActionListener cancelListener )
```

This method is called by the `showDialog()` method to create a new dialog. However, if you require additional control over the dialog (including the ability to configure the dialog title, modality, action listeners for the buttons, and so on) you can call this method directly.

```
public Color getColor()
public void setColor( Color color )
public void setColor( int r, int g, int b )
public void setColor( int c )
```

This group of methods provides the capability to access and manage the current color selection from within the color chooser instance.

8.4   The file chooser

If you have previously used AWT, you may recall Sun's attempt to provide standard dialog boxes, including the file selection dialog in the FileDialog class. Unfortunately, the file selector dialog in AWT was implemented using a peer class mapped to the operating system's standard file selector (if available). Though the FileDialog class does allow Java applications to access files from the operating system, it suffers from some serious drawbacks.

If the operating system vendor does not supply a standard dialog, then AWT must provide one, which will undoubtedly differ from file selection dialogs in other applications. Also, if the operating system vendor elects to change or replace the API to access the standard dialog, your application may no longer work properly (until a new version of AWT is released). Finally, if your application uses a specific file extension to designate its files (for example, text files traditionally use *.TXT), there is no convenient way to add this type as the default file type in the standard file dialog.

Swing alleviates many of these problems by providing a new file selection dialog called JFileChooser. This class implements all of the functionality found in the AWT FileDialog class, but does so with a pure Java solution. This means that you, as a developer, have more access and more control over the operation of the class, and you are no longer at the mercy of an operating system vender's whims.

Listing 8.6 contains the source code to open a JFileChooser dialog and retrieve a file selection from the user. The example code dumps the file selection string and other interesting pieces of information into the Java console window. Figure 8.8 shows the result of running this code listing.

```
// Imports
import java.awt.*;
import java.awt.event.*;
import com.sun.java.swing.*;
```

Listing 8.6   JFileChooser example

```
class TestFrame
      extends        JFrame
      implements     ActionListener
{
   // Instance attributes used in this example
   private JPanel      topPanel;
   private JButton     buttonFile;

   // Constructor of main frame
   public TestFrame()
   {
      // Set the frame characteristics
      setTitle( "File Chooser Application" );
      setSize( 300, 100 );
      setBackground( Color.gray );

      // Create a panel to hold all other components
      topPanel = new JPanel();
```

Listing 8.6   JFileChooser example (continued)

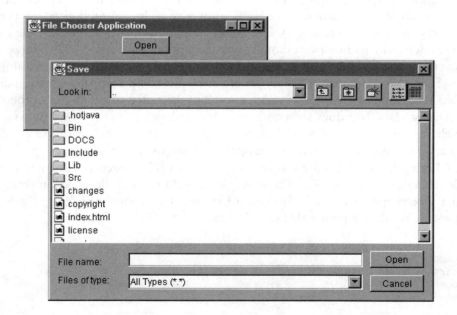

Figure 8.8   JFileChooser program output

```
        topPanel.setLayout( new FlowLayout() );
        getContentPane().add( topPanel );

        // Create a button to start the dialog
        buttonFile = new JButton( "Open" );
        topPanel.add( buttonFile );
        buttonFile.addActionListener( this );
    }

    // ActionListener handler to listen for button clicks
    // within this application frame
    public void actionPerformed( ActionEvent event )
    {
        if( event.getSource() == buttonFile )
        {
            // Create an instance of the file chooser dialog
            JFileChooser fileChooser = new JFileChooser();

            // Configure some file type parameters
            fileChooser.addChooseableFileType(
                    "Text Files (*.txt)", "*.txt", null );
            fileChooser.addChooseableFileType(
                    "Word Files (*.doc)", "*.doc", null );
            fileChooser.addChooseableFileType(
                    "My Files (*.my)", "*.my", null );

            // Do some personalized text changes
            fileChooser.setOkayTitle( "Yep!" );
            fileChooser.setCancelTitle( "No way!" );

            // Get a selection from the user
            int returnValue = fileChooser.showDialog( null );
            if( returnValue == 0 )  // User selected OK
            {
                // Figure out what file the user selected
                TypedFile selectedFile = fileChooser.getSelectedFile();
                String selectedFileString = selectedFile.toString();
                System.out.println( "Selected File = "
                                        + selectedFileString );
            }
            else
            {
                System.out.println( "User cancelled operation" );
            }
        }
    }
}
```

Listing 8.6   JFileChooser example (continued)

```
// Main entry point for this example
public static void main( String args[] )
{
    // Create an instance of the test application
    TestFrame mainFrame = new TestFrame();
    mainFrame.setVisible( true );
}
}
```

Listing 8.6   JFileChooser example (continued)

8.4.1   JFileChooser variables

```
protected Vector choosableTypes
```

This variable contains a vectored array of choosable file types. These items are shown in the combo box at the bottom of the file chooser dialog.

```
protected String typesTitle
protected String locationTitle
protected String okayTitle
protected String cancelTitle
protected static String DefaultPrompt
protected static String DefaultTypesTitle
protected static String DefaultLocationTitle
protected static String DefaultOkayTitle
protected static String DefaultCancelTitle
```

This group of variables holds strings pertinent to the file chooser dialog. Each of the titles and labels within the file chooser is under program control, allowing the programmer to change the displayed text at any time.

```
protected String okayCommand
protected String cancelCommand
protected static String DefaultOkayCommand
protected static String DefaultCancelCommand
```

These variables hold the strings associated with action commands for the OK and Cancel operations. The action strings are under programmer control and can be changed if these actions are being handled by the application.

```
protected JDirectoryPane directoryPane
```

This variable holds the instance of the JDirectoryPane owned by the file chooser dialog. In the user interface, this pane is represented by the central scrollable window containing the list of files and directories.

8.4.2   JFileChooser constructors

```
public JFileChooser()
```

This constructor creates a new instance of the file chooser, which, by default, loads the file list with the contents of the user's home directory.

```
public JFileChooser( String path )
```

This constructor creates a new instance of the file chooser, which, by default, loads the file list starting at the specified path.

```
public JFileChooser( File directory )
```

This constructor creates a new instance of the file chooser, which, by default, loads the file list starting at the path specified in the supplied file descriptor.

8.4.3   JFileChooser significant method groupings

```
public String getPrompt()
public void setPrompt(String prompt)
public String getTypesTitle()
public void setTypesTitle(String prompt)
public String getLocationTitle()
public void setLocationTitle(String locationTitle)
public String getOkayTitle()
public void setOkayTitle(String okayTitle)
public String getCancelTitle()
public void setCancelTitle(String cancelTitle)
```

This group of methods manages the various text labels displayed within the JFileChooser instance. Each of the text labels can be individually configured, which permits dialogs to easily support different languages and localizations.

```
public JDirectoryPane getDirectoryPane()
```

This method retrieves the JDirectoryPane instance used by the file chooser.

```
public TypedFile getSelectedFile()
```

The getSelectedFile() method can be called after the user selects the OK button in the file chooser dialog. This method returns a TypedFile instances containing information regarding the file selected by the user.

```
public void performOkay()
public void performCancel()
```

The OK and Cancel operations in the file chooser dialog can be imitated programmatically using the methods in this group.

```
public String getOkayCommand()
public void setOkayCommand(String okayCommand)
public String getCancelCommand()
public void setCancelCommand(String cancelCommand)
```

This group of methods controls the action commands produced within the file chooser dialog instance. If a custom handler inside the application is handling these actions, the command strings can be changed to suit the program's particular needs.

```
public int showDialog(Component parent)
```

This method initiates the file selection process by opening the chooser dialog on the user's display. Since the file chooser dialog is modal, this method will not return until the user selects either the OK or Cancel button.

```
public void addChooseableFileType( String presentationName,
                                   String extension, Icon icon )
public void addChooseableFileType( String presentationName,
                                   String extensions[], Icon icon )
public void addChooseableFileType( FileType type )
public Enumeration enumerateChoosableFileTypes()
public Vector getChoosableFileTypes()
public boolean isChoosableFileType( FileType t )
public void setChoosableFileTypes(FileType types[])
```

This group of methods controls and maintains the list of choosable file types. In the user interface, this list is represented by the combo box at the bottom of the dialog.

8.5   Internal frames

Most graphical user interfaces in use today offer the ability to embed windows (or Frames, in the Java world) inside parent frames, allowing the child frame to move freely within its parent and to be minimized, maximized, or restored. Microsoft Windows users will recognize this capability as the Multi-Document Interface (MDI).

Previous to the release of Swing, MDI was foreign to Java developers; however, with Swing, the features of the MDI are easily accessible. Note that Swing refers to embedded windows as internal frames and implements them in the JInternalFrame class.

UI GUIDELINE

Help the user manage internal frames by using same type document windows. In general, users run into window management problems with internal frames; the UI should support easy switching between windows of same type documents (for example, as a menu option). Users run into more serious problems managing internal frames with different document types, and you should seriously consider redesigning in order to avoid this scenario altogether.

Like other frames and dialogs we have discussed, an internal frame supports a single component pane onto which all panels and other embellishments are added. Also, since an internal frame is a container (by virtue of extending JComponent), it can support toolbars, menus, tabbed panes, and all other Swing derived components. Let's take a look at an example.

```java
// Imports
import java.awt.*;
import java.awt.event.*;
import com.sun.java.swing.*;

class TestFrame
        extends        JFrame
        implements     ActionListener
{
    // Instance attributes used in this example
    private JPanel         topPanel;
    private JMenuItem      menuFileNew;
    private JDesktopPane   desktopPane;

    // Constructor of main frame
    public TestFrame()
    {
        // Set the frame characteristics
        setTitle( "Internal Frame Application" );
        setSize( 600, 400 );
        setBackground( Color.gray );

        // Create a panel to hold all other components
        topPanel = new JPanel();
        topPanel.setLayout( new BorderLayout() );
        getContentPane().add( topPanel );
```

Listing 8.7A   Sample frame class

```
            // Create an application menu
            JMenu menuFile = new JMenu( "File" );
            menuFile.setMnemonic( 'F' );
            menuFileNew = CreateMenuItem( menuFile, "New",
                            'N', "Create a new internal frame" );
            JMenuBar menuBar = new JMenuBar();
            menuBar.add( menuFile );
            setJMenuBar( menuBar );

            // Create a desktop pane to support the internal
            // frame interface
            desktopPane = new JDesktopPane();
            topPanel.add( desktopPane, BorderLayout.CENTER );
        }

    public void actionPerformed( ActionEvent event )
    {
        System.out.println( event );

        // Create a new internal frame and add it to the desktop panel
        TestInternalFrame internalFrame = new TestInternalFrame();
        desktopPane.add( internalFrame, JLayeredPane.PALETTE_LAYER );
    }


    public JMenuItem CreateMenuItem( JMenu menu, String sText,
                            int acceleratorKey, String sToolTip )
    {
        // Create the item
        JMenuItem menuItem = new JMenuItem();

        // Add the item text
        menuItem.setText( sText );

        // Add the accelerator key
        if( acceleratorKey > 0 )
            menuItem.setMnemonic( acceleratorKey );

        // Add the optional tool tip text
        if( sToolTip != null )
            menuItem.setToolTipText( sToolTip );

        // Add an action handler to this menu item
        menuItem.addActionListener( this );

        menu.add( menuItem );

        return menuItem;
    }
```

Listing 8.7A Sample frame class (continued)

```
    // Main entry point for this example
    public static void main( String args[] )
    {
        // Create an instance of the test application
        TestFrame mainFrame = new TestFrame();
        mainFrame.setVisible( true );
    }
}
```

Listing 8.7A   Sample frame class (continued)

Listing 8.7A contains all of the code needed to create the main frame, including the JDesktopPane instance that acts as a container for any internal frame that the user creates. Note that the internal frames will be added to the palette layer of the desktop pane, which, by convention, is the layer where frames of this type should be inserted.

```
// Imports
import java.io.*;
import java.awt.*;
import java.awt.event.*;
import com.sun.java.swing.*;

class TestInternalFrame
        extends JInternalFrame
{
    // Instance attributes used in this example
    private JPanel         topPanel;
    private JScrollPane    scrollPane1;

    // Constructor of main frame
    public TestInternalFrame()
    {
        // Configure the internal frame embellishments
        setClosable( true );
        setMaximizable( true );
        setIconifiable( true );
        setResizable( true );

        // Set the frame characteristics
        setTitle( "Internal Frame" );
        setSize( 300, 200 );
```

Listing 8.7B   TestInternalFrame class

```
        setBackground( Color.gray );

        // Create a panel to hold all other components
        topPanel = new JPanel();
        topPanel.setLayout( new BorderLayout() );
        getContentPane().add( topPanel );

        // Populate the panel with something the user
        // can play with
        CreateTopPane( topPanel );
    }

    // Create a scrollable pane containing a source code file
    private void CreateTopPane( JPanel topPanel )
    {
        // Create a text area
        JTextArea area = new JTextArea();

        // Load a file into the text area, catching any exceptions
        try {
            FileReader fileStream = new FileReader( "TestFrame.java" );
            area.read( fileStream, "TestFrame.java" );

        }
        catch( FileNotFoundException e )
        {
            System.out.println( "File not found" );
        }
        catch( IOException e )
        {
            System.out.println( "IOException occurred" );
        }

        // Create the scrolling pane for the text area
        scrollPane1 = new JScrollPane();
        scrollPane1.getViewport().add( area );
        topPanel.add( scrollPane1, BorderLayout.CENTER );
    }
}
```

Listing 8.7B TestInternalFrame class (continued)

Listing 8.7B contains the source code to implement an internal frame. This code first sets frame widgets to control minimizing, maximizing, and restoring the frame, as well as the close button to dispose of the frame instance. All of the window operations are managed automatically by the desktop pane in the main frame, so you do not need to add extra code to support them. The remainder of listing 8.7B implements a scrollable pane with a text area containing a sample source file. The results produced by executing the source code in listings 8.7A and 8.7B is shown in figure 8.9.

Notice that each time the New menu option is selected, the program creates a new instance of an internal frame which it adds to the desktop pane. Each internal frame operates independently of its siblings, and there is no limitation on adding internal frames supporting different functionality. For example, you could create internal frames for toolbar palettes, text editors, or graphics display, and they could all be visible simultaneously.

8.5.1 JInternalFrame constants

```
public static final String CONTENT_PANE_PROPERTY
public static final String MENU_BAR_PROPERTY
public static final String TITLE_PROPERTY
public static final String LAYERED_PANE_PROPERTY
public static final String ROOT_PANE_PROPERTY
public static final String GLASS_PANE_PROPERTY
public static final String IS_SELECTED_PROPERTY
public static final String IS_CLOSED_PROPERTY
public static final String IS_MAXIMUM_PROPERTY
```

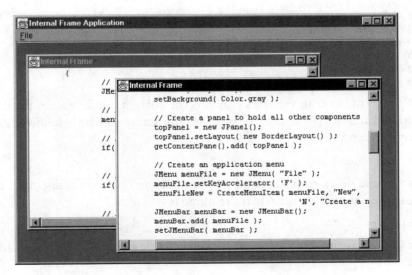

Figure 8.9   JInternalFrame program output

```
public static final String IS_ICON_PROPERTY
public static final String CONTENT_PANE_PROPERTY
public static final String MENU_BAR_PROPERTY
public static final String TITLE_PROPERTY
public static final String LAYERED_PANE_PROPERTY
public static final String ROOT_PANE_PROPERTY
public static final String GLASS_PANE_PROPERTY
public static final String IS_SELECTED_PROPERTY
public static final String IS_CLOSED_PROPERTY
public static final String IS_MAXIMUM_PROPERTY
public static final String IS_ICON_PROPERTY
```

The constants defined in the JInternalFrame class are all static strings holding the names of bound properties. These constants are used internally by the class, and, as a result, you should have little need for them.

8.5.2 JInternalFrame variables

```
protected JRootPane rootPane
```

This variable holds an instance of the root pane. The root pane is the only component added to the internal frame—all other components must be added to the root pane.

```
protected boolean closable
protected boolean isClosed
protected boolean maximizable
protected boolean isMaximum
protected boolean iconable
protected boolean isIcon
protected boolean resizable
protected boolean isSelected
```

This group of boolean variables contains the current configuration parameters for the internal frame. These control whether the frame can be minimized, maximized, iconified, and so on.

```
protected Icon frameIcon
```

This variable holds an instance of the frame icon. This icon is displayed in the upper-left corner of the title bar when the frame is visible.

```
protected String title
```

This variable maintains a copy of the current title string for the internal frame instance.

```
protected JDesktopIcon desktopIcon
```

The variable maintains an instance of the icon displayed when the internal frame is minimized (iconified).

8.5.3   JInternalFrame constructors

```
public JInternalFrame()
```

This constructor creates an instance of an internal frame with default parameters.

```
public JInternalFrame( String title )
```

This constructor creates an instance of an internal frame with the specified title string.

```
public JInternalFrame( String title, boolean resizable )
```

This constructor creates an instance of an internal frame with the specified title string. The specified flag controls the resizability of the window.

```
public JInternalFrame( String title, boolean resizable,
                        boolean closable )
```

This constructor creates an instance of an internal frame with the specified title string. The specified flag controls the resizability of the window. The availability of a Close button is controlled by the supplied boolean value.

```
public JInternalFrame( String title, boolean resizable,
                        boolean closable, boolean maximizable )
```

This constructor creates an instance of an internal frame with the specified title string. The specified flag controls the resizability of the window. The availability of Close and Maximize buttons is controlled by the supplied boolean values.

```
public JInternalFrame( String title, boolean resizable,
                        boolean closable, boolean maximizable,
                        boolean iconifiable )
```

This constructor creates an instance of an internal frame with the specified title string. The specified flag controls the resizability of the window. The availability of Close, Maximize, and Minimize buttons is controlled by the supplied boolean values.

8.5.4   JInternalFrame significant method groupings

```
public JMenuBar getMenuBar()
public void setMenuBar( JMenuBar m )
```

These methods control and manage an instance of a JMenuBar assigned to this internal frame instance. Like JFrame, JInternalFrame can support the addition of a menu bar, even if its owner frame already has one.

```
public Container getContentPane()
public void setContentPane(Container c)
public JLayeredPane getLayeredPane()
public void setLayeredPane(JLayeredPane layered)
public Component getGlassPane()
public void setGlassPane(Component glass)
public JRootPane getRootPane()
protected void setRootPane(JRootPane root)
```

This group of methods manages the various panes available to an internal frame instance. Note that all programmer-written components must be added to one of these preassigned panes. It is not possible to add components directly to an internal frame.

```
public void setVisible(boolean b)
public void setClosable(boolean b)
public boolean isClosable()
public boolean isClosed()
public void setClosed(boolean b) throws PropertyVetoException
public void setResizable(boolean b)
public boolean isResizable()
public void setIconifiable(boolean b)
public void setIcon(boolean b) throws PropertyVetoException
public boolean isIconifiable()
public boolean isIcon()
public void setMaximizable(boolean b)
public boolean isMaximum()
public void setMaximum(boolean b) throws PropertyVetoException
```

This large group of methods manages the display states that an internal frame instance supports. This include the minimized/maximized states, a state to control whether the frame can be closed, and control of the resizability of the frame.

```
public String getTitle()
public void setTitle(String title)
```

This method group manages the string displayed in the title bar of the internal frame.

```
public void moveToFront()
public void moveToBack()
public void toFront()
```

```
public void toBack()
```

When several internal frame instances are present in the desktop pane, they can become buried. This group of methods allows the programmer to control where a frame is displayed in the window stack. Frames can be moved to the front or back of the stack by using these methods.

```
public synchronized void addInternalFrameListener(
                         InternalFrameListener l)
public synchronized void removeInternalFrameListener(
                         InternalFrameListener l)
```

These two methods are used to add or remove an internal frame listener. This type of listener can detect changes to the internal frame such as when the frame is moved or resized, iconified, restored to its original size, and so on.

8.6   Chapter summary

In this chapter, we have discussed the classes needed to implement dialogs. The JDialog class permits the developer to create generic dialog boxes that can contain any other Swing and/or AWT components. Dialog boxes are used when an application needs to deviate from its main task to display information or request data input by the user.

Next, we examined the JOptionPane class, which can be used to display simple messages, errors, and warnings to the user. The class is a functional extension of the MessageBox API available on the Windows platform. JOptionPane allows a developer to create a simple input form to request information from the user. Input can be acquired from a simple text field or from a combo box.

Then we looked at the JColorChooser class, which allows the user to select a color using either RGB slider controls or an HSB pinwheel. This class can be used as a complex component which can be integrated into a complete design or can be presented as a complete dialog requiring no developer intervention. Examples for each form were shown in this chapter.

In a similar vein, we discussed the JFileChooser class, which gives your programs a finished look. This class can be used to request a filename from the user, usually as part of a save or load operation. JFileChooser replaces the AWT FileDialog class and offers a standard look-and-feel across all target Java platforms.

Finally, we studied the JInternalFrame class. The availability of internal frames allows Java developers the same type of capabilities that Windows developers currently have with the MDI. The ability to display multiple frames within an application allows us to expand the types of functions that we can present to a user. For example, we can now offer palettes, floating toolbars, and so on—all within the same application frame.

9

List boxes

A list box is simply a user interface control containing a collection of similar items from which the user can make one or more selections. This is the premise behind the AWT List control, which presents a Java component equivalent to list box objects found in all other graphics interfaces. The List class provides the basic functionality to add and remove items, display them (including the ability to scroll through long lists) and to allow the user to make selections. Though List is adequate for many applications, it falls short when you need to perform special operations, such as rendering lists of graphics or other peculiar data.

Swing provides a completely different approach to list management by supplying an entirely new list box component in a class called JList. In addition to the capabilities of the AWT List class, JList also has the ability to display graphics, with or without associated text, and also provides some additional event handling.

> *FYI*   Though many of the methods in the JList API are similar to those of AWT's List class, the two classes are generally incompatible. If you are planning to port an existing AWT application that uses List, you will need to do some additional work to correctly implement JList replacements.

Unlike AWT List, JList is a lightweight component, so it implements its display and data handling capabilities in separate models. Throughout our discussion of Swing's list box class, we will examine some techniques to create and manage special models, and we will generate some advanced examples to demonstrate key features. First, we will start by looking at a simple example of an application using a JList component.

9.1 A simple JList example

Listing 9.1 shows the source code needed to implement a simple list box example using the Swing API. This example generates a static list from which the user can make a selection. Currently, this code provides no mechanism to detect the selections made, nor does it include the capability to scroll the list, if required. We will add these features as we progress through this chapter.

```java
// Imports
import java.awt.*;
import java.awt.event.*;
import com.sun.java.swing.*;

class TestFrame
      extends JFrame
{
    // Instance attributes used in this example
    private JPanel  topPanel;
    private JList   listbox;

    // Constructor of main frame
    public TestFrame()
    {
        // Set the frame characteristics
        setTitle( "Simple ListBox Application" );
        setSize( 300, 100 );
        setBackground( Color.gray );

        // Create a panel to hold all other components
        topPanel = new JPanel();
        topPanel.setLayout( new BorderLayout() );
        getContentPane().add( topPanel );

        // Create some items to add to the list
        String listData[] =
        {
            "Item 1",
            "Item 2",
            "Item 3",
            "Item 4"
        };

        // Create a new list box control
        listbox = new JList( listData );
        topPanel.add( listbox, BorderLayout.CENTER );
    }

    // Main entry point for this example
    public static void main( String args[] )
    {
        // Create an instance of the test application
        TestFrame mainFrame = new TestFrame();
        mainFrame.setVisible( true );
    }
}
```

Listing 9.1   Simple JList application

FYI The JList class has no provision to handle scrolling. If your list contains more information than can be shown in the space provided, you need to add the list to a JScrollPane instance. This is identical to the technique used for JTextArea and for any other component capable of displaying more information than you have space for.

If you are familiar with the AWT List class, you will see that there isn't an add method in the JList class. JList does not store the data shown in the list; instead, it relies on a data model to manage that task. Listing 9.1 included an array of strings (the data model, for this sample) and associated that data with the user interface when the JList object was constructed.

As you will see later in this chapter, the use of a separate data model opens up many new opportunities for list boxes within your application. With AWT, if you want to display dynamic data from a data array in a list, you are required to copy the data from the array into the List instance using the add() method. With the JList class in Swing, all you need to do is identify the data array as the JList instance's data model, which reduces the amount of code you need to write and maintain.

Figure 9.1 shows the output produced by the simple example presented in listing 9.1. Notice that you can use the mouse to click on any of the items to highlight them. This example is quite simple, but, as you will soon see, the JList component can be much more complex.

9.2   A more advanced JList example

The previous example demonstrated the most basic list box example which included only static data and supported no selection management. However, there is much more to the JList class. Let's create a more advanced list box application to demonstrate some of the functionality provided by this useful Swing component.

Figure 9.1
JList application output

In this sample, we want to show a list box that will be dynamically updated by the user. Additionally, we must provide the capability to add new text to the list, so we will create an Add button and a text field into which the user can type. Also, since the user may want to delete items, we will create a Remove button and, to it, attach code to delete list items. Finally, we will intercept list selections and transfer the selected item back into the text field.

UI GUIDELINE

Design a list that doesn't require horizontal scrolling. As noted previously, users can get a little annoyed with horizontal scrolling and might ignore horizontally occluded data. Use concise terms for list items.

Listing 9.2 presents the source code for this more complex list box example. A string vector has replaced the static string array (of listing 9.1) so that the code can dynamically insert and remove strings. Additionally, since the list may grow beyond the bounds of the application frame, the list instance has been added to a scrolling pane, and it will automatically attach scroll bars when required.

```
// Imports
import java.util.*;
import java.awt.*;
import java.awt.event.*;
import com.sun.java.swing.*;
import com.sun.java.swing.event.*;

class TestFrame
        extends          JFrame
        implements       ActionListener,
                         ListSelectionListener
{
    // Instance attributes used in this example
    private      JPanel          topPanel;
    private      JList           listbox;
    private      Vector          listData;
    private      JButton         addButton;
    private      JButton         removeButton;
    private      JTextField      dataField;
    private      JScrollPane     scrollPane;

    // Constructor of main frame
```

Listing 9.2   Advanced JList application

```
public TestFrame()
{
    // Set the frame characteristics
    setTitle( "Advanced List Box Application" );
    setSize( 300, 100 );
    setBackground( Color.gray );

    // Create a panel to hold all other components
    topPanel = new JPanel();
    topPanel.setLayout( new BorderLayout() );
    getContentPane().add( topPanel );

    // Create the data model for this example
    listData = new Vector();

    // Create a new list box control
    listbox = new JList( listData );
    listbox.addListSelectionListener( this );

    // Add the list box to a scrolling pane
    scrollPane = new JScrollPane();
    scrollPane.getViewport().add( listbox );
    topPanel.add( scrollPane, BorderLayout.CENTER );

    CreateDataEntryPanel();
}

public void CreateDataEntryPanel()
{
    // Create a panel to hold all other components
    JPanel dataPanel = new JPanel();
    dataPanel.setLayout( new BorderLayout() );
    topPanel.add( dataPanel, BorderLayout.SOUTH );

    // Create some function buttons
    addButton = new JButton( "Add" );
    dataPanel.add( addButton, BorderLayout.WEST );
    addButton.addActionListener( this );

    removeButton = new JButton( "Delete" );
    dataPanel.add( removeButton, BorderLayout.EAST );
    removeButton.addActionListener( this );

    // Create a text field for data entry and display
    dataField = new JTextField();
    dataPanel.add( dataField, BorderLayout.CENTER );
}
```

Listing 9.2   Advanced JList application (continued)

```
// Handler for list selection changes
public void valueChanged( ListSelectionEvent event )
{
    // See if this is a list box selection and the
    // event stream has settled
    if( event.getSource() == listbox
                    && !event.getValueIsAdjusting() )
    {
        // Get the current selection and place it in the
        // edit field
        String stringValue = (String)listbox.getSelectedValue();
        if( stringValue != null )
            dataField.setText( stringValue );
    }
}

// Handler for button presses
public void actionPerformed( ActionEvent event )
{
    if( event.getSource() == addButton )
    {
        // Get the text field value
        String stringValue = dataField.getText();
        dataField.setText( "" );

        // Remove this item from the list and refresh
        if( stringValue != null )
        {
            listData.addElement( stringValue );
            listbox.setListData( listData );
            scrollPane.revalidate();
            scrollPane.repaint();
        }
    }

    if( event.getSource() == removeButton )
    {
        // Get the current selection
        int selection = listbox.getSelectedIndex();
        if( selection >= 0 )
        {
            // Add this item to the list and refresh
            listData.removeElementAt( selection );
            listbox.setListData( listData );
            scrollPane.revalidate();
            scrollPane.repaint();
```

Listing 9.2   Advanced JList application (continued)

```
                    // As a nice touch, select the next item
                    if( selection >= listData.size() )
                        selection = listData.size() - 1;
                    listbox.setSelectedIndex( selection );
                }
            }
        }

        // Main entry point for this example
        public static void main( String args[] )
        {
            // Create an instance of the test application
            TestFrame mainFrame = new TestFrame();
            mainFrame.setVisible( true );
        }
    }
```

Listing 9.2   Advanced JList application (continued)

The output of listing 9.2 is shown in figure 9.2. Initially, the list in the center of the frame is empty; however, by typing text and pressing the Add button, items can be added to the list. The vertical scroll bar (and horizontal scroll bar, if necessary) appears whenever the number of items in the list exceeds the frame size.

9.3   Listening for list activity

The code in listing 9.2 implements a ListSelectionListener that is responsible for detecting user list selections. The list box attaches the listener code using the following line:

```
        listbox.addListSelectionListener( this );
```

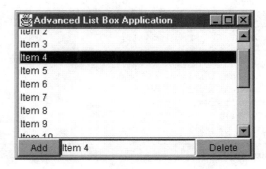

Figure 9.2
Advanced JList application output

The `valueChanged()` method is called any time the user selects an item from the list. When this occurs, the code determines the current list selection and copies its text to the text field. The `valueChanged()` method, like other action handlers shown previously, uses the `event.getSource()` call to determine the component generating the event.

```
if( event.getSource() == listbox
            && !event.getValueIsAdjusting() )
```

But, this line of code does something else, too. List selection events are generated in clusters, one for each item that is being deselected, one for each selected item, and one final event that indicates that the selection values are no longer changing. This final event is the one the program needs to detect, while all others can be disregarded. To accomplish this, the code uses the event's `getValueIsAdjusting()` method.

9.4   Custom data model

The examples shown in listings 9.1 and 9.2 implement the default data model built into Swing. This suggests that even though you didn't specifically make a copy of the data while elements were being added to the list, a copy operation was still occurring. For large arrays of list data, this can negatively effect performance.

Being a lightweight component, JList easily accepts the replacement of its data model with a custom version implemented by a programmer. In listing 9.3A, we revisit the simple list example, however, you might notice that the example does not include a string array or a vector holding any list strings. Instead, the code creates an instance of the `CustomListModel` class (see listing 9.3B). Except for the addition of a scrolling pane, this example is otherwise unchanged from the first simple list example shown in listing 9.1.

```
// Imports
import java.util.*;
import java.awt.*;
import java.awt.event.*;
import com.sun.java.swing.*;
import com.sun.java.swing.event.*;

class TestFrame
        extends JFrame
```

Listing 9.3A   Custom data model application

```
{
    // Instance attributes used in this example
    private    JPanel             topPanel;
    private    JList              listbox;
    private    CustomListModel    listData;
    private    JScrollPane        scrollPane;

    // Constructor of main frame
    public TestFrame()
    {
        // Set the frame characteristics
        setTitle( "Custom Data Model List Application" );
        setSize( 300, 100 );
        setBackground( Color.gray );

        // Create a panel to hold all other components
        topPanel = new JPanel();
        topPanel.setLayout( new BorderLayout() );
        getContentPane().add( topPanel );

        // Create the data model for this example
        listData = new CustomListModel();

        // Create a new list box control
        listbox = new JList( listData );

        // Add the list box to a scrolling pane
        scrollPane = new JScrollPane();
        scrollPane.getViewport().add( listbox );
        topPanel.add( scrollPane, BorderLayout.CENTER );
    }

    // Main entry point for this example
    public static void main( String args[] )
    {
        // Create an instance of the test application
        TestFrame mainFrame = new TestFrame();
        mainFrame.setVisible( true );
    }
}
```

Listing 9.3A   Custom data model application

Listing 9.3B shows the CustomListModel class, which is responsible for answering requests for list element data. Notice that the code does not store list elements in an array or vector—instead, data are manufactured on the fly. A custom data model for a list extends the AbstractListModel class, and, as such, it must implement two methods.

The first of these, `getSize()`, returns the number of items in the model. In our case, the method returns a constant value of `300`. The second method, `getElementAt()`, returns the actual list item at the specified item offset (starting at zero). In our example, we manufacture the value string using the format Item n, where n is the index number.

```
// Imports
import com.sun.java.swing.*;

class CustomListModel
    extends      AbstractListModel
{
    // Return the size of the list
    public int getSize()
    {
        return 300;
    }
    // Return an element from the list
    public Object getElementAt( int index )
    {
        return "Item " + index;;
    }
}
```

Listing 9.3B   Custom data model class

The output of listing 9.3 is a 300-element list, shown in figure 9.3. Note that, since there is no actual data array in the example, everything you see when you run the code is artificial. For large, static lists, this is an excellent technique to reduce the memory requirements of your application and improve its overall performance.

9.5   Basic custom list rendering

But wait, there's more! So far, all of the JList examples shown in this chapter included only textual data. This is adequate in most situations, but we can improve the appearance of our Java applications by adding graphics to the list and changing the font and color used to display list elements. Much like the custom data model shown previously, the viewer can also be replaced simply by adding a custom renderer to the list.

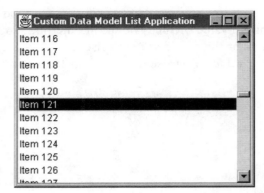

Figure 9.3
Custom data model application output

UI GUIDELINE

Simulate UI components using graphics in lists. Small graphics (such as 16 by 16 pixels) can add a lot of visual appeal to a list. Consider drawing UI components, such as checkboxes or radio buttons, as graphics to enable custom selection behaviors in list controls.

Listings 9.4A and 9.4B make up an application that implements a simple list like the example shown in listing 9.1; however, the example also provides a custom cell renderer, which has the responsibility of drawing each element in the list. Items can be drawn differently depending on whether or not they are selected, including the foreground and background colors and the font. The example shown here displays the selected item in a 24-point font and changes the background color of the selection to red. Notice, also, that this example includes images for each item to help the user better identify the style associated with each selection, greatly improving the user experience with this application.

```
// Imports
import java.awt.*;
import java.awt.event.*;
import com.sun.java.swing.*;

class TestFrame
        extends JFrame
{
```

Listing 9.4A   Custom rendering list example

```
// Instance attributes used in this example
private    JPanel      topPanel;
private    JList       listbox;

// Constructor of main frame
public TestFrame()
{
    // Set the frame characteristics
    setTitle( "Rendered ListBox Application" );
    setSize( 300, 160 );
    setBackground( Color.gray );

    // Create a panel to hold all other components
    topPanel = new JPanel();
    topPanel.setLayout( new BorderLayout() );
    getContentPane().add( topPanel );

    // Create some items to add to the list
    String listData[] =
    {
        "Circles",
        "Bubbles",
        "Thatch",
        "Pinstripes"
    };

    // Create a new list box control
    listbox = new JList( listData );
    listbox.setCellRenderer( new CustomCellRenderer() );
    topPanel.add( listbox, BorderLayout.CENTER );
}

// Main entry point for this example
public static void main( String args[] )
{
    // Create an instance of the test application
    TestFrame mainFrame = new TestFrame();
    mainFrame.setVisible( true );
}
}
```

Listing 9.4A   Custom rendering list example (continued)

The CustomCellRenderer class first loads the required images in its constructor, then waits for the list box to request a rendering operation. The getListCellRendererComponent() method performs the actual rendering, determining the colors and font required to display the item. Additionally, this method assigns the correct image to the item being drawn.

```java
// Imports
import java.awt.*;
import com.sun.java.swing.*;

class CustomCellRenderer
    extends        JLabel
    implements     ListCellRenderer
{
    private    ImageIcon  image[];

    public     CustomCellRenderer()
    {
        setOpaque(true);

        // Pre-load the graphics images to save time
        image = new ImageIcon[4];
        image[0] = new ImageIcon( "circles.gif" );
        image[1] = new ImageIcon( "bubbles.gif" );
        image[2] = new ImageIcon( "thatch.gif" );
        image[3] = new ImageIcon( "pinstripe.gif" );
    }

    public Component getListCellRendererComponent(
            JList list, Object value, int index,
            boolean isSelected, boolean cellHasFocus )
    {
        // Display the text for this item
        setText(value.toString());

        // Set the correct image
        setIcon( image[index] );

        // Draw the correct colors and font
        if( isSelected )
        {
            // Set the color and font for a selected item
            setBackground( Color.red );
            setForeground( Color.white );
            setFont( new Font( "Roman", Font.BOLD, 24 ) );
        }
        else
        {
            // Set the color and font for an unselected item
```

Listing 9.4B   Custom cell renderer class

```
            setBackground( Color.white );
            setForeground( Color.black );
            setFont( new Font( "Roman", Font.PLAIN, 12 ) );
        }

        return this;
    }
}
```

Listing 9.4B   Custom cell renderer class (continued)

Figure 9.4 shows the output produced by listing 9.4B. Notice that the selected item, Thatch, is presented in a much larger font than the other items, and each item includes an associated image indicating graphically what the text is describing.

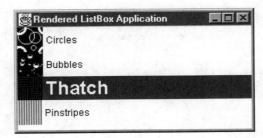

Figure 9.4
Custom rendering list application output

9.6   Advanced custom list rendering

But, that's still not all! The custom renderer in listing 9.4 extended the JLabel control and used it to draw what is essentially a label in the space provided for each item in the list. Though the addition of a graphic provided a unique interface, it still exhibits some limitations for some applications.

Well, the good news is that JLabel is only one of several classes that can be displayed in a list box. You can also display instances of JButton, JTextField, JCheckBox, and so on—even JTextArea (a multiline component nestled into a list box item). Here's the code:

```
// Imports
import java.awt.*;
import java.awt.event.*;
import com.sun.java.swing.*;

class TestFrame
      extends JFrame
{
    // Instance attributes used in this example
    private     JPanel      topPanel;
    private     JList       listbox;

    // Constructor of main frame
    public TestFrame()
    {
        // Set the frame characteristics
        setTitle( "Advanced Rendered ListBox Application" );
        setSize( 300, 160 );
        setBackground( Color.gray );

        // Create a panel to hold all other components
        topPanel = new JPanel();
        topPanel.setLayout( new BorderLayout() );
        getContentPane().add( topPanel );

        // Create some items to add to the list
        String listData[] =
        {
            "Chapter 1\nIntroduction",
            "Chapter 2\nA Java Refresher",
            "Chapter 3\nSwing Basics",
            "Chapter 4\nPanels, Panes and More Layout Managers"
        };
        // Create a new list box control
        listbox = new JList( listData );
        listbox.setCellRenderer( new CustomCellRenderer() );
        topPanel.add( listbox, BorderLayout.CENTER );
    }
    // Main entry point for this example
    public static void main( String args[] )
    {
        // Create an instance of the test application
        TestFrame mainFrame = new TestFrame();
        mainFrame.setVisible( true );
    }
}
```

Listing 9.5A   Advanced custom rendering list example

Listing 9.5A is still based on the first example shown in the chapter, and includes almost no new functionality when compared to the previous example listing 9.1. Notice, in listing 9.5A, the values loaded into the list:

```
"Chapter 1\nIntroduction",
"Chapter 2\nA Java Refresher",
"Chapter 3\nSwing Basics",
"Chapter 4\nPanels, Panes and More Layout Managers"
```

Each value includes a \n new line character to force a line break in the middle of the text. Listing 9.5B implements a custom cell renderer, but, this time, it extends JTextArea instead of JLabel. Since JTextArea does not support graphics, we have abandoned the icons from the previous example.

```
// Imports
import java.awt.*;
import com.sun.java.swing.*;
import com.sun.java.swing.border.*;

class CustomCellRenderer
    extends         JTextArea
    implements      ListCellRenderer
{
    public Component getListCellRendererComponent(
            JList list, Object value, int index,
            boolean isSelected, boolean cellHasFocus )
    {
        setBorder( new BevelBorder( BevelBorder.RAISED ) );

        // Display the text for this item
        setText(value.toString());

        // Draw the correct colors and font
        if( isSelected )
        {
            // Set the color and font for a selected item
            setBackground( Color.red );
            setForeground( Color.white );
        }
        else
        {
            // Set the color and font for an unselected item
            setBackground( Color.lightGray );
            setForeground( Color.black );
        }
```

Listing 9.5B   Advanced custom cell renderer class

```
        return this;
    }
}
```

Listing 9.5B   Advanced custom cell renderer class

The result is a nicely formatted list resembling the screen output shown in figure 9.5. Note that, although I elected to eliminate the font changes included with the previous example, the JTextArea class does support them. Since the height of each list item is determined when constructed, it is possible to cause display clipping if the font is set to a large value.

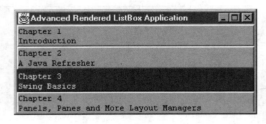

Figure 9.5
Advanced custom rendering list application output

9.7   JList constructors

`public JList()`

This constructor creates an instance of a JList object with an empty data model.

`public JList( ListModel dataModel )`

This constructor creates an instance of a JList object with the data model specified in the supplied parameter. The data model must not be empty.

`public JList( Object listData[] )`

This constructor creates an instance of a JList object with the data specified in the supplied array. This array is inserted into a default list model.

`public JList(Vector listData)`

This constructor creates an instance of a JList object with the data specified in the supplied vector. This array is inserted into a default list model.

9.8   JList significant method groupings

```
public Object getPrototypeCellValue()
public void setPrototypeCellValue(Object prototypeCellValue)
```

These methods managed the cell prototype value. The prototype value is used to calculate the width of each cell in the list. Using a cell prototype is much more efficient than inspecting each item in the list to determine the maximum width.

```
public int getFixedCellWidth()
public void setFixedCellWidth( int width )
public int getFixedCellHeight()
public void setFixedCellHeight( int height )
```

These methods are used to determine and control the width and height of each cell in the list.

```
public ListCellRenderer getCellRenderer()
public void setCellRenderer( ListCellRenderer cellRenderer )
```

These methods manage the delegate class used to paint each cell in the list.

```
public Color getSelectionForeground()
public void setSelectionForeground(Color selectionForeground)
public Color getSelectionBackground()
public void setSelectionBackground(Color selectionBackground)
```

As the names suggest, these methods manage the foreground and background colors used to display the currently selected item. A custom cell renderer can override these values, or that renderer can reference these colors during a painting operation.

```
public int getVisibleRowCount()
public void setVisibleRowCount(int visibleRowCount)
```

These methods detect and control the number of rows visible within a list. The row count (overall height) of a JList instance can be managed at run time with these methods.

```
public int getFirstVisibleIndex()
public int getLastVisibleIndex()
public void ensureIndexIsVisible( int index )
```

The methods in this group are used to determine the index of the first or last index visible in the list. Additionally, the ensureIndexIsVisible() method can force any item into the visible region of the list.

```
public int locationToIndex( Point location )
public Point indexToLocation( int index )
```

These methods are used to calculate the correlation of a list item, referenced by index, and an actual pixel location within the list. These methods are typically used to determine which item is currently under the mouse pointer.

```
public Rectangle getCellBounds( int index1, int index2 )
```

This method returns a rectangular region bound by two list items specified by index numbers.

```
public ListModel getModel()
public void setModel( ListModel model )
public void setListData( Object listData[] )
public void setListData( Vector listData )
```

These methods are used to manage the data referenced in the list. Data can be stored within a custom data model, a simple array, or a vectored array. Any time data is changed dynamically, one of the set methods shown here must be called to update the list.

```
public void addListSelectionListener(ListSelectionListener listener)
public void removeListSelectionListener(
                    ListSelectionListener listener)
```

These methods manage the presence of a list selection listener for the current JList instance. A list selection listener intercepts events generated by the list object when the user changes the current selection.

```
public int getSelectionMode()
public void setSelectionMode(int selectionMode)
```

These methods control the selection mode used in the list instance. The mode is limited to:

- SINGLE_SELECTION   for selecting only one item at a time
- SINGLE_INTERVAL_SELECTION   to allow selection of single contiguous blocks of items
- MULTIPLE_INTERVAL_SELECTION   to allow multiple item or block selection

```
public int getAnchorSelectionIndex()
public int getLeadSelectionIndex()
public int getMinSelectionIndex()
public int getMaxSelectionIndex()
```

This group of methods returns list indices based on various restrictions. For example, the first selected item in a range of selections can be determined with the getAnchorSelectionIndex() method.

```
public boolean isSelectedIndex(int index)
public boolean isSelectionEmpty()
public void clearSelection()
public int[] getSelectedIndices()
public void setSelectedIndex(int index)
public void setSelectedIndices(int indices[])
public Object[] getSelectedValues()
public int getSelectedIndex()
public Object getSelectedValue()
public void setSelectedValue( Object anObject, boolean shouldScroll )
public void setSelectionInterval( int anchor, int lead )
public void addSelectionInterval( int anchor, int lead )
public void removeSelectionInterval( int index0, int index1 )
```

This method group manages information about the selections within the list object. Additionally, selections can be added or removed with methods from this group.

```
public void setValueIsAdjusting(boolean b)
public boolean getValueIsAdjusting(boolean b)
```

These two methods manage the state of the is value adjusting flag.

9.9 Chapter summary

In this chapter, we have examined the Swing JList class, which is a super-set of the AWT List control. However, unlike List, JList requires a separate data model to hold the item values it displays. This makes porting AWT List code to JList a much more extensive exercise than for most other Swing-based components.

We began this chapter with a simple list example which contained only four static items and offered no scrolling capability. This example showed that creating lists with the JList class can be quite simple.

Next, we started to examine custom data models. The second example shown in this chapter used a vectored data array, which permitted us to add or remove list items at run time. This example was followed closely by a third example that used no data array at all. Instead, a completely custom data model was used to manufacture the requested data on the fly.

Finally, we got our first taste of custom display rendering, by replacing the UI delegate with a new one of our own design. We created a simple example that changed the font and color of the list and any selected items, but we also added graphics to perk up the user interface. In the final example, we created an interesting multiline list box, where every list element used two lines instead of the typical one line.

In the next chapter, we will expand on the idea of lists by studying a completely new Swing class which implements a more complex form of list called the hierarchical tree. As you will see, we can employ much of what we already know about lists when we use trees in our applications.

10

Trees

In the last chapter, we examined the Swing JList, and, though it differed from the AWT List component in implementation, the two classes are equivalent functionally. In this chapter, we will discuss the hierarchical tree control—a class which is now a part of the standard Java tool set. This component is familiar to Windows API programmers, but so far unknown to Java, excluding many of the third party libraries.

List boxes are great for displaying simple lists of information from which the user can make single or multiple selections; however, in many situations, a list is inadequate. For example, if you were writing a program containing several general selection topics, and each of these topics could be subdivided into many specific subtopics, you would require a list of subtopics for each general topic. Not only would these numerous list boxes consume vital screen real estate, but also, a presentation of dozens of lists would intimidate your users. Another difficulty with this type of interface is the huge amount of code you would need to write to support it. For four or five separate lists, you could still manage a scenario like this, but what if you had a hundred general topics?

A better solution to this problem is to implement a single control containing all of the lists. Not only does this greatly reduce the amount of code that must be written and maintained, but also, it greatly simplifies the interface presented to the user. The key to this solution is the hierarchical tree, since it can nest lists of lists, to any depth required. The tree control gets its name from the series of collapsible/expandable branches it can contain. Each of the tree's branches can be divided into successively more specific branches, and there is no practical limit to the number of items that each branch can hold, nor to the nesting of subbranches.

In Swing, the hierarchical tree is implemented in the JTree class, which, like all other Swing components, is derived from JComponent. Since JTree is indirectly based on the Container class, it reaps all of the benefits we have seen with other Swing classes, including the ability to contain a collection of (almost) any other components. But, of course, we need to start with a much more basic example of a tree application.

10.1 Basic tree implementation

In this section, we will examine most of the aspects of creating and displaying Swing JTree components. We will start with a simple example and work our way through to more advanced data modeling and display characteristics support by the class. At the conclusion of this section, you will know how to create any sort of tree you want, including trees with default characteristics and tree instances that implement custom graphical images and data formats.

GUIDELINE

Novice software users have problems working with hierarchical data structures. If you are designing for a more sophisticated user, this is not an issue. But, for the average user, try to avoid using a tree control that doesn't already strongly conform to an existing UI metaphor with which users are comfortable. This may mean using a tree in combination with a list to display lowest level tree nodes (for example, Windows Explorer). Trees have the unfortunate side effect of encouraging the creation of deep nested structures that become difficult for the user to navigate and manage.

10.1.1 A basic JTree example

In the first example, we will create a simple tree containing only a few items and having no ability to add or remove items. Additionally, this example will include a scrollable pane, which will become more important as we add features to our application. The icons shown in this example are defaults provided by Swing, but, later in this chapter, we will do a little work to change these.

```
// Imports
import java.awt.*;
import java.awt.event.*;
import com.sun.java.swing.*;

class TestFrame
      extends JFrame
{
    // Instance attributes used in this example
    private JPanel    topPanel;
    private JTree     tree;
    private JScrollPane scrollPane;

    // Constructor of main frame
    public TestFrame()
    {
        // Set the frame characteristics
        setTitle( "Simple Tree Application" );
        setSize( 300, 100 );
```

Listing 10.1   Simple JTree example

```
        setBackground( Color.gray );

        // Create a panel to hold all other components
        topPanel = new JPanel();
        topPanel.setLayout( new BorderLayout() );
        getContentPane().add( topPanel );

        // Create a new tree control
        tree = new JTree();

        // Add the list box to a scrolling pane
        scrollPane = new JScrollPane();
        scrollPane.getViewport().add( tree );
        topPanel.add( scrollPane, BorderLayout.CENTER );
    }

    // Main entry point for this example
    public static void main( String args[] )
    {
        // Create an instance of the test application
        TestFrame mainFrame = new TestFrame();
        mainFrame.setVisible( true );
    }
}
```

Listing 10.1   Simple JTree example

Listing 10.1 is a short example, creating a JTree instance. Notice that the code does not perform any sort of item insertion, so, this tree should be empty. Actually, when no specific data model has been specified, JTree reverts to a sample model which is impractical, but which is quite suitable to demonstrate the use of JTree.

Figure 10.1 shows the output produced by listing 10.1. Aside from the cute content of the tree, notice that, when the program is executed, the tree is initially collapsed down to the root level. Opening the root expands it, showing the next level of indentation. Notice the change in icon for the lowest element of the tree. This is the default operation for the simple tree.

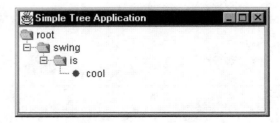

Figure 10.1
Simple JTree example output

10.1.2 Adding new tree items

Doubtless, many would argue that the code in listing 10.1 is adequate; but, because this first example uses the sample data model, it is generally useful only for demonstration purposes. Adding branches and items to a tree instance involves a bit of additional code, but the process of creating and using the JTree class will remain clear. Study the following sample code:

```java
// Imports
import java.awt.*;
import java.awt.event.*;
import com.sun.java.swing.*;
import com.sun.java.swing.tree.*;

class TestFrame
       extends JFrame
{
    // Instance attributes used in this example
    private JPanel    topPanel;
    private JTree     tree;
    private JScrollPane scrollPane;

    // Constructor of main frame
    public TestFrame()
    {
        // Set the frame characteristics
        setTitle( "More Advanced Tree Application" );
        setSize( 300, 100 );
        setBackground( Color.gray );

        // Create a panel to hold all other components
        topPanel = new JPanel();
        topPanel.setLayout( new BorderLayout() );
        getContentPane().add( topPanel );

        // Create data for the tree
        DefaultMutableTreeNode root
                  = new DefaultMutableTreeNode( "Deck" );

        DefaultMutableTreeNode itemClubs
                  = new DefaultMutableTreeNode( "Clubs" );
        addAllCard( itemClubs );
        root.add( itemClubs );

        DefaultMutableTreeNode itemDiamonds
                  = new DefaultMutableTreeNode( "Diamonds" );
```

Listing 10.2   More advanced JTree example

```
        addAllCard( itemDiamonds );
        root.add( itemDiamonds );

        DefaultMutableTreeNode itemSpades
                = new DefaultMutableTreeNode( "Spades" );
        addAllCard( itemSpades );
        root.add( itemSpades );

        DefaultMutableTreeNode itemHearts
                = new DefaultMutableTreeNode( "Hearts" );
        addAllCard( itemHearts );
        root.add( itemHearts );

        // Create a new tree control
        DefaultTreeModel treeModel = new DefaultTreeModel( root );
        tree = new JTree( treeModel );

        // Add the tree to a scrolling pane
        scrollPane = new JScrollPane();
        scrollPane.getViewport().add( tree );
        topPanel.add( scrollPane, BorderLayout.CENTER );
    }

    // Helper method to write an entire suit of cards to the
    // current tree node
    public void addAllCard( DefaultMutableTreeNode suit )
    {
        suit.add( new DefaultMutableTreeNode( "Ace" ) );
        suit.add( new DefaultMutableTreeNode( "Two" ) );
        suit.add( new DefaultMutableTreeNode( "Three" ) );
        suit.add( new DefaultMutableTreeNode( "Four" ) );
        suit.add( new DefaultMutableTreeNode( "Five" ) );
        suit.add( new DefaultMutableTreeNode( "Six" ) );
        suit.add( new DefaultMutableTreeNode( "Seven" ) );
        suit.add( new DefaultMutableTreeNode( "Eight" ) );
        suit.add( new DefaultMutableTreeNode( "Nine" ) );
        suit.add( new DefaultMutableTreeNode( "Ten" ) );
        suit.add( new DefaultMutableTreeNode( "Jack" ) );
        suit.add( new DefaultMutableTreeNode( "Queen" ) );
        suit.add( new DefaultMutableTreeNode( "King" ) );
    }

    // Main entry point for this example
    public static void main( String args[] )
    {
        // Create an instance of the test application
        TestFrame mainFrame = new TestFrame();
```

Listing 10.2   More advanced JTree example (continued)

```
        mainFrame.setVisible( true );
    }
}
```

Listing 10.2   More advanced JTree example (continued)

Listing 10.2 contains the code required to generate a JTree instance containing all of the cards in a deck of playing cards. The key feature in this application is the use of the DefaultMutableTreeNode class, which is a general-purpose node item compatible with the Swing graphical tree component. Each child node is inserted into its parent node using the add() method, and any child node can itself act as a parent for subsequent child nodes.

The root is a special node because it is the ultimate parent of all of the other tree nodes. It is inserted into the tree's data model, which, in the case of listing 10.2, is an instance of the DefaultTreeModel class. This is the model that a JTree instance should use, unless a custom data model is used. We will discuss custom data models for JTree next.

The results produced by executing the code shown in listing 10.2 have been captured in figure 10.2. Notice that once a node is added to one of the suits (Clubs, for example), the node becomes a branch with a folder-like icon and the addition of a graphic (+/-) to the left of the entry, which can be used to expand or collapse the branch.

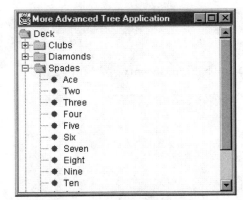

Figure 10.2
More advanced JTree example output

10.1.3 Custom data models

When we were discussing the JList class in the previous chapter, you got your first taste of Swing's custom data models. The JList class is not unique in its ability to manage data using a custom model—JTree also supports custom data modeling, though, because of the hierarchical nature of a tree, the model is a bit more complex.

In the following example, we will recreate the tree containing the deck of cards; however, this example will use a custom data model to manufacture the cards within each suit. The result is an application consisting of approximately the same number of code lines, but with much better performance, particularly for large data sets.

```
// Imports
import java.awt.*;
import java.awt.event.*;
import com.sun.java.swing.*;
import com.sun.java.swing.tree.*;

class TestFrame
        extends JFrame
  {
    // Instance attributes used in this example
    private JPanel      topPanel;
    private JTree       tree;
    private JScrollPane scrollPane;

    // Constructor of main frame
    public TestFrame()
    {
        // Set the frame characteristics
        setTitle( "Custom Data Model Tree Application" );
        setSize( 300, 200 );
        setBackground( Color.gray );

        // Create a panel to hold all other components
        topPanel = new JPanel();
        topPanel.setLayout( new BorderLayout() );
        getContentPane().add( topPanel );

        // Create data for the tree
        DefaultMutableTreeNode root
                = new DefaultMutableTreeNode( "Deck" );

        CreateSuit( root, "Clubs" );
        CreateSuit( root, "Diamonds" );
        CreateSuit( root, "Spades" );
```

Listing 10.3A   Custom data model application example

```
        CreateSuit( root, "Hearts" );

        // Create a new tree control
        MyDataModel treeModel = new MyDataModel( root );
        tree = new JTree( treeModel );

        // Add the tree to a scrolling pane
        scrollPane = new JScrollPane();
        scrollPane.getViewport().add( tree );
        topPanel.add( scrollPane, BorderLayout.CENTER );
    }

    public void CreateSuit( DefaultMutableTreeNode root,
                                String suitName )
    {
        DefaultMutableTreeNode itemSuit
                    = new DefaultMutableTreeNode( suitName );
            for( int iCtr = 0; iCtr < 13; iCtr++ )
                itemSuit.add( new DefaultMutableTreeNode( "" ) );

        root.add( itemSuit );
    }

    // Main entry point for this example
    public static void main( String args[] )
    {
        // Create an instance of the test application
        TestFrame mainFrame = new TestFrame();
        mainFrame.setVisible( true );
    }
}
```

Listing 10.3A   Custom data model application example (continued)

Listing 10.3A recreates the main class for the application that creates a JTree holding every card in a deck. The `CreateSuit()` method adds an entire suit to the deck tree; however, the cards added all consist of an empty string, which is shorter, and hence, faster to manage.

```
// Imports
import java.util.*;
import com.sun.java.swing.*;
import com.sun.java.swing.tree.*;

class MyDataModel
```

Listing 10.3B   Custom data model application example

```
extends      DefaultTreeModel
{
    private DefaultMutableTreeNode root;
    private String rootName = "";
    private String cardArray[] = {
                        "Ace", "Two", "Three", "Four",
                        "Five", "Six", "Seven", "Eight",
                        "Nine", "Ten", "Jack", "Queen",
                        "King"
                    };
    public MyDataModel( TreeNode root )
    {
        super( root );
        DefaultMutableTreeNode parentNode =
                    (DefaultMutableTreeNode)root;
        rootName = (String)parentNode.getUserObject();
    }
    public Object getChild( Object parent, int index )
    {
        DefaultMutableTreeNode parentNode =
                            (DefaultMutableTreeNode)parent;
        String parentName = (String)parentNode.getUserObject();

        if( parentName.equals( rootName ) )
            return super.getChild( parent, index );
        else
            return new DefaultMutableTreeNode( cardArray[index] );
    }
}
```

Listing 10.3B   Custom data model application example (continued)

Listing 10.3B contains the code for the custom data model class that extends DefaultTreeModel. Though we could have overridden other methods from the parent class, only the getChild() method is handled. In this method, the code ignores any tree node (the suits, in our example) whose parent is the root node: however, for nodes that do not belong to the root node (the cards, in our example), the get-Child() method instead uses a lookup table to generate the node name. The result is an application that is not only faster, but also uses much less dynamic memory.

Remember that strings in Java are immutable, so any opportunity to eliminate them or replace them with static strings should be exploited. Custom data models for the Swing JTree class can often provide this opportunity.

10.1.4 Custom rendering

In addition to handling custom data modeling, the JTree class also supports custom rendering of individual items within the list. This is useful for adding graphics or changing the font of specific items in the tree. For example, it may be important, in your application, to display top-level items with bolded text to highlight their importance, or you may want to add an icon image to each tree item to help denote its significance. These capabilities are added to a tree by using custom rendering.

GUIDELINE **Imitate UI components by using graphics in trees.** Consider drawing UI components (for example, check boxes) to allow for disjointed selections within the tree and tri-state check boxes (for example, a gray check box) on parent nodes to show the partially disjointed selections of the children below.

In listings 10.4A and 10.4B, we again re-create the playing card tree example, but this time we will implement a custom renderer class to handle some special features. For example, the top-level items (the suits) include graphics for each of the suits in a deck of cards, and the individual cards also include graphics. I stopped short of displaying the entire graphic for each card, but doing so would require only minor changes to the rendering method presented here.

```
// Imports
import java.awt.*;
import java.awt.event.*;
import com.sun.java.swing.*;
import com.sun.java.swing.tree.*;

class TestFrame
        extends JFrame
{
```

Listing 10.4A   Custom rendered JTree application example

```
// Instance attributes used in this example
private JPanel  topPanel;
private JTree   tree;
private JScrollPane scrollPane;

// Constructor of main frame
public TestFrame()
{
    // Set the frame characteristics
    setTitle( "Custom Rendered Tree Application" );
    setSize( 300, 200 );
    setBackground( Color.gray );

    // Create a panel to hold all other components
    topPanel = new JPanel();
    topPanel.setLayout( new BorderLayout() );
    getContentPane().add( topPanel );

    // Create data for the tree
    DefaultMutableTreeNode root
            = new DefaultMutableTreeNode( "Deck" );

    DefaultMutableTreeNode itemClubs
            = new DefaultMutableTreeNode( "Clubs" );
    addAllCard( itemClubs );
    root.add( itemClubs );

    DefaultMutableTreeNode itemDiamonds
            = new DefaultMutableTreeNode( "Diamonds" );
    addAllCard( itemDiamonds );
    root.add( itemDiamonds );

    DefaultMutableTreeNode itemSpades
            = new DefaultMutableTreeNode( "Spades" );
    addAllCard( itemSpades );
    root.add( itemSpades );

    DefaultMutableTreeNode itemHearts
            = new DefaultMutableTreeNode( "Hearts" );
    addAllCard( itemHearts );
    root.add( itemHearts );

    // Create a new tree control
    DefaultTreeModel treeModel = new DefaultTreeModel( root );
    tree = new JTree( treeModel );

    // Tell the tree it is being rendered by our application
    tree.setCellRenderer( new CustomCellRenderer() );
```

Listing 10.4A   Custom rendered JTree application example

```
        // Add the tree to a scrolling pane
        scrollPane = new JScrollPane();
        scrollPane.getViewport().add( tree );
        topPanel.add( scrollPane, BorderLayout.CENTER );
    }

    // Helper method to write an entire suit of cards to the
    // current tree node
    public void addAllCard( DefaultMutableTreeNode suit )
    {
        suit.add( new DefaultMutableTreeNode( "Ace" ) );
        suit.add( new DefaultMutableTreeNode( "Two" ) );
        suit.add( new DefaultMutableTreeNode( "Three" ) );
        suit.add( new DefaultMutableTreeNode( "Four" ) );
        suit.add( new DefaultMutableTreeNode( "Five" ) );
        suit.add( new DefaultMutableTreeNode( "Six" ) );
        suit.add( new DefaultMutableTreeNode( "Seven" ) );
        suit.add( new DefaultMutableTreeNode( "Eight" ) );
        suit.add( new DefaultMutableTreeNode( "Nine" ) );
        suit.add( new DefaultMutableTreeNode( "Ten" ) );
        suit.add( new DefaultMutableTreeNode( "Jack" ) );
        suit.add( new DefaultMutableTreeNode( "Queen" ) );
        suit.add( new DefaultMutableTreeNode( "King" ) );
    }

    // Main entry point for this example
    public static void main( String args[] )
    {
        // Create an instance of the test application
        TestFrame mainFrame = new TestFrame();
        mainFrame.setVisible( true );
    }
}
```

Listing 10.4A Custom rendered JTree application example

Listing 10.4A is almost identical to the code shown in previous examples. It creates a tree instance and inserts all of the pertinent data: however, it has an additional line to notify the tree that we will provide a custom renderer.

The code in listing 10.4B constitutes the rendering code for this application. To save time during execution, the class implements a constructor to load the graphics that will be used to display the cards and suits. The `getTreeCellRendererComponent()` method, which must be provided as a requirement of the TreeCellRender implementation used by this class, is responsible for the actual drawing of tree cells.

In our example, getTreeCellRendererComponent() determines what it is drawing (based on the text in the specified tree node) and then assigns the correct image to the displayed items. Additionally, this method sets the correct foreground color, depending on the selection state of the item.

FYI Currently, the background color of the tree item cannot be set within the rendering method (at least, setting it has no effect). It is unknown whether this limitation is a Swing bug or a feature. To work around this problem, a paint() method is required within the custom rendering class.

```
// Imports
import com.sun.java.swing.*;
import com.sun.java.swing.tree.*;
import java.awt.*;

public class CustomCellRenderer
       extends     JLabel
       Implements  TreeCellRenderer
{
    private     ImageIcon       deckImage;
    private     ImageIcon[]     suitImages;
    private     ImageIcon[]     cardImages;
    private     boolean         bSelected;

    public CustomCellRenderer()
    {
        // Load the images
        deckImage = new ImageIcon( "deck.gif" );

        suitImages = new ImageIcon[4];
        suitImages[0] = new ImageIcon( "clubs.gif" );
        suitImages[1] = new ImageIcon( "diamonds.gif" );
        suitImages[2] = new ImageIcon( "spades.gif" );
        suitImages[3] = new ImageIcon( "hearts.gif" );

        cardImages = new ImageIcon[13];
        cardImages[0] = new ImageIcon( "ace.gif" );
        cardImages[1] = new ImageIcon( "two.gif" );
        cardImages[2] = new ImageIcon( "three.gif" );
        cardImages[3] = new ImageIcon( "four.gif" );
        cardImages[4] = new ImageIcon( "five.gif" );
```

Listing 10.4B   CustomCellRenderer class code

```java
        cardImages[5] = new ImageIcon( "six.gif" );
        cardImages[6] = new ImageIcon( "seven.gif" );
        cardImages[7] = new ImageIcon( "eight.gif" );
        cardImages[8] = new ImageIcon( "nine.gif" );
        cardImages[9] = new ImageIcon( "ten.gif" );
        cardImages[10] = new ImageIcon( "jack.gif" );
        cardImages[11] = new ImageIcon( "queen.gif" );
        cardImages[12] = new ImageIcon( "king.gif" );
    }

    public Component getTreeCellRendererComponent( JTree tree,
                Object value, boolean bSelected, boolean bExpanded,
                    boolean bLeaf, int iRow, boolean bHasFocus )
    {
        // Find out which node we are rendering and get its text
        DefaultMutableTreeNode node = (DefaultMutableTreeNode)value;
        String labelText = (String)node.getUserObject();

        this.bSelected = bSelected;

        // Set the correct foreground color
        if( !bSelected )
            setForeground( Color.black );
        else
            setForeground( Color.white );

        // Determine the correct icon to display
        if( labelText.equals( "Deck" ) )
            setIcon( deckImage );
        else if( labelText.equals( "Clubs" ) )
            setIcon( suitImages[0] );
        else if( labelText.equals( "Diamonds" ) )
            setIcon( suitImages[1] );
        else if( labelText.equals( "Spades" ) )
            setIcon( suitImages[2] );
        else if( labelText.equals( "Hearts" ) )
            setIcon( suitImages[3] );
        else if( labelText.equals( "Ace" ) )
            setIcon( cardImages[0] );
        else if( labelText.equals( "Two" ) )
            setIcon( cardImages[1] );
        else if( labelText.equals( "Three" ) )
            setIcon( cardImages[2] );
        else if( labelText.equals( "Four" ) )
            setIcon( cardImages[3] );
        else if( labelText.equals( "Five" ) )
            setIcon( cardImages[4] );
```

Listing 10.4B   CustomCellRenderer class code (continued)

```
        else if( labelText.equals( "Six" ) )
            setIcon( cardImages[5] );
        else if( labelText.equals( "Seven" ) )
            setIcon( cardImages[6] );
        else if( labelText.equals( "Eight" ) )
            setIcon( cardImages[7] );
        else if( labelText.equals( "Nine" ) )
            setIcon( cardImages[8] );
        else if( labelText.equals( "Ten" ) )
            setIcon( cardImages[9] );
        else if( labelText.equals( "Jack" ) )
            setIcon( cardImages[10] );
        else if( labelText.equals( "Queen" ) )
            setIcon( cardImages[11] );
        else if( labelText.equals( "King" ) )
            setIcon( cardImages[12] );

        // Add the text to the cell
        setText( labelText );

        return this;
    }

    // This is a hack to paint the background. Normally, a JLabel can
    // paint its own background, but due to an apparent bug or
    // limitation in the TreeCellRenderer, the paint method is
    // required to handle this.
    public void paint( Graphics g )
    {
        Color   bColor;
        Icon    currentI = getIcon();

        // Set the correct background color
        bColor = bSelected ? SystemColor.textHighlight : Color.white;
        g.setColor( bColor );

        // Draw a rectangle in the background of the cell
        g.fillRect( 0, 0, getWidth() - 1, getHeight() - 1 );

        super.paint( g );
    }
}
```

Listing 10.4B CustomCellRenderer class code (continued)

The output produced by this application is shown in figure 10.3. Notice that each of the suits displays its correct image and each card shows a graphic of the number (or letter) on the card, along with the text. In order to reduce the number

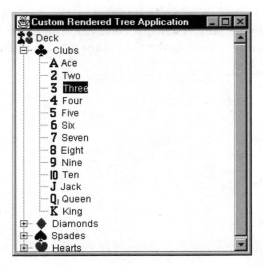

Figure 10.3
Custom rendering JTree output

of graphics needed for this example, the images for the cards are all black (so, red cards have black numbers); however, updating this to include the additional graphics for red numbers is a simple exercise.

10.1.5 Editing tree nodes

One concept that we have not touched on yet is node editing. In a manner similar to custom rendering, we can also perform custom editing of any item in a tree control. JTree supports three techniques for editing tree nodes. The easiest is to simply call the setEditable() method like this:

```
tree.setEditable( true );
```

In this mode, the tree values are editable using a simple text editor—not very intriguing, but, for many applications, this is exactly what you will need.

The second technique is to create a real custom editor for the tree, and this is what we will do in listing 10.5. In this sample, we create a tree instance and set the default cell editor to point to a combo box which allows node changes only from the list of selections.

The third technique for tree editing is to replace the `DefaultCellEditor()` reference in listing 10.5 with a class that implements `CellEditor`. You can refer to the online Swing documentation for details about the CellEditor implementation.

```
// Imports
import java.awt.*;
import java.awt.event.*;
import com.sun.java.swing.*;

class TestFrame
      extends JFrame
 {
    // Instance attributes used in this example
    private JPanel       topPanel;
    private JTree        tree;
    private JScrollPane scrollPane;

    // Constructor of main frame
    public TestFrame()
    {
        // Set the frame characteristics
        setTitle( "Editable Tree Application" );
        setSize( 300, 100 );
        setBackground( Color.gray );

        // Create a panel to hold all other components
        topPanel = new JPanel();
        topPanel.setLayout( new BorderLayout() );
        getContentPane().add( topPanel );

        // Create a new tree control
        tree = new JTree();
        tree.setEditable( true );

        // Create a combo box of editing options
        JComboBox box = new JComboBox();
        box.addItem( "Swing" );
        box.addItem( "Java" );
        box.addItem( "neat" );
        box.addItem( "funky" );
        box.addItem( "life" );
        box.addItem( "awesome" );
        box.addItem( "cool!" );

        // Add a cell editor to the tree
        tree.setCellEditor( new DefaultCellEditor( box ) );
```

Listing 10.5   Editable JTree example

```
        // Add the tree to a scrolling pane
        scrollPane = new JScrollPane();
        scrollPane.getViewport().add( tree );
        topPanel.add( scrollPane, BorderLayout.CENTER );
    }

    // Main entry point for this example
    public static void main( String args[] )
    {
        // Create an instance of the test application
        TestFrame mainFrame = new TestFrame();
        mainFrame.setVisible( true );
    }
}
```

Listing 10.5   Editable JTree example (continued)

Figure 10.4 shows the output produced as a result of executing this sample. In this example, the cell editor is set to an instance of JComboBox. In addition to this class, the cell editor can also be configured to use a JTextField or JCheckBox instance, but the implementation is the same as the one shown here.

10.2 Listening for tree actions

In the examples shown so far, no provision has been made to detect when the user actually makes a selection or performs some other significant action on a JTree instance. In this section, we will discuss the types of selection listeners supported by the JTree class. Examples of each of these listeners are included in this section.

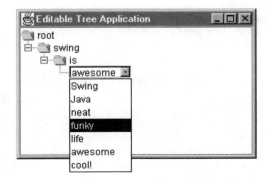

Figure 10.4
Editable JTree application output

10.2.1 Listening for tree selections

The listener we will examine is the `TreeSelectionListener`, which is responsible for handling events generated as a result of the user making item selections. Listing 10.6 contains the code required to create a tree and handle user selection events through the provision of the `valueChanged()` method. Inside this method, the application extracts the current selection from the user and displays this information in the Java console display

In the `valueChanged()` method, you will notice another Swing class named `TreePath`. This class is used to contain and describe all aspects of a path, including the string it contains and details about its parent and child relationships. For details on the `TreePath` class, see the Swing online documentation.

```java
// Imports
import java.awt.*;
import java.awt.event.*;
import com.sun.java.swing.*;
import com.sun.java.swing.event.*;
import com.sun.java.swing.tree.*;

class TestFrame
        extends         JFrame
        implements      TreeSelectionListener
  {
    // Instance attributes used in this example
    private     JPanel          topPanel;
    private     JTree           tree;
    private     JScrollPane     scrollPane;

    // Constructor of main frame
    public TestFrame()
    {
        // Set the frame characteristics
        setTitle( "TreeSelectionListener Application" );
        setSize( 300, 100 );
        setBackground( Color.gray );

        // Create a panel to hold all other components
        topPanel = new JPanel();
        topPanel.setLayout( new BorderLayout() );
        getContentPane().add( topPanel );

        // Create a new tree control
        tree = new JTree();
```

Listing 10.6   Example JTree application with a selection listener

```
            // Add a selection listener
            tree.addTreeSelectionListener( this );

            // Add the tree to a scrolling pane
            scrollPane = new JScrollPane();
            scrollPane.getViewport().add( tree );
            topPanel.add( scrollPane, BorderLayout.CENTER );
    }

    // Handle tree item selections
    public void valueChanged( TreeSelectionEvent event )
    {
        if( event.getSource() == tree )
        {
            // Display the full selection path
            TreePath path = tree.getSelectionPath();
            System.out.println( "Selection path="
                                + path.toString() );

            // Get the text for the last component
            System.out.println( "Selection="
                                + path.getLastPathComponent() );
        }
    }

    // Main entry point for this example
    public static void main( String args[] )
    {
        // Create an instance of the test application
        TestFrame mainFrame = new TestFrame();
        mainFrame.setVisible( true );
    }
}
```

Listing 10.6   Example JTree application with a selection listener (continued)

10.2.2 Listening for tree expansions

Determination of the tree node selected by a user is the most common function an application developer will implement, but there is another user action that generates events from the JTree class. A Swing-based program can intercept events caused by the user expanding or collapsing a node in a tree object. You can use this for many purposes—for example, you can enable or disable specific program features depending on the expansion state of a specific node in the tree.

Listing 10.7 contains a sample application implementing a tree object with an attached expansion listener. When the user expands a tree branch, the treeExpanded() method is called, which displays the full path of the expanded node. In a similar fashion, when a node is collapsed, the treeCollapsed() method handles the event.

```java
// Imports
import java.awt.*;
import java.awt.event.*;
import com.sun.java.swing.*;
import com.sun.java.swing.event.*;
import com.sun.java.swing.tree.*;

class TestFrame
        extends          JFrame
        implements       TreeExpansionListener
  {
    // Instance attributes used in this example
    private    JPanel          topPanel;
    private    JTree           tree;
    private    JScrollPane     scrollPane;

    // Constructor of main frame
    public TestFrame()
    {
        // Set the frame characteristics
        setTitle( "TreeExpansionListener Application" );
        setSize( 300, 300 );
        setBackground( Color.gray );

        // Create a panel to hold all other components
        topPanel = new JPanel();
        topPanel.setLayout( new BorderLayout() );
        getContentPane().add( topPanel );

        // Create a new tree control
        tree = new JTree();

        // Add a selection listener
        tree.addTreeExpansionListener( this );

        // Add the tree to a scrolling pane
        scrollPane = new JScrollPane();
        scrollPane.getViewport().add( tree );
        topPanel.add( scrollPane, BorderLayout.CENTER );
    }

    // Handle tree item expansion
    public void treeExpanded( TreeExpansionEvent event )
```

Listing 10.7 Example JTree application with an expansion listener

```
        {
            if( event.getSource() == tree )
            {
                // Display the full selection path
                TreePath path = event.getPath();
                System.out.println( "Node Expanded=" + path.toString() );
            }
        }

        // Handle tree item expansion
        public void treeCollapsed( TreeExpansionEvent event )
        {
            if( event.getSource() == tree )
            {
                // Display the full selection path
                TreePath path = event.getPath();
                System.out.println( "Node Collapsed=" + path.toString() );
            }
        }

        // Main entry point for this example
        public static void main( String args[] )
        {
            // Create an instance of the test application
            TestFrame mainFrame = new TestFrame();
            mainFrame.setVisible( true );
        }
    }
```

Listing 10.7   Example JTree application with an expansion listener (continued)

10.3   Tips and tricks for enhancing trees

There are many, more subtle aspects of the JTree component that we have not discussed so far in this chapter. These features involve adding simple, one line or two line extensions to your code to effect changes (in some cases, dramatic changes) in the character of the tree control. In this section, we will quickly examine some of these nuances.

10.3.1 Hiding the root node

A major apparent drawback of a JTree component instance is the presence of a root node within the visible window. Often, it is undesirable to display this top-level node in your application since, in many situations, the root is simply a nonfunctional container for all other nodes in the tree. Fortunately, it is simple to hide the root node from the user's view by adding a line like the following to your application:

```
tree.setRootVisible( false );
```

The root node's visibility can be controlled during the normal execution process of an application, so, it is also possible to toggle the root as part of some user configurable feature in the program.

10.3.2 Expanding and collapsing the tree

In addition to tree expansion and collapse events generated by the user, JTree also provides a programmatic interface to these functions. First, there are two distinct techniques for identifying a node: by index number and by `TreePath`. `TreePath` is the simple container for node data which we saw in the previous section, while the index number is a unique tag identifying the node (The node index count is zero-based).

The methods that are provided for expanding and collapsing tree nodes are:

```
tree.expandPath( path );
tree.collapsePath( path );
tree.expandPath( index );
tree.collapsePath( index );
```

So, for example, if you wanted to expand whatever node the user has selected, you could execute the following code:

```
tree.expandPath( tree.getSelectedPath() );
```

10.3.3 Selecting and deselecting nodes

The final aspect of the JTree class which we will discuss is the technique used to select and deselect nodes within the tree. This capability is useful for building special features into an application. For example, if you add code to perform a search of the tree data, you need a method of highlighting items when they are found.

To select nodes, you again have the option of referencing the item by its index number or by a `TreePath` data structure, which is how you most likely access the node. To select a node specified in a given `TreePath`, use code similar to the following:

```
TreePath path = …
tree.setSelectionPath( path );
```

JTree provides a method used to clear selections, as well. This is useful for deselecting all highlighted items, particularly if the tree allows multiple selections. Using this method, you can avoid having to keep track of every selected item. The format of this method is:

```
tree.clearSelection();
```

It is also possible to remove single nodes from the selection group. Some sample code to perform this task follows:

```
TreePath path = …
tree.removeSelectionPath( path );
```

10.4 JTree class information

This section lists the constants variables and methods for the JTree class.

10.4.1 JTree constants

```
public static final String CELL_RENDERER_PROPERTY
public static final String TREE_MODEL_PROPERTY
public static final String ROOT_VISIBLE_PROPERTY
public static final String SHOWS_ROOT_HANDLES_PROPERTY
public static final String ROW_HEIGHT_PROPERTY
public static final String CELL_EDITOR_PROPERTY
public static final String EDITABLE_PROPERTY
public static final String LARGE_MODEL_PROPERTY
public static final String SELECTION_MODEL_PROPERTY
public static final String VISIBLE_ROW_COUNT_PROPERTY
public static final String INVOKES_STOP_CELL_EDITING_PROPERTY
```

JTree provides several constants used to access the various properties within the class. Though you can access these constants, you will probably have little need of them in normal use of the JTree component.

10.4.2 JTree variables

```
protected transient TreeModel treeModel
```

This variable holds the instance of the current tree model used by the JTree instance.

```
protected transient TreeSelectionModel selectionModel
```

This variable holds the instance of the current selection model used by the JTree instance.

```
protected boolean rootVisible
```

If true, this flag indicates that the root node of the tree is visible; otherwise, the root is not shown to the user.

```
protected transient TreeCellRenderer cellRenderer
```

This variable holds the instance of the current tree cell renderer object used by the JTree instance for the renderer to draw node items.

```
protected int rowHeight
```

The `rowHeight` variable contains an integer value indicating the height of each row in the table. If this value is less than or equal to zero, the cell renderer will be used to determine the height of each row.

```
protected boolean showsRootHandles
```

This boolean flag controls whether or not there should be handles shown at the top level of the tree. If the root node is not shown, it is recommended that this flag be set as true.

```
protected transient TreeCellEditor cellEditor
```

This variable holds the instance of the current tree cell editor object used by the JTree instance.

```
protected int visibleRowCount
```

This variable contains an integer value representing the number of rows of the table that are visible in the user interface.

```
protected boolean editable
protected boolean largeModel
protected boolean invokesStopCellEditing
```

These boolean variables control other miscellaneous characteristics of the JTree instance.

10.4.3 JTree constructors

```
public JTree()
```

This constructor creates an instance of a JTree component providing a sample data model.

```
public JTree( Object value[] )
```

This constructor creates an instance of a JTree component providing a default data model that receives the data contained in the supplied object array.

```
public JTree( Vector value )
```

This constructor creates an instance of a JTree component providing a default data model that receives the data contained in the supplied vectored array of objects.

```
public JTree( Hashtable value )
```

This constructor creates an instance of a JTree component providing a default data model that receives the data contained in the supplied hash table.

```
public JTree( TreeNode root )
```

This constructor creates an instance of a JTree component providing a default data model with the root node specified. By default, the asksAllowsChildren flag is false, so the leaf state of nodes is determined by the isLeaf() method.

```
public JTree( TreeNode root, boolean asksAllowsChildren )
```

This constructor creates an instance of a JTree component providing a default data model with the root node specified. If the asksAllowsChildren flag is false, the leaf state of nodes is determined by the isLeaf() method: otherwise, the getAllowsChildren() method is supported.

```
public JTree( TreeModel newModel )
```

This constructor creates an instance of a JTree component providing a specified data model containing the tree data.

10.4.4 JTree significant method groups

```
public TreeCellRenderer getCellRenderer()
public void setCellRenderer(TreeCellRenderer x)
```

This group of methods manages the cell renderer used for the JTree instance. When the tree object is constructed, the DefaultTreeCellRenderer is instantiated.

```
public void setEditable(boolean flag)
public boolean isEditable()
public void setCellEditor(TreeCellEditor cellEditor)
public TreeCellEditor getCellEditor()
public void setInvokesStopCellEditing(boolean newValue)
public boolean getInvokesStopCellEditing()
public boolean isPathEditable(TreePath path)
```

```
public boolean isEditing()
public boolean stopEditing()
public void startEditingAtPath(TreePath path)
public TreePath getEditingPath()
```

These methods manage and control the characteristics of the cell editor for the JTree instance. Though the tree object will create a default cell editor, a new one can be created and inserted.

```
public TreeModel getModel()
public void setModel(TreeModel newModel)
```

This group of methods manages the data model used for the JTree instance. When the tree object is constructed, the `DefaultTreeModel` is instantiated.

```
public boolean isRootVisible()
public void setRootVisible(boolean rootVisible)
public void setShowsRootHandles(boolean newValue)
public boolean getShowsRootHandles()
```

The methods in this group control the presence or absence of the root node and root handles in the tree's user interface.

```
public void setRowHeight(int rowHeight)
public int getRowHeight()
public boolean isFixedRowHeight()
```

These methods control the height of each row shown in the tree. The JTree class supports both fixed and variable row heights, which are controlled by either the default cell renderer or by a custom rendering class provided by the developer.

```
public void setLargeModel(boolean newValue)
public boolean isLargeModel()
```

This group of methods manages the large data model flag, which controls how the tree reacts to large data. Note that not all user interfaces support a large model.

```
public int getRowCount()
```

This method returns the number of rows contained in the tree. Each item in the tree is considered a row, regardless of its expansion state.

```
public void setSelectionPath(TreePath path)
public void setSelectionPaths(TreePath paths[])
public void setSelectionRow(int row)
public void setSelectionRows(int rows[])
public void addSelectionPath(TreePath path)
public void addSelectionPaths(TreePath paths[])
```

```
public void addSelectionRow(int row)
public void addSelectionRows(int rows[])
public void setSelectionInterval(int index0, int index1)
public void addSelectionInterval(int index0, int index1)
public void removeSelectionInterval(int index0, int index1)
public void removeSelectionPath(TreePath path)
public void removeSelectionPaths(TreePath paths[])
public void removeSelectionRow(int row)
public void removeSelectionRows(int rows[])
public void clearSelection()
public Object getLastSelectedPathComponent()
public TreePath getSelectionPath()
public TreePath[] getSelectionPaths()
public int[] getSelectionRows()
public int getSelectionCount()
public int getMinSelectionRow()
public int getMaxSelectionRow()
public int getLeadSelectionRow()
public TreePath getLeadSelectionPath()\
public boolean isRowSelected(int row)
public boolean isSelectionEmpty()
public boolean isPathSelected(TreePath path)
```

This large group of methods manages selections within the tree object. Single nodes can be added or removed from the selection group; however, entire ranges of items can also be handled with ease. This group also provides several methods to determine not only the range of selected nodes, but also the minimum and maximum indices for selected nodes.

```
public boolean isExpanded(TreePath path)
public boolean isExpanded(int row)
public boolean isCollapsed(TreePath path)
public boolean isCollapsed(int row)
public void expandPath(TreePath path)
public void expandRow(int row)
public void collapsePath(TreePath path)
public void collapseRow(int row)
```

This group of methods manages the visible state of the tree nodes within the user interface. Any parent node can be expanded or collapsed programmatically with these methods, and the current state can be determined with the boolean method in this group.

```
public void makeVisible(TreePath path)
public boolean isVisible(TreePath path)
public Rectangle getPathBounds(TreePath path)
public Rectangle getRowBounds(int row)
```

```
public void scrollPathToVisible(TreePath path)
public void scrollRowToVisible(int row)
```

With these methods, the developer can control the visibility of a specified node within the user interface. With these methods, it is possible to reposition the tree viewport to display any node you choose.

```
public TreePath getPathForRow(int row)
public int getRowForPath(TreePath path)
public TreePath getPathForLocation(int x, int y)
public int getRowForLocation(int x, int y)
public TreePath getClosestPathForLocation(int x, int y)
public int getClosestRowForLocation(int x, int y)
```

This group of methods act as helpers to resolve row-to-path and path-to-row conversions. Additionally, some of these methods resolve node to X-, Y-coordinate conversions, which can be used when handling mouse events.

```
public void setSelectionModel( TreeSelectionModel selectionModel )
public TreeSelectionModel getSelectionModel()
```

This group of methods manages the selection model used for the JTree instance. When the tree object is constructed, the `DefaultTreeSelectionModel` is instantiated.

```
public void addTreeExpansionListener( TreeExpansionListener tel )
public void removeTreeExpansionListener( TreeExpansionListener tel )
public void addTreeSelectionListener(TreeSelectionListener tsl )
public void removeTreeSelectionListener( TreeSelectionListener tsl )
```

The four methods shown here control the listeners supported by the JTree class. A tree object supports two listeners: one for selection events and one for tree node expansion and collapse.

10.5 Chapter summary

This chapter encapsulated most of what you need to know to create graphical tree components in your Swing-based Java applications. We started by examining a simple tree example that implemented a sample data model, allowing us to create a small sample from which to build the other examples in this chapter. In a more advanced example, we created a hierarchical tree containing all of the cards in a deck and used the tree to divide each suit.

Next, we examined the subject of custom data models within a tree component and rebuilt the card deck code example. Instead of accessing a large dynamic array inside the default data model, the custom data model manufactured its data single static array, eliminating the duplication for the cards in each suit. The result was a smaller, faster application that would exhibit even better performance as the size of the data model increases.

In the third segment of this chapter, we examined custom rendering, which allowed us to add pizzazz to the revamped card application. In the new sample, each suit was represented by a graphic rendering of the correct symbol, and each card in the tree displayed a graphic representing its value. Custom rendering empowers us to create almost any sort of presentation we choose—be it color and font changes (depending on what the tree is displaying), or the addition of animated graphics.

Following custom rendering, we quickly studied the (closely related) editing capabilities of JTree, which allow the user to modify the contents of nodes in the tree hierarchy. By default, Swing supports editors for text fields, combo boxes, and check boxes, but, with a bit more work, new TreeCellEditor classes can be implemented to support other types of editing.

Finally, we looked at some of the subtler, but no less important, aspects of Swing's JTree. With the addition of just a few lines of code, an application can present a tree without a root node, programmatically expanding or collapsing selected nodes.

In the next chapter, we will complete our examination of the Swing components by taking an in-depth look at the table component, sometimes referred to as a spreadsheet component or a grid. Then, we will move into the final segment of this book to discuss more advanced topics in Swing and the Java environment.

11

Tables

For the final chapter of part 2, we will cover a particularly interesting topic—tables. In the two previous chapters, you were introduced to Swing's list box and graphical tree controls, both of which are useful for displaying large amounts of data. But, in many situations, they are inappropriate because they simply cannot display enough data. So, in many applications, you will need to display a grid of data consisting of rows and columns similar to a spreadsheet.

Swing's JTable control is a Java component that provides the power to present large amounts of data in a simple two-dimensional display, and it supports custom data modeling and display rendering. There is no equivalent to JTable in the standard AWT component library; however, many third-party venders do offer spreadsheet components. Though JTable's look is similar to these spreadsheet components, it does not have the same feel. The JTable class has some limitations that will prevent you from using it as a spreadsheet, but it supports many features that make it superior to a simple spreadsheet component.

UI GUIDELINE **Use a consistent tabular presentation.** There are style guides devoted entirely to tables. Some of the rules are: centering and bolding column headings, left aligning row headers and text, right aligning numerical data, and bolding of totals. Acceptable deviations include aligning the column header with the data below (for example, right aligning column headers with right aligned numerical data below). Also, you will need to determine what happens to the data display when the user resizes columns—the view of the data should remain contiguous. Whatever rules you follow or establish, be consistent throughout your table implementation.

11.1 Basic table use

Like other advanced components in the Swing library, JTable implementations can be as simple or as complex as you wish. For example, in its simplest form, you can implement a JTable-based application with just a few lines of code, or, with much more code, you can offer custom data modeling and display rendering. The results are directly proportional to the amount of code you write.

In this section, we will start by creating two simple examples. The first will only display a small amount of data. In the second example, we will add scrolling capability and implement some JTable features.

11.1.1 The simplest of table examples

This example contains code to generate a tree column table with four rows of numerical data, and, as you will see, even in this simple example we get a lot of functionality with very little code.

```
// Imports
import java.awt.*;
import com.sun.java.swing.*;

class TestFrame
      extends JFrame
{
    // Instance attributes used in this example
    private JPanel       topPanel;
    private JTable       table;
    private JScrollPane scrollPane;

    // Constructor of main frame
    public TestFrame()
    {
        // Set the frame characteristics
        setTitle( "Simple Table Application" );
        setSize( 300, 200 );
        setBackground( Color.gray );

        // Create a panel to hold all other components
        topPanel = new JPanel();
        topPanel.setLayout( new BorderLayout() );
        getContentPane().add( topPanel );

        // Create columns names
        String columnNames[] = { "Column 1", "Column 2", "Column 3" };

        // Create some data
        String dataValues[][] =
        {
            { "12", "234", "67" },
            { "-123", "43", "853" },
            { "93", "89.2", "109" },
            { "279", "9033", "3092" }
        };

        // Create a new table instance
        table = new JTable( dataValues, columnNames );

        // Add the table to a scrolling pane
```

Listing 11.1 Simple JTable sample source code

```
        scrollPane = table.createScrollPaneForTable( table );
        topPanel.add( scrollPane, BorderLayout.CENTER );
    }

    // Main entry point for this example
    public static void main( String args[] )
    {
        // Create an instance of the test application
        TestFrame mainFrame = new TestFrame();
        mainFrame.setVisible( true );
    }
}
```

Listing 11.1   Simple JTable sample source code (continued)

Listing 11.1 implements arrays containing the column names and sample data, which are added to the table when it is constructed. The example also includes scrolling capability with a simple call to the `createScrollPaneForTable()` method.

Figure 11.1 shows the execution results of this example. Clicking the left mouse button on an individual cell will highlight the entire row and select the individual cell (notice the select rectangle surrounding the 89.2 value. The example appears quite simple at first, but there is more than meets the eye.

If you reduce the height of the window, the vertical scroll bar appears by default. Resizing the frame in the horizontal direction automatically adds the horizontal scroll bar. Another feature that the application inherits is the ability to reorganize and resize the columns. For example, placing the mouse pointer on a

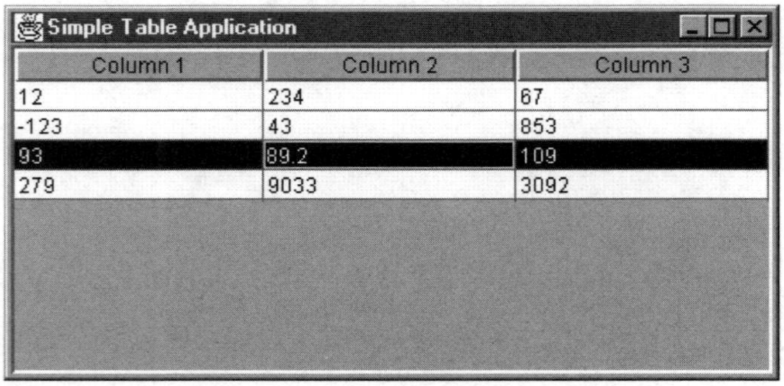

Figure 11.1   Simple JTable sample output

column name and dragging it (with the left mouse button pressed) allows the entire column to be moved to a new position. When the mouse button is released, the selected column is dropped into its new location and the entire table is repainted to accommodate the adjustment. Placing the mouse pointer on the vertical separator between two column headers causes the pointer to change to a resize indicator. Holding down the left mouse button while dragging resizes the columns.

11.1.2 A more complex table example

Many JTable features (column movement, and so forth) are enabled by default, so even our simple example was more advanced than we might have expected. Our second example shows a few of the somewhat more advanced features of the JTable class.

This example builds on the first by using loader methods to load an array of eight columns by 100 rows. Additionally, the table is configured to show only the vertical grid lines and to allow simultaneous row and column selection. Listing 11.2 contains all of the source code for this example.

```
// Imports
import java.awt.*;
import java.util.*;
import com.sun.java.swing.*;
import com.sun.java.swing.table.*;

class TestFrame
        extends JFrame
{
    // Instance attributes used in this example
    private JPanel      topPanel;
    private JTable      table;
    private JScrollPane scrollPane;

    private String      columnNames[];
    private String      dataValues[][];

    // Constructor of main frame

    public TestFrame()
    {
        // Set the frame characteristics
        setTitle( "Advanced Table Application" );
```

Listing 11.2   More complex JTable sample source code

```
        setSize( 300, 200 );
        setBackground( Color.gray );

        // Create a panel to hold all other components
        topPanel = new JPanel();
        topPanel.setLayout( new BorderLayout() );
        getContentPane().add( topPanel );

        // Create columns
        CreateColumns();
        CreateData();

        // Create a new table instance
        table = new JTable( dataValues, columnNames );

        // Configure some of JTable's parameters
        table.setShowHorizontalLines( false );
        table.setRowSelectionAllowed( true );
        table.setColumnSelectionAllowed( true );

        // Change the selection color
        table.setSelectionForeground( Color.white );
        table.setSelectionBackground( Color.red );

        // Add the table to a scrolling pane
        scrollPane = table.createScrollPaneForTable( table );
        topPanel.add( scrollPane, BorderLayout.CENTER );
    }

    public void CreateColumns()
    {
        // Create column string labels
        columnNames = new String[8];

        for( int iCtr = 0; iCtr < 8; iCtr++ )
            columnNames[iCtr] = "Col:" + iCtr;
    }

    public void CreateData()
    {
        // Create data for each element
        dataValues = new String[100][8];

        for( int iY = 0; iY < 100; iY++ )
        {
            for( int iX = 0; iX < 8; iX++ )
            {
                dataValues[iY][iX] = "" + iX + "," + iY;
```

Listing 11.2   More complex JTable sample source code (continued)

```
        }
     }
  }

  // Main entry point for this example
  public static void main( String args[] )
  {
     // Create an instance of the test application
     TestFrame mainFrame = new TestFrame();
     mainFrame.setVisible( true );
  }
}
```

Listing 11.2   More complex JTable sample source code (continued)

Figure 11.2 shows the result produced by executing this code. Notice that with this example, when an individual cell is selected, a cross-hair selection pattern is formed, centered around the selected cell. In this sample, the foreground and background colors for the selection region have been altered for effect (JTable supports color changes for the selection area).

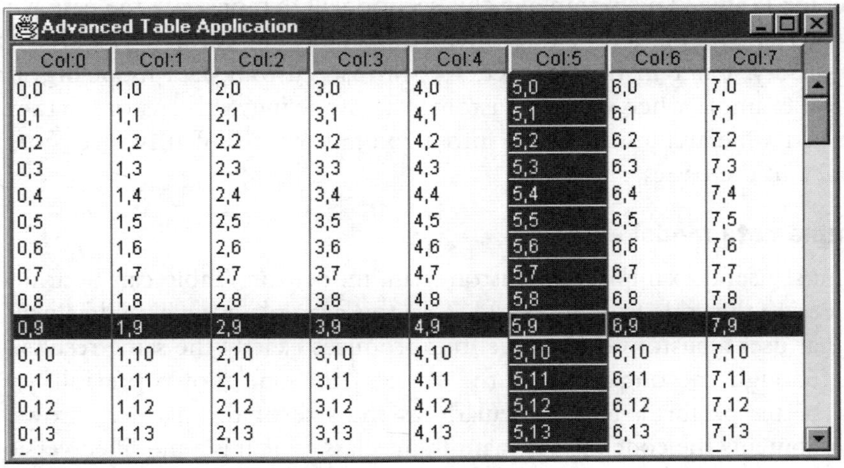

Figure 11.2   More complex JTable sample output

IMHO   This example implements a relatively large array of data. The JTable class in the 1.0 release of Swing does not handle large data particularly well, resulting in generally poor performance. If your application demands large arrays (more than 2,000 elements), you should probably consider a grid component from a third-party vendor.

11.2   Adding a custom data model

As with most other Swing components, JTable supports the replacement of its data model in order to improve performance or to help reduce the size of the code required for a given application. The custom data model feature used in JTable is actually simpler than the one used for (for example) the JTree class because JTable manages a simple two-dimensional matrix of data rather than a convoluted array of nested information. With a custom data model, JTable supports additional data elements for each cell (used, typically, with custom data rendering to control how cells are displayed).

In this section, we will examine the benefits of supporting a custom data model for JTable. The example in this section will demonstrate the ease with which a custom data model can be implemented, its better performance, and its extended functionality. Later in this chapter, we will use custom data modeling in a more practical example when we link custom data modeling with custom data rendering to embed a hierarchical data tree into a column of a JTable instance. For now, we will stick to the basics.

11.2.1 A simple data model example

The most useful example of a custom data model for JTable can be found by re-engineering the code from listing 11.2. In this example, we will build a new application that uses a custom data model but produces exactly the same results as listing 11.2. Though the output looks the same as the one shown previously, it offers much better performance, particularly as the size of the data set grows. Listing 11.3A contains the code for the main frame class, which is a modified version of the previous example.

Notice that in this source code listing, the `CreateData()` method has been removed—it is no longer required because the custom data model generates the data set. Also, the `CreateColumns()` method has been changed. Since the code no

```java
// Imports
import java.awt.*;
import java.util.*;
import com.sun.java.swing.*;
import com.sun.java.swing.table.*;

class TestFrame
       extends JFrame
 {
    // Instance attributes used in this example
    private JPanel      topPanel;
    private JTable      table;
    private JScrollPane scrollPane;

    private String      columnNames[];
    private String      dataValues[][];

    // Constructor of main frame
    public TestFrame()
    {
        // Set the frame characteristics
        setTitle( "Custom Table Data Model Application" );
        setSize( 300, 200 );
        setBackground( Color.gray );

        // Create a panel to hold all other components
        topPanel = new JPanel();
        topPanel.setLayout( new BorderLayout() );
        getContentPane().add( topPanel );

        // Create the custom data model
        CustomDataModel customDataModel = new CustomDataModel();

        // Create a new table instance
        table = new JTable( customDataModel );

        // Create columns
        CreateColumns();

        // Configure some of JTable's parameters
        table.setShowHorizontalLines( false );
        table.setRowSelectionAllowed( true );
        table.setColumnSelectionAllowed( true );

        // Change the selection color
        table.setSelectionForeground( Color.white );
        table.setSelectionBackground( Color.red );
```

Listing 11.3A   Custom data modeling JTable sample source code

```
        // Add the table to a scrolling pane
        scrollPane = table.createScrollPaneForTable( table );
        topPanel.add( scrollPane, BorderLayout.CENTER );
    }

    public void CreateColumns()
    {
        // Say that we are manually creating the columns
        table.setAutoCreateColumnsFromModel( false );

        for( int iCtr = 0; iCtr < 8; iCtr++ )
        {
            // Manually create a new column
            TableColumn column = new TableColumn( iCtr );
            column.setHeaderValue( (Object)("Col:" + iCtr) );

            // Add the column to the table
            table.addColumn( column );
        }
    }

    // Main entry point for this example
    public static void main( String args[] )
    {
        // Create an instance of the test application
        TestFrame mainFrame = new TestFrame();
        mainFrame.setVisible( true );
    }
}
```

Listing 11.3A   Custom data modeling JTable sample source code (continued)

longer uses an instance of the DefaultDataModel class (instantiated automatically by JTable in the previous example), the application is now required to create its own columns. To accomplish this, the CreateColumns() method reverts to first principles by creating an instance of a TableColumn object and populating it with the appropriate text before adding it to the table. Also, since the example now generates its own column data, it notifies the table not to attempt to determine this information from the data. It does this by calling JTable's setAutoCreateColumns-FromModel() method.

Listing 11.3B holds the code for the custom data model, which extends the AbstractTableModel class and provides four methods called by the JTable code when data is accessed. Since the data model is now synthesized, the getValueAt() method simply determines the row and column being accessed and generates a string representing the cell data.

The `getColumnCount()` method returns a value of zero, which may not be what you expected. Remember, though, that this method returns the number of columns managed by the table code. In the `CreateColumns()` method in listing 11.3A, we informed the table that it should not attempt to generate any of its own columns. As a result, the value of `getColumnCount()` is zero.

```
// Imports
import com.sun.java.swing.*;
import com.sun.java.swing.table.*;

class CustomDataModel
        extends      AbstractTableModel
{

    public Object getValueAt( int iRowIndex, int iColumnIndex )
    {
        return "" + iColumnIndex + "," + iRowIndex;
    }

    public void setValueAt( Object aValue, int iRowIndex,
                                      int iColumnIndex )
    {
        // All data is manufactured - nothing to do here
    }

    public int getColumnCount()
    {
        // Return 0 because we handle our own columns
        return 0;
    }

    public int getRowCount()
    {
        // Return the number of rows in this table
        return 500;
    }
}
```

Listing 11.3B   CustomDataModel source code

As indicated previously, custom data models are much more useful when used in conjunction with custom rendering. In the next section, we will discuss rendering, and, in the last section of this chapter, we will merge both topics to create an interesting and powerful application.

11.3 Adding custom rendering

With other Swing user interface classes, we discussed techniques to add custom rendering support. This usually involves creating a new rendering object that extends an abstract class supplied by Swing. With the JTable class, rendering is accomplished using a mechanism similar to the other Swing classes we have seen. If you are comparing JTable to most third-party grid components, the greater flexibility of JTable rendering is obvious because it allows developers more display options for the contents of each cell.

In this section, we will generate some sample code to demonstrate the sorts of things you can accomplish with custom rendering. As usual, we will begin simply and continue to build on the sample to include the full complement of rendering features. Since we have already seen much of the actual rendering code, only the rendering engine for the JTable will be new to you.

11.3.1 Simple table cell rendering

Let's start by looking at an example program that implements a custom rendered JTable. The sample presented here implements the custom rendering on top of the modified code from the first example in this chapter. Instead of displaying numerical (X, Y) data, the code revisits the card deck example from the previous chapter; however, the display is in tabular form rather than in a tree. Each column represents a suit in the deck, with each cell drawn as a graphical suit and a card number.

Listing 11.4A contains the code for the main frame of the application. The only significant notable in this file is the call to the JTable's `setCellRenderer()` method, which informs the table object that all of its drawing will be handled by an external rendering class.

```
// Imports
import java.awt.*;
import java.util.*;
import com.sun.java.swing.*;
import com.sun.java.swing.table.*;

class TestFrame
      extends JFrame
 {
    // Instance attributes used in this example
```

Listing 11.4A   Custom rendering JTable sample source code

```
private JPanel      topPanel;
private JTable      table;
private JScrollPane scrollPane;

private String      columnNames[];
private String      dataValues[][];

// Constructor of main frame
public TestFrame()
{
    // Set the frame characteristics
    setTitle( "Custom Cell Rendering Application" );
    setSize( 300, 200 );
    setBackground( Color.gray );

    // Create a panel to hold all other components
    topPanel = new JPanel();
    topPanel.setLayout( new BorderLayout() );
    getContentPane().add( topPanel );

    // Create the custom data model
    CustomDataModel customDataModel = new CustomDataModel();

    // Create a new table instance
    table = new JTable( customDataModel );

    // Create columns
    CreateColumns();

    // Configure some of JTable's parameters
    table.setShowHorizontalLines( false );
    table.setRowSelectionAllowed( true );
    table.setColumnSelectionAllowed( true );

    // Change the selection color
    table.setSelectionForeground( Color.white );
    table.setSelectionBackground( Color.red );

    // Add the table to a scrolling pane
    scrollPane = table.createScrollPaneForTable( table );
    topPanel.add( scrollPane, BorderLayout.CENTER );
}

public void CreateColumns()
{
    // Say that we are manually creating the columns
    table.setAutoCreateColumnsFromModel( false );
    for( int iCtr = 0; iCtr < 4; iCtr++ )
    {
```

Listing 11.4A   Custom rendering JTable sample source code (continued)

```
                // Manually create a new column
                TableColumn column = new TableColumn( iCtr );
                column.setHeaderValue( (Object)("Col:" + iCtr) );

                // Add a cell renderer for this class
                column.setCellRenderer( new CustomCellRenderer() );

                // Add the column to the table
                table.addColumn( column );
            }
        }

        // Main entry point for this example
        public static void main( String args[] )
        {
            // Create an instance of the test application
            TestFrame mainFrame = new TestFrame();
            mainFrame.setVisible( true );
        }
    }
}
```

Listing 11.4A   Custom rendering JTable sample source code (continued)

Listing 11.4B contains the code for the custom table cell renderer, implementing a method named getTableCellRendererComponent() to handle the drawing of individual cells. This method determines if the item it is drawing is selected or has the focus, and uses this information to control the foreground color. Because of the restrictions noted in a previous chapter with regard to painting the background color, this class also provides a paint() method, which uses the selection and focus flags as well.

The developers of Swing wisely decided to design custom rendering to ensure as much commonality as possible between the various user interface components. For this reason, you should notice remarkable similarities between the custom renderer presented here and those shown in previous chapters. You may observe that the code in listing 11.4B does not change the font, but we implemented this capability in the JList rendering example in chapter 9. You can duplicate the font changing code in this example, if desired.

```
import java.awt.*;
import com.sun.java.swing.*;
import com.sun.java.swing.table.*;
```

Listing 11.4B   CustomCellRender source code

```
class CustomCellRenderer
    extends         JLabel
    implements      TableCellRenderer
{
    private boolean     isSelected;
    private boolean     hasFocus;
    private ImageIcon[] suitImages;

    public CustomCellRenderer()
    {
        suitImages = new ImageIcon[4];
        suitImages[0] = new ImageIcon( "clubs.gif" );
        suitImages[1] = new ImageIcon( "diamonds.gif" );
        suitImages[2] = new ImageIcon( "spades.gif" );
        suitImages[3] = new ImageIcon( "hearts.gif" );
    }

    public Component getTableCellRendererComponent( JTable table,
                Object value, boolean isSelected, boolean hasFocus,
                int row, int column )
    {
        String sText = (String)value;
        this.isSelected = isSelected;
        this.hasFocus = hasFocus;

        if( isSelected )
            setForeground( Color.red );
        else
            setForeground( Color.black );
        if( hasFocus )
            setForeground( Color.cyan );

        setIcon( suitImages[column] );

        setText( "" + row );
        return this;
    }

    // This is a hack to paint the background. Normally, a JLabel can
    // paint its own background, but due to an apparent bug or
    // limitation in the TableCellRenderer, the paint method is
    // required to handle this.
    public void paint( Graphics g )
    {
        Color   bColor;
        Icon    currentI = getIcon();

        // Set the correct background color
```

Listing 11.4B CustomCellRender source code (continued)

```
        if( isSelected )
            bColor = Color.cyan;
        else
            bColor = Color.white;
        if( hasFocus )
            bColor = Color.red;
        g.setColor( bColor );

        // Draw a rectangle in the background of the cell
        g.fillRect( 0, 0, getWidth() - 1, getHeight() - 1 );

        super.paint( g );
    }
}
```

Listing 11.4B   CustomCellRender source code (continued)

The application implemented in listings 11.4A, 11.4B, and 11.4C also includes a custom data model, which is similar to previous examples. The only difference is in the number of rows in the model—thirteen, in this case. Listing 11.4C is provided only for reference.

```
// Imports
import com.sun.java.swing.*;
import com.sun.java.swing.table.*;

class CustomDataModel
        extends      AbstractTableModel
{
    public Object getValueAt( int iRowIndex, int iColumnIndex )
    {
        return "" + iColumnIndex + "," + iRowIndex;
    }

    public void setValueAt( Object aValue, int iRowIndex,
                                      int iColumnIndex )
    {
        // All data is manufactured - nothing to do here
    }

    public int getColumnCount()
    {
        // Return 0 because we handle our own columns
        return 0;
```

Listing 11.4C   CustomDataModel source code

```
    }
    public int getRowCount()
    {
        return 13;
    }
}
```

Listing 11.4C CustomDataModel source code

Figure 11.3 shows the output produced by this program. Each cell contains the individual card value, though, in this example, card numbers start at zero and there are no face cards. Since much of the data, particularly the graphics, are replicated from one cell to the next, the example is not particularly practical. The only purpose of this example is to demonstrate that each cell can be individually displayed. You can easily draw completely different graphic images for each cell.

In the last section of this chapter, we will create a more interesting example in which a column of the table will be rendered as a hierarchical tree. This will require a more complex data model, and, in order to represent the model graphically, we will need to implement a more advanced custom cell renderer.

11.4 Rendering column headers

In the previous section, you saw how to render the individual cells of a table, but tables also contain another key piece of information—the column headers. By default, JTable renders a column header as a gray box with black text and a beveled border—not particularly inspiring. Fortunately, a table column header is really just another type of cell, and, as such, we can modify it to suit our own needs.

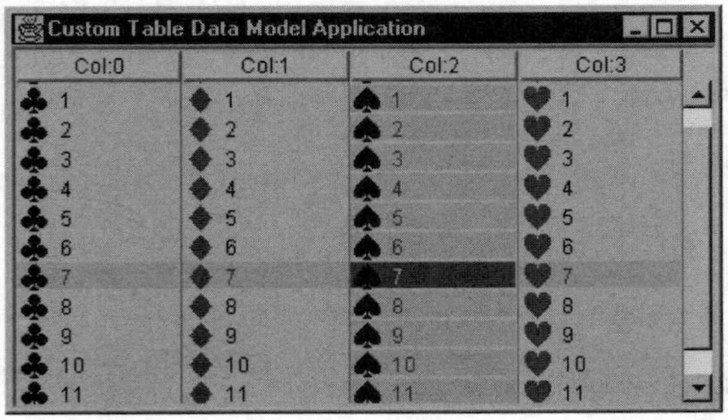

Figure 11.3
Custom renderer program output

In this section, we will discuss rendering techniques for the column headers of a JTable instance. As you will see, the syntax for accomplishing this is just a slight modification of our previous cell rendering examples. In fact, we could render the headers using the same code if we wanted to, but, in the examples presented in this section, we will exploit more interesting aspects of the column header.

11.4.1 Simple header rendering

Listing 11.5A shows the source code for the main frame of the header rendering application. This code is virtually identical to the code in the previous example, except that, in this case, the call to `setCellRender()` in the `CreateColumns()` class method has been replaced with a call to JTable's `setHeaderRender()` method. This new method call informs the table instance that the specified rendering class is taking responsibility for drawing the column headers.

```
// Imports
import java.awt.*;
import java.util.*;
import com.sun.java.swing.*;
import com.sun.java.swing.table.*;

class TestFrame
      extends JFrame
{
    // Instance attributes used in this example
    private JPanel    topPanel;
    private JTable    table;
    private JScrollPane scrollPane;

    private String    columnNames[];
    private String    dataValues[][];

    // Constructor of main frame
    public TestFrame()
    {
        // Set the frame characteristics
        setTitle( "Custom Header Rendering Application" );
        setSize( 300, 200 );
        setBackground( Color.gray );

        // Create a panel to hold all other components
        topPanel = new JPanel();
        topPanel.setLayout( new BorderLayout() );
```

Listing 11.5A   Custom header rendering sample frame source code

```
        getContentPane().add( topPanel );

        // Create the custom data model
        CustomDataModel customDataModel = new CustomDataModel();

        // Create a new table instance
        table = new JTable( customDataModel );

        // Create columns
        CreateColumns();

        // Configure some of JTable's parameters
        table.setShowHorizontalLines( false );
        table.setRowSelectionAllowed( true );
        table.setColumnSelectionAllowed( true );

        // Change the selection color
        table.setSelectionForeground( Color.white );
        table.setSelectionBackground( Color.red );

        // Add the table to a scrolling pane
        scrollPane = table.createScrollPaneForTable( table );
        topPanel.add( scrollPane, BorderLayout.CENTER );
    }

    public void CreateColumns()
    {
        // Say that we are manually creating the columns
        table.setAutoCreateColumnsFromModel( false );

        for( int iCtr = 0; iCtr < 4; iCtr++ )
        {
            // Manually create a new column
            TableColumn column = new TableColumn( iCtr );
            column.setHeaderValue( (Object)("Col:" + iCtr) );

            // Add a cell renderer for this class
            column.setHeaderRenderer( new CustomHeaderRenderer() );

            // Add the column to the table
            table.addColumn( column );
        }
    }

    // Main entry point for this example
    public static void main( String args[] )
    {
        // Create an instance of the test application
        TestFrame mainFrame = new TestFrame();
```

Listing 11.5A   Custom header rendering sample frame source code (continued)

```
        mainFrame.setVisible( true );
    }
}
```

Listing 11.5A   Custom header rendering sample frame source code (continued)

The actual header rendering class, CustomHeaderRenderer, is shown in listing 11.5B. Since a column header is just a specialized type of cell, it makes sense that this class implements a TableCellRender. However, in the getTableCellRendererComponent() method, we can ignore the row value and the boolean flag containing the selection and focus state.

The rendering code first sets the alignment of the text and icon such that the text will be positioned underneath the icon and both attributes will be centered within the header label. Next, a border is applied which, in this case, is a titled border showing the true column label used in the table. Finally, the method performs a bit of its own data modeling by determining the column (0 through 3) and assigning the label text to the appropriate card suit.

```
import java.awt.*;
import com.sun.java.swing.*;
import com.sun.java.swing.border.*;
import com.sun.java.swing.table.*;

class CustomHeaderRenderer
    extends         JLabel
    implements      TableCellRenderer
{
    private boolean     isSelected;
    private boolean     hasFocus;
    private ImageIcon[] suitImages;

    public CustomHeaderRenderer()
    {
        suitImages = new ImageIcon[4];
        suitImages[0] = new ImageIcon( "clubs.gif" );
        suitImages[1] = new ImageIcon( "diamonds.gif" );
        suitImages[2] = new ImageIcon( "spades.gif" );
        suitImages[3] = new ImageIcon( "hearts.gif" );
    }

    public Component getTableCellRendererComponent( JTable table,
            Object value, boolean isSelected, boolean hasFocus,
```

Listing 11.5B   CustomHeaderRenderer source code

```
                    int row, int column )
  {
    // Retreive the text to display
    String sText = (String)value;

    // Set all sorts of interesting alignment options
    setVerticalAlignment( SwingConstants.CENTER );
    setHorizontalAlignment( SwingConstants.CENTER );
    setHorizontalTextPosition( SwingConstants.CENTER );
    setVerticalTextPosition( SwingConstants.BOTTOM );

    // Assign a border
    setBorder( new TitledBorder( new EtchedBorder(), sText ) );

    // Populate the icon and text
    setIcon( suitImages[column] );

    // Set the text to the correct suit
    switch( column )
    {
        case 0:
            setText( "Clubs" );
            break;
        case 1:
            setText( "Diamonds" );
            break;
        case 2:
            setText( "Hearts" );
            break;
        case 3:
            setText( "Spades" );
            break;
    }

    return this;
  }
}
```

Listing 11.5B   CustomHeaderRenderer source code (continued)

 This example also requires the CustomDataModel.java file shown in the previous example. Since this file is unchanged from the one shown in listing 11.4C, it has been omitted.

Figure 11.4 illustrates the output produced by this example. Notice the dramatic difference between the headers shown here and those of the default JTable rendering engine. Like table cells, the possibilities for the content of custom rendered headers is virtually limitless—you can display just about anything you wish to, even if you use only the simple JLabel derivative shown in the previous two examples.

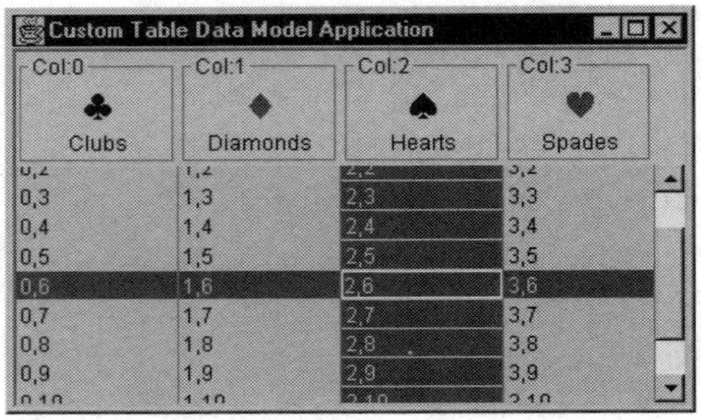

Figure 11.4
Custom header renderer program output

11.5 Listening for table actions

In all of the shown examples so far in this chapter, no effort has been made to detect changes in the characteristics or attributes of the table. Many situations demand that the application immediately detect changes initiated by the user, so we need to examine the mechanisms supported by JTable to recognize user activity. These events can be sorted into two basic categories: cell selections made by the user, and user-invoked changes to the table itself. In this section, we will examine the possible events that a Swing-based table object generates, and we will develop some simple examples to demonstrate how to listen for and handle these events.

11.5.1 Detecting table selections

The first type of action we will study is the user-invoked selection, which usually involves a mouse click to select a single cell or a drag operation to select a range of values from the table. In chapter 10, we created an application containing a JList instance, and implemented a `ListSelectionListener` to handle selections. JTable and JList share many common concepts and, fortunately, handle selection listeners in exactly the same way. You already know how to detect user selections in a JList, so, all we need to do here is to develop a simple example which includes user-invoked selections.

```java
// Imports
import java.awt.*;
import com.sun.java.swing.*;
import com.sun.java.swing.event.*;
import com.sun.java.swing.table.*;

class TestFrame
        extends        JFrame
        implements     ListSelectionListener
 {
    // Instance attributes used in this example
    private JPanel      topPanel;
    private JTable      table;
    private JScrollPane scrollPane;

    // Constructor of main frame
    public TestFrame()
    {
        // Set the frame characteristics
        setTitle( "Simple Table Application" );
        setSize( 300, 200 );
        setBackground( Color.gray );

        // Create a panel to hold all other components
        topPanel = new JPanel();
        topPanel.setLayout( new BorderLayout() );
        getContentPane().add( topPanel );

        // Create columns names
        String columnNames[] = { "Column 1", "Column 2", "Column 3" };

        // Create some data
        String dataValues[][] =
        {
            { "12", "234", "67" },
            { "-123", "43", "853" },
            { "93", "89.2", "109" },
            { "279", "9033", "3092" }
        };

        // Create a new table instance
        table = new JTable( dataValues, columnNames );

        // Handle the listener
```

Listing 11.7   Table selection example source code

```
        ListSelectionModel selectionModel = table.getSelectionModel();
        selectionModel.addListSelectionListener( this );

        // Add the table to a scrolling pane
        scrollPane = table.createScrollPaneForTable( table );
        topPanel.add( scrollPane, BorderLayout.CENTER );
    }

    // Handler for list selection changes
    public void valueChanged( ListSelectionEvent event )
    {
        // See if this is a valid table selection
        if( event.getSource() == table.getSelectionModel()
                    && event.getFirstIndex() >= 0 )
        {
            // Get the data model for this table
            DefaultTableModel model =
                        (DefaultTableModel)table.getModel();

            // Determine the selected item
            String string = (String)model.getValueAt(
                            table.getSelectedRow(),
                            table.getSelectedColumn() );

            // Display the selected item
            System.out.println( "Value selected = " + string );
        }
    }

    // Main entry point for this example
    public static void main( String args[] )
    {
        // Create an instance of the test application
        TestFrame mainFrame = new TestFrame();
        mainFrame.setVisible( true );
    }
}
```

Listing 11.7   Table selection example source code (continued)

Listing 11.7 illustrates code implementing the cell selection mechanism provided by the JTable class. To enable selection events, the code adds a ListSelectionListener to the table's selection model. This is accomplished by executing the following code:

```
// Handle the listener
ListSelectionModel selectionModel = table.getSelectionModel();
selectionModel.addListSelectionListener( this );
```

The `valueChanged()` method is required in order to implement `ListSelectionListener`. In this example, this method first determines if the event originates from our JTable instance's selection model, and then it ensures that the event references a valid selection. To access the selected cell, the code references the table's data model and simply extracts the data based on the selected row and column.

11.5.2 Detecting column property changes

The second significant series of events produced by table activity relate to manipulations of the column presentation. Any time the user moves a column from one place to another, or adds a new column, the table generates an event—more specifically a column model change event. To intercept these events, a listener must be associated with the table's column model. This is done using the following code:

```
// Handle the listener
DefaultTableColumnModel columnModel =
            (DefaultTableColumnModel)table.getColumnModel();
columnModel.addColumnModelListener( this );
```

Then all that remains is the implementation of the column model listener methods:

```
public void columnAdded( TableColumnModelEvent event )
public void columnRemoved( TableColumnModelEvent event )
public void columnMoved( TableColumnModelEvent event )
public void columnMarginChanged( ChangeEvent event )
public void columnSelectionChanged( ListSelectionEvent event )
```

Let's take a look at an example that demonstrates the implementation of a column model listener and its association to a table. Listing 11.8 shows the source code to implement the methods required to support the `TableColumnModelListener` interface.

```
// Imports
import java.awt.*;
import com.sun.java.swing.*;
import com.sun.java.swing.event.*;
import com.sun.java.swing.table.*;

class TestFrame
        extends       JFrame
        implements    TableColumnModelListener
```

Listing 11.8 Column property change example

```
{
    // Instance attributes used in this example
    private JPanel      topPanel;
    private JTable      table;
    private JScrollPane scrollPane;

    // Constructor of main frame
    public TestFrame()
    {
        // Set the frame characteristics
        setTitle( "Simple Table Application" );
        setSize( 300, 200 );
        setBackground( Color.gray );

        // Create a panel to hold all other components
        topPanel = new JPanel();
        topPanel.setLayout( new BorderLayout() );
        getContentPane().add( topPanel );

        // Create columns names
        String columnNames[] = { "Column 1", "Column 2", "Column 3" };

        // Create some data
        String dataValues[][] =
        {
            { "12",  "234",  "67" },
            { "-123", "43",  "853" },
            { "93",  "89.2", "109" },
            { "279", "9033", "3092" }
        };

        // Create a new table instance
        table = new JTable( dataValues, columnNames );

        // Add the table to a scrolling pane
        scrollPane = table.createScrollPaneForTable( table );
        topPanel.add( scrollPane, BorderLayout.CENTER );

        // Handle the listener
        DefaultTableColumnModel columnModel =
                    (DefaultTableColumnModel)table.getColumnModel();
        columnModel.addColumnModelListener( this );
    }

    // Handler called when a column is added
    public void columnAdded( TableColumnModelEvent event )
    {
        System.out.println( "columnAdded" );
```

Listing 11.8 Column property change example (continued)

```
    }

    // Handler called when a column is removed
    public void columnRemoved( TableColumnModelEvent event )
    {
        System.out.println( "columnRemoved" );
    }

    // Handler called when a column is moved
    public void columnMoved( TableColumnModelEvent event )
    {
        System.out.println( "columnMoved" );
    }

    // Handler called when the column margin is changed
    public void columnMarginChanged( ChangeEvent event )
    {
        int iColumn = table.getSelectedColumn();
        if( iColumn >= 0 )
        {
            System.out.println( "columnMarginChanged=" + iColumn );
        }
    }

    // Handler called when the column selection changes
    public void columnSelectionChanged( ListSelectionEvent event )
    {
        int iColumn = table.getSelectedColumn();
        if( iColumn >= 0 )
        {
            System.out.println( "columnSelectionChanged=" + iColumn );
        }
    }

    // Main entry point for this example
    public static void main( String args[] )
    {
        // Create an instance of the test application
        TestFrame mainFrame = new TestFrame();
        mainFrame.setVisible( true );
    }
}
```

Listing 11.8   Column property change example (continued)

11.6 Other tips and tricks

We have now covered all of the important aspects of Swing's JTable, and you should now be familiar enough with it to create some interesting applications using this powerful class. But there are a few more tips and tricks that will help you make better use of JTable. In this section, we will briefly discuss some of the more subtle issues regarding tables and some simple techniques you can apply to help create more appealing applications.

11.6.1 Eliminating the annoying gray background

You may have noticed, from the examples in this chapter, that if you stretch out a frame containing an instance of JTable, you will see a gray background. None of the applications in this chapter custom-colored this background, so there it is—by default. It will quickly become annoying to the user, especially if the table has a white background. Eliminating this annoying gray background from your applications is really quite simple, once you understand its origin.

In all of the examples presented in this chapter, the JTable instance was inserted into a scrolling pane created for us by the table itself when the create-ScrollPaneForTable() method was called. The gray background, shown when the frame area is larger than the table component, is actually the background color of the scrolling pane, and it can easily be changed. In the examples in this chapter, the source code to create the scrolling pane appears like this:

```
// Add the table to a scrolling pane
scrollPane = table.createScrollPaneForTable( table );
topPanel.add( scrollPane, BorderLayout.CENTER );
```

To eliminate the gray background, modify this code so it now looks like:

```
// Add the table to a scrolling pane
scrollPane = table.createScrollPaneForTable( table );
scrollPane.getViewport().setBackground( Color.white );
topPanel.add( scrollPane, BorderLayout.CENTER );
```

This code applies the white color to the background of the scrolling pane's viewport, and that corrects the problem. Note that, if your application is rendering cells with a different background color, change the Color.white in the code above to the correct color for your cell background.

11.6.2 Intercepting mouse and keyboard events

In some situations (you will see one in the next section), you need to have additional control over the table to perform special tasks. For example the application may perform a special task when the mouse is positioned over a particular column or cell, or you may want to handle a special keyboard sequence. By default, the JTable class does not give you this capability, so, in order to handle the mouse or keyboard, some alternative method must be developed.

Fortunately, JTable is a Java class, and, like any other class, it can be sub-classed. Sub-classing allows the developer to take control of normally unsupported aspects of the JTable control, including special mouse and keyboard handling. Consider the following code snippet:

```
class MyTable
        extends      JTable
        implements   MouseListener
{
    public MyTable( DefaultDataModel model )
    {
        super( model );

    // Configure the table
    setFont( new Font( "Helvetica", Font.PLAIN, 12 ) );
    setColumnSelectionAllowed( false );
    setSelectionMode( ListSelectionModel.SINGLE_SELECTION );
    setShowGrid( false );
    setIntercellSpacing( new Dimension( 0, 1 ) );
    setAutoCreateColumnsFromModel( false );
    sizeColumnsToFit( true );

    // Prevent table column reordering
    JTableHeader header = getTableHeader();
    header.setUpdateTableInRealTime( false );
    header.setReorderingAllowed( false );

        // Attach a mouse listener
        addMouseListener( this );
    }
    public void mouseClicked( MouseEvent e )
    {
        int iMouseX = e.getX();
        int iMouseY = e.getY();

        int iSelectedColumn = columnAtPoint(
                        new Point( iMouseX, iMouseY ) );
        int iSelectedRow = rowAtPoint( new Point( iMouseX, iMouseY ) );
```

```
          .
          .
          .
    }
public void mouseEntered( MouseEvent e )
{
}
public void mouseExited( MouseEvent e )
{
}
public void mousePressed( MouseEvent e )
{
}
public void mouseReleased( MouseEvent e )
{
}
}
```

This subclass of JTable allows custom configuration of the table within the constructor, and it also implements a mouse listener. The example partially implements the `mouseClicked()` method in order to show you how to convert a mouse position into an absolute cell location. With this information, you can perform any special task you require, and the next section will present an example of some code where this is necessary.

11.7 Putting it all together

Since you now know almost everything you need to regarding the JTable class, we can develop a much more intricate application based on this powerful class. In this section, we will create an application that employs all of the features we have covered in this chapter. These features include custom rendering, custom data models, mouse interactions, and a host of special tricks. The finished product will be an example from which you can extract any parts that are suitable for your own applications.

This example creates a simulated server-administrator application which uses a JTable instance to display server information, including the server site name, an associated location, and a server status. All of the server information is fabricated for this example—the emphasis of this code is to demonstrate the capabilities of JTable. The user interface presentation includes columns of information and a hierarchical tree; however, due to limitations of the JTable class, we cannot simply insert an instance of JTree. Instead, the code presented in this section implements a rudimentary tree display for the first column of the table.

Listing 11.9A contains the code for the main applications frame. It creates an instance of the custom data model class (CustomDataModel) and populates it with data. We will see the implementation for this class later. Next, the main frame creates an instance of the subclassed table (MyTable), assigning the data model to it. The code in this listing should be relatively straightforward, since it is simply a modified version of the frame code presented in previous examples in this chapter.

```
// Imports
import java.awt.*;
import java.util.*;
import com.sun.java.swing.*;
import com.sun.java.swing.table.*;

class TestFrame
        extends JFrame
{
    // Instance attributes used in this example
    private JPanel      topPanel;
    private JTable      table;
    private JScrollPane scrollPane;

    private String      columnNames[];
    private String      dataValues[][];

    // Constructor of main frame
    public TestFrame()
    {
        // Set the frame characteristics
        setTitle( "Advanced JTable Application" );
        setSize( 500, 200 );
        setBackground( Color.gray );

        // Create a panel to hold all other components
        topPanel = new JPanel();
        topPanel.setLayout( new BorderLayout() );
        getContentPane().add( topPanel );

        // Create the custom data model and insert some data
        CustomDataModel customDataModel = new CustomDataModel();

        int iParent = customDataModel.InsertParent( "JavaSoft",
                                "www.javasoft.com", "OK" );
```

Listing 11.9A   Advanced JTable main frame source code

```
        customDataModel.InsertChild( iParent, "Developer Tools",
                            "/developer", "OK" );
        customDataModel.InsertChild( iParent, "Products",
                            "/products", "Unavailable" );
        customDataModel.InsertChild( iParent, "Marketing",
                            "/marketing", "OK" );

        iParent = customDataModel.InsertParent( "Netscape",
                            "www.netscape.com", "OK" );
        customDataModel.InsertChild( iParent, "Products",
                            "/products", "OK" );
        customDataModel.InsertChild( iParent, "Client Tools",
                            "/navigator", "Unavailable" );
        customDataModel.InsertChild( iParent, "Server Tools",
                            "/servers", "OK" );

        iParent = customDataModel.InsertParent( "Microsoft",
                            "www.microsoft.com", "Delayed" );
        customDataModel.InsertChild( iParent, "Operating Systems",
                            "/windows", "OK" );
        customDataModel.InsertChild( iParent, "Java",
                            "/java", "Unavailable" );
        customDataModel.InsertChild( iParent, "Games",
                            "/games", "OK" );
        customDataModel.InsertChild( iParent, "Office97",
                            "/office", "OK" );

        // Create a new table instance
        table = new MyTable( customDataModel );

        // Add the table to a scrolling pane
        scrollPane = table.createScrollPaneForTable( table );
        scrollPane.getViewport().setBackground( Color.white );
        topPanel.add( scrollPane, BorderLayout.CENTER );
    }

    // Main entry point for this example
    public static void main( String args[] )
    {
        // Create an instance of the test application
        TestFrame mainFrame = new TestFrame();
        mainFrame.setVisible( true );
    }
}
```

Listing 11.9A   Advanced JTable main frame source code (continued)

The code shown in listing 11.9B implements a new table class called MyTable, which has been subclassed from the Swing JTable class. This new class also implements a `MouseListener` to detect mouse clicks in the table. This code is necessary to determine when the user clicks on the tree expansion button (the +/- box in the image) associated with server nodes in the tree.

The constructor configures the table as specified and creates the columns (Server, Location, and Status). For each of these columns, the code assigns a custom cell renderer and a header renderer. Finally, the constructor adds a mouse listener to intercept mouse clicks from the user.

The `mouseClicked()` method converts the mouse location to a table row/column position to ensure that the click occurred in the first column (we ignore clicks elsewhere). Next, this method determines if the click occurred within the area occupied by the expansion button. If it does, the code expands or collapses the tree, as required.

```java
// Imports
import java.awt.*;
import java.awt.event.*;
import com.sun.java.swing.*;
import com.sun.java.swing.table.*;

class MyTable
        extends         JTable
        implements      MouseListener
{
    private CustomDataModel model = null;

    public MyTable( CustomDataModel model )
    {
        super( model );

        this.model = model;

        // Configure the table
        setFont( new Font( "Helvetica", Font.PLAIN, 12 ) );
        setColumnSelectionAllowed( false );
        setSelectionMode( ListSelectionModel.SINGLE_SELECTION );
        setShowGrid( false );
        setIntercellSpacing( new Dimension( 0, 1 ) );
        setAutoCreateColumnsFromModel( false );
        sizeColumnsToFit( true );

        // Prevent table column reordering
```

Listing 11.9B   MyTable class source code

```
        JTableHeader header = getTableHeader();
        header.setUpdateTableInRealTime( false );
        header.setReorderingAllowed( false );

        // Added our columns into the column model
        TableColumn newColumn = new TableColumn();
        newColumn.setCellRenderer( new CustomCellRenderer( model ) );
        newColumn.setHeaderValue( "Server" );
        newColumn.setHeaderRenderer( new CustomHeaderRenderer() );
        addColumn( newColumn );

        newColumn.setCellRenderer( new CustomCellRenderer( model ) );
        newColumn.setHeaderValue( "Location" );
        newColumn.setHeaderRenderer( new CustomHeaderRenderer() );
        addColumn( newColumn );

        newColumn.setCellRenderer( new CustomCellRenderer( model ) );
        newColumn.setHeaderValue( "Status" );
        newColumn.setHeaderRenderer( new CustomHeaderRenderer() );
        addColumn( newColumn );

        // Attach a mouse listener
        addMouseListener( this );
    }

    public void mouseClicked( MouseEvent e )
    {
        int iMouseX = e.getX();
        int iMouseY = e.getY();

        int iSelectedColumn = columnAtPoint(
                            new Point( iMouseX, iMouseY ) );
        int iSelectedRow = rowAtPoint( new Point( iMouseX, iMouseY ) );

        if( iSelectedRow >= 0 && iSelectedRow < model.getRowCount() )
        {
            // Get the type of service we are rendering
            MyTableNode node = (MyTableNode)
                    model.vectorDisplayService.elementAt( iSelectedRow );

            // Test to see if the user clicked on the
            // expand/collapse button
            if( iSelectedColumn == 0 && iMouseX >= 4 && iMouseX <= 12
                            && node.typeString.equals( model.SERVER ) )
            {
                // Expand the tree
                if( node.iChildren == 0 && node.iActualChildren > 0 )
                {
```

Listing 11.9B   MyTable class source code (continued)

```
                    model.ExpandParent( node );
                    repaint();
                }
                else if( node.iChildren > 0 )
                {
                    model.CollapseParent( node );
                    repaint();
                }
            }
        }
    }

    public void mouseEntered( MouseEvent e )
    {
    }

    public void mouseExited( MouseEvent e )
    {
    }

    public void mousePressed( MouseEvent e )
    {
    }

    public void mouseReleased( MouseEvent e )
    {
    }
}
```

Listing 11.9B   MyTable class source code (continued)

Every row in the table loosely equates to a tree node, and contains the displayed information and data critical to controlling the graphical tree. Listing 11.9C shows a structure used to hold the data for each row of the table. Note that there are two types of nodes in the table: SERVER and RESOURCE.

```
class MyTableNode
{
    public int iParentOffset;
    public int iChildren;          // Number of visible children
    public int iActualChildren;    // Number of children that the
                                   // node actually has

    public String typeString;
```

Listing 11.9C   MYTableNode class source code

```
    public String nameString;
    public String locationString;
    public String statusString;

    public MyTableNode()
    {
        typeString = "";
        nameString = "";
        locationString = "";
        statusString = "";

        iParentOffset = 0;
        iChildren = 0;
        iActualChildren = 0;
    }

    public MyTableNode( MyTableNode node, int iOffset )
    {
        this.typeString = new String( node.typeString );
        this.nameString = new String( node.nameString );
        this.locationString = new String( node.locationString );
        this.statusString = new String( node.statusString );

        this.iParentOffset = iOffset;
        this.iChildren =   node.iChildren;
        this.iActualChildren = node.iActualChildren;
    }
}
```

Listing 11.9C   MYTableNode class source code (continued)

Listing 11.9D shows the code used to render the column headers for the table. Similar code was shown in a previous example. This rendering code is completely independent from the code used to render the cells.

```
import java.awt.*;
import com.sun.java.swing.*;
import com.sun.java.swing.border.*;
import com.sun.java.swing.table.*;

class CustomHeaderRenderer
    extends       JLabel
    implements    TableCellRenderer
{
```

Listing 11.9D   CustomHeaderRenderer class source code

```
public Component getTableCellRendererComponent( JTable table,
        Object value, boolean isSelected, boolean hasFocus,
        int row, int column )
{
    // Retrieve the text to display
    String sText = (String)value;

    // Set all sorts of interesting alignment options
    setVerticalAlignment( SwingConstants.CENTER );
    setHorizontalAlignment( SwingConstants.LEFT );

    // Assign a border
    setBorder( new EtchedBorder() );

    // Set the text to the correct value
    switch( column )
    {
        case 0:
            setText( "Server" );
            break;
        case 1:
            setText( "Location" );
            break;
        case 2:
            setText( "Status" );
            break;
    }

    return this;
}
}
```

Listing 11.9D   CustomHeaderRenderer class source code

The custom cell renderer is shown in listing 11.9E. This code, though it appears complex, is actually quite similar to the cell renderer shown in a previous listing. Since only the first column contains an image, the renderer determines if the column being rendered is the server column. If so, a determination is made to ensure that the correct icon is drawn—there is an icon for each possible state and node type (icons depict: a server with no children, a server in an expanded state, a server in a collapsed state, and two resource images). The final stage of the cell rendering is to display the correct text in the cell. This is accomplished by extracting the string information from the data structure of the node being rendered.

The final source file in this example, shown in listing 11.9F, implements a class called CustomDataModel. This class manages the data model used for the custom

```
import java.awt.*;
import com.sun.java.swing.*;
import com.sun.java.swing.border.*;
import com.sun.java.swing.table.*;

class CustomCellRenderer
    extends          JLabel
    implements       TableCellRenderer
{
    private boolean            isSelected;
    private boolean            hasFocus;
    private CustomDataModel     model;
    private ImageIcon[]        images;

    public CustomCellRenderer( CustomDataModel model )
    {
        this.model = model;

        // Create all of the images
        images = new ImageIcon[5];
        images[0] = new ImageIcon("server.gif");
        images[1] = new ImageIcon("server+.gif");
        images[2] = new ImageIcon("server-.gif");
        images[3] = new ImageIcon("resource.gif");
        images[4] = new ImageIcon("resource_last.gif");
    }

    public Component getTableCellRendererComponent(
            JTable renderTable, Object value, boolean isSelected,
            boolean hasFocus, int iRowIndex, int iColumnIndex )
    {
        MyTable table = (MyTable)renderTable;
        this.hasFocus = hasFocus;
        this.isSelected = isSelected;

        if( iRowIndex < model.getRowCount() )
        {
            // Get the node we are rendering
            MyTableNode node = (MyTableNode)
                model.vectorDisplayService.elementAt( iRowIndex );

            // Draw the correct text color depending on the
            // selection state
            if( hasFocus || isSelected )
                setForeground( Color.white );
            else
                setForeground( Color.black );
```

Listing 11.9E   CustomCellRenderer class source code

```
        // Draw the correct icon for this service
        if( iColumnIndex == 0 )
        {
            if( node.typeString.equals( model.SERVER ) )
            {
                // Get a reference to the shadow parent
                int iShadowParent = model.GetShadowNode(
                            node.nameString, model.SERVER );
                MyTableNode shadow = (MyTableNode)model.
                            vectorService.elementAt( iShadowParent );

                if( node.iChildren == 0 && shadow.iChildren == 0 )
                        setIcon( images[0] );
                else if( node.iChildren == 0
                            && shadow.iChildren > 0 )
                    setIcon( images[1] );
                else
                    setIcon( images[2] );
            }
            else
            {
                // Get a reference to the parent node
                int iParent = iRowIndex - node.iParentOffset;
                MyTableNode parent = (MyTableNode)model.
                        vectorDisplayService.elementAt( iParent );

                if( iParent + parent.iChildren <= iRowIndex )
                    setIcon( images[4] );
                else
                    setIcon( images[3] );
            }
        }
        else
            setIcon( null );

        // Draw the node text
        switch( iColumnIndex )
        {
            case 0:
                setText( node.nameString );
                break;
            case 1:
                setText( node.locationString );
                break;
            case 2:
                setText( node.statusString );
```

Listing 11.9E CustomCellRenderer class source code (continued)

```
                    break;
        }
    }

    return this;
    }

    // This is a hack to paint the background. Normally, a JLabel can
    // paint its own background, but, due to an apparent bug or
    // limitation in the TableCellRenderer, the paint method is
    // required to handle this.
    public void paint( Graphics g )
    {
        Color   bColor;

        // Set the correct background color
        if( isSelected || hasFocus )
            bColor = Color.red;
        else
            bColor = Color.white;
        g.setColor( bColor );

            // Draw a rectangle in the background of the cell
        g.fillRect( 0, 0, getWidth(), getHeight() - 1 );

        super.paint( g );
    }
}
```

Listing 11.9E   CustomCellRenderer class source code (continued)

table, including the data handling for the graphical tree. The first four methods in the source file are required to implement a data model, and you have already seen examples of these in a previous sample. The remaining methods manage the data requirements of the graphical tree, including the capability to insert new parent (SERVER) and child (RESOURCE) objects.

We won't exhaustively discuss the inner workings of this source file; however, there is a particular point that needs clarification. The model includes two different data vectors that appear to contain matching information, but, in fact, only one of these vectors is guaranteed to hold a complete copy of the data for all nodes in the tree. The other vector, vectorDisplayService, contains only those nodes that are visible in the tree—child nodes hidden as a result of a collapsed tree are not contained in this vector. All methods that access or manipulate data elements must ensure that the data in both remains synchronized.

```java
// Imports
import java.util.*;
import java.io.*;
import com.sun.java.swing.*;
import com.sun.java.swing.table.*;

class CustomDataModel
          extends      AbstractTableModel
{
    // Constant node types
    public static  String  SERVER     = "0";
    public static  String  RESOURCE   = "1";

    // Vectored arrays to hold grid data
    public Vector vectorService;
    public Vector vectorDisplayService;

    public CustomDataModel()
    {
        super();

        // Create instances of the vector data arrays
        vectorService = new Vector();
        vectorDisplayService = new Vector();
    }

    public int getColumnCount()
    {
        // Return 0 because we handle our own columns
        return 0;
    }

    public int getRowCount()
    {
        return vectorDisplayService.size();
    }

    public Object getValueAt( int iRowIndex, int iColumnIndex )
    {
        if( iRowIndex >= 0 && iRowIndex < vectorDisplayService.size() )
        {
            // Get the node we are referencing
            MyTableNode node = (MyTableNode)
                    vectorDisplayService.elementAt( iRowIndex );

            switch( iColumnIndex )
            {
                case 0:
```

Listing 11.9F CustomCellRenderer class source code

```
                    return node.nameString;
            case 1:
                return node.locationString;
            case 2:
                return node.statusString;
        }
    }

    return "";
}

public void setValueAt( Object aValue,
                    int iRowIndex, int iColumnIndex )
{
    // Get the node we are referencing
    MyTableNode node = (MyTableNode)
            vectorDisplayService.elementAt( iRowIndex );

    switch( iColumnIndex )
    {
        case 0:
            node.nameString = (String)aValue;
            break;
        case 1:
            node.locationString = (String)aValue;
            break;
        case 2:
            node.typeString = (String)aValue;
            break;
    }

    // Update the node
    vectorDisplayService.setElementAt( node, iRowIndex );
}

public synchronized int GetDisplayNode(
                        String string, String type )
{
    MyTableNode node;
    for( int iCtr = 0; iCtr < vectorDisplayService.size(); iCtr++ )
    {
        node = (MyTableNode)vectorDisplayService.elementAt( iCtr );
        if( node.nameString.equalsIgnoreCase( string )
                        && node.typeString.equals( type ) )
            return iCtr;
    }
    return -1;
```

Listing 11.9F CustomCellRenderer class source code (continued)

```java
    }
public synchronized int GetShadowNode(
                        String string, String type )
{
    MyTableNode node;
    for( int iCtr = 0; iCtr < vectorService.size(); iCtr++ )
    {
        node = (MyTableNode)vectorService.elementAt( iCtr );
        if( node.nameString.equalsIgnoreCase( string )
                        && node.typeString.equals( type ) )
            return iCtr;
    }
    return -1;
}

// Expand the specified parent node
public void ExpandParent( MyTableNode node )
{
    // Determine the parent offsets
    int iParent = GetDisplayNode( node.nameString, SERVER );
    int iShadowParent = GetShadowNode( node.nameString, SERVER );
    MyTableNode shadow = (MyTableNode)
                        vectorService.elementAt( iShadowParent );

    if( shadow.iChildren > 0 )
    {
        // Reinsert the children
        MyTableNode child;
        for( int iCtr = 0; iCtr < shadow.iChildren; iCtr++ )
        {
            // Insert items from the shadow parent back into the
            // display parent record
            child = (MyTableNode)new MyTableNode( (MyTableNode)
                        vectorService.elementAt( iShadowParent
                        + iCtr + 1 ), iCtr + 1 );
            vectorDisplayService.insertElementAt( child,
                                    iParent + iCtr + 1 );
        }

        // Update the parent record
        node.iChildren = shadow.iChildren;
        vectorDisplayService.setElementAt( node, iParent );
    }
}

// Collapse the specified parent node
```

Listing 11.9F   CustomCellRenderer class source code (continued)

```
public void CollapseParent( MyTableNode node )
{
    // Determine the parent offsets
    int iParent = GetDisplayNode( node.nameString, SERVER );

    // Remove any children
    for( int iCtr = node.iChildren; iCtr > 0; iCtr-- )
        vectorDisplayService.removeElementAt( iParent + iCtr );

    // Update the parent record
    node.iChildren = 0;
    vectorDisplayService.setElementAt( node, iParent );
}

// Insert a new parent node into the tree
public int InsertParent( String nameString,
                    String locationString, String statusString )
{
    // Create a new child record
    MyTableNode node = (MyTableNode)new MyTableNode();
    node.typeString = SERVER;
    node.nameString = nameString;
    node.locationString = locationString;
    node.statusString = statusString;
    vectorDisplayService.addElement( node );

    // Add data to the shadow data area
    node = (MyTableNode)new MyTableNode();
    node.typeString = SERVER;
    node.nameString = nameString;
    node.locationString = locationString;
    node.statusString = statusString;
    vectorService.addElement( node );

    return vectorDisplayService.size() - 1;
}

// Insert a new child node into the tree within the
// specified parent node
public void InsertChild( int iParent, String nameString,
                    String locationString, String statusString )
{
    // Get the node we are referencing
    MyTableNode parent = (MyTableNode)
            vectorDisplayService.elementAt( iParent );

    // Create a new child record
    MyTableNode node = (MyTableNode)new MyTableNode();
```

Listing 11.9F   CustomCellRenderer class source code (continued)

```
            node.typeString = RESOURCE;
            node.nameString = nameString;
            node.locationString = locationString;
            node.statusString = statusString;

            // Set the offset
            parent.iChildren++;
            parent.iActualChildren++;
            node.iParentOffset = parent.iChildren;

            // Insert the new node
            if( iParent + parent.iChildren >= vectorDisplayService.size() )
                vectorDisplayService.addElement( node );
            else
                vectorDisplayService.insertElementAt( node, iParent
                                            + parent.iChildren );

            // Update the parent record
            vectorDisplayService.setElementAt( parent, iParent );

            // Add data to the shadow data area, too
            node = (MyTableNode)new MyTableNode();
            node.typeString = RESOURCE;
            node.nameString = nameString;
            node.locationString = locationString;
            node.statusString = statusString;

            int iShadowParent = GetShadowNode( parent.nameString, SERVER );
            parent = (MyTableNode)vectorService.elementAt( iShadowParent );
            parent.iChildren++;
            parent.iActualChildren++;
            node.iParentOffset = parent.iChildren;
            if( iParent + parent.iChildren >= vectorService.size() )
                vectorService.addElement( node );
            else
                vectorService.insertElementAt( node, iShadowParent
                                            + parent.iChildren );
            vectorService.setElementAt( parent, iShadowParent );
    }
}
```

Listing 11.9F   CustomCellRenderer class source code (continued)

FYI This example has a known limitation. Only a single level of nesting can occur within the tree column. For example, server nodes can have one or more resource children, but resources cannot have children. This restriction will limit the use of this code in some applications.

The example presented in this section, when executed, produces the output shown in figure 11.5. Notice the added appeal offered by the graphical tree, which is fully functional. The addition of a tree to a JTable instance seems to be a subject of recurring questions in Java-related USENET new groups, and now you know how to handle this advanced topic.

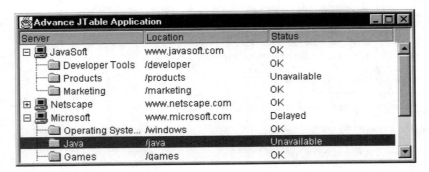

Figure 11.5   Advanced JTable example output

11.8   JTable class information

This section lists the constants variables and methods for the JTable class.

11.8.1 JTable constants

```
public static final int AUTO_RESIZE_LAST_COLUMN
public static final int AUTO_RESIZE_OFF
public static final int AUTO_RESIZE_ALL_COLUMNS
```

These constants contain flags to control the resize state of columns in the table. These constants are used as parameters to the `setAutoResizeMode()` method.

11.8.2 JTable variables

```
protected TableModel dataModel
protected TableColumnModel columnModel
protected ListSelectionModel selectionModel
```

These variables hold instances of the various models associated with a JTable object.

```
protected JTableHeader tableHeader
```

This variable holds the instance of the table headers for this JTable object. The header holds particulars, such as, the column object.

```
protected int rowHeight
protected int rowMargin
```

These variables contain information to manage the attributes of a table row.

```
protected Color gridColor
```

The color of the grid lines drawn in the table is stored in this variable.

```
protected boolean showHorizontalLines
protected boolean showVerticalLines
protected boolean autoCreateColumnsFromModel
protected boolean rowSelectionAllowed
```

These boolean flags contain information about the states of particular modes within the JTable object.

```
protected int autoResizeMode
```

The value of this variable determines if the table object automatically resizes the width of the columns to occupy the entire width of the table. It is also used to decide how the resizing is done.

```
protected Dimension preferredViewportSize
```

This variable is used by the scrolling pane instance associated with the table object. It determines the initial visible area for the table.

```
protected transient Component editorComp
```

When the table is performing a cell editing operation, this variable holds an instance of the component used to handle the editing operation.

```
protected transient TableCellEditor cellEditor
```

This variable holds an instance of the cell editor used by this table object.

```
protected transient int editingRow
```

```
protected transient int editingColumn
```

When editing table cells, these variables contain the row and column address of the cell being edited.

```
protected Hashtable defaultRenderersByColumnClass
protected Hashtable defaultEditorsByColumnClass
```

These variables are used to keep track of the default cell editors and renderers known to this table object.

```
protected Color selectionForeground
protected Color selectionBackground
```

These variables contain the colors of the foreground and background used to draw selected text. These values are overridden by any custom cell render code.

11.8.3 JTable constructors

```
public JTable()
```

This constructor creates an instance of the JTable class that is initialized with a default data model, column model, and selection model.

```
public JTable( TableModel dm )
```

This constructor creates an instance of the JTable class that is initialized with a default column model and selection model, and with the specified data model.

```
public JTable( TableModel dm, TableColumnModel cm )
```

This constructor creates an instance of the JTable class that is initialized with a default selection model. The data model and column models specified are assigned to the instance.

```
public JTable( TableModel dm,
                TableColumnModel cm, ListSelectionModel sm )
```

This constructor creates an instance of the JTable class that is initialized with the specified selection model, data model, and column model.

```
public JTable( int numColumns, int numRows )
```

This constructor creates an instance of the JTable class that is initialized with a default data model, column model, and selection model. The data model contains an array of empty cells specified by the number of rows and column from the caller. By default, the column names will have the form "A", "B", "C", and so on.

```
public JTable( Vector data, Vector columnNames )
```

This constructor creates an instance of the JTable class that is initialized with a default data model, column model, and selection model. The data model receives the data from the first vector parameter. The second vector is transferred to the default column model.

```
public JTable( Object data[][], Object columnNames[] )
```

This constructor creates an instance of the JTable class that is initialized with a default data model, column model, and selection model. The data model receives the data from the first object array parameter. The second array is transferred to the default column model.

11.8.4 JTable significant method groups

```
public static JScrollPane createScrollPaneForTable(JTable aTable)
```

This method creates an instance of a JScrollPane object and attaches it to the JTable object.

```
public void setTableHeader(JTableHeader newHeader)
public JTableHeader getTableHeader()
```

These methods manage the header associated with the JTable object. The table header object holds information about the columns and their characteristics.

```
public void setRowHeight(int newHeight)
public int getRowHeight()
```

These methods manage the height of the rows within the JTable object. A custom cell renderer can override the row height.

```
public void setIntercellSpacing(Dimension newSpacing)
public Dimension getIntercellSpacing()
```

The methods in this group manage the space between cells within the table. The intercell spacing can be overridden by a custom cell renderer.

```
public void setGridColor(Color newColor)
public Color getGridColor()
public void setShowGrid(boolean b)
public void setShowHorizontalLines(boolean b)
public void setShowVerticalLines(boolean b)
public boolean getShowHorizontalLines()
public boolean getShowVerticalLines()
```

These methods control the color of the grid lines and determine if the grid lines are visible within the table. The grid lines in the horizontal and vertical planes are individually configurable with methods from this group.

```
public void setAutoResizeMode(int mode)
public int getAutoResizeMode()
public void sizeColumnsToFit(boolean lastColumnOnly)
```

This group of methods controls the automatic sizing of columns. This feature resizes the columns whenever the owner panel is resized.

```
public void setAutoCreateColumnsFromModel(boolean createColumns)
public boolean getAutoCreateColumnsFromModel()
public void createDefaultColumnsFromModel()
```

These methods manage the creation of columns within the table. Columns can be generated automatically from the data model; however, column creation can be overridden if the developer manually creates them.

```
public void setDefaultRenderer( Class columnClass,
                                TableCellRenderer renderer )
public TableCellRenderer getDefaultRenderer( Class columnClass )
public void setDefaultEditor( Class columnClass,
                              TableCellEditor editor )
public TableCellEditor getDefaultEditor(Class columnClass)
```

The methods in this group return instances of the default model owned by the table object.

```
public void setSelectionMode(int selectionMode)
public void setRowSelectionAllowed(boolean flag)
public void setColumnSelectionAllowed(boolean flag)
public boolean getColumnSelectionAllowed()
public void setCellSelectionEnabled(boolean flag)
public boolean getCellSelectionEnabled()
public void selectAll()
public void clearSelection()
public void setRowSelectionInterval( int index0, int index1 )
public void setColumnSelectionInterval( int index0, int index1 )
public void addRowSelectionInterval( int index0, int index1 )
public void addColumnSelectionInterval( int index0, int index1 )
public void removeRowSelectionInterval( int index0, int index1 )
public void removeColumnSelectionInterval( int index0, int index1 )
public int getSelectedRow()
public int getSelectedColumn()
public int[] getSelectedRows()
public int[] getSelectedColumns()
public int getSelectedRowCount()
```

```
public int getSelectedColumnCount()
public boolean isRowSelected(int row)
public boolean isColumnSelected(int column)
public boolean isCellSelected(int row, int column)
```

This large group of methods manages all aspects of cell selection in a JTable instance. Selection resolution can be performed at the row, column, or individual cell level. Selections can be returned as a single item or an array of items.

```
public Color getSelectionForeground()
public void setSelectionForeground(Color selectionForeground)
public Color getSelectionBackground()
public void setSelectionBackground(Color selectionBackground)
```

These methods control the foreground and background colors used to identify the selected cells, rows, and columns within the JTable.

```
public TableColumn getColumn(Object identifier)
public int convertColumnIndexToModel(int viewColumnIndex)
public int convertColumnIndexToView(int modelColumnIndex)
public String getColumnName(int column)
public Class getColumnClass(int column)
public void addColumn(TableColumn aColumn)
public void removeColumn(TableColumn aColumn)
public void moveColumn( int column, int targetColumn )
```

The methods in this group are responsible for retrieving information about columns and for controlling the organization of columns within the table. Columns can be added, removed, or moved with these methods.

```
public int getRowCount()
public int getColumnCount()
```

These methods return the count of rows and columns within the JTable instance's data model.

```
public Object getValueAt( int row, int column )
public void setValueAt( Object aValue, int row, int column )
```

The methods shown here are responsible for retrieving and setting the values of individual cells in the table. The cell location is identified by its row and column values.

```
public boolean isCellEditable( int row, int column )
public boolean editCellAt( int row, int column )
public boolean editCellAt( int row, int column, EventObject e )
public boolean isEditing()
public Component getEditorComponent()
```

```
public int getEditingColumn()
public int getEditingRow()
public TableCellEditor getCellEditor()
public void setCellEditor(TableCellEditor anEditor)
public void setEditingColumn(int aColumn)
public void setEditingRow(int aRow)
```

These methods manage the editing features of the JTable class. Individual cells can be edited using either the default editor or one specified programmatically.

```
public void setModel(TableModel newModel)
public TableModel getModel()
public void setColumnModel(TableColumnModel newModel)
public TableColumnModel getColumnModel()
public void setSelectionModel(ListSelectionModel newModel)
public ListSelectionModel getSelectionModel()
```

This group of methods manages the models used by the JTable class. By default, the table will assign default model objects which can be retrieved with methods from this group, or new custom models can be attached to the table.

11.9 Chapter summary

In this chapter, we examined the many facets of the JTable class, which is responsible for managing and displaying two-dimensional data arrays. As indicated, JTable supports many significant features, such as column reordering, and selection, avoiding additional coding on your part.

After presenting some basic examples of table applications, we examined some of the more advanced aspects of JTable. First, we discussed the concept of custom data modeling, which involves replacing the default model created by the table with a new one of our own design. In the example for this, we re-engineered a previous example such that all data displayed in the table was manufactured rather than recalled from a large data array. The result of this effort is a faster application, especially for larger data sets.

Next, we examined custom display rendering, a feature that permits developers to replace the default drawing of table cells and headers with a new rendering engine of their own design. In the examples for this section, we presented code to redraw cells, add graphics, and change the selection colors of the table. Then, we authored an application to alter the format of the headers. In this example, we replaced the default column header with larger headers (including a graphic and a title) and modified the border used to draw them.

Finally, we developed a much larger application based on JTable which used all of the concepts reviewed in this chapter. In this example, we replaced one of the default column displays with a graphical tree of our own design, clearly demonstrating the flexibility that the JTable class offers us.

This is the end of part 2 of this book, and we have now examined all of the important components and classes provided by the Swing portion of the Java Foundation Classes. There are, of course, many more classes in Swing that we did not touch upon; however, the purpose of this book is to help bring you up to speed, and, to that end, we have covered only the important classes that you will use in everyday work.

Part III

Advanced topics

*I*n part 3 of this book, we will take a look at some of the more obscure and advanced topics related to Swing and to Java. If you are already content with what you know about Swing, these topics will only be of passing interest; however, the final chapter, which deals with optimization in Java and Swing applications, is worthy of some attention. We will also study in greater detail the pluggable look-and-feel interface built into Swing, which is important if you are planning to build platform independent applications.

12

Creating custom look-and-feel

In this chapter

- What is look-and-feel?
- Listing available look-and-feel libraries
- Creating a custom look-and-feel

12.1 Model-View-Controller architecture revisited

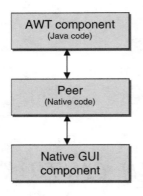

**Figure 12.1
AWT look–and-feel**

In chapter 3 of this book, we discussed the MVC architecture built into the Java 1.1 JDK; however, even though MVC was supported in the version 1.1 virtual machine, the AWT user interface classes were not based on MVC. Instead, AWT components were based on a peer model in which a portion of the component was written using native code (usually C) specific to the operating system platform (see figure 12.1). The dependence on the operating system implies that AWT components take on the same look-and-feel as native applications. For example, on the Microsoft Windows platform, Java applications closely resemble other Windows applications.

With the JFC user interface components, the MVC model is fully integrated (see figure 12.2), allowing complete control over how the component displays itself, how it manages its data, and how it handles interactions with the user. Since JFC user interface components have an MVC heritage, we are free to replace any of these modules with one of our own design. In many of the sample applications shown in this book, we have already seen examples of replacement data models and viewers, though we did not formally change the look-and-feel of the component.

In this chapter, we will explore the look-and-feel aspects of Swing components, and we will create some examples of familiar components—but with a completely new appearance. If you are interested in other variations of component look-

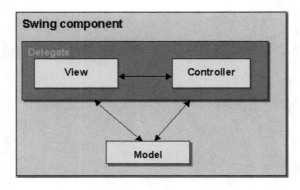

**Figure 12.2
JFC (Swing) look-and-feel architecture**

and-feel in JFC, you can study the source code for the look-and-feel libraries included with JFC.

12.2 Why create a look-and-feel?

The obvious question with regard to JFC's look-and-feel support is, "Why would anyone care?" There are many answers to this simple question, and we will investigate them in more detail as we progress through this chapter, but let's take a quick overview of the advantages of custom look-and-feel.

12.2.1 Corporate standard user interface

The obvious advantage of the look-and-feel capabilities built into JFC is the power it provides to create a standard user interface. With intranets supporting custom applications (now a standard feature in many companies) there is a definite appeal to creating programs that look and feel the same, even across different operating systems.

A common user interface for all corporate applications can save a company a great deal of time and money otherwise lost to employee training. JFC provides corporations with the power to invest modestly to create a standard user interface and apply it to all network applications throughout the corporation.

12.2.2 Ease of portability

You may have heard the "Write Once, Run Everywhere" slogan made famous by Sun while promoting the Java language; however, this promise was never really realized until the release of JFC. Generally, Java code (with AWT) can be written and completely debugged on one platform, but, due to differences in virtual machines across operating systems, this can cause problems ranging from minor user interface misrepresentation to more major inconsistencies (possibly, causing the application to crash during use, or simply refusing to start). The real problem is not Java, but AWT—more specifically, the hoops that the AWT designers had to jump through to make the user interface components portable.

With JFC, these problems are ancient history. Using the look-and-feel libraries built into JFC, applications can be written and debugged using a single common user interface. When the applications are ported to other platforms, the user interface appears identical. Though JFC supplies several look-and-feel libraries, these may be undesirable in some situations—some libraries run only on a single platform, others are just not appealing to users on some platforms. A custom look-and-feel can help meet the demands of all users, and simplify the transfer of code from one platform to another.

12.2.3 New component creation

Though JFC supplies several look-and-feel libraries, there may still be times when you are unable to find the exact component you need. Creating a custom look-and-feel permits you to create a new component (actually, a new feel for an existing component) while still using the controller and/or viewer portions of a similar component. For example, assume you have an application that needs a component resembling a button, but, to meet your requirements, the button must look like something completely different—such as, an octagonal stop sign or a three-dimensional metallic button.

To save you hours of effort creating a completely new user interface component, you can take portions of the existing button class and augment them with a new look. Redesigning every component in the user interface library sounds intimidating, but as you will see from examples in this chapter, much of this code is simple and repetitive.

GUIDELINE

Be careful about using a custom look-and-feel. It may seem blatantly obvious, but remember that users on your target platform(s) already use software and a UI that they are familiar with, so any deviation will create a learning curve. Use the power of custom look-and-feel with due caution.

12.3 UIManager and JFC look-and-feel

Before you can appreciate what is involved in building your own look-and-feel, we should examine the existing user interfaces supported by JFC, and, more importantly, how the look-and-feel of an application is handled. An object called the UIManager, which is created as part of the startup procedure for a JFC application, controls the entire look-and-feel interface for an application.

UIManager is responsible for loading the default look-and-feel library when the application starts, and for providing an interface allowing a new look-and-feel to be loaded at runtime. Later in this chapter, when we create our own custom look-and-feel library, we will use UIManager to install it for the application we will use for testing our user interface. Let's take a closer look at UIManager using a sample application.

12.3.1 Listing available look-and-feel libraries

Listing 12.1 contains an application that lists all of the look-and-feel libraries currently supported by the JFC installation. It accomplishes this task by accessing the static instance of the UIManager object for this application, calling the `getInstalledLookAndFeels()` method to obtain the list of user interfaces available.

```java
// Imports
import java.awt.*;
import com.sun.java.swing.*;

class TestFrame
       extends JFrame
{
    // Instance attributes used in this example
    private JPanel     topPanel;

    // Constructor of main frame
    public TestFrame()
    {
        // Set the frame characteristics
        setTitle( "Available L&F Application" );
        setSize( 300, 200 );
        setBackground( Color.gray );

        // Create a panel to hold all other components
        topPanel = new JPanel();
        topPanel.setLayout( new BorderLayout() );
        getContentPane().add( topPanel );

        // Crete a text area to display the results
        JTextArea area = new JTextArea();
        topPanel.add( area, BorderLayout.CENTER );
        area.setText( "This system supports the following " +
                      "list of pluggable L&F libraries:\n\n" );

        // Get the LAF list
        UIManager.LookAndFeelInfo laf[]
                   = UIManager.getInstalledLookAndFeels();

        // List each item in the text area
        for( int iCtr = 0; iCtr < laf.length; iCtr++ )
```

Listing 12.1   Look-and-feel list application source code

```
        {
            area.append( "LAF #" + iCtr + ":\t" + laf[iCtr].getName()
                    + "\n\t" + laf[iCtr].getClassName() + "\n" );
        }
    }

    // Main entry point for this example
    public static void main( String args[] )
    {
        // Create an instance of the test application
        TestFrame mainFrame = new TestFrame();
        mainFrame.setVisible( true );
    }
}
```

Listing 12.1   Look-and-feel list application source code (continued)

The results produced by this application will vary depending on the number of look-and-feel libraries on your system. Figure 12.3 shows one possible combination of library names and paths to the class responsible for this user interface.

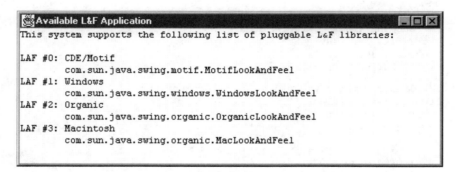

Figure 12.3   Look-and-feel list output

12.3.2 Changing the current look-and-feel

JFC can support as many look-and-feel user interfaces as you care to create, so we will examine the techniques we can apply to dynamically change the interface either during program initialization or at run time. To handle this, our applications need to call the UIManager's `setLookAndFeel()` method, which assigns the specified look-and-feel.

Listing 12.2 extends the previous application to include the ability to change the user interface to any one of the available look-and-feel libraries. It creates an array of buttons (one for each look-and-feel) and allows the user to choose which interface should be used for the program.

```java
// Imports
import java.awt.*;
import java.awt.event.*;
import com.sun.java.swing.*;
import com.sun.java.swing.border.*;

class TestFrame
        extends         JFrame
        implements      ActionListener
{
    // Instance attributes used in this example
    private JPanel      topPanel;
    private JTextArea   area;
    private JButton     lafButtons[];

    // Constructor of main frame
    public TestFrame()
    {
        // Set the frame characteristics
        setTitle( "Selectable L&F Application" );
        setSize( 300, 200 );
        setBackground( Color.gray );

        // Create a panel to hold all other components
        topPanel = new JPanel();
        topPanel.setLayout( new BorderLayout() );
        getContentPane().add( topPanel );

        // Create a panel to store LAF selection buttons
        JPanel buttonPanel = new JPanel();
        buttonPanel.setLayout( new FlowLayout() );
        buttonPanel.setBorder( new BevelBorder( BevelBorder.RAISED ) );
        topPanel.add( buttonPanel, BorderLayout.NORTH );

        // Create a text area to display the results
        area = new JTextArea();
        topPanel.add( area, BorderLayout.CENTER );

        // Get the LAF list
        UIManager.LookAndFeelInfo laf[]
                    = UIManager.getInstalledLookAndFeels();
```

Listing 12.2   Look-and-feel selection application source code

```
        // Create a button for each LAF
        lafButtons = new JButton[ laf.length ];
        for( int iCtr = 0; iCtr < laf.length; iCtr++ )
        {
            lafButtons[iCtr] = new JButton( laf[iCtr].getName() );
            buttonPanel.add( lafButtons[iCtr] );
            lafButtons[iCtr].setActionCommand(
                                laf[iCtr].getClassName() );
            lafButtons[iCtr].addActionListener( this );
        }
    }

    public void actionPerformed( ActionEvent event )
    {
        // Set the look-and-feel according to the button press
        try {
            UIManager.setLookAndFeel( event.getActionCommand() );
            SwingUtilities.updateComponentTreeUI( this );

            area.append( "Look-and-Feel: "
                            + event.getActionCommand() + "\n" );
        }
        catch( Exception e )
        {
            area.append( "L&F unavailable: "
                            + event.getActionCommand() + "\n" );
        }
    }

    // Main entry point for this example
    public static void main( String args[] )
    {
        // Create an instance of the test application
        TestFrame mainFrame = new TestFrame();
        mainFrame.setVisible( true );
    }
}
```

Listing 12.2   Look-and-feel selection application source code (continued)

Figure 12.4 shows the different user interfaces we can achieve with this program. This figure shows the look-and-feel for Motif, Windows, and Organic, respectively. The Organic user interface is a special library developed by Sun specifically for JFC. In addition to the basic display format, Organic also includes support for themes which allow the application to assign different color schemes to the user

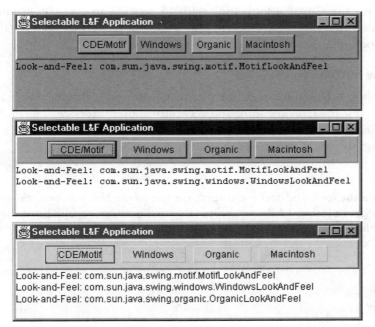

**Figure 12.4
Look-and-feel selection
application output**

interface without altering its visual format. Organic does not ship with JFC, but is available from the Sun Java web site at `http://www.javasoft.com`.

12.4 Creating a new look

Creating components with a new look-and-feel is definitely not for the faint-hearted. Unless you crave the satisfaction of creating your own custom user interface, you will probably be content with the look-and-feel libraries provided in JFC. However, if you are a user interface designer and you want to tap into the power that custom look-and-feel offers, then this is the section you need to read.

In this section, we will create a look-and-feel library called Chrome, which is based on the existing Basic look-and-feel user interface. This allows us to create components one at a time while still providing Basic defaults for those components not yet implemented with the new interface.

The goal for the Chrome look-and-feel is to provide an interface having the appearance of polished metal. Ultimately, this look-and-feel could include all user interface components, but we will implement only a few.

12.4.1 Building a new button

Listing 12.3A shows the source code for the main TestFrame class in this example, which is used to test the Chrome look-and-feel button user interface. The code first sets the Chrome look-and-feel for the program, then creates four buttons, including both text and graphics, and draws them with this new user interface.

FYI When the look-and-feel is changed, the use of the JFC component does not change. In listing 12.3A we create JButton instances, regardless of the look-and-feel library loaded for the application.

```
// Imports
import java.awt.*;
import java.awt.event.*;
import com.sun.java.swing.*;
import com.sun.java.swing.border.*;

class TestFrame
        extends JFrame
 {
    // Instance attributes used in this example
    private JPanel      topPanel;
    private JButton     clubsButton;
    private JButton     diamondsButton;
    private JButton     heartsButton;
    private JButton     spadesButton;

    // Constructor of main frame
    public TestFrame()
    {
        // Set the look-and-feel according to the button press
        try {
            UIManager.setLookAndFeel( "Chrome.ChromeLookAndFeel" );
            SwingUtilities.updateComponentTreeUI( this );
            System.out.println( "L&F Loaded" );
        }
```

Listing 12.3A   Custom look-and-feel selection main frame source code

```
        catch( Exception e )
        {
            System.out.println( "L&F unavailable" );
        }

        // Set the frame characteristics
        setTitle( "Custom L&F Application" );
        setSize( 300, 200 );
        setBackground( Color.gray );

        // Create a panel to hold all other components
        topPanel = new JPanel();
        topPanel.setLayout( new FlowLayout() );
        getContentPane().add( topPanel );

        // Create instances of chrome buttons
        JButton clubsButton = new JButton( "Clubs",
                            new ImageIcon( "clubs.gif" ) );
        topPanel.add( clubsButton );

        JButton diamondsButton = new JButton( "Diamonds",
                            new ImageIcon( "diamonds.gif" ) );
        topPanel.add( diamondsButton );

        JButton spadesButton = new JButton( "Spades",
                            new ImageIcon( "spades.gif" ) );
        topPanel.add( spadesButton );

        JButton heartsButton = new JButton( "Hearts",
                            new ImageIcon( "hearts.gif" ) );
        topPanel.add( heartsButton );
    }

    // Main entry point for this example
    public static void main( String args[] )
    {
        // Create an instance of the test application
        TestFrame mainFrame = new TestFrame();
        mainFrame.setVisible( true );
    }
}
```

Listing 12.3A Custom look-and-feel selection main frame source code (continued)

We can implement a new look-and-feel library in one of several ways. If you are creating an entire user interface which implements every JFC component, you can extend the LookAndFeel class; however, you will have a great deal of work to do. An easier approach to creating a new look-and-feel is to extend one that already exists. In the case of Chrome, we will minimize the amount of work required by extending the Basic look-and-feel that comes with JFC.

Listing 12.3B shows the source code to implement the Chrome look-and-feel. In this example, the `initClassDefaults` provides the mechanism to set the user interfaces we will implement in the library. In this case, we plan to implement only the ButtonIU.

The `initComponentDefaults()` is a special method that defines some new attributes for any ComponentUI classes we create. This method defines the names and default values for any colors and fonts we will support within our user interface, dictating how our components appear. Supporting this mechanism (as opposed to hard coding fonts and colors) is one of the central ideas behind the look-and-feel technology built into JFC. We can put defaults in place for our interface, but we allow these values to be changed by the developer, if desired. The Organic look-and-feel uses the default interface to change the colors and fonts for all of the components, and allows support for different look-and-feel themes.

```
package Chrome;

import java.io.Serializable;
import java.awt.*;
import com.sun.java.swing.*;
import com.sun.java.swing.plaf.*;
import com.sun.java.swing.plaf.basic.*;

public class ChromeLookAndFeel
    extends          BasicLookAndFeel
    implements       Serializable
{
    // Set up the UIs that we will implement
    protected void initClassDefaults( UIDefaults defaults )
    {
        // Give the basic LAF first crack at initialization
        super.initClassDefaults( defaults );

        String packageName = "Chrome.";
        Object[] uiDefaults =
        {
            "ButtonUI", packageName + "ChromeButtonUI"
        };

        // Add the ui defaults to the look-and-feel
```

Listing 12.3B ChromeLookAndFeel class source code

```
        defaults.putDefaults( uiDefaults );
}

// Return an identifier for this class
public String getID()
{
    return "Chrome";
}

// Return the name of our look-and-feel
public String getName()
{
    return "Chrome Look and Feel";
}

// Return a description of the LAF
public String getDescription()
{
    return "Up to Speed Chrome Look and Feel";
}

// Our LAF is not native
public boolean isNativeLookAndFeel()
{
    return false;
}

// Our LAF is always supported
public boolean isSupportedLookAndFeel()
{
    return true;
}

protected void initComponentDefaults(UIDefaults table)
{
    super.initComponentDefaults( table );

    Object[] defaults =
    {
        "Button.HighBackground", getHighBackground(),
        "Button.LowBackground", getLowBackground(),
        "Button.font", getFont()
    };

    // Add our defaults to the default table
    table.putDefaults( defaults );
}
```

Listing 12.3B ChromeLookAndFeel class source code (continued)

```
// *** Fonts
FontUIResource dialogPlain12 = new FontUIResource(
                              "Dialog", Font.PLAIN, 12 );

// *** Colors
ColorUIResource white = new ColorUIResource( Color.white );
ColorUIResource gray = new ColorUIResource( Color.gray );

public FontUIResource getFont() { return dialogPlain12; }
public ColorUIResource getHighBackground() { return white; }
public ColorUIResource getLowBackground() { return gray; }
}
```

Listing 12.3B   ChromeLookAndFeel class source code (continued)

The ChromeButtonUI class, which is the biggest class in this section, implements all aspects of the button face, excluding the border. Though, at first, this source code seems intimidating, it is really quite simple, and in fact, later in this chapter, you will discover that we have actually done much more work than we need to. The first three methods defined (`createUI()`, `installUI()`, and `uninstallUI()`) are responsible for setting up and removing this component user interface from the look-and-feel. These methods are largely repeated in each component interface, and will become commonplace if you are implementing an entire look-and-feel. Equally repetitive are the next eight methods, which are responsible for controlling the minimum, maximum, and preferred sizes, as well as the default margins for the component.

Take special note of the first three attributes in this class:

```
private final static Color defaultLowColor
               = UIManager.getColor( "Button.LowBackground" );

private final static Color defaultHighColor
               = UIManager.getColor( "Button.HighBackground" );
protected final static Font defaultFont
               = UIManager.getFont( "Button.font" );
```

When we discussed the ChromeLookAndFeel class, I noted the presence of default color and font values that we could use for all ComponentUI classes defined under the Chrome look-and-feel umbrella. The ChromeButtonUI class references these attributes to obtain the color and font values it uses to draw the button.

If you examine the source code for the Basic look-and-feel, you will notice an ample supply of default properties for every conceivable color and font, but you are not restricted to these simple user interface characteristics. The BasicLookAndFeel class also defines defaults for borders, icons, and even ToolTips, all of which it will readily change to suit your needs. This allows new look-and-feel libraries to be developed much more quickly than would be achievable without this support. The Metal look-and-feel developed as part of Sun's Swing project, uses these attributes extensively, avoiding a lot of unnecessary implementation of paint handling. The MetalButtonUI class, which implements a new look-and-feel for JButton, was implemented with less than 50 lines of code.

All of the real work for the custom user interface is handled by the paint method, which, like any other `paint()` method in Java, is invoked by the VM when the component needs to be redrawn. In listing 12.3C, the `paint()` method has been broken into three basic parts. The first two are responsible for painting the icon and text, and are essentially unchanged from the original BasicButtonUI class. The third part of the painting process draws the background of the button, which is the most interesting part of this example. The `PaintBackground()` method in listing 12.3C draws the chrome background for the button.

```java
package Chrome;

import java.io.*;
import java.awt.*;
import java.awt.event.*;
import com.sun.java.swing.*;
import com.sun.java.swing.plaf.*;
import com.sun.java.swing.plaf.basic.*;
import com.sun.java.swing.border.*;

public class ChromeButtonUI
    extends        ButtonUI
    implements     Serializable
{
    private final static Color defaultLowColor
                    = UIManager.getColor( "Button.LowBackground" );
    private final static Color defaultHighColor
                    = UIManager.getColor( "Button.HighBackground" );
    protected final static Font defaultFont
                    = UIManager.getFont( "Button.font" );
    private final static Border defaultBorder
                    = new CompoundBorder(
                            new BevelBorder( BevelBorder.RAISED ),
                            BasicMarginBorder.getMarginBorder() );
```

Listing 12.3C   ChromeButtonUI class source code

```
protected static final int        textIconGap = 3;
protected static ButtonUI         buttonUI;
private     ChromeButtonListener  listener;

public static ComponentUI createUI( JComponent c )
{
    if (buttonUI == null)
        buttonUI = new ChromeButtonUI();

    return buttonUI;
}

public void installUI( JComponent c )
{
    // Add listeners for mouse activity
    listener = new ChromeButtonListener( c );
    c.addMouseListener( listener );
    c.addMouseMotionListener( listener );

    // Assign the default font to this item
    if( c.getFont() == null
            || c.getFont() instanceof UIResource )
        c.setFont( defaultFont );

    // If there is no border, assign the default border
    if( c.getBorder() == null
                || c.getBorder() instanceof UIResource )
        c.setBorder( defaultBorder );
    // Force this button to be opaque by default
    c.setOpaque( true );
}

public void uninstallUI( JComponent c )
{
    // Remove the mouse listeners
    c.removeMouseListener( listener );
    c.removeMouseMotionListener( listener );

    // Remove the border
    if( c.getBorder() == defaultBorder )
        c.setBorder( null );
}

public void paint( Graphics g, JComponent c )
{
    AbstractButton ab    = (AbstractButton)c;
    ButtonModel    bm    = ab.getModel();
```

Listing 12.3C   ChromeButtonUI class source code (continued)

```
    Dimension        size= ab.getSize();

    g.setFont( c.getFont() );
    FontMetrics fm = g.getFontMetrics();

    // Layout the label text
    Rectangle viewRect = new Rectangle( size );
    Rectangle iconRect = new Rectangle();
    Rectangle textRect = new Rectangle();
    String text = SwingUtilities.layoutCompoundLabel(
        fm, ab.getText(), ab.getIcon(),
        ab.getVerticalAlignment(),
        ab.getHorizontalAlignment(),
        ab.getVerticalTextPosition(),
        ab.getHorizontalTextPosition(),
        viewRect, iconRect, textRect, textIconGap );

    // Determine the offset of pixels during a button press
    int shiftOffset = 0;
    if( bm.isArmed() && bm.isPressed() )
        shiftOffset = 1;

    // Paint background
    PaintBackground( g, ab, size, shiftOffset );

    // Draw Icon
    PaintIcon( g, ab, size, shiftOffset, iconRect );

    // Draw Text
    PaintText( g, ab, shiftOffset, textRect, text );
}

public void PaintText( Graphics g, AbstractButton ab,
            int shiftOffset, Rectangle textRect, String text )
{
    FontMetrics    fm     = g.getFontMetrics();
    ButtonModel    bm     = ab.getModel();

    if( text != null && text.length() != 0 )
    {
        if( bm.isEnabled() )
        {
            g.setColor( ab.getForeground() );
          BasicGraphicsUtils.drawString( g, text,
                    bm.getMnemonic(),
                    textRect.x + shiftOffset,
                    textRect.y + fm.getAscent() + shiftOffset);
        }
```

Listing 12.3C   ChromeButtonUI class source code (continued)

```
            else
            {
                g.setColor( defaultLowColor.brighter() );
                BasicGraphicsUtils.drawString( g, text,
                        bm.getMnemonic(),
                        textRect.x, textRect.y + fm.getAscent() );
                g.setColor( defaultLowColor.darker() );
                BasicGraphicsUtils.drawString( g, text,
                        bm.getMnemonic(), textRect.x - 1,
                        textRect.y + fm.getAscent() - 1 );
            }
        }
    }

    public void PaintIcon( Graphics g, AbstractButton ab,
                Dimension size, int shiftOffset, Rectangle iconRect )
    {
        ButtonModel bm = ab.getModel();

        if( ab.getIcon() != null )
        {
            Icon icon = null;
            if( !bm.isEnabled() )
                icon = ab.getDisabledIcon();
            else if( bm.isPressed() && bm.isArmed() )
                icon = ab.getPressedIcon();
            else if( bm.isRollover() )
                icon = ab.getRolloverIcon();

            if( icon == null )
                icon = ab.getIcon();
            if( bm.isPressed() && bm.isArmed() )
                icon.paintIcon( ab, g, iconRect.x + shiftOffset,
                                iconRect.y + shiftOffset);
            else
                icon.paintIcon( ab, g, iconRect.x, iconRect.y );
        }
    }

    public void PaintBackground( Graphics g, AbstractButton ab,
                                Dimension size, int shiftOffset )
    {
        if( ab.isOpaque() )
        {
            // Draw the correct button background
            if( shiftOffset == 0 )
            {
```

Listing 12.3C   ChromeButtonUI class source code (continued)

```
                ChromeUtilities.DrawHalf( defaultLowColor,
                        defaultHighColor, g, size, 0, 1 );
                ChromeUtilities.DrawHalf( defaultLowColor,
                        defaultHighColor, g, size, size.height/2, -1 );
            }
            else
            {
                ChromeUtilities.DrawHalf( defaultLowColor,
                        defaultHighColor, g, size, 0, -1 );
                ChromeUtilities.DrawHalf( defaultLowColor,
                        defaultHighColor, g, size, size.height/2, 1 );
            }
        }
    }

    public Dimension getMinimumSize( JComponent c )
    {
        return getPreferredSize( c );
    }

    public Dimension getMaximumSize( JComponent c )
    {
        return getPreferredSize( c );
    }

    public Dimension getPreferredSize( JComponent c )
    {
        if( ( c.getComponentCount() > 0 )
                        || !( c instanceof AbstractButton ) )
        {
            return null;
        }

        AbstractButton ab = (AbstractButton)c;
        Icon icon = ab.getIcon();
        String text = ab.getText();
        Font font = ab.getFont();
        FontMetrics fm = ab.getToolkit().getFontMetrics (font);
        Rectangle viewRect = new Rectangle( Short.MAX_VALUE,
                                        Short.MAX_VALUE );
        Rectangle iconRect = new Rectangle();
        Rectangle textRect = new Rectangle();
        SwingUtilities.layoutCompoundLabel( fm, text, icon,
                ab.getVerticalAlignment(), ab.getHorizontalAlignment(),
                ab.getVerticalTextPosition(),
                ab.getHorizontalTextPosition(),
```

Listing 12.3C ChromeButtonUI class source code (continued)

```
                    viewRect, iconRect, textRect, textIconGap );
        // Find union of icon and text rectangles
        Rectangle rect = iconRect.union( textRect );
        Insets insets = getInsets( c );
        rect.width += insets.left + insets.right;
        rect.height += insets.top + insets.bottom;
        return rect.getSize();
    }

    public Insets getDefaultMargin( AbstractButton b )
    {
        // Return the default margins for this control
        return new Insets (2, 5, 2, 5);
    }

    public Insets getInsets( JComponent c )
    {
        Border border = c.getBorder();
        Insets insets = ( ( border != null )
                ? border.getBorderInsets (c)
                : new Insets (0,0,0,0));
        return insets;
    }
}
```

Listing 12.3C   ChromeButtonUI class source code (continued)

The code in listing 12.3C deliberately overrides some methods that do not need to be addressed by our code. Methods such as setMinimumSize(), setMaximumSize(), and setPreferredSize() have been overridden in this example simply to show you that you can do this in your own code. If your button interface demands certain dimensional restrictions, you can implement these methods to prevent a size outside of your acceptable limits. Otherwise, we would not implement these methods for the Chrome button because they add no additional value to our code.

The previous listing references a method named SwingUtilities. DrawHalf(). This method is responsible for drawing one half of the chrome appearance. Since any component that has a chrome look will need to execute this code, we create a separate class containing a static method that can be called by a UI class in the Chrome look-and-feel library. You can add any other common methods to this utility class. Listing 12.3D shows this method.

```java
package Chrome;

import java.io.*;
import java.awt.*;
import java.awt.event.*;
import com.sun.java.swing.*;
import com.sun.java.swing.plaf.*;
import com.sun.java.swing.plaf.basic.*;
import com.sun.java.swing.border.*;

public class ChromeUtilities
{
    // Draw one half of the button
    public static void DrawHalf( Color defaultLowColor,
                    Color defaultHighColor, Graphics g,
                    Dimension size, int start, int direction )
    {
        // Determine the increment
        int inc = size.height / 2;

        // Determine the amount of change for each color
        int redDelta = (defaultHighColor.getRed()
                    - defaultLowColor.getRed()) / inc;
        int greenDelta = (defaultHighColor.getGreen()
                    - defaultLowColor.getGreen()) / inc;
        int blueDelta = (defaultHighColor.getBlue()
                    - defaultLowColor.getBlue()) / inc;

        Color color = defaultLowColor;

        // Loop through each increment to draw the correct color
        for( int iCtr = 0; iCtr <= inc; iCtr++ )
        {
            g.setColor( color );

            // Draw the line in the correct location
            if( direction < 0 )
                g.drawLine( 0, start + inc - iCtr, size.width,
                                    start + inc - iCtr );
            else
                g.drawLine( 0, start + iCtr, size.width, start + iCtr );

            // update the color
            int red = color.getRed() + redDelta;
```

Listing 12.3D   ChromeUtilities class source code

```
                    int green = color.getGreen() + greenDelta;
                    int blue = color.getBlue() + blueDelta;

                    // Make sure we don't run out of range
                    if( red > 255 ) red = defaultHighColor.getRed();
                    if( green > 255 ) green = defaultHighColor.getGreen();
                    if( blue > 255 ) blue = defaultHighColor.getBlue();

                    color = new Color( red, green, blue );
                }
            }
        }
```

Listing 12.3D   ChromeUtilities class source code (continued)

The final segment of the Chrome button user interface is the mouse listener, which is shown in listing 12.3E. This code is responsible for handling mouse clicks and drag operations over the button in order to ensure that the correct icon is drawn and that the background reflects and selection. This code is attached to the button when the `installUI()` method is called in the ChromeButtonUI class.

```
package Chrome;

import java.io.*;
import java.awt.*;
import java.awt.event.*;
import com.sun.java.swing.*;

class ChromeButtonListener
    implements Serializable,
                    MouseListener,
                    MouseMotionListener
{
    private      AbstractButton ab;

    public ChromeButtonListener( JComponent c )
    {
        // Save a copy of the component we are listening to
        ab = (AbstractButton)c;
    }

    public void mouseDragged( MouseEvent event )
    {
        ButtonModel bm = ab.getModel();
```

Listing 12.3E   ChromeButtonListener class source code

```
        if (bm.isPressed())
        {
            Graphics g = ab.getGraphics();
            if( g != null )
            {
                Rectangle r = g.getClipBounds();
                if( r.contains( event.getPoint() ) )
                    bm.setArmed( true );
                else
                    bm.setArmed( false );
            }
        }
    }

public void mouseMoved( MouseEvent event )
{
}

public void mouseClicked( MouseEvent event )
{
}

public void mousePressed( MouseEvent event )
{
    ButtonModel    bm            = ab.getModel();
    bm.setArmed( true );
    bm.setPressed( true );
}

public void mouseReleased( MouseEvent event )
{
    ButtonModel    bm            = ab.getModel();
    bm.setPressed ( false );
}

public void mouseEntered( MouseEvent event )
{
    ButtonModel    bm            = ab.getModel();
    if( ab.getRolloverIcon() != null )
        bm.setRollover( true );
}

public void mouseExited( MouseEvent event )
{
    ButtonModel    bm            = ab.getModel();
    if( ab.getRolloverIcon() != null )
        bm.setRollover( false );
```

Listing 12.3E   ChromeButtonListener class source code (continued)

```
    }
}
```

Listing 12.3E   ChromeButtonListener class source code (continued)

   The Basic look-and-feel provides an adequate listener to meet our needs for the chrome button; however, in your own user interface, you may wish to change how the button reacts to mouse events. In order to show an example of how this is accomplished, we have implemented listener code in listing 12.3E. This code should be omitted if you are simply building a different button face and retaining the existing mouse control—BasicButtonUI will look after this for us.

Figure 12.5
Chrome look-and-feel output

Figure 12.5 shows the output of this example. Notice that all instances of JButton now have a raised and polished appearance, and, when the buttons are pressed, the colors reverse such that the button then appears depressed. Since we extended the Basic JFC look-and-feel, all other components would still appear as they normally would, but you can just as easily replace every other component in the user interface. Most of the work involved is repetitive, so you can simply cut and paste common code between components and, relatively quickly, have a new user interface up and running.

12.4.2 Building chrome menus

In the Chrome button user interface, we created several classes, and implemented a lot of code just to make a button work correctly. The good news is that the ButtonUI derivatives are one of the hardest classes to work with, and you have now mastered it. Fortunately, not every ComponentUI requires this sort of effort.

To extend our Chrome look-and-feel even further, let's create a chrome menuing system. As you will see, this requires much less code because we can take some short cuts that reuse code from the Basic parent menu classes. To completely replace the application menu, we will need to implement classes for MenuBarUI,

`MenuUI`, and `MenuItemUI` (we will ignore check box and radio button menu items in this example).

The ChromeMenuBarUI class, shown in listing 12.4A extends the BasicMenuUI class, so, we can save time by using this parent's code for all functions except painting. The paint method looks remarkably like a scaled-down version of the one we used previously in the ChromeButtonUI class.

```java
package Chrome;

import com.sun.java.swing.*;
import java.awt.*;

import com.sun.java.swing.plaf.*;
import com.sun.java.swing.plaf.basic.*;

public class ChromeMenuBarUI extends BasicMenuBarUI
{
    private final static    Color   defaultLowColor
                        = UIManager.getColor( "Menu.LowBackground" );
    private final static    Color   defaultHighColor
                        = UIManager.getColor( "Menu.HighBackground" );

    public static ComponentUI createUI( JComponent c )
    {
        return new ChromeMenuBarUI();
    }

    public void paint( Graphics g, JComponent c )
    {
        Dimension   size    = c.getSize();

        g.setColor( defaultLowColor );

        // Calculate the shading grades
        int incs = size.height / 2;

        // initial colors
        Color color = defaultLowColor;
        int delta = (255 - color.getRed()) / incs;

        // Draw the background
        ChromeUtilities.DrawHalf( defaultLowColor,
                defaultHighColor, g, size, 0, 1 );
        ChromeUtilities.DrawHalf( defaultLowColor,
                defaultHighColor, g, size, size.height / 2, -1 );
```

Listing 12.4A   ChromeMenuBarUI class source code

```
        }
    }
```

Listing 12.4A   ChromeMenuBarUI class source code

To draw menus, we need to do a little more work. Menus function much like buttons, so we need to write a `paint()` method that can handle the background shading, text, and graphics. Listing 12.4B shows the source code to implement a chrome menu.

```java
package Chrome;

import java.awt.*;

import com.sun.java.swing.*;
import com.sun.java.swing.plaf.*;
import com.sun.java.swing.plaf.basic.*;

public class ChromeMenuUI extends BasicMenuUI
{
    private     final static  Color   defaultLowColor
                            = UIManager.getColor( "Menu.LowBackground" );
    private     final static  Color   defaultHighColor
                            = UIManager.getColor( "Menu.HighBackground" );
    protected   static final  int     textIconGap = 3;

    public static ComponentUI createUI( JComponent c )
    {
        return new ChromeMenuUI();
    }

    public void paint( Graphics g, JComponent c )
    {
        AbstractButton    ab       = (AbstractButton)c;
        ButtonModel       bm       = ab.getModel();
        Dimension         size     = c.getSize();

        g.setFont( c.getFont() );
        FontMetrics fm = g.getFontMetrics();

        // Layout the label text
        Rectangle viewRect = new Rectangle( size );
        Rectangle iconRect = new Rectangle();
        Rectangle textRect = new Rectangle();
```

Listing 12.4B   ChromeMenuUI class source code

```
        String text = SwingUtilities.layoutCompoundLabel(
            fm, ab.getText(), ab.getIcon(),
            ab.getVerticalAlignment(),
            ab.getHorizontalAlignment(),
            ab.getVerticalTextPosition(),
            ab.getHorizontalTextPosition(),
            viewRect, iconRect, textRect, textIconGap );

        // Determine the offset of pixels during a button press
        int shiftOffset = 0;
        if( bm.isSelected() )
            shiftOffset = 1;

        // Paint background
        PaintBackground( g, ab, size, shiftOffset );

        // Draw Icon
        PaintIcon( g, ab, size, iconRect );

        // Draw Text
        PaintText( g, ab, textRect, text );
    }

    public void PaintText( Graphics g, AbstractButton ab,
                    Rectangle textRect, String text )
    {
        FontMetrics     fm      = g.getFontMetrics();
        ButtonModel     bm      = ab.getModel();

        if( text != null && text.length() != 0 )
        {
            if( bm.isEnabled() )
            {
                g.setColor( ab.getForeground() );
                BasicGraphicsUtils.drawString( g, text,
                        bm.getMnemonic(),
                        textRect.x, textRect.y + fm.getAscent());
            }
            else
            {
                g.setColor( defaultLowColor.brighter() );
                BasicGraphicsUtils.drawString( g, text,
                        bm.getMnemonic(),
                        textRect.x, textRect.y + fm.getAscent() );
                g.setColor( defaultLowColor.darker() );
                BasicGraphicsUtils.drawString( g, text,
                        bm.getMnemonic(),
```

Listing 12.4B   ChromeMenuUI class source code (continued)

```
                                    textRect.x - 1,
                                    textRect.y + fm.getAscent() - 1 );
                }
            }
        }

    public void PaintIcon( Graphics g, AbstractButton ab,
                    Dimension size, Rectangle iconRect )
    {
        ButtonModel    bm    = ab.getModel();

        if( ab.getIcon() != null )
        {
            Icon icon = null;
            if( !bm.isEnabled() )
                icon = ab.getDisabledIcon();
            else if( bm.isPressed() && bm.isArmed() )
                icon = ab.getPressedIcon();
            else if( bm.isRollover() )
                icon = ab.getRolloverIcon();

            if( icon == null )
                icon = ab.getIcon();
            if( bm.isPressed() && bm.isArmed() )
                icon.paintIcon( ab, g, iconRect.x, iconRect.y );
            else
                icon.paintIcon( ab, g, iconRect.x, iconRect.y );
        }
    }

    public void PaintBackground( Graphics g, AbstractButton ab,
                                Dimension size, int shiftOffset )
    {
        if( ab.isOpaque() )
        {
            // Draw the correct button background
            if( shiftOffset == 0 )
            {
                ChromeUtilities.DrawHalf( defaultLowColor,
                        defaultHighColor, g, size, 0, 1 );
                ChromeUtilities.DrawHalf( defaultLowColor,
                        defaultHighColor, g, size, size.height / 2, -1 );
            }
            else
            {
                ChromeUtilities.DrawHalf( defaultLowColor,
                        defaultHighColor, g, size, 0, -1 );
```

Listing 12.4B   ChromeMenuUI class source code (continued)

```
                ChromeUtilities.DrawHalf( defaultLowColor,
                    defaultHighColor, g, size, size.height / 2, 1 );
            }
        }
    }
}
```

Listing 12.4B   ChromeMenuUI class source code (continued)

To complete the chrome implementation of the menu system, we need to manage the drawing of JMenuItem instances. Listing 12.4C shows the code for this. Notice that this code is almost a duplication of the code used to handle ChromeMenuUI drawing.

```
package Chrome;

import java.awt.*;

import com.sun.java.swing.*;
import com.sun.java.swing.plaf.*;
import com.sun.java.swing.plaf.basic.*;

public class ChromeMenuItemUI extends BasicMenuItemUI
{
    private     final static  Color   defaultLowColor
                    = UIManager.getColor( "Menu.LowBackground" );
    private     final static  Color   defaultHighColor
                    = UIManager.getColor( "Menu.HighBackground" );
    protected   static final  int      textIconGap = 3;

    public static ComponentUI createUI( JComponent c )
    {
        return new ChromeMenuItemUI();
    }

    public void paint( Graphics g, JComponent c )
    {
        AbstractButton      ab          = (AbstractButton)c;
        ButtonModel         bm          = ab.getModel();
        Dimension           size        = c.getSize();

        g.setFont( c.getFont() );

        FontMetrics fm = g.getFontMetrics();
```

Listing 12.4C   ChromeMenuItemUI class source code

```
        // Layout the label text
        Rectangle viewRect = new Rectangle( size );
        Rectangle iconRect = new Rectangle();
        Rectangle textRect = new Rectangle();
        String text = SwingUtilities.layoutCompoundLabel(
            fm, ab.getText(), ab.getIcon(),
            ab.getVerticalAlignment(),
            ab.getHorizontalAlignment(),
            ab.getVerticalTextPosition(),
            ab.getHorizontalTextPosition(),
            viewRect, iconRect, textRect, textIconGap );

        // Determine the offset of pixels during a button press
        int shiftOffset = 0;
        if( bm.isSelected() )
            shiftOffset = 1;

        // Paint background
        PaintBackground( g, ab, size, shiftOffset );

        // Draw Icon
        PaintIcon( g, ab, size, iconRect );

        // Draw Text
        PaintText( g, ab, textRect, text );
    }

    public void PaintText( Graphics g, AbstractButton ab,
                   Rectangle textRect, String text )
    {
        FontMetrics   fm    = g.getFontMetrics();
        ButtonModel   bm    = ab.getModel();

        if( text != null && text.length() != 0 )
        {
            if( bm.isEnabled() )
            {
                g.setColor( ab.getForeground() );
                BasicGraphicsUtils.drawString( g, text,
                        bm.getMnemonic(),
                        textRect.x,
                        textRect.y + fm.getAscent());
            }
            else
            {
                g.setColor( defaultLowColor.brighter() );

                BasicGraphicsUtils.drawString( g, text,
```

Listing 12.4C   ChromeMenuItemUI class source code (continued)

```
                                    bm.getMnemonic(),
                            textRect.x, textRect.y + fm.getAscent() );
                    g.setColor( defaultLowColor.darker() );
                    BasicGraphicsUtils.drawString( g, text,
                                    bm.getMnemonic(),
                            textRect.x - 1,
                            textRect.y + fm.getAscent() - 1 );
            }
        }
}

public void PaintIcon( Graphics g, AbstractButton ab,
                Dimension size, Rectangle iconRect )
{
    ButtonModel     bm          = ab.getModel();

    if( ab.getIcon() != null )
    {
        Icon icon = null;
        if( !bm.isEnabled() )
            icon = ab.getDisabledIcon();
        else if( bm.isPressed() && bm.isArmed() )
            icon = ab.getPressedIcon();
        else if( bm.isRollover() )
            icon = ab.getRolloverIcon();

        if( icon == null )
            icon = ab.getIcon();
        if( bm.isPressed() && bm.isArmed() )
            icon.paintIcon( ab, g, iconRect.x, iconRect.y );
        else
            icon.paintIcon( ab, g, iconRect.x, iconRect.y );
    }
}

public void PaintBackground( Graphics g, AbstractButton ab,
                            Dimension size, int shiftOffset )
{
    if( ab.isOpaque() )
    {
        g.setColor( defaultLowColor );

        // Draw the correct button background
        if( shiftOffset == 0 )
        {
            ChromeUtilities.DrawHalf( defaultLowColor,
```

Listing 12.4C   ChromeMenuItemUI class source code (continued)

```
                              defaultHighColor, g, size, 0, 1 );
              ChromeUtilities.DrawHalf( defaultLowColor,
                      defaultHighColor, g, size, size.height / 2, -1 );
          }
          else
          {
              ChromeUtilities.DrawHalf( defaultLowColor,
                      defaultHighColor, g, size, 0, -1 );
              ChromeUtilities.DrawHalf( defaultLowColor,
                      defaultHighColor, g, size, size.height / 2, 1 );
          }
      }
  }
}
```

Listing 12.4C   ChromeMenuItemUI class source code (continued)

Figure 12.6 shows the new chrome menu created with the user interface code from listings 12.4A-C. Adding a simple menu hierarchy to the existing sample application produced this example. Admittedly, the appearance of this menu will not be appealing to some users, but the advantage of custom look-and-feel is that you now have the knowledge required to change it.

The point of this exercise is to show that adding new user interface components is really quite simple. If all you want to do is change the visual part of the component, you can cut and paste in the same way we did here. Since we are deriving all of our classes from their Basic look-and-feel equivalents, we can let the parent do all the work. However, if you want to add new characteristics (such as additional keyboard support) then you need to develop more code to support them. In any case, use what you can from the parent class to save coding time.

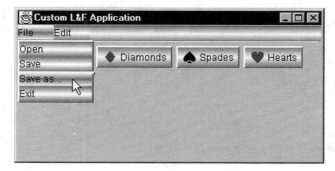

Figure 12.6
Chrome menu output

12.4.3 Supporting themes

One of the late additions to the Swing Look-and-Feel interface was support for themes. Themes are simply different color schemes supported by the look-and-feel library that can be changed at run time without affecting how the application is written. The Organic and Metal look-and-feel classes both support themes, and, as you will see here, implementation of themes is really quite simple.

You may ask, "Why would anyone care about themes?" If you are building an application that exploits Java's full potential of platform independence, you have no assurance that your color scheme will appeal to all users. In fact, some of your users may be using desktop systems (such as Sun SparcStation or Windows NT) which support millions of colors, but others may be running your code on a PDA which may not support color at all. Color rendering on a monochrome screen is usually handled poorly, so you need to address this issue, and the way to manage it with Swing is to implement color themes.

Since the Chrome look-and-feel is, for the most part, already monochrome, we will not add this code to our project; however, if you are going to create a theme, you need to know how it is accomplished, so we will use Chrome in all of the code shown here. Most of this code was simply taken from the existing Metal look-and-feel and modified to meet our needs.

The first task is to associate themes with the ChromeLookAndFeel class shown earlier. To do this, we need to add a new attribute to track the current theme. Listing 12.5A shows the updated ChromeLookAndFeel class source code.

```
package Chrome;

import java.io.Serializable;
import java.awt.*;
import com.sun.java.swing.*;
import com.sun.java.swing.plaf.*;
import com.sun.java.swing.plaf.basic.*;

public class ChromeLookAndFeel
    extends      BasicLookAndFeel
{
    private static ChromeTheme currentTheme;

    // Return the name of our look-and-feel
    public String getName()
    {
```

Listing 12.5A   ChromeLookAndFeel update source code

```
        return "Chrome Look and Feel";
    }

    // Return an identifier for this class
    public String getID()
    {
        return "Chrome";
    }

    // Return a description of the LAF
    public String getDescription()
    {
        return "Up to Speed Chrome Look and Feel";
    }

    // Our LAF is not native
    public boolean isNativeLookAndFeel()
    {
        return false;
    }

    // Our LAF is always supported
    public boolean isSupportedLookAndFeel()
    {
        return true;
    }

    // Set up the UIs that we will implement
    protected void initClassDefaults( UIDefaults defaults )
    {
        // Give the basic LAF first crack at initialization
        super.initClassDefaults( defaults );

        String packageName = "Chrome.";
        Object[] uiDefaults =
        {
            "MenuBarUI", packageName + "ChromeMenuBarUI",
            "MenuUI", packageName + "ChromeMenuUI",
            "MenuItemUI", packageName + "ChromeMenuItemUI",
            "ButtonUI", packageName + "ChromeButtonUI"
        };

        // Add the ui defaults to the look-and-feel
        defaults.putDefaults( uiDefaults );
    }

    protected void initComponentDefaults(UIDefaults table)
    {
```

Listing 12.5A ChromeLookAndFeel update source code (continued)

```
        super.initComponentDefaults( table );

    Object[] defaults =
    {
        "Button.HighBackground", getHighBackground(),
        "Button.LowBackground", getLowBackground(),
        "Button.font", getFont()
    };

    // Add our defaults to the default table
    table.putDefaults( defaults );
}

protected void createDefaultTheme()
{
    if( currentTheme == null)
        currentTheme =  new DefaultChromeTheme();
}

public UIDefaults getDefaults()
{
    // Create the default theme for this look-and-feel
    createDefaultTheme();

    // return the table of defaults
    UIDefaults table = super.getDefaults();
    currentTheme.addCustomEntriesToTable( table );

    return table;
}

public static void setCurrentTheme( ChromeTheme theme )
{
    if (theme == null)
    {
        throw new NullPointerException("Can't have null theme");
    }

    // Set the new theme
    currentTheme = theme;
}

public FontUIResource getFont() { return currentTheme.getFont(); }
public ColorUIResource getHighBackground()
                    { return currentTheme.getHighBackground(); }
public ColorUIResource getLowBackground()
                { return currentTheme.getLowBackground(); }
}
```

Listing 12.5A   ChromeLookAndFeel update source code (continued)

In the code shown in listing 12.5A, we referenced some new classes. The first of these was the class, ChromeTheme, which is an abstract class that defines the format of all themes used by the Chrome look-and-feel. This class is shown in listing 12.5B.

```
package Chrome;

import java.awt.*;
import com.sun.java.swing.*;
import com.sun.java.swing.plaf.*;

public abstract class ChromeTheme
{
    public abstract String getName();

    public abstract FontUIResource getFont();

    public abstract ColorUIResource getHighBackground();
    public abstract ColorUIResource getLowBackground();

    public void addCustomEntriesToTable( UIDefaults table ) {}
}
```

Listing 12.5B   ChromeTheme class

From the ChromeTheme class, we derive all possible themes for our look-and-feel. The first theme we define is the DefaultChromeTheme class, which implements the default colors and fonts that were originally defined in the ChromeLookAndFeel class. Listing 12.5C contains the code to build the default theme for our Chrome look-and-feel.

```
package Chrome;

import java.io.Serializable;
import java.awt.*;
import com.sun.java.swing.*;
import com.sun.java.swing.plaf.*;
import com.sun.java.swing.plaf.basic.*;

public class DefaultChromeTheme extends ChromeTheme
{
    FontUIResource dialogPlain12 = new FontUIResource(
                        "Dialog", Font.PLAIN, 12 );
```

Listing 12.5C   DefaultChromeTheme class

```
    ColorUIResource white = new ColorUIResource( Color.white );
    ColorUIResource gray = new ColorUIResource( Color.gray );

    public String getName()
    {
        return "Default";
    }

    public FontUIResource getFont() { return dialogPlain12; }

    public ColorUIResource getHighBackground() { return white; }
    public ColorUIResource getLowBackground() { return gray; }

    public void addCustomEntriesToTable( UIDefaults table ) {}
}
```

Listing 12.5C   DefaultChromeTheme class (continued)

To create another theme, we can derive a second class from ChromeTheme. In this example, we will choose a distinctive red color to draw the buttons, and we will enlarge the font to 14 points from the default 12 points. The source code for the RedChromeTheme class is shown in listing 12.5D.

```
package Chrome;

import com.sun.java.swing.*;
import com.sun.java.swing.plaf.*;

public class RedChromeTheme extends ChromeTheme
{
    FontUIResource dialogPlain12 = new FontUIResource(
                              "Dialog", Font.PLAIN, 14 );
    ColorUIResource white = new ColorUIResource( Color.white );
    ColorUIResource red = new ColorUIResource( Color.red );

    public String getName()
    {
        return "Red";
    }

    public FontUIResource getFont() { return dialogPlain12; }

    public ColorUIResource getHighBackground() { return white; }
    public ColorUIResource getLowBackground() { return red; }

    public void addCustomEntriesToTable( UIDefaults table ) {}
}
```

Listing 12.5D   RedChromeTheme class

Now that the themes have been created, you need to know how to select them from the main TestFrame class. To accomplish this, you need to call the setCurrentTheme() method that we added to the ChromeLookAndFeel class. Modify the TestFrame class and replace the current look-and-feel setting code with the code shown below:

```
// Create an instance of the chrome LAF
   ChromeLookAndFeel laf = new ChromeLookAndFeel();

   // Set the Red theme
   laf.setCurrentTheme( new RedChromeTheme() );

   // Set the look-and-feel
   try {
       UIManager.setLookAndFeel( laf );
       SwingUtilities.updateComponentTreeUI( this );
       System.out.println( "L&F Loaded" );
   }
   catch( Exception e )
   {
       System.out.println( "L&F unavailable" );
   }
```

12.5 Chapter summary

In this chapter, we have started to dig much deeper into Swing and JFC by examining the plugable look-and-feel interface. We started by revisiting the MVC architecture and briefly describing its benefit to application building with JFC. We examined the UIManager and developed some applications that enumerate the look-and-feel libraries supported by JFC, permitting the user interface to be reconfigured with the click of a button.

Next, we started to create our own look-and-feel user interface called Chrome, which displays components with a polished metal finish. We started our interface by implementing a ChromeButtonUI class, which we added to our look-and-feel in order to manage the drawing of standard JButton components. Finally, we added support for chromed menus and menu items (reusing much of the code implemented in the Basic UI classes) with our own UI classes containing only a method to handle our specific painting requirements.

Optimizing JFC applications

13

In this chapter
- Using optimization tools to find code bottlenecks
- General Java performance tuning
- Special tips for tuning JFC programs

13.1 Why optimize?

For the last chapter of this book, I thought it would be a great idea to discuss optimization of Java programs and, more specifically, applications based on JFC. Without question, code optimization is one of my favorite topics. Since the Java compiler builds bytecode (which is an interpreted intermediate machine code) optimization is extremely important—every bytecode instruction that can be eliminated will result in better performance of your applications.

Java has received a bit of criticism from some developers who experienced poor performance with Java, but these criticisms are, for the most part, rooted in a lack of understanding of the language. Extensive UI applications written in Java can be every bit as responsive as a similar program written in C++. There is no question that C++ can crunch numbers better than a Java interpreter, but we will demonstrate how to narrow this gap, as well. It is my hope that this chapter will be a rewarding experience for you and will help you write better code.

We will discuss many of the reasons that Java code can run slowly, and we will discuss solutions and workarounds to some of these problems. To help us write faster (and possibly smaller) Java applications, we will not only examine some of the performance tools available, but we will also create a few of our own which you can use in your applications. So, let's dig in and have some fun.

13.2 Using optimization tools

The greatest assistant in the war against poor performance is a code profiler. These utilities provide detailed feedback about where an executing application spends its time, offering a clear indicator of what parts of an application require the most attention during the optimization phase of your project. Though the list of competent Java profilers is growing, we will concentrate on only two.

13.2.1 A poorly performing test case

For our work with profilers, we will need a test application which we know is poorly written and requires a significant amount of time to execute. Listing 13.1 is an example of such a program. It contains an iterating loop and some poorly written internals designed specifically to produce bad performance; however, even though we know this is an example of a poorly written program, it contains code commonly found in many programs. Software development cycles today are so tight that, often, overall code quality (and usually performance) suffers as a direct result of trying to adhere to a product development schedule. So, we will assume that the code in listing 13.1 is fairly representative of the code that many developers write.

```
class MainClass
{
    public static void main( String args[] )
    {
        int constantMultiplier = 2;

        for( int iCtr = 0; iCtr < 20000; iCtr++ )
        {
            String string = new String( "Option: " );
            int tempValue = iCtr * constantMultiplier;
            String valueString = new String( "" + iCtr );

            myMethod( string, valueString, tempValue, iCtr );

        }
    }

    public static void myMethod( String string, String valueString,
                                    int tempValue, int iCtr )

    {
        System.out.println( string + valueString + "," + tempValue );
    }
}
```

Listing 13.1   Example of a poorly performing application

13.2.2 Sun's JDK profiler

The first profiler we will examine is the free one built into every JDK installation. When the Java VM is started for an application, you have the option of specifying that the code should be profiled. This is accomplished like this:

```
Java_g -prof:out.txt MainClass
```

 In order to get accurate profiling information, you must build your code to include debugging information. The VM must be executed with java_g, rather than java, so it will use the debugging data.

This command executes the program as it normally would; however, behind the scenes, the VM is collecting run time information about the methods being called, the amount of time expended for each line, and so on. The results of this command produce a file, OUT.TXT, containing the profile information. As you can see, this data (shown in the following listing) is quite confusing, but we will attempt to decode it.

```
count callee caller time
183335 java/lang/Character.forDigit(II)C
       java/lang/Integer.toString(II)Ljava/lang/String; 1176
183335 java/lang/StringBuffer.ensureCapacity(I)V
       java/lang/StringBuffer.append(C)Ljava/lang/StringBuffer; 892
183335 java/lang/StringBuffer.append(C)Ljava/lang/StringBuffer;
       java/lang/Integer.toString(II)Ljava/lang/String; 3633
183335 java/lang/StringBuffer.copyWhenShared()V
       java/lang/StringBuffer.append(C)Ljava/lang/StringBuffer; 293
160000 java/lang/System.arraycopy(Ljava/lang/Object;ILjava/lang/Object;II)V
       java/lang/String.getChars(II[CI)V 352
80000 java/lang/String.length()I java/lang/StringBuffer.append
       (Ljava/lang/String;)Ljava/lang/StringBuffer; 113
80000 sun/io/CharToByte8859_1.flush([BII)I
       java/io/OutputStreamWriter.flushBuffer()V 359
80000 java/lang/StringBuffer.copyWhenShared()V java/lang/StringBuffer.append
       (Ljava/lang/String;)Ljava/lang/StringBuffer; 143
80000 java/lang/String.getChars(II[CI)V java/lang/StringBuffer.append
       (Ljava/lang/String;)Ljava/lang/StringBuffer; 830
80000 java/lang/StringBuffer.ensureCapacity(I)V java/lang/StringBuffer.append
       (Ljava/lang/String;)Ljava/lang/StringBuffer; 374
60000 java/lang/String.<init>(Ljava/lang/StringBuffer;)V
       java/lang/StringBuffer.toString()Ljava/lang/String; 1276
60000 java/io/OutputStream.flush()V java/io/BufferedOutputStream.flush()V 48
60000 java/io/BufferedOutputStream.flushBuffer()V
       java/io/BufferedOutputStream.flush()V 5064
60000 java/lang/StringBuffer.getValue()[C
       java/lang/String.<init>(Ljava/lang/StringBuffer;)V 100
60000 java/lang/StringBuffer.setShared()V
       java/lang/String.<init>(Ljava/lang/StringBuffer;)V 132
60000 java/lang/StringBuffer.length()I
       java/lang/String.<init>(Ljava/lang/StringBuffer;)V 83
40000 java/io/BufferedWriter.ensureOpen()V
       java/io/BufferedWriter.flushBuffer()V 65
40000 java/io/BufferedWriter.write(Ljava/lang/String;II)V
       java/io/Writer.write(Ljava/lang/String;)V 1879
40000 sun/io/CharToByte8859_1.convert([CII[BII)I
       java/io/OutputStreamWriter.write([CII)V 7772
40000 java/lang/Math.min(II)I
       java/io/BufferedWriter.write(Ljava/lang/String;II)V 99
40000 java/lang/StringBuffer.copyWhenShared()V
       java/lang/StringBuffer.reverse()Ljava/lang/StringBuffer; 81
```

```
40000  java/lang/String.<init>(Ljava/lang/String;)V
       MainClass.main([Ljava/lang/String;)V 1145
40000  java/io/PrintStream.write([BII)V
       java/io/OutputStreamWriter.flushBuffer()V 6865
40000  java/lang/String.getChars(II[CI)V
       java/io/BufferedWriter.write(Ljava/lang/String;II)V 506
40000  java/lang/StringBuffer.toString()Ljava/lang/String;
       java/lang/Integer.toString(II)Ljava/lang/String; 1182
40000  java/lang/StringBuffer.reverse()Ljava/lang/StringBuffer;
       java/lang/Integer.toString(II)Ljava/lang/String; 1138
40000  java/lang/StringBuffer.<init>(I)V
       java/lang/Integer.toString(II)Ljava/lang/String; 411
40000  java/io/FileOutputStream.write([BII)V
       java/io/BufferedOutputStream.flushBuffer()V 4660
40000  java/io/OutputStreamWriter.write([CII)V
       java/io/BufferedWriter.flushBuffer()V 8832
40000  java/io/OutputStreamWriter.ensureOpen()V
       java/io/OutputStreamWriter.flushBuffer()V 75
40000  java/io/BufferedWriter.ensureOpen()V
       java/io/BufferedWriter.write(Ljava/lang/String;II)V 73
40000  java/io/OutputStreamWriter.ensureOpen()V
       java/io/OutputStreamWriter.write([CII)V 80
40000  java/lang/String.getChars(II[CI)V
       java/lang/String.<init>(Ljava/lang/String;)V 635
40000  java/io/PrintStream.ensureOpen()V java/io/PrintStream.write([BII)V 94
40000  java/lang/System.arraycopy(Ljava/lang/Object;ILjava/lang/Object;II)V
       java/io/BufferedOutputStream.write([BII)V 83
40000  java/lang/Integer.toString(II)Ljava/lang/String;
       java/lang/String.valueOf(I)Ljava/lang/String; 10145
40000  java/io/BufferedOutputStream.write([BII)V
       java/io/PrintStream.write([BII)V 615
40000  java/io/BufferedOutputStream.flush()V
       java/io/PrintStream.write([BII)V 5458
40000  java/lang/StringBuffer.append(Ljava/lang/String;)
       Ljava/lang/StringBuffer; MainClass.myMethod(Ljava/lang/String;
       Ljava/lang/String;II)V 1360
40000  java/io/FileOutputStream.writeBytes([BII)V
       java/io/FileOutputStream.write([BII)V 4260
20000  java/io/PrintStream.ensureOpen()V
       java/io/PrintStream.write(Ljava/lang/String;)V 35
20000  java/io/PrintStream.ensureOpen()V java/io/PrintStream.newLine()V 59
20000  java/io/PrintStream.print(Ljava/lang/String;)V
       java/io/PrintStream.println(Ljava/lang/String;)V 14250
20000  java/lang/StringBuffer.append(Ljava/lang/String;)Ljava/
       lang/StringBuffer; java/lang/StringBuffer.append(I)
       Ljava/lang/StringBuffer; 807
20000  java/io/Writer.write(Ljava/lang/String;)V
       java/io/BufferedWriter.newLine()V 1066
```

```
20000 java/lang/StringBuffer.append(Ljava/lang/String;)Ljava/
      lang/StringBuffer; java/lang/StringBuffer.<init>(
      Ljava/lang/String;)V 797
20000 java/io/PrintStream.write(Ljava/lang/String;)V
      java/io/PrintStream.print(Ljava/lang/String;)V 14168
20000 java/lang/String.indexOf(I)I
      java/io/PrintStream.write(Ljava/lang/String;)V 1210
20000 java/lang/String.valueOf(Ljava/lang/Object;)Ljava/
      lang/String; MainClass.myMethod(Ljava/lang/String;
      Ljava/lang/String;II)V 134
20000 java/io/Writer.write(Ljava/lang/String;)V
      java/io/PrintStream.write(Ljava/lang/String;)V 1002
20000 java/lang/String.valueOf(I)Ljava/lang/String;
      MainClass.main([Ljava/lang/String;)V 4961
20000 java/io/BufferedWriter.flushBuffer()V
      java/io/PrintStream.newLine()V 1980
20000 java/io/BufferedWriter.flushBuffer()V
      java/io/PrintStream.write(Ljava/lang/String;)V 7483
20000 java/io/BufferedWriter.newLine()V java/io/PrintStream.newLine()V 1150
20000 java/lang/StringBuffer.toString()Ljava/lang/String;
      MainClass.myMethod(Ljava/lang/String;Ljava/lang/String;II)V 590
20000 java/io/OutputStreamWriter.flushBuffer()V
      java/io/PrintStream.write(Ljava/lang/String;)V 3982
20000 java/io/OutputStreamWriter.flushBuffer()V
      java/io/PrintStream.newLine()V 4510
20000 java/io/PrintStream.newLine()V
      java/io/PrintStream.println(Ljava/lang/String;)V 8336
20000 java/io/PrintStream.println(Ljava/lang/String;)V
      MainClass.myMethod(Ljava/lang/String;Ljava/lang/String;II)V 22803
20000 java/lang/String.indexOf(II)I java/lang/String.indexOf(I)I 1133
20000 java/lang/StringBuffer.<init>(I)V
      java/lang/StringBuffer.<init>(Ljava/lang/String;)V 148
20000 MainClass.myMethod(Ljava/lang/String;Ljava/lang/String;II)V
      MainClass.main([Ljava/lang/String;)V 32820
20000 java/lang/StringBuffer.<init>(Ljava/lang/String;)V
      MainClass.myMethod(Ljava/lang/String;Ljava/lang/String;II)V 1204
20000 java/lang/String.length()I
      java/lang/StringBuffer.<init>(Ljava/lang/String;)V 33
20000 java/lang/StringBuffer.append(I)Ljava/lang/StringBuffer;
      MainClass.myMethod(Ljava/lang/String;Ljava/lang/String;II)V 6283
20000 java/lang/String.toString()Ljava/lang/String;
      java/lang/String.valueOf(Ljava/lang/Object;)Ljava/lang/String; 24
20000 java/io/BufferedOutputStream.flush()V java/io/PrintStream.newLine()V
228
20000 java/lang/String.valueOf(I)Ljava/lang/String;
      java/lang/StringBuffer.append(I)Ljava/lang/StringBuffer; 5347
6 java/lang/System.gc()V  java/lang/StringBuffer.<init>(I)V 167
4 java/lang/System.gc()V  MainClass.main([Ljava/lang/String;)V 77
```

```
4 java/lang/String.<init>(II[C)V <unknown caller> 0
1 java/lang/Object.<init>()V java/lang/String.<init>(Ljava/lang/String;)V 0
1 java/lang/Float.floatToIntBits(F)I java/lang/Math.<clinit>()V 0
1 java/lang/String.length()I java/io/Writer.write(Ljava/lang/String;)V 0
1 java/lang/System.gc()V  sun/io/CharToByte8859_1.convert([CII[BII)I 19
1 java/lang/Float.<clinit>()V <unknown caller> 0
1 java/lang/Class.getPrimitiveClass(Ljava/lang/String;)Ljava/lang/Class;
       java/lang/Double.<clinit>()V 0
1 MainClass.main([Ljava/lang/String;)V <unknown caller> 39594
1 java/lang/Double.longBitsToDouble(J)D java/lang/Double.<clinit>()V 0
1 java/lang/String.length()I java/lang/String.<init>(Ljava/lang/String;)V 0
1 java/lang/Class.getPrimitiveClass(Ljava/lang/String;)Ljava/lang/Class;
       java/lang/Float.<clinit>()V 0
1 java/lang/System.gc()V
       java/lang/StringBuffer.toString()Ljava/lang/String; 23
1 java/lang/Double.doubleToLongBits(D)J java/lang/Math.<clinit>()V 0
1 java/lang/Double.<clinit>()V <unknown caller> 0
1 java/lang/Math.<clinit>()V <unknown caller> 20
handles_used: 1010, handles_free: 26214, heap-used: 105184, heap-free: 733672
sig   count  bytes   indx
[C     145 18802      5
[B       5 19200      8
*** tab[979] p=1d78558 cb=f80140 cnt=609 ac=1 al=0
   Ljava/lang/String; 609 7308
   [Ljava/lang/String; 1 0
*** tab[946] p=1d78348 cb=f830b0 cnt=22 ac=0 al=0
   Ljava/util/Locale; 22 352
*** tab[941] p=1d782f8 cb=f800a8 cnt=2 ac=1 al=4
   Ljava/lang/ThreadGroup; 2 80
   [Ljava/lang/ThreadGroup; 1 16
*** tab[899] p=1d78058 cb=f80000 cnt=3 ac=2 al=8
   Ljava/lang/Thread; 3 132
   [Ljava/lang/Thread; 2 32
*** tab[603] p=1d76dd8 cb=f83b50 cnt=2 ac=0 al=0
   Ljava/io/BufferedWriter; 2 48
*** tab[414] p=1d76208 cb=f80868 cnt=2 ac=0 al=0
   Ljava/io/BufferedOutputStream; 2 24
*** tab[398] p=1d76108 cb=f80828 cnt=1 ac=0 al=0
   Ljava/io/FileInputStream; 1 4
*** tab[392] p=1d760a8 cb=f80810 cnt=1 ac=0 al=0
   Ljava/io/FileDescriptor; 1 4
*** tab[384] p=1d76028 cb=f807f0 cnt=2 ac=0 al=0
   Ljava/io/FileOutputStream; 2 8
*** tab[376] p=1d75fa8 cb=f807d0 cnt=1 ac=0 al=0
   Ljava/io/BufferedInputStream; 1 24
*** tab[370] p=1d75f48 cb=f807b8 cnt=2 ac=0 al=0
   Ljava/io/PrintStream; 2 48
*** tab[358] p=1d75e88 cb=f80788 cnt=2 ac=0 al=0
```

```
  Ljava/io/OutputStreamWriter; 2 48
*** tab[38] p=1d74a88 cb=f80288 cnt=1 ac=0 al=0
  Ljava/util/Properties; 1 20
*** tab[36] p=1d74a68 cb=f80280 cnt=1 ac=0 al=0
  Ljava/util/Hashtable; 1 16
*** tab[28] p=1d749e8 cb=f80260 cnt=203 ac=2 al=1002
  Ljava/util/HashtableEntry; 203 3248
  [Ljava/util/HashtableEntry; 2 4008
```

In order to decipher the meaning of this list, we will use the single line shown below. You will find this line of data in the OUT.TXT file generated by the profiler.

```
20000 MainClass.myMethod(Ljava/lang/String;Ljava/lang/String;II)V
      MainClass.main([Ljava/lang/String;)V 32820
```

The format of this line is "`count callee caller time`" where:

- `count`   indicates the number of times the method is called
- `callee`   is the name of the method called
- `caller`   lists the method which invoked the called method
- `time`   is the total elapsed time measured in milliseconds used to execute the called method

From the sample line, you can see that the `myMethod()` code is called 20,000 times from `main()`, and used 32.82 seconds, or 1.641 milliseconds per call.

We won't dwell on Sun's profiler because you are likely to shy away from it. The output it produces is quite informative, but requires a great deal of developer intervention in order to manually sift through the volumes of data produced. As we will see next, Sun offers a tool that enhances the abilities of its profiler by automatically performing the laborious task of examining the raw profiler data

13.2.3 Profiling with Java workshop

The JDK is not the only place Sun provides a profiler. In fact, the Sun Java Work-Shop product also includes a profiler which is arguably the best profiler for Java today. This profiler allows you view method execution time at a millisecond resolution, and this value can include or exclude the time used by anything else an individual method executes.

Figure 13.1 shows the profiler output produced by the test program in listing 13.1. Since our sample includes only two methods, the output is quite simple. In the top window, the main method is highlighted; the middle window shows the

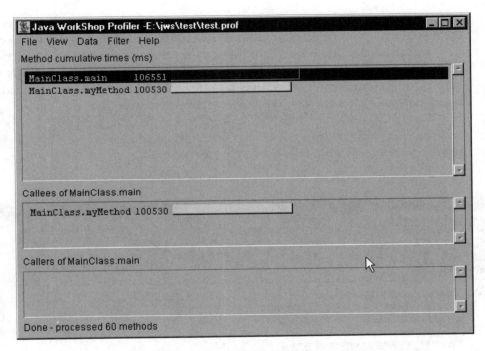

Figure 13.1 Java WorkShop profiler output for test application

times used by any methods that `main()` calls; and the lower window would show the times for any caller methods, if there were any.

Figure 13.1 shows that our untuned example required 106.551 seconds to execute. With some quick performance tuning, we can reduce this time to approximately 98 seconds. This 8.6 percent time saving doesn't sound significant, but remember, this is only one method call. In a much more complex application, you can usually save more time than this, so, profiling is definitely a worthwhile exercise. One of the easiest ways to accomplish this task is with Sun's Java Workshop profiler tool.

13.2.4 Profiling with OptimizeIt

Fortunately, there is an even better tool for profiling Java code—OptimizeIt, which has been developed specifically for tuning Java applications. Its downside is that it comes with a price tag attached but this tool is well worth its modest price. Appendix B contains an overview of OptimizeIt and other tools you may want to acquire.

Figure 13.2 shows a sample of the output produced when the sample application (listing13.1) is executed. In this case, it shows that the program spends 96.65 percent of its time within `MainClass.myMethod()`, which is not unexpected since this method handles the console output. However, note that our sample spends over 8 percent of its time handling strings. Strings in Java are notorious for poor performance, and we will look at ways to eliminate some of these bottlenecks and improve on others a little later in this chapter.

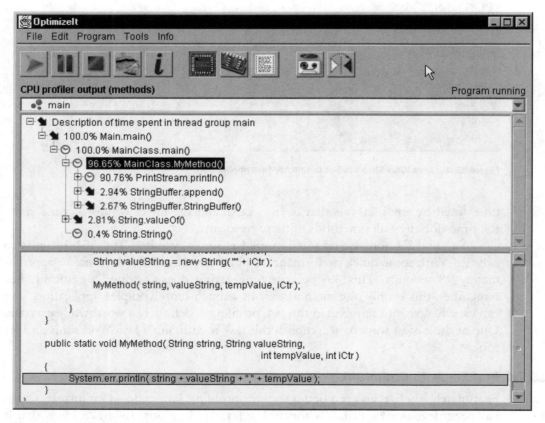

Figure 13.2 OptimizeIt output for test application

OptimizeIt is an excellent tool that all Java developers concerned with performance should have in their toolboxes. This application faithfully details where CPU time is being spent with an application or applet. Unfortunately, OptimizeIt only indicates performance as a percentage of total execution time, rather than absolute time. This does make it more difficult to tune specific methods with the tool, but OptimizeIt's benefits far outweigh any disadvantages.

13.2.5 A custom profiler class

The tools we have reviewed so far tap into an application from the outside. Though both the Sun Java profiler and OptimizeIt are each powerful in their own right, they are hampered by the fact that they cannot penetrate into the internals of the application. These tools are unable to determine exactly how much time is required to execute groups of source code lines—or even a single line.

To address these issues, we can implement a special class that we can use to determine elapsed time between two or more lines of code. It is important to note that once we start adding code to an application for profiling purposes, we begin to affect the real performance of the program—basically, the profiling code is also profiling itself. For this reason, we must ensure that whatever code we add is optimized as much as possible, in order to minimize the effect that profiling has on overall performance.

Listing 13.2A shows the code for the DebugProfile class, which simply keeps track of the profile start time and the time of each `Print()` method invocation. From this information, it is easy to determine how long a task takes, as well as how much time has elapsed between one or more lines of code.

```
class DebugProfile
{
    private long   lStart = 0;
    private long   lLast  = 0;
    private String titleString;

    public DebugProfile( String titleString )
    {
        this.titleString = titleString;
    }

    public void Print( String string )
    {
```

Listing 13.2A DebugProfile class source code

```
        // Keep track of the current elpased time and the
        // time from start
        long lCurrent = System.currentTimeMillis();
        if( lStart == 0 )
        {
            lLast = lCurrent;
            lStart = lCurrent;
        }

        // Display the string along with a time stamp
        System.out.println( titleString + "\t" + (lCurrent-lStart)
                        + "\t" + (lCurrent-lLast) + "\t" + string );

        // Save the last time
        lLast = lCurrent;
    }
}
```

Listing 13.2A   DebugProfile class source code (continued)

Listing 13.2B shows the modified MainClass source code containing the profiling code. Notice that in the constructor for the profiler object, there is a string called Main. This string is prefixed to any printed profile data, so it can be used to identify the part of the code to which the profile information is referring. This is especially useful if you are profiling several methods in the code at the same time.

```
class MainClass
{
    public static void main( String args[] )
    {
        DebugProfile log = new DebugProfile( "Main" );

        int constantMultiplier = 2;

        log.Print( "Starting Loop" );
        for( int iCtr = 0; iCtr < 1000; iCtr++ )
        {
            log.Print( "Iteration:" + iCtr );

            String string = new String( "Option: " );
            int tempValue = iCtr * constantMultiplier;
            String valueString = new String( "" + iCtr );

            myMethod( string, valueString, tempValue, iCtr );
```

Listing 13.2B   Sample MainClass source code with profiling

```
            log.Print( "Done iteration:" + iCtr );
        }
        log.Print( "Finished Loop" );
    }

    public static void myMethod( String string, String valueString,
                                 int tempValue, int iCtr )
    {
        System.out.println( string + valueString + "," + tempValue );
    }
}
```

Listing 13.2B   Sample MainClass source code with profiling (continued)

The partial list below shows the results of the profiling class. It indicates the profile name (Main, in this case) followed by two columns: the first showing the time from the start, and the second showing the time from the last print. From this information, we can determine that the program consumes 30 milliseconds to execute the line containing the for statement the first time through. This time can be attributed to initializing the loop control (iCtr).

```
Main    0       0       Starting Loop
Main    30      30      Iteration:0
Main    30      0       Done iteration:0
Main    30      0       Iteration:1
Main    30      0       Done iteration:1
```

The times shown are absolute, but do include any time consumed by the profiling code itself; however, since any time used by the profiling code is relatively constant, the displayed time values are representative of the real time used by the application.

The best way to use the DebugProfile class is in conjunction with a tool like OptimizeIt. The profiling tool can narrow down the search for hot spots in the code, and the DebugProfile class can zoom right in to individual lines of slow code.

 Currently, the DebugProfile class writes its output to the system console stream, which may not be desirable in some applications. The source code could be modified to write to a file stream in order to archive logged profile data; however, file streaming will increase the impact that the profiling code has on overall performance of the application that it is testing.

13.2.6 Native compilation—the easy way out

Making applications run fast is of prime concern to any serious developer. We can spend huge amounts of time in an attempt to steal back CPU cycles from poorly performing applications, an effort which is critical for VM-interpreted Java code. But squeezing every last unnecessary instruction out of a program may still result in unacceptable performance, so, we need to seek an alternative.

Some of the newer Java development environments are now addressing this issue; however, there is a significant technical cost associated with these tools. Some development environments now offer the ability to compile the Java code to a platform native executable—which may not increase performance by an order of magnitude, but, in most situations, the increase is significant. At the present time, the only mainstream environment supporting native compilation is Symantec's Visual Café product, but others will undoubtedly follow. You can find more information concerning native code compilers at:

`http://www.roaster.com/news/dec97/1201/pr/133.html`.

There is an important distinction between native compilation and optimization. Native compilation is simply a lazy technique for improving the performance of a Java application by generating native machine code, but it comes at the expense of platform independence. For example, a compiled Java program for Microsoft Windows will not run on a Sun Solaris system because they use different CPUs; however, if you are targeting a single platform or you are prepared to recompile your application on each target platform, you may want to investigate native compilation.

To see the effect of native compilation, we need to run some rudimentary benchmark tests. These tests were performed on a Compaq DeskPro 300Mhz Pentium II system with 128MB of memory. The looping code from listing 13.1 (with 20,000 iterations) requires an average of 10.85 seconds to run as an interpreted Java application. The same program, when compiled to a native application, requires just 7.2 seconds.

Before you begin thinking that native compilation will save you from the evils of optimization, we should test an optimized version of the sample code. In the same situation and on the same hardware, the speed-tuned version of listing 13.1, shown below, requires just 6.4 seconds to complete the loop test with 20,000 iterations.

```
class MainClass
{
  public static void main( String args[] )
  {
```

```
DebugProfile log = new DebugProfile( "Main" );

log.Print( "Starting Loop" );
int iCtr = 0;
while( iCtr < 20000 )
{
    System.out.println( "Option: " + iCtr + "," + (iCtr << 2) );
    iCtr++;
}
log.Print( "Finished Loop" );
    }
}
```

13.3 General rules for Java optimization

In the previous section we examined some of the techniques and tools available for determining where Java applications and applets contain performance bottlenecks. Except for the noticeable differences between the original poorly performing sample in listing 13.1, and the final optimized version, we have not discussed why some code is slow, nor has there been any attempt to solve this problem.

In this section, we will outline some of the common performance problems associated with writing Java code and the techniques you can employ to eliminate them from your applications. The rules described in this section apply to all types of Java code. In the next section, we will focus in on ways you can improve the performance of JFC-based code.

 The golden rule of optimization: In a typical program, 90 percent of the total execution time will occur within 10 percent of the code (Some people use an 80 percent/20 percent ratio). Using a profiling tool like OptimizeIt, determine where the bulk of the execution time is occurring and concentrate on improving the performance there—ignore the 90 percent of the code where 10 percent of the time is spent. There is little gained by improving the performance of code that is executed only once or twice. The most common place to find performance problems occurs within loops.

13.3.1 Loop optimization

Loops in the code can pose special performance problems. If a loop contains a poorly written section of code, this problem becomes compounded by each iteration of the loop. Let's examine some of the more common ways to improve looping performance.

IMHO — Be careful when altering code that already works well. Attempts to optimize a program can sometimes introduce subtle bugs.

Object creation in loops

Study the following code fragment which shows code that most developers would write:

```
for( int iCtr = 0; iCtr < 20000; iCtr++ )
{
   String stringValue = new String( "Sample:" + iCtr );
   System.out.println( stringValue );
}
```

Notice that a new String object is created within the loop, and, as a side effect, the object is destroyed at the end of each loop iteration—leaving fragmented memory for the Java garbage collector (GC) to clean up. Since strings in Java are immutable, we can do little to improve on the implied append operation when the loop value is added to the string, but the implied object creation can be eliminated. Look at the following improved code:

```
String stringValue = new String( "Sample:" );
for( int iCtr = 0; iCtr < 20000; iCtr++ )
{
   System.out.println( stringValue + iCtr );
}
```

In this case, the string is created only once, eliminating the 20,000 object creations in the previous example, and, equally important, the 20,000 fragmented chunks of memory left for GC to handle.

Loop unrolling

Another way to improve loop performance is to reduce the number of iterations that the loop control must manage. The code to handle the loop control is definitely significant, so, reducing the number of iterations can dramatically improve performance—especially for loops that execute a single line of code. Consider the following code:

```
for( int iCtr = 0; iCtr < 20000; iCtr++ )
{
   arrayA[iCtr] = iCtr * 12.5;
}
```

To reduce the number of iterations by a factor of two, and significantly improve performance, we could write this code as:

```
for( int iCtr = 0; iCtr < 20000; iCtr += 2 )
{
   arrayA[iCtr] = iCtr * 12.5;
   arrayA[iCtr+1] = (iCtr+1) * 12.5;
}
```

In this second example, each iteration of the loop increments the control by two rather than one. This means that instead of the original 20,000 iterations the code now executes only 10,000.

IMHO   In the process of optimizing an application, it is quite easy to obfuscate the code, which can be a real headache later on when you need to maintain the program. Optimizing code generally sacrifices its readability.

Loop elimination

Another technique commonly used by optimizing compilers is a technique known as loop elimination, which eliminates the loop if doing so will result in smaller, faster code. Let's assume that we have the following code, which iterates a loop just three times:

```
String stringValue = new String( "Sample:" );
for( int iCtr = 0; iCtr < 3; iCtr++ )
{
   System.out.println( stringValue + iCtr );
}
```

A better way to implement this is to unfold the loop into three lines of code.

```
String stringValue = new String( "Sample:" );
System.out.println( stringValue + 0 );
System.out.println( stringValue + 1 );
System.out.println( stringValue + 2 );
```

Though the code produced might be larger in some situations, it will execute faster because it eliminates the code required to manage the loop iteration.

13.3.2 String handling

Strings in the Java language have become notorious for causing performance problems within programs, and, in this regard, it is unfortunate that strings are so convenient. There are several techniques that can be implemented to either reduce the use of the Java String class or to better control them. We will concentrate on two of the most important ones.

Using StringBuffer

String concatenation is quite slow in Java, due largely to its immutable strings. When one string is added to another, the Java VM creates a third string containing the added result. The garbage collector thread is trusted to remove the old data. Consider the following code:

```
String string1 = new String( "" );
for( int iCtr = 0; iCtr < 20000; iCtr++ )
string1 = string1 + "A";
```

On a test system, this code required an average of 7.93 seconds to complete.

The StringBuffer class, though often ignored by Java developers, offers vastly better performance than its String cousin does. Furthermore, it is simple to convert a StringBuffer to a String instance, if it is required. Let's rewrite the previous code using a StringBuffer instead of a String:

```
StringBuffer string2 = new StringBuffer( "" );
for( int iCtr = 0; iCtr < 20000; iCtr++ )
    string2.append( "A" );
string1 = string2.toString();
```

This code required one more line of code, so it will generate a slightly larger footprint; however, on the same test machine, this code requires just 0.15 seconds to execute—that's almost 50 times faster!

 Using StringBuffer is probably the most likely way to improve performance in your application, so it deserves special mention. Where possible eliminate the use of the String class. Instead, replace strings with instances of String-Buffer and use the `toString()` method to convert them to strings if required.

Reducing string manipulations

Another way to improve performance with strings is to eliminate unnecessary manipulations, especially in and around loops. For example, consider the following code:

```
for( int iCtr = 0; iCtr < 100; iCtr++ )
{
    String stringValue = anotherString + " value of this is "
                            + testString + ":" + iCtr );
    System.out.println( stringValue );
}
```

In this example, the string addition is performed for every iteration of the loop, so, the common elements should be factored out to produce tighter code. This is actually a form of code movement, which we will examine in the next section. The previous example should be written as:

```
String stringValue = anotherString + " value of this is "
                        + testString + ":";
for( int iCtr = 0; iCtr < 100; iCtr++ )
{
    System.out.println( stringValue + iCtr );
}
```

13.3.3 Numerical data handling

Java offers a number of opportunities to improve performance when handling numerical values. Calculations (particularly in loops) can present performance problems which can easily be optimized out, sacrificing little in terms of readability. Let's examine a few of the problems around numerical data, and ways in which we can solve them.

Strength reduction

A simple technique to improve performance of integer calculations is known as strength reduction, and though this technique does compromise code readability somewhat, it can offer a significant performance boost. Consider the following code:

```
int value = otherValue * 16;
```

This line of code requires a multiplication operation. The value 16 is actually a binary weighted value of 2^4, so we can easily eliminate the multiplication operation by using a bit shift of 4, resulting in better performance. Thus we can rewrite the code as:

```
int value = otherValue << 4;
```

Eliminating common sub-expressions

It is quite easy to implement code containing common subexpressions. To improve performance, these redundant calculations should be factored out. Look at the following code:

```
float x = value * ( lowRange / hiRange ) * deltaX;
float y = value * ( lowRange / hiRange ) * deltaY;
```

Notice the two lines of code contain common subexpressions that can be factored. This code would be more efficiently written as:

```
float rangeValue = value * ( lowRange / hiRange );
float x = rangeValue * deltaX;
float y = rangeValue * deltaY;
```

Code motion

When performing numerical calculations, we need to avoid performing unnecessary operations within loops. Calculation of values invariant to the loop should be moved outside the looping code. This technique is known as code motion. Consider the following code fragment:

```
for( int iCtr = 0; iCtr < valueArray.length; iCtr++ )
{
   valueArray[iCtr] *= currentTime * 1000;
}
```

In this sample, the calculation currentTime * 1000 is invariant. This code should be written as:

```
int invariantValue = currentTime * 1000;
for( int iCtr = 0; iCtr < valueArray.length; iCtr++ )
{
   valueArray[iCtr] *= invariantValue;
}
```

Improving integer math

Let's examine one final technique to make integer addition and subtraction faster. Look at the following code:

```
int iValue = 10;
```

```
iValue = iValue + 27;
```

Though this code seems harmless enough, it is actually less efficient than the alternative. This code generates the following bytecode:

```
;int iValue = 10;
0  bipush 10
2  istore_1

;iValue = iValue + 27;
3  iload_1
4  bipush 27
6  iadd
7  istore_1
```

A better way to achieve the same result is to use the autoincrement or autodecrement operator:

```
int iValue = 10;
iValue += 27;
```

This source code generates a slightly shorter stream of bytecode:

```
;int iValue = 10;
0  bipush 10
2  istore_1
3  iinc 1 27
```

As you can see, instead of the original 4 bytecode instructions, the new code executes only one, saving 3 bytes in the process. Incidentally, the ++ and — operators generate similarly tight code and should always be used instead of adding one to an integer.

13.3.4 Native code

One final technique you can employ to tune performance is to exchange slower Java code with native C code; however, this technique is undesirable because it greatly complicates the development environment in which you need to work. Once a decision to implement native code has been made, you need to support not only your existing Java environment, but also whatever native language development environment you decide to use.

While the use of native methods provides the ultimate performance boost to Java code, it presents some serious drawbacks. For example, in addition to the build process complications noted previously, the use of native methods also sacrifices platform independence. If you are writing code targeted to several different platforms, do not use native methods.

13.3.5 Other tips for optimizing Java code

Avoid synchronized methods and variables

When implementing multiple threads in an application, is it sometimes impossible to avoid synchronized methods and variables, and careless use of the synchronized keyword can substantially degrade program performance. A synchronized method requires about 30 percent more CPU time to set up and execute than a normal method, so only apply synchronization if it is required. Since use of threads is discouraged in JFC-based programs (more on this in the next section), it should be easy to avoid synchronized methods and variables.

13.4 Optimizing JFC applications

So far in this chapter, we have focussed on improving the general performance of Java applications, identifying common techniques that can be applied to any code (including JFC). In this section, we will focus only on the performance issues for JFC and Swing—including ways in which we can apply multithreading to JFC applications to help improve performance (as well as some other tricks that I have learned from my often painful experiences with JFC).

13.4.1 Adding threads to a JFC application

If you are familiar with Java, then you probably already understand how Java's threads can help improve perceived performance by allowing simultaneous execution of two or more unrelated tasks. This inherent capability in Java means that you can create and manage the user interface on one thread and handle the data collection portion of your program (for example) on another thread. At some point during program execution, the two threads inevitably interact, but, with careful coding and synchronization, it works.

Swing components pose special problems in a multithreaded application, and they require a unique approach. Once a Swing component has been realized (its paint() method has been called), any code that affects it, or that it affects, must be executed on the event-dispatching thread. This restriction might imply that Swing-based programs must be single threaded, but Swing offers some alternative techniques for threading, and some methods in the Swing classes are thread-safe.

FYI In JComponent, the `repaint()`, `revalidate()`, and `invalidate()` methods can be safely used within threads. They can be called from any thread executing within the application. The `repaint()` and `revalidate()` methods queue requests until the event-dispatch thread can process them.

To allow serialized execution of tasks within the event-dispatch thread, Swing provides two methods in the SwingUtilities class (see the following table). These methods virtualize the concept of multithreading by queuing tasks until it is safe for the event-dispatch thread to execute them.

`invokeLater()`	This method asks the event-dispatch thread to execute the specified code while the program continues to execute. Once the event-dispatch thread reaches the queued request, it will be executed, but there is no guarantee when this action will be performed.
`invokeAndWait()`	This method accepts a runnable class and requests that the event-dispatching thread execute it. The program will wait until the task has been completed.

IMHO Whenever possible, you should use the `invokeLater()` method rather than `invokeAndWait()`. If you must use `invokeAndWait()` make sure that the code it executes does not lock any other threads; otherwise, you can run into a potential deadlock situation.

The following code fragment shows the `invokeLater()` method in use. This method requires that the code to be executed is implemented within a runnable class. Within the `run()` method of this sample, you can execute any code you want, including code that manipulates one or more Swing components.

```
class RunnableClass implements Runnable
{
   public void run()
   {
       // Do work here
   }
};
SwingUtilities.invokeLater( new RunnableClass() );
```

Though this chapter has focused on techniques you can use to make your programs faster, using `invokeLater()` will not necessarily directly help you improve performance; however, internally in JFC, placing tasks on the event-dispatch thread improves how code is managed and executed, which does result in better performance.

13.4.2 Using JFC timers to reduce CPU usage

When creating separate threads in JFC applications (using the `invokeLater()` method), there will inevitably be times when you want the thread code to execute for the life of the program, coming to life on a regular basis to perform some low priority task. For example, let's say we are building a program to display the time in a window. We can create a thread to retrieve the time and display it, but there is little point in performing this task more than once per second. We could implement our thread code like this:

```
public void run()
{
   while( 1 == 1 )
   {
      // Load the time

      // Display the time

      sleep( 1000 );
   }
}
```

The problem with this approach should be fairly obvious. Once the `sleep()` method is called, our program really loses control over the CPU. Internally, `sleep()` presumably executes on a one millisecond interval, checking the elapsed time, and timing out after 1,000 milliseconds. This means that even though our code is effectively idle, it can still be consuming CPU cycles.

JFC offers a better approach by providing an event driven timer class which generates an action event when the specified time has elapsed. Using the Timer class, the code fragment above can be rewritten:

```
class MyClass
{
   Timer   myTimer;

   public MyClass()
   {
      .
      .
      .
```

```
        myTimer = new Timer( 1000, this );
        myTimer.start();
        myTimer.setRepeats( true );
    }

    public void actionPerformed( ActionEvent event )
    {
        if( event.getSource() == myTimer )
        {
            // Load the time

            // Display the time
        }
    }
}
```

The code creates a timer with a 1,000 millisecond repeatable interval which invokes the `actionPerformed()` method to fetch the time and display it. With this mechanism, we eliminate the constant CPU usage incurred with the `sleep()` method, and, as a pleasant side effect, the code becomes much cleaner.

13.4.3 Other tips for optimizing JFC applications

There are a number of other minor tips and tricks you can use to improve the performance or size of a JFC-based application.

Optimizing custom renderers

Customer renderers for Swing components are a great place to concentrate on performance tuning. In the renderer for a JTable instance, the code is executed for each visible cell, so any performance problems will manifest themselves in the form of a sluggish user interface.

If the custom rendering code involves changing fonts, you have the potential for problems. Look at the following code:

```
public Component getTableCellRendererComponent( JTable xcTable,
                    Object value, boolean hasFocus,
                    boolean isSelected, int iRowIndex,
                    int iColumnIndex )
{
    // Draw the service name
    setFont(new Font( "Helvetica", Font.BOLD, 12 ) );
    setText( value.toString() );
}
```

In this example, the font is set every time the renderer is called (for every visible cell in the table). Creating a new font instance is a relatively time consuming operation, so you certainly don't want to perform this operation within a rendering method. Instead, implement a constructor that creates the font as a class attribute, then reference this in the renderer code when setting the font. If the renderer uses several fonts, depending on the data it is displaying, create a font attribute for each font.

Use Basic look-and-feel

If you are more concerned with size than performance (an issue applet developers can appreciate), then avoid using a look-and-feel other than the Basic one. All other stock look-and-feel class libraries are based on Basic, so using Motif, for example, requires both the Basic and the Motif library, resulting in the code footprint increasing by approximately 175K bytes. Since the JAR file for both look-and-feels must be loaded, there are also performance considerations for the applet/application startup time.

13.5   Chapter summary

In this final chapter we deviated somewhat from the JFC and Swing focus to investigate reasons for poor performance in Java code. The first part of this chapter was devoted to general improvements in Java performance, including standard optimization techniques that apply to most languages. We examined some of the weapons at our disposal in the war against poor performance, including optimizers such as OptimizeIt, and a DebugProfile class that you can embed in your own code to determine the execution duration for even single lines of code.

Next, we examined some of the performance techniques applicable to JFC-based programs. We discussed reasons to avoid using Java threads, and the alternative provision made by JFC—the `invokeLater()` method. The Swing Timer class was presented as an alternative to building threads that poll in order to execute periodic maintenance code (such as, garbage collection). Timer provides a much cleaner event-driven approach to help reduce the CPU consumption of idle threads.

Finally, we discussed some of the other miscellaneous tips you can apply to make Swing-based applications run faster. The primary message of this section is to eliminate costly code from rendering methods. Renders are called frequently, so any performance concerns will quickly compound to produce an application that runs very slowly.

Since this is the last chapter of the book, we have to say good-bye. I hope that this book has helped you to consolidate and clarify the information available for

JFC, and, in particular, the Swing user interface library. Good-luck with your Swing-based designs!

In the appendices, you will find a wealth of information about Java develop environments and available tools. Appendix C contains a list of information sources available on the Internet.

A
Visual development tools

In this appendix

■ A review of some visual development tools
  for Java applications

Building Java applications today no longer requires using a text editor to create source files and compiling them with the command-line compiler from Sun's JDK. However, it may be wise to compile all release builds with Sun's JDK just to ensure absolute compatibility across all of the target platforms for the application. Events in the past, with Microsoft and Sun arguing over VM compatibility, have taught us all something about trusting the ubiquity of the Java VM.

Today, several vendors offer much better environments in which to build Java applications. This new breed of tools offers a completely integrated development environment with debugging capability, and some include code profiling. Most of these tools (and all of the tools discussed here) offer the power to create applications visually by allowing components to be laid out graphically, then connecting them functionally using simple mouse clicks or menu selections. The result can be a complete Java application created without writing a single line of code. Often, the visual tools will provide insufficient capability, so, all of these tools offers a mechanism to allow developers to integrate user-written code as well.

This section will examine some of the most popular visual tools available for Java development. This list is not all-inclusive and is certainly not an endorsement of these tools over others currently available. The tools described in this section are sold by large software companies, but, with a bit of searching in the Internet, you can undoubtedly find other acceptable Java development environments for free.

A.1   IBM VisualAge for Java

IBM has made some very heavy investments in Java, and one of the key components in its strategy is a product called VisualAge for Java. VisualAge for Java is an extremely powerful and complex tool that many users may find intimidating. Like the other products in IBM's VisualAge family, the Java tool is based on the VisualAge engine. This engine does not use traditional files to store source code. Instead, VisualAge stores all of its source code in a repository. This permits advanced capabilities, such as automatic revision control and editing-while-debugging, but users more familiar with the Microsoft Developer Studio may be unnerved by the inability to examine source files any time they choose. Fortunately, VisualAge for Java does provide an export capability for release builds of source and class files.

Figure A.1 shows a screen depicting the typical usage of VisualAge for Java, illustrating three commonly referenced windows. The window in the upper-left corner contains the repository view that allows the user to browse and examine all of

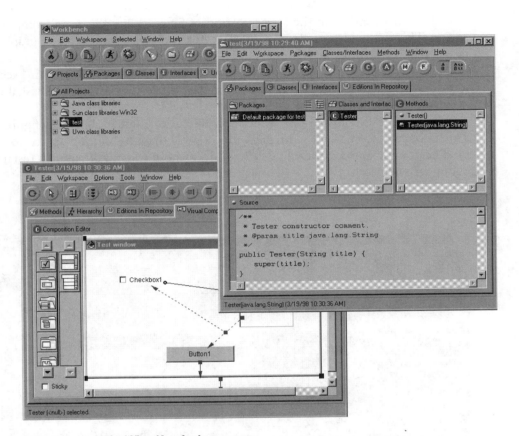

Figure A.1   A typical VisualAge for Java screen

the source code currently managed by VisualAge. Developers who have used IBM's VisualAge for SmallTalk product will already know about the code repository, but those more familiar with Microsoft's development environment will initially find this concept a bit confusing. Unfortunately, unlike VisualAge for SmallTalk, the Java tool is unable to compress the repository, so there is potential for extreme growth of the associated data file on disk.

The window in the upper-right side of the screen shot in figure A.1 shows the Workbench. This window is where typical users will spend most of their time working, as it permits package and class selection, and source code editing.

The final window in the lower portion of figure A.1 is the visual composition editor. This window provides an interface for users to create screens graphically rather than by writing Java code. All connections between components are shown graphically through the use of arrow-headed lines. In theory, this is an excellent idea, but, as the design becomes more complex, the VisualAge for Java visual composer screen begins to get very congested.

VisualAge for Java also provides a powerful debugger, shown in figure A.2. This debugger, combined with the code registry, has the unique ability to allow modification of source code while debugging without forcing the user to restart the debugger session.

The IBM web site for VisualAge Java is at

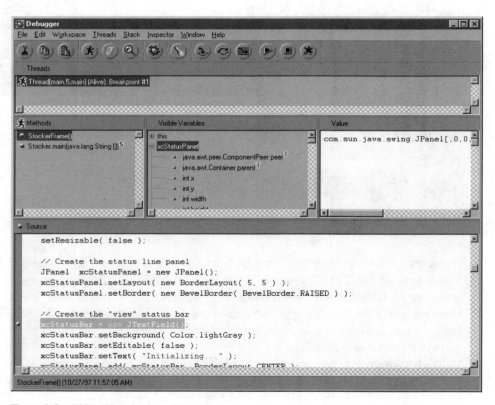

Figure A.2   A VisualAge for Java debugger

`http://www.software.ibm.com/ad/vajava/`.

This site contains complete specifications, pricing information, and a trial version of the program that can be downloaded for free. This site is also an excellent place to find out about current Java news.

A.2   Symantec Visual Café

Another exciting environment for Java development originates from Symantec—Visual Café. This integrated editor, compiler, and debugger really lives up to its name. This tool assists the user in quickly implementing complete Java applications visually. Like VisualAge for Java, Visual Café fully supports an environment which allows the user to write Java code manually and then compile it and run it. It also has a more seamless technique (than VisualAge for Java) for visually creating dialogs, frames, and so on, which doesn't require the user to write the Java code behind them. Visual Café also includes a very nice feature for graphically displaying and editing the class hierarchy of an application. This is shown in figure A.3.

Figure A.4 is a screen shot of Symantec Visual Café, showing several of the many windows used in a typical session. Unlike VisualAge for Java, Visual Café is more toolbar driven. (Note the impressive toolbar at the top of the screen.) The Project Window in the upper-left corner contains a list of the Java files needed to construct the application. The user can click on these files to manually edit the Java source code at any time, as shown in the source code window in the lower right-hand corner.

The two frames in the upper-center and upper-right corners of figure A.4 contain portions of the visual builder, showing the representation of the frame being created and a property sheet of the selected component. Unlike VisualAge for Java, Café shows a grid in its visual builder, and components added to the layout are automatically sized and positioned according to this grid. Café does not apply connection lines on the visual diagram the way VisualAge does. Instead, it allows for logic connections using a connection wizard. This has the benefit of maintaining a clear visual representation of the dialog or frame under construction, but it offers no clear indication of how the visual components interact. The ability to toggle a connection view would be a welcome feature in both VisualAge for Java and Visual Café (as well as for Borland's JBuilder, which will be examined next).

Finally, Visual Café offers a feature unconnected to visual application creation, but it deserves an honorable mention. With Café, developers can compile Java code to native Microsoft Windows executables and DLLs. This provides significantly improved performance on the Windows platform and still allows non-Windows users to use the application class files. Native code output is a very nice touch, and this feature alone may win Symantec many votes of approval for Visual Café.

Symantec provides a wealth of information about Visual Café at their web site at:

```
http://www.symantec.com/domain/cafe/deved/index.html.
```

A.3   Borland JBuilder

Borland International is less of an industry force now than it was in their days as a powerhouse in the C/C++ and Pascal worlds. However, with the release of their JBuilder product, Borland might regain their previous stature. JBuilder is a com-

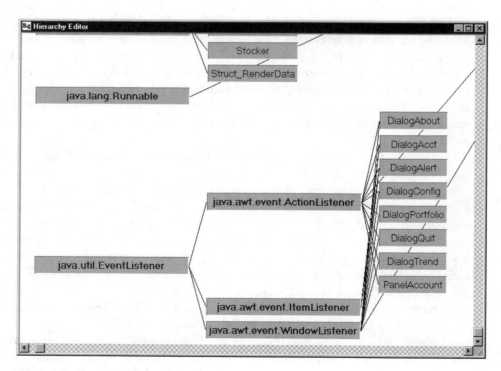

Figure A.3   Visual Café class display

pletely integrated development environment for Java, and it includes a visual builder. Figure A.5 is a screen shot of JBuilder showing the toolbar and the three panes normally visible to the user. Borland appears to have adopted the best features from Microsoft's Developer Studio product and combined them with the best features of Visual Café.

JBuilder does not offer a native code compiler, and its visual tool (shown in figure A.6) is not as smoothly integrated as those found in Café or VisualAge for Java, but JBuilder is a solid product that is certainly worth a test drive.

Figure A.6 shows a very simple frame creation in the visual builder. Like Symantec's Café, JBuilder also provides a separate property/events window that

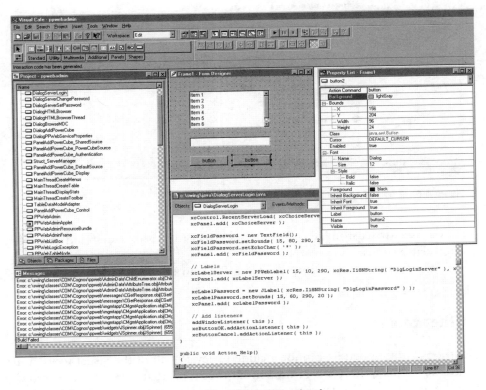

Figure A.4   A screen shot of Symantec Visual Café Professional

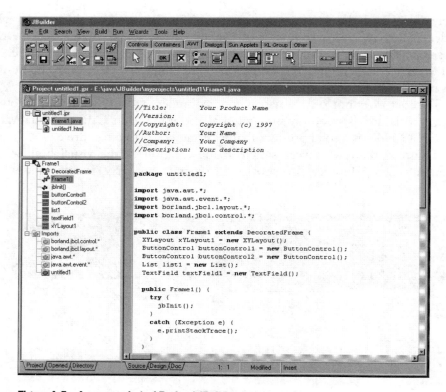

Figure A.5   A screen shot of Borland JBuilder

allows users to customize the components in the visual panel and to specify their interrelationships.

For further information regarding Borland JBuilder, visit its web site at:

```
http://www.borland.com/jbuilder/
```

A.4   Other tools

Although this appendix cannot include reviews of all of the visual tools available to Java developers, there are a number of other tools that deserve some recognition—and new tools and updates are emerging into the marketplace on a daily basis.

Sun offers two tools to assist with the visual development of Java programs. Java Workshop, shown in figure A.7, is a typical development environment offering

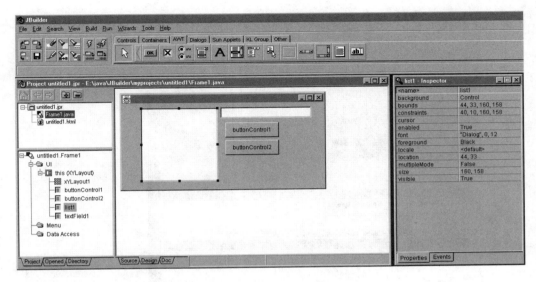

Figure A.6   JBuilder visual designer

visual composition and the ability to interface user-written Java code. Java Studio offers a complete visual environment in which users can create complete applications and applets without writing any Java code.

Java Workshop and Java Studio are available from Sun at:

```
http://shop.sun.com/.
```

This site provides sales information for the products and a thirty-day test version of each tool.

Another excellent product comes from Bulletproof Corporation—JDesigner Pro, which is a complete and comprehensive tool, at a reasonable price. JDesigner offers a visually oriented design environment and even supports an ODBC interface for database application developers.

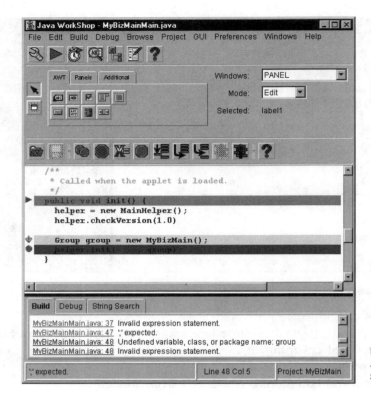

Figure A.7
A screen shot of
Sun's Java Workshop

B *Other* *tools*

Visual development environments only partially complete the developer's arsenal of Java tools. None of the development tools described in appendix A provides any sort of code validation or optimization—both of which are crucial in the Java world. Since Java is a bytecode interpreted language, performance can easily suffer if care is not taken when coding, so developers must rely on optimization tools to assist them. Also, portability can be compromised without the developer being aware of it, so developers need some form of validation tool to indicate where portability concerns might crop up.

In this appendix, we will review some of the tools available to help Java developers write better code. Many of these tools are freely available from web sites on the Internet, and others are available for a modest charge. You will find that even the retail products are well worth the cost if you plan to write production Java code.

B.1 PureCheck

PureCheck is one part of Sun Microsystems' 100 percent Pure Java initiative, which intends to make Java the industry standard. It is a tool designed to report portability conflicts in Java code. This utility scans compiled Java class files, ZIP archives, and JAR files looking for code that might sacrifice platform independence.

 If your application depends on external .JAR or .ZIP files or other classes, make sure these are specified as input to the PureCheck program. Otherwise, undefined reference errors will be reported.

The tool is quite simple to use, requiring only a list of compiled files for which the check will occur. The utility scans these files (a process that can take several minutes for larger applications) and creates a report showing all instances in the code where warnings or errors have occurred (see figure B.1).

Once the Analyze phase is completed, the user can inquire about the details of any portability errors reported for the code. Figure B.2 shows an example of a typical error screen, indicating, among other things, that the erroneous class DialogServerChangePassword contains a hard-coded path to a file.

If the finished application must run on platforms other than the one on which it was developed, then PureCheck is an absolute requirement. Fortunately, the PureCheck utility can be downloaded for free from Sun's web site at:

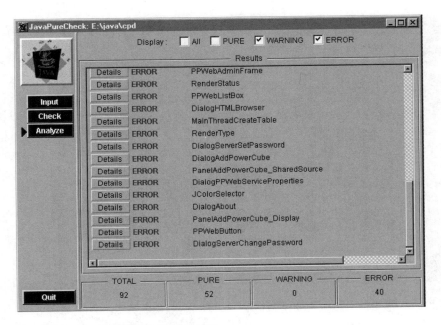

Figure B.1   The PureCheck report screen

http://www.suntest.com/100percent/tools.html.

B.2   Jikes Debugger

Most of the debuggers provided with Java-integrated development environments are adequate for simple debugging. However, few of them stand up to the pounding they may get when attempting to debug larger, more complex applications or applications which require remote debugging and testing.

Fortunately, Derek Lieber (of the Java Tools Group at IBM's Watson Research Center) invested some time to create a simply superb utility called the Jikes Debugger (JD). JD offers all of the typical features found in most integrated development environments, but it offers the improvement of showing all of the required information at the same time without requiring the developer to sift through dozens of independent data panes. Additionally, the Jikes Debugger can debug applications across a network, an uncommon feature among Java debuggers.

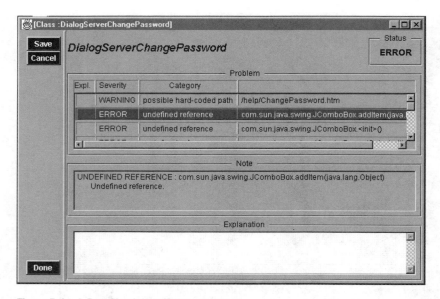

Figure B.2   A PureCheck detailed error screen

Figure B.3 contains a screen capture for the Jikes Debugger, showing the process of an executing application. Note that virtually everything a developer could ever need is visible, including local variables, threads, and even the console output.

The best feature of JD is that IBM has made it available for no charge. You can download the current release from its web site at:

```
http://www.alphaworks.ibm.com/alphapreview_tools.
```

This site also contains several other utilities that may be of interest, including the Jikes compiler, which promises faster compilation and an intelligent incremental build facility.

B.3   OptimizeIt

So far, we have discussed some tools for building applications and for debugging them, but we have not described any tools for improving the performance of an application. Naturally, there are many products of varying degrees of capability and

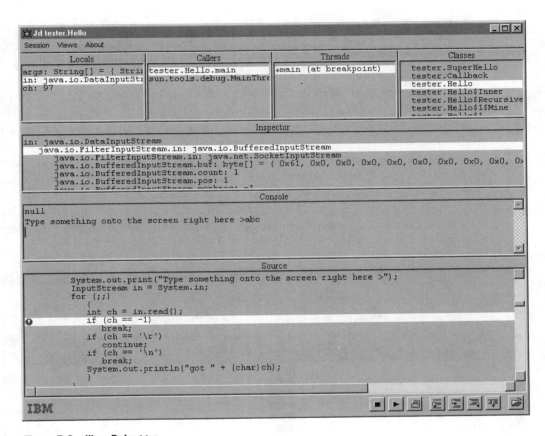

Figure B.3 Jikes Debugger

quality available, but one particular product stands out— OptimizeIt, from Intuitive Systems, Inc. In chapter 13, we examined techniques for using OptimizeIt to fine-tune Java code for performance. Here, you will see the merits of OptimizeIt as we use it to find performance problems in some sample code.

OptimizeIt can analyze a running Java application or applet and identify where performance improvements can be made, and it also displays a graph identifying each class in the application and how often it is called. The graph helps you to identify methods in your code that have to service a large number callers, which is often an indicator that some class or method is a traffic bottleneck.

Figure B.4 shows the typical call heap for a running application. This diagram shows that the java.lang.String class is the most frequently called class in this application. Since internal classes such as String are part of the Java run time library, no performance improvement can be made. As a result, the graph can become cluttered with classes external to the application. Fortunately, OptimizeIt provides a filtering feature to eliminate such distracting data. However, it is important to note that the extensive use of an internal class could indicate that a better algorithm might be needed.

To find out exactly how much time is required for each method of a running application, the user needs to switch to OptimizeIt's CPU Profiler mode of operation. In this mode, data is collected by a recorder and is displayed once the recorder is stopped. The ability to start and stop the data recorder at any time offers a high level of granularity when performing tests. For example, OptimizeIt can determine

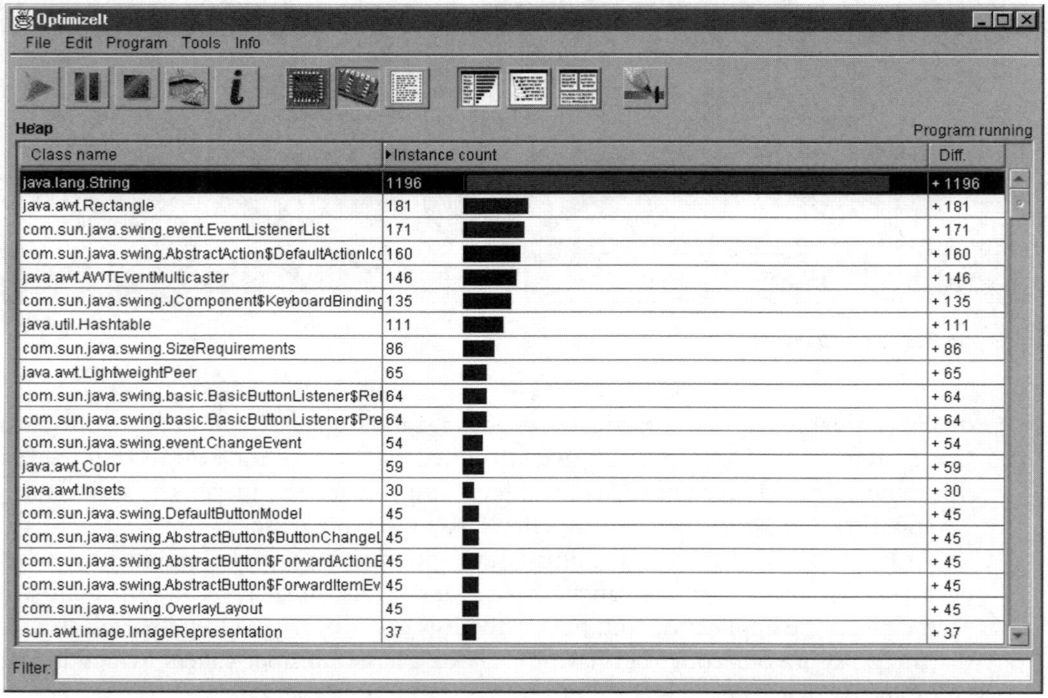

Figure B.4 OptimizeIt main screen

the time required for displaying and populating a specific dialog within an application. Figure B.5 shows an example of this function.

Although there may be many other code profilers for Java, OptimizeIt is definitely one that deserves some serious consideration. Intuitive Systems offers a thirty-day trial version of OptimizeIt that can be downloaded from its web site at:

```
http://www.optimizeit.com.
```

B.4 DashO optimizer

Another technique for optimizing Java code is to find a tool that makes its best attempt to do all the work for you. PreEmptive Solutions offers a tool called DashO

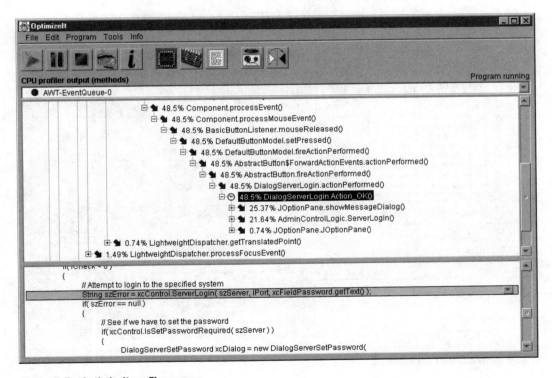

Figure B.5 OptimizeIt profiler screen

that helps take some of the guesswork out of optimization. Figure B.6 illustrates a typical session with DashO.

The program itself does not conjure any real magic; rather, it applies some of the performance tuning techniques we discussed in chapter 13. Some users may find DashO a bit unnerving because there is no real indication of how it changes your code. Many developers will find manual tuning techniques much more pleasing.

A thirty-day trial version of DashO can be downloaded directly from the Pre-Emptive Solutions web site at:

```
http://www.preemptive.com/dasho.
```

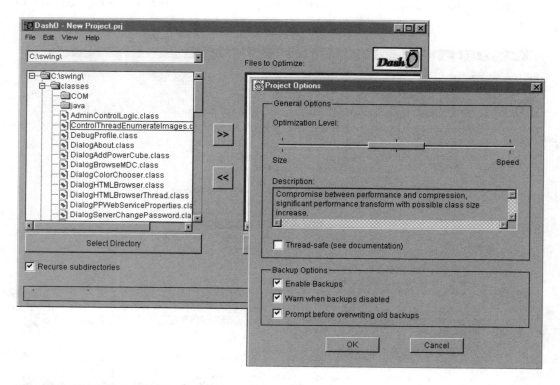

Figure B.6   The DashO optimizer

This concludes our examination of the most commonly used development tools available for Java. This list is far from exhaustive, but it should provide enough information to get you started. No doubt, some users will prefer a text editor and a JDK compiled solution, but for most developers, an integrated development environment will save countless hours of time, particularly at the debugging stage of a project.

C Sources of information

The Internet has become an incredible library of information. The wealth and detail of Java information is simply amazing. This appendix outlines some of the most common places to find information about Java and Swing. For clarity, the information sources are grouped by general subject and, where appropriate, are identified by company or author.

C.1 Search engines

Internet search engines are usually the quickest tool for locating useful information. Browser URLs for a number of the more common search engines follow:

```
http://www.altavista.digital.com/
http://www.excite.com/
http://www.infoseek.com/
http://www.lycos.com/
http://www.search.com/
http://www.yahoo.com/
```

C.2 Tools

The Internet contains an abundance of excellent tools for Java development. The following is a list of commonly available tools and related support pages.

Manufacturer/Tool	URL
Borland JBuilder	http://www.borland.com/jbuilder/
IBM VisualAge for Java	http://www.software.ibm.com/ad/vajava/
IBM Jikes Debugger	http://www.alphaworks.ibm.com/alphapreview_tools
Intuitive Systems Inc. OptimizeIt	http://www.optimizeit.com
Microsoft Inc. Internet Explorer	http://www.microsoft.com/ie/download/
Netscape Inc. Communicator	http://www.netscape.com/download/client_download.html
PreEmptive Solutions DashO	http://www.preemptive.com/dasho
Sun Microsystems PureCheck	http://www.suntest.com/100percent/tools.html

Manufacturer/Tool	URL
Sun Microsystems HotJava Browser	`http://java.sun.com/products/hotjava/1.1.2/index.html`
Sun Microsystems Java Workshop	`http://shop.sun.com`
Sun Microsystems Java Runtime Environment	`http://java.sun.com/products/jdk/1.1/jre` (JDK 1.1.x) `http://java.sun.com/products/jdk/1.2/jre` (JDK 1.2)
Sun Microsystems JavaBeans	`http://java.sun.com/beans/index.html`
Symantec Visual Café for Java	`http://www.symantec.com/domain/cafe/deved/index.html`

C.3   Documentation

The Internet also includes many useful documents. The following list shows some of the sites for useful information about Java and Swing.

Description	URL
Java Frequently Asked Questions	`http://java.sun.com/products/jdk/faq.html`
JDK Known and Fixed Bugs	`http://java.sun.com/products/jdk/1.1/bugs.html`
Java Developer Connection	`http://developer.javasoft.com/developer/index.html`
Java Class Libraries	`http://java.sun.com/products/jdk/1.1/docs/api/packages.html`
JavaBeans API	`http://java.sun.com/products/jdk/1.1/docs/guide/beans/index.html`
Java Foundation Classes White Paper	`http://java.sun.com/marketing/collateral/foundation_classes.html`
AmbySoft A Java Coding Convention	`http://www.ambysoft.com/javaCodingStandards.html`
Developer.com	`http://java.developer.com`
Gamelan	`http://www.gamelan.com/`
JavaWorld	`http://www.javaworld.com`
Think in Java	`http://www.EckelObjects.com`
The Swing Connection	`http://java.sun.com/products/jfc/swingdoc-current/`

Description	URL
Java Guidelines	http://www.chimu.com/publications/javaStandards/index.html

C.4   Tutorials

Not all tutorials require you to buy a book. There are some very nice Java and Swing tutorials available in the Internet for free. Here is a partial list.

Description	URL
The Sun Java Tutorial	http://java.sun.com/docs/books/tutorial/
Swing Tutorial (Requires free registration for Java Developer Connection)	http://developer.javasoft.com/developer/onlineTraining/swing/index.html
Dick Baldwin's Java Programming Tutorials	http://www.phrantic.com/scoop/onjava.html
The Java Tutor	http://www1.mercury.com/java-tutor/

References

D

Ambler, S. *Java Coding Convention Summary Document*. AmbySoft, Inc., 1997.
`http://www.ambysoft.com/javaCodingStandards.html`.

Bartlett, N., A. Leslie, and S. Simkin, *Java Programming Explorer*. Scottsdale, AZ: The Coriolis Group, 1996.

Bell, D. *Make Java Fast: Optimize!*. JavaWorld. IDG Publications, 1997.
`http://www.javaworld.com/javaworld/jw-04-1997/jw-04-optimize.html`.

Bergman, E., and E. Johnson, *Towards Accessible Human-Computer Interaction*. Sun Microsystem, 1995.
`http://www.sun.com/access/updt.HCI.advance.html`.

ChiMu Corporation. *Java Guidelines*. ChiMu Corporation, 1998.
`http://www/chimu.com/publications/javaStandards/index.html`.

Cooper, A. *The Essentials of User Interface Design*. Foster City, CA: IDG Books Worldwide, 1995.

Flanagan, D. *Java in a Nutshell*. 2nd ed. Sepbastopol, CA: O'Reilly and Associates, Inc., 1997.

Fowler, Amy. *Mixxing Heavy and Lightweight Components*. The Swing Connection. Sun Microsystems, 1998.
`http//java.sun.com/products/jfc/swingdoc-current/mixing.html`.

Gamma, E., R. Helm, R. Johnson, and J. Vlissides, *Design Patterns : Elements of Reusable Object-Oriented Software*. Reading, MA: Addison-Wesley Publishing Co., 1995.

Geary, D. *JFC's Swing, Part I: Model/View/Controller*. Java Report, November 1997. pp. 28-38.

IBM. *Common User Access Advanced Interface Design Reference*. Systems Application Architecture Library, IBM: 1991.

Lemay, L., and C. Perkins, *Teach Yourself Java in 21 Days*. Indianapolis, IN: Sams Publishing, Inc., 1995.

MageLang Institute. *Swing Short Course, Part I*. San Mateo, CA: MageLang Institute, 1997.
`http://developer.javasoft.com/onlineTrainging/swing/swing.htm`.

MageLang Institute. *Swing Short Course, Part II*. San Mateo, CA: MageLang Institute, 1997.
`http://developer.javasoft.com/onlineTrainging/swing2/swing.htm`.

Muller, H., and K. Walrath, *All About Threads*. The Swing Connection. Palo Alto, CA: Sun Microsystems, 1998.
`http://java.sun.com/products/ifc/swingdoc-archive/threads.html`.

Petrich, D., and D. Flanagan, *Netscape IFC in a Nutshell*. Sepbastopol, CA: O'Reilly and Associates, Inc., 1997. (ISBN 1-56592-343-X)

The Windows Interface Guidelines for Software Design: An Application Design Guide. Redmond WA: Microsoft Press, 1995.

Zukowski, J. *Java AWT Reference*. Sepbastopol, CA: O'Reilly and Associates, Inc., 1997.

Index

The Awesome Power of JavaBeans
  by Lawrence H. Rodrigues
  ISBN: 1-884777-56-2
  $44.95
  545 pages
  Available spring 1998

Java Foundation Classes: Swing Reference
  by Stephen C. Drye, William C. Wake
  ISBN: 1 884777-67-8
  $39.95
  700 pages
  Available summer 1998

For electronic browsing and ordering of these, and other Manning books, visit:
  http://www.manning.com.

Distributed Programming with Java
  by Qusay H. Mahmoud
  ISBN: 1-884777-65-1
  $43.95
  450 pages
  Available fall 1998

Server-Based Java Programming
  by Piroz Mohseni
  ISBN: 1-884777-71-6
  $42.95
  375 pages
  Available fall 1998

For electronic browsing and ordering of these, and other Manning books, visit:
http://www.manning.com.

Java Network Programming / 2nd edition
  by Merlin Hughes, et al
  ISBN: 1-884777-49-X
  $44.95
  750 pages
  Available summer 1998

Java Servlets by Example
  by Alan R. Williamson
  ISBN: 1-884777-66-X
  $49.95
  550 pages
  Available fall 1998

For electronic browsing and ordering of these, and other Manning books, visit:
  http://www.manning.com.